Dedicated to:

Benjamin T. Zeigler
Ernest "Chip" Helms

Francis Marion
and the
Snow's Island Community

Myth, History, and Archaeology

Steven D. Smith

Funded by:
The Florence County Historical Society
Snow's Island Research Fund, South Carolina Archaeological Trust

United Writers Press
Asheville, N.C.

Francis Marion and the Snow's Island Community
Myth, History, and Archaeology

Copyright © 2024 by Steven D. Smith
Second Edition

All rights reserved. No part of this book may be used in any form or reproduced by any means without written permission from the publisher with the exception of brief passages quoted in reviews, critical articles, or essays.

Published by:
United Writers Press
Asheville, NC 28803
www.UWPnew.com

ISBN: 978-1-952248-16-0 (trade paper)

ISBN: 978-1-952248-15-3 (eBook)

Library of Congress Control Number: 2020919724

Cover Art: Derived from an image of the John Blake White painting, *General Marion Inviting a British Officer to Share His Meal*. His slave, Oscar Marion, kneels at the left of the group.

Unless otherwise noted, images herein have been reproduced from the author's dissertation, entitled "Archaeological Perspectives on Partisan Communities: Francis Marion at Snow's Island in History, Landscape, and Memory," or are believed to be in the public domain.

Printed in the U.S.A.

General Francis Marion Inviting a British Officer to Share a Meal
Oil on canvas ca. 1820-1840, 28.5 x 35.5 inches
Collection, The Oakland Club, Pineville, S.C.

This oil painting of a British officer visiting Marion's camp is owned and proudly exhibited at the Oakland Club (formerly Bluford Plantation), Berkeley County, S.C. Stephen Motte, Curator of Collections and Interpretation at the Florence County Museum believes it is an early rendition of the "sweet potato" scene that predates the iconic 1836 painting by famed artist John Blake White (cover). Motte notes that Marion's appearance "seems to be lifted directly" from a description by early biographer William Dobein James:

> [Marion] was rather below middle stature of men, lean and swarthy. His body was well set, but his knees and ankles were badly formed: his nose aquiline; his chin projecting; his forehead was large and high, and his eyes black and piercing.

Indeed, James describes Marion's dress as "a close round bodied crimson jacket, [and]…a leather cap." Motte concludes, "In its composition and treatment of the subject matter, the painting lacks refinement or grandeur, which is precisely why it succeeds where other versions of Marion and the British Officer have fallen short." The painting is in many ways a more reliable rendition of Marion at Snow's Island than White's 1836 version, and perhaps the most accurate depiction of Francis Marion at his Snow's Island camp. Although it lacks historical documentation, the location of the painting, as well as the similarities in skill level, stylistic preferences, subject matter, dimensions, and apparent date range indicate an artist who fits White's profile and may have been a student of White's.

Sincere thanks are due to The Oakland Club for permission to publish the painting.

CONTENTS

Acknowledgments ix
Foreword: The Road From Camden xv
Preface xxi
    A Note About This Edition.. xxiii
Prologue xxv

Chapter 1: Francis Marion, Partisan Warrior 1
    Snow's Island 5
    Francis Marion's Early History..5
    Marion's Tactics 8

Chapter 2: An Archaeological Perspective 15
    Archaeological Concepts of Community 16
    Community and Landscape..18
    Other Perspectives of Partisan Communities 19
    A Theoretical Statement...21
    Remembering Francis Marion and Snow's Island 22
    Methods 23
    Weaknesses of the Methods 25

Chapter 3: The Settlement of the Snow's Island Community 33
    The Snow's Island Regional Landscape..33
    Development of the Colonial Community..44

Chapter 4: The Pre-Revolutionary Snow's Island Community.............................55
    Core Families...58
    Second Tier Families...81
    Third Tier Families 86

Chapter 5: The War Begins 93

Chapter 6: Marion and the Partisans: 17 August 1780 To 13 April 1781 103
    17 August 1780 to 3 December 1780 104
    4 December 1780 to 31 January 1781 117
    1 February to 13 April 1781 126

Chapter 7: Marion and Greene 145
    14 April 1781 to July 1781 146
    August 1781 to December 1782...151
    The Resistance Within the Resistance 159

Chapter 8: The Archaeology and Landscape of the Snow's Island Community 171

- Archaeological Methods 172
- 38Fl380 Witherspoon's Ferry 176
- 38Fl409, 38Fl410, 38Fl411 Port's Ferry 178
- 38MA205 Richardson's 181
- 38MA212 Hickory Hill 181
- 38MA55 The Tanyard 183
- 38MA207 Dunham's [Dunnam's] Bluff 186
- 38MA165 Dunham's Bluff Redoubt 202
- 38MA81 Richbourg's 204
- 38FL280 and 38FL281 Snow's Island 204
- 38FL282 Goddard's Plantation 207
- 38WG170 Black Mingo, 38WG171 Black Mingo North 213
- 38MA206 Blue Savannah 215
- Burch's [Burches] Mill, 38FL46 and 38FL50 217
- The Partisan Community Landscape 220

Chapter 9: Francis Marion, Snow's Island, and American Memory 235

- Horry, Weems, James, and Simms 236
- Marion, the Swamp Fox 242
- Snow's Island in American Memory 245
- Francis Marion, Memory, and Living Legend 249

Chapter 10: Francis Marion at Snow's Island 265

- A Historical Review of the Snow's Island Community 266
- The Landscape of Partisan Communities and Partisans 270
- The Archaeological Manifestation of Partisan Communities 274
- Partisan Communities Remembered 276
- Francis Marion, the Partisan Community, and Communities of Resistance 277

Bibliography 285

- Primary Sources (Manuscripts, Diaries, Collections, Papers) 285
- Published Primary Sources 287
- Primary Sources Consulted 290
- Secondary Sources 290
- Map Figures 309
- Newspapers 309

Index 311

About the Author 323

ACKNOWLEDGMENTS

Numerous people influenced, shaped, assisted, and guided my research over 30-plus years. I sincerely apologize to those who have faded from memory.

This book is a significant revision of my Ph.D. dissertation. Bringing this to a much more readable book was the inspiration and support of Ben Zeigler, Tom Tisdale, and editor Ms. Vally M. Sharpe. Financial assistance for publication was provided by the Florence County Historical Society and the Snow's Island Research Fund of the South Carolina Archaeological Trust. Special thanks to an anonymous donor who put us over the top.

The original dissertation committee included chair Kenneth G. Kelly, and members Joanna L. Casey, Tom Leatherman, Ed Carr, and Larry Babits. Charlie Cobb also read and commented on many drafts. Sincere thanks to all.

I have been assisted by a core of outstanding friends and colleagues, including historians and archivists Sam Fore, the late Mike Scoggins, Charles Lesser, Tracy Power, Ross St. George, Christine R. Swager, John Oller, Jim Piecuch, Tom Powers, Terry Lipscomb, Robin Copp, Henry Fulmer, Graham Duncan, Charles Baxley, David Ruewer, and David Moltke-Hansen. Archeologists include Audrey Dawson, Sean Taylor, Chris Clement, Alaina Williams, Jon Leader, Mark Brooks and especially my long-time colleague, Jim Legg. Local Marion County historians and genealogists include Deryl Young, Jo Church Dickerson, Maxcy Foxworth, Nell Morris, Joanna Brown, and "Tres" Hyman. Friends who assisted in all sorts of ways include Doraine and Luther Wannamaker, the late Bill Chandler, Spencer Barker, Jack Buchanan, David Neilan, David Adams, Neil Myers, Kevin Rooney, Gretchen Hudgins, Brett Cullen, Colonel [Ret] George and Carole Summers, Dick Watkins, and John Allison.

Research for the dissertation was funded by the Sonoco Products Company (thanks to Ed Drayton), the American Battlefield Protection Program, National Park Service (thanks Kris McMasters), the Francis Marion Trail Commission (thanks to Ben Zeigler, Fred Carter, and Bob Barrett), The South Carolina Lowcountry Council of Governments (Ginnie Kozak), and numerous contributors to the Snow's Island Research Fund, especially Ernest "Chip" Helms and John Frierson. I was graciously provided funding to write the dissertation by two grants from the Robert L. Stephenson Fund and the South Carolina Archaeological Research Trust. I also received a much-appreciated fellowship from the South Carolina Battleground Trust (thanks, Blake Hallman and the late Mike Taylor). Brock Shattuck and Tamara S. Wilson drafted the maps. Although nothing herein was discovered or written *sine numine*, remaining errors and omissions are mine alone.

List of Abbreviations

CP	Cornwallis Papers, National Archives of Great Britain
CP-SCDAH	Cornwallis Papers, South Carolina Department of Archives and History
GP	Papers of General Nathanael Greene
GP-WCL	Papers of General Nathanael Greene, William Clements Library
PCC	Papers of the Continental Congress
SCL-USC	South Caroliniana Library, University of South Carolina
SRNC	State Records of North Carolina

Selected Principal Events of the American Revolution with Emphasis on South Carolina

19 April 1775	Battle of Lexington and Concord, Massachusetts
28 June 1776	Battle of Fort Sullivan, Sullivan's Island, South Carolina
19 October 1779	British Capture of Savannah, Georgia
12 May 1780	British Capture of Charleston, South Carolina
16 August 1780	Battle of Camden, South Carolina
17 January 1781	Battle of Cowpens, South Carolina
15 March 1781	Battle of Guilford Court House, North Carolina
25 April 1781	Battle of Hobkirk's Hill, South Carolina
8 September 1781	Battle of Eutaw Springs, South Carolina
19 October 1781	American Capture of Yorktown, Virginia
14 December 1782	British leave Charleston, South Carolina
2 September 1783	Treaty of Paris ends the war

List of Tables

Table 4.1. Snow's Island Third-Tier Community Members 87

Table 7.1. Supplies received from Snow's Island community 154
Table 7.2. Supplies/Provisions from Snow's Island community, 1782. 160
Table 7.3. Snow's Island community partisan service 161
Table 7.4. 1790 slave population by family in the Snow's Island community 166

Table 8.1. Lead Shot from 38MA207 199
Table 8.2. Lead shot from 38FL282 211

List of Illustrations/Paintings

General Marion Inviting a British Officer to Share His Meal (1836) .... Cover
General Francis Marion Inviting a British Officer to Share a Meal (The Oakland Club) v
General Francis Marion 1
Sketch of Mason Locke Weems ("Parson" Weems) 23
Colonel Peter Horry in Uniform 23
Horatio Gates 100
General Nathanael Greene 118
General Daniel Morgan 124
Lieutenant Colonel Henry Lee 125
Peter Horry 236

List of Figures

Figure 1.1. Snow's Island (USGS The National Map, modified by Brock Shattuck) 3
Figure 1.2. Greater Snow's Island community region (Tamara S. Wilson) 4
Figure 3.1. Snow's Island community core and outer regions (T.S. Wilson) 34
Figure 3.2. Detail of 1783 plat of James Michie's forfeited estate
(SCDAH, S126102:334,166) 36
Figure 3.3. Greater Pee Dee River drainage in South Carolina (T.S. Wilson) 37
Figure 3.4. Ferries around Snow's Island (USGS The National Map,
modified by Brock Shattuck) 42
Figure 3.5. Detail of Henry Mouzon's 1775 map of North and South Carolina depicting
Snow's Island and environs (S.C. Department of Archives and History) 43
Figure 3.6. Detail of James Cook's 1773 Map of the Province of South Carolina
depicting Snow's Island and environs (University of S.C. Caroliniana Library) 43
Figure 3.7. Britton's Neck and Lower Marion District from *Mills' Atlas* (1825)
depicting various place names in the Snow's Island region 45
Figure 3.8. Detail of 1943 USGS Johnsonville, South Carolina, topographic map,
15-minute quadrangle, revised 1946 46
Figure 3.9. Detail of John Stuart-William Faden's 1780 Map of South Carolina
depicting Queensborough (S.C. Department of Archives and History). 49
Figure 4.1. General locations of Snow's Island community core families
in the Snow's Island region (Brock Shattuck) 56
Figure 4.2. General locations of Snow's Island second tier families (T.S. Wilson) 57
Figure 4.3. Mrs. Phyllis Canady's cadastral map of Britton families on Britton's Neck
(Bass-Canady Correspondence, permission, Deryl Young and Marion County
Historical Center, Marion County, South Carolina) 59
Figure 4.4. Plat of Thomas Port's 336 acres and Dunham's Bluff
(SCDAH, S213184:6,68) 75
Figure 4.5. Detail of 1913 Florence County school district map
(S.C. Department of Archives and History) 85
Figure 4.6. Detail of Marion County map, surveyed by Harlee, 1815,
enlarged by P.Y. Bethea 1882 (SCDAH) 85
Figure 6.1. Marion's Battles and Skirmishes 1 (Brock Shattuck) 106
Figure 6.2. Marion's Battles and Skirmishes 2 (Brock Shattuck) 114
Figure 6.3. William Snow's receipt for cattle requisitioned for the men at
Marion's Snow's Island camp (A.A. 7197, SCDAH) 121
Figure 6.4. Watson's march toward Snow's Island (T.S. Wilson) 130
Figure 7.1. Detail of Charleston District from *Mills' Atlas* (1825) depicting
location of Fairlawn, Moncks Corner, and Wadboo Plantation 153

xiv | *Francis Marion and the Snow's Island Community*

List of Figures (cont.)

Figure 8.1. General location of Archaeological sites discussed in Chapter 8......................173

Figure 8.2. Detail of Williamsburg District, Mills' Atlas, depicting Witherspoon's Ferry and "Marion's Camp"..177

Figure 8.3. General location of archaeological site 38FL380 (USGS The National Map, modified by Brock Shattuck) 179

Figure 8.4. General location of Port's Ferry archaeological sites 38FL409, 38FL410, and 38FL411 (USGS The National Map, modified by Brock Shattuck)............180

Figure 8.5. General location of archaeological site 38MA205 (Richardson's) and Todd's Site (USGS The National Map, modified by Brock Shattuck)..182

Figure 8.6. General location of sites and landscape features on Britton's Neck. A=38MA207, 38MA165, 38MA81 site complex, B=Rae's Causeway, C=Widow Jenkins Home, D=38MA212 Hickory Hill, E= Relic Collector Camp, F= Potato Bed Ferry (USGS The National Map, modified by Brock Shattuck) 184

Figure 8.7. General location of archaeological site 38MA55, the Tanyard (USGS The National Map, modified by Brock Shattuck)...185

Figure 8.8. General location of archaeological sites 38MA207, 38MA165, and 38MA81188 (USGS The National Map, modified by Brock Shattuck) 187

Figure 8.9. Plat Snow's Island Public Improvements Ferries-Petitions 1813 (SCDAH) ...189

Figure 8.10. Site 38MA207 (Sean Taylor)...193

Figure 8.11. Block "I" silver sleeve button and "piece of eight" from 38MA207...............194

Figure 8.12. A 2-lb. cannon ball with British "broad arrow" from 38MA207....................194

Figure 8.13. Feature 1 profile from 38MA207 195

Figure 8.14. Rattlesnake button found at Dunham's Bluff in 1924 (Stokes 1926).............203

Figure 8.15. Profile of Dunham's Bluff redoubt (Sean Taylor)..203

Figure 8.16. General locations of sites 38FL280, 38FL281, and 38FL382 (USGS The National Map, modified by Brock Shattuck)..206

Figure 8.17. Goddard's Plantation on *Mills' Atlas* (1825)...208

Figure 8.18. Structure 1 at 38FL282 (James B. Legg)..210

Figure 8.19. Structure 2 at 38FL282 (Mona M. Grunden)..212

Figure 8.20. General location of sites 38WG170 and 38WG171 (USGS The National Map, modified by Brock Shattuck)..214

Figure 8.21. Thomas M. Munnerlyn 1865 plat depicting blue savannah and homestead (Marion Deed Book II:92, courtesy Jo Church Dickerson)...............................217

Figure 8.22. General locations of sites 38FL46, 38FL50, and suspected location of Burch's Mill (USGS The National Map, modified by Brock Shattuck) 219

FOREWORD
The Road from Camden

On the afternoon of August 15, 1780, a motley group of about 20 soldiers of varying backgrounds and affiliations rode out of the camp of General Horatio Gates near Camden, South Carolina and headed southeast. Their leader was Lieutenant Colonel Francis Marion, a senior Continental officer who had avoided capture by the British at the surrender of Charleston several months before, but was nevertheless without a formal command. Marion's followers consisted of similarly displaced and detached Continental soldiers, as well as neighbors from his home on the Santee River, all united in a desire to continue the fight for American independence despite almost complete British control of South Carolina and the Southern theater as a whole.

Marion and his men had arrived in Gates's camp only a few days before to offer their services to the hero of Saratoga, who had marched into South Carolina in early August. Gates had been sent South by the order of the Continental Congress itself and, with approximately 4,100 men (mostly militia) under his command, he was poised to challenge the strategically important British garrison at Camden. It was entirely possible, if not likely, that the liberation of South Carolina was about to begin, and Marion and his followers wanted to be a part of that process.

Whatever their hopes and expectations might have been, the reception Marion and his men received from Gates's "Grand Army" had not been warm; in fact, Gates and his officers had been dismissive if not derisive of the group. Colonel Otho Williams, Gates's Deputy Adjutant General, later recalled:

> Col. Marion, a gentleman of South Carolina, had been with the army a few days, attended by a very few followers, distinguished by small leather caps, and the wretchedness of their attire; their number did not exceed twenty men and boys, some white, some black, and all mounted, but most of them miserably equipped; their appearance was in fact so burlesque, that it was with much difficulty the diversion of the regular soldiery was restrained by the officers; and the General himself was glad

of an opportunity of detaching Col. Marion, at his own instance, towards the interior of South Carolina, with orders to watch the motions of the enemy and furnish intelligence.

That "opportunity" was a chance for Gates to rid himself of an awkward supernumerary and his ill-equipped retinue, and the "interior of South Carolina" to which Gates sent them was a place of seemingly little strategic importance—the remote and swampy Pee Dee region in the Northeastern portion of the state.

It was from the Pee Dee that the Williamsburg Militia, a group consisting primarily of first and second generation Scots-Irish immigrants, had written to Gates, and possibly to Marion himself, requesting a professional soldier to command them. Led by Major John James, the Williamsburg Militia had bristled at British commander Henry Clinton's June 3 proclamation that all paroles given to Americans who had surrendered were void; that South Carolinians would thereafter be considered British subjects, and thus they could be required to fight for His Majesty and against their friends and neighbors.

This issue seems to have galvanized support for American independence in the Pee Dee and among the members of the Williamsburg Militia and their community. As recalled by Major James's son some forty years later, "news of the approach of Gates having arrived, a public meeting of this people was called, and it was unanimously resolved to take up arms in defense of their country." The Williamsburg Militia then went into camp at a crossing of the Lynches River known as Witherspoon's Ferry, just a few miles upriver from Snow's Island, to await a commander.

Marion's journey from Gates's camp to the command of a remote militia force proved to be richly ironic. Having sent Marion off to a backwater where he and his ragtag followers would be out of the way of the Grand Army's liberation of South Carolina, Gates saw that army overwhelmingly defeated at Camden the next day. Gates fled the battlefield, his career and reputation ruined, and Camden would go down as one of the greatest American defeats of the War, an apparent end to any hopes for the cause of American independence in the South.

By contrast, Marion, who heard the first shots of the battle of Camden from his overnight encampment in the predawn hours of August 16, rode toward a more prominent and successful, if not essential role in the achievement of American independence. Almost certainly unbeknownst to Marion at the time, when he arrived at Witherspoon's Ferry on August 17 and took command of the Williamsburg Militia, his was soon to be one of only a handful of organized forces resisting the British occupation of South Carolina, and the only such force in the eastern half of the state. Gates's army had been annihilated at Camden the day before, and Thomas Sumter and his force of 800 regulars and militia would be routed at Fishing Creek the next day.

Francis Marion's dismissal thus became his salvation, and would begin his transition as a leader from professional journeyman to partisan genius. For most of the autumn of 1780, Marion and the Williamsburg Militia, joined by other militia regiments from around the Pee Dee region, kept the American cause alive in South Carolina, harassing British lines of supply and communication and, perhaps more importantly, preventing the organization and consolidation of Loyalist forces in the eastern third of the state. Thereafter, from 1781 to the end of the War, Marion and his militia would play a central role in the reduction of British and Loyalist strongholds from the South Carolina midlands to the coast, ultimately leading to the final withdrawal of British forces from the state in December 1782.

That Marion was able to achieve such success in command of a militia force was unprecedented in European warfare. Indeed the whole idea of "commanding" militia was anathema to professional officers, Marion included. Specifically with regard to Marion's appointment to command militia in the Pee Dee, Peter Horry later noted:

> Gen'l Marion always said it was a skulking position—their [Militia's] officers dare not force the men for fear of losing their commissions…no people can war with success because all are rulers.

The idea of militia officers fearing their men and all militia men being rulers speaks to the democratic aspect of militia organization in the American colonies in the eighteenth century. Not surprisingly, settlers in the Backcountry of South Carolina, particularly Scots-Irish Presbyterians, tended to resist authority and outside organization and discipline. An important measure of Marion's genius is that he adapted to this dynamic rather than trying to change it. He did not seek to impose professional discipline on the loosely organized group of individuals that constituted his command; rather, he molded his tactics to fit their needs and abilities, relying on small patrols, mounted attacks, and disruption of supply lines as an alternative to frontal infantry assaults designed take and hold positions.

Marion's men were in fact as close to all being individually independent— all being "rulers" to use Horry's words—as any fighting force in the modern era, often choosing, with Marion's reluctant acquiescence, when to come and go, returning home to see to their domestic duties, and reporting back to camp when chores were done. Indeed, as Steve Smith astutely points out in the following chapters, Marion used the loose organization of his command to his advantage, allowing his militia to disappear quickly into the surrounding community in the face of a superior opposing force. In so doing, Marion began the practice of guerrilla warfare three decades before that term was first used in reference to native resistance to Napoleon's invasion of Spain.

In 1780 and 1781, Marion was thus as much in charge of a community as he was a military command, and that community had its geographic center in an around the confluence of the Lynches and the Great Pee Dee Rivers. Bordering this confluence on the west and south, and itself protected on the west and south by Clark's Creek, is Snow's Island, an area of several thousand acres of river swamps interspersed with ridges of high ground, ideal for evasion and concealment.

In a practical and literal sense, Snow's Island became Marion's base during the key months of his partisan campaigns in 1780 and 1781, and would come to occupy central place in the later Marion myth. In that myth, Snow's Island would be Marion's Athelney, the Sherwood Forest of his brigade, a secretive place of safety so evocatively captured in John Blake White's painting *General Marion Inviting a British Officer to Share His Meal*, which was completed in 1836.

But in the work that follows, Steve Smith both broadens and deepens our understanding of Snow's Island and Francis Marion, putting both in the context of their greatest significance—the partisan community that both supported and was supported by Marion's campaigns. With a fresh perspective, and using tools unemployed by previous Marion biographers, Smith examines the larger Marion story with reference to that community, its familial, religious, and commercial relationships, as well as the intricacies of the alliances, feuds, and aspirations that defined and informed it.

Using archaeology as a point of departure, Steve Smith's work takes the reader on a journey through a complex and richly peopled landscape, telling the story of Marion, his men, and their world as no Marion biographer or scholar has done before. What emerges is a picture of the Francis Marion story that is as complete as the available record allows—one that is at the same time objective, detailed, and intimate. It is a picture that begins to demarcate the reality of the context of Marion's campaigns from the mythology that the children and grandchildren of his militia men nurtured and promulgated as they became wealthy in the cotton boom, many moving West, in the first half of the nineteenth century.

The world we see in *Francis Marion and the Snow's Island Community: Myth, History, and Archaeology* is the world into which Francis Marion passed on his journey from Camden to Witherspoon's Ferry. The essence of Marion's genius and the basis for his achievements can be found in his relationship to that world. All who love history and love our Country should be grateful to Steve Smith for exploring that relationship and helping us to understand and appreciate it.

Benjamin T. Zeigler
President, Florence County Historical Society
Chairman, Francis Marion Trail Commission, 2005-2009

PREFACE

"We don't really know a lot about Francis Marion." Back in the 1990s, when I first began to lecture on Francis Marion, I often started my presentation with those words. Even then, before the emergence of a lot of new scholarship on Marion since 2000, that statement was not completely accurate. What I meant was that, although there are numerous Marion biographies going back to the early 19th century, all these efforts heavily relied on the first full biography written by Peter Horry and Mason Locke Weems in 1809.

Weems, a clergyman who was also an itinerant book salesman, had recently won wide fame for his biography of George Washington. He was soon looking for a new subject and met Peter Horry who had written a memoir of his exploits with Francis Marion. Weems saw the opportunity to do for Francis Marion what he had done for George Washington. Essentially what he did was turn Washington, and then Marion, into larger than life heroes, which the new country of America rapidly absorbed as paragons of national identity. Later, another antebellum biographer, William Gilmore Simms, finished the process, and Marion's name spread across the continent as new counties, towns, streets, were named in his honor. So, a lot of what we think we know about Francis Marion has been tainted by Weems' mythology, confusing facts and fancy. Some facts are also controversial or subject to debate. At a conference devoted to Marion, I once heard a participant say about another, "He knows so much that just isn't true!" Weems, Simms, and other 19th century biographers have left modern scholars to sort through myth and legend to extract the real Francis Marion.

The first 20 years of the 21st century, however, has seen a surge in what I like to call "Marionology" including: the publishing of a 1938 "local history" biography by William Willis Boddie in 2000, the publication of Marion's Orderly Book in 2006, a tactical analysis of Marion campaigns by Scott Aiken in 2016, numerous re-published editions of William Gilmore Simms's *The Life of Marion* (including a 2016 edition by the University of South Carolina Press, with an introduction I wrote), and a completely new full biography in

2016 by John Oller, in which Oller incorporated much of this new knowledge. Our knowledge of Marion's military exploits have also increased as a result of now easily accessible primary sources like General Nathanael Greene's Revolutionary War correspondence in thirteen volumes (1976-2005), which include all of Marion's correspondence with Greene, the publication of British General Charles Cornwallis's Revolutionary War correspondence in 2010, and the on-line publication of Revolutionary War soldiers' pension applications, including Marion's men, by *Fold3.com*. In 2003, an annual symposium devoted to Marion was established in Manning, South Carolina, bringing Marion scholars together annually to present their research on their favorite hero. The following year saw the establishment of the Swamp Fox Murals Trail Society in Clarendon County. In 2005, the Francis Marion Trail Commission was created by the South Carolina state legislature to define a heritage tourism trail dedicated to Marion's campaigns in the northeastern part of the state. The legislature followed up on that in 2007 to declare February 27 Francis Marion Memorial Day.

Today, Marion scholars are still left with the legends and myths, but these scholarly activities and public endorsements clearly indicate an enduring fascination with Francis Marion and that our knowledge of Francis Marion has greatly expanded in the last twenty years. One is left wondering: 1) how can we further sort fact and fiction of Marion's life and 2) what more can be known?

The sorting of fact and fiction will never be complete, but this book attempts to demonstrate what new can be learned. What follows is a different perspective on the life and campaigns of Francis Marion. This perspective envisions Francis Marion through the lens of anthropology, and specifically that branch of anthropology called archaeology. It goes beyond mere fragmentary documents. It combines the documentary evidence with material evidence, cultural evidence, and tradition (folk or oral history) to create this new perspective. Furthermore, this book does not focus on Marion per se but instead on his soldiers and those Carolinians who supported his soldiers. It relates the story of a particular South Carolina community that resisted British rule and, under the leadership of Francis Marion, won their independence. That community consisted of Whig partisans living on and around a place known as Snow's Island, South Carolina. Readers familiar with this tract of land, surrounded by the Pee Dee River, Lynches River, and Clark's Creek in the northeastern part of South Carolina, also know that it was the site of Francis Marion's camp during the fall and winter of 1780-1781. As the cliché goes, it was the "lair of the Swamp Fox."

This book is not another Marion biography. Everything about Marion's military career detailed herein is described with a focus on Marion's relationship with the people who lived on and around Snow's Island, within a radius of 15 miles. Further, the book focuses on the period in Marion's career where he was the leader of a partisan band of rebels when his primary retreat was in and around Snow's Island. Other periods of Marion's career are summarized.

Along the way, I hope readers will learn something about how archaeologists do their job of revealing the past. This book is part history, part archaeology, and all detective story. Some of it may be technical and detailed—most archaeological discoveries are not "Eureka!" moments, but rather the result of slow digging, first through archives and libraries, then through the dirt, then in laboratories, and then back to the archives. Only then do short passages in obscure documents and small items found in the ground uncover facts that reveal entirely new visions of the past.

A Note About This Edition

This book is a significant revision of my dissertation, originally completed in the fall of 2010. Dissertations are written not only to present new, original research but also to demonstrate a Ph.D. candidate's command of his discipline, knowledge of the subject, and in archaeology, his methodology, presentation of data, and analysis—all in fine and excruciating detail. In other words, it can be quite ponderous.

In this version, I have attempted to reduce the wordiness, eliminate the academic jargon, and remove all the required in-text citations essential in a dissertation and presented them as endnotes to increase readability. There are quite a few asides in the endnotes that will be of interest to historians of Marion. Full citations for the notes appear in the bibliography in the back of the book.

At the same time, I have attempted to retain some of the flavor, so that readers can see how archaeologists go about their work. For instance, I have included, but significantly shortened, Chapter 2, wherein I describe an anthropological approach to Marion's Snow's Island community and explain how this theory guides the documentary and archaeological research presented in subsequent chapters. I have also updated passages and included new information as a result of my continuing research and interest in Francis Marion. The original dissertation included a chapter discussing the whole Marion mythology. I have kept that chapter and it also has been updated

Hopefully, this book will be of interest to followers and admirers of Francis Marion and to people who want to know how an archaeologist goes about researching the past.

Finally, I have chosen to describe Marion as a partisan warrior and the people who lived around Snow's Island at the time as a partisan community. The word "partisan" has had many meanings since its first use, originating as early as the 16th century. At that time, it was used to describe guards for an officer. By the 17th century, it meant an officer of lightly armed cavalry. Today, it is often used synonymously for guerillas or irregulars. Partisan (or guerrilla) warfare also describes a type of mobile warfare in which raids, ambushes, and surprise are strategic elements. A common modern use of the word describes people in Yugoslavia during World War II as engaged in guerrilla warfare.

I have settled on the term "partisan" warfare in this book for several reasons. First, it was the word used at the time of the American Revolution for light troops using irregular tactics and/or independently operating and commanded light troops used to reconnoiter, attack convoys and escorts, and plant ambushes. George Washington preferred the term Petit Guerre [sic, *la Petite Guerre*]. The term partisan was also applied to mobile light infantry and cavalry, such as Colonel Henry Lee's Partisan Corps, the 18th century equivalent to a combined arms unit consisting of cavalry and infantry.

In Marion's case, the word partisan also had the connotation of non-regulars (armed civilians) fighting against regular soldiery. Marion's partisans were not full-time professional soldiers, but citizen soldiers using guerrilla or irregular tactics.

Steven D. Smith
January 2021

PROLOGUE

In the spring of 1782, being the seventh year of the American Revolution, a Loyalist colonel named Robert Gray wrote a long essay entitled *Observations on the War in Carolina*. In it, he described South Carolina as "a piece of patch work, the inhabitants of every settlement, when united in sentiment being in arms for the side they liked best and making continual inroads into one another's settlements." One of those pieces of patch work, the people living on and surrounding Snow's Island, South Carolina, were "united in sentiment" against the British crown. This community of partisans had joined the rebellion as early as 1775 and had stubbornly refused to surrender, even when Charleston fell in 1780. They had supplied food, forage, and blood to the rebellion, and under the leadership of General Francis Marion, had become an obstacle to British control of the southern colonies. This book is their story.

History is said to be the biography of society. Society is composed of individuals—and the biography of an individual who has exerted a wide influence in the community of which he was a member is actually the history of that community.

— Anonymous Review of "The Study of History" —
Southern Quarterly Review, July 10, 1846

CHAPTER 1
FRANCIS MARION, PARTISAN WARRIOR

General Francis Marion (1732-1795) is widely regarded as the most successful partisan of the American Revolution. He would be called a partisan both by his British enemies and his biographers.[1]

His British enemies begrudgingly admitted his expertise.[2] For example, in the fall of 1780, Lord Charles Cornwallis, commander of the British forces in South Carolina, wrote to Sir Henry Clinton that:

> Col. Marion has so wrought on the minds of the People, partly by the terror of his threats & cruelty of his punishments, and partly by the Promise of Plunder, that there was scarce an Inhabitant between the Santee and Pee Dee that was not in Arms against us…[3]

In Marion's case, the word partisan also had the connotation of non-regulars (armed civilians) fighting against regular soldiery. Thus, Francis Marion was both a partisan himself and a *commander* of partisans. Typical of innumerable analyses of Marion's place in the history of guerrilla warfare is this recent summation:

Francis Marion, in his late forties at the time, became the symbol of American guerrilla resistance. A teetotaling Huguenot, Francis Marion commanded a ragtag band of irregulars, including young boys and ex-slaves. They made their own clothes and weapons and shot their pistols with bullets made of pewter. Numbering no more than several hundred at its peak strength, Marion's force became skilled in night and dawn raids against British outposts. He and his men would ride as many as sixty miles at a stretch along clay paths and marches of South Carolina in order to surprise a Tory or redcoat force. After the war, many of Marion's guerrilla paths became permanent roads. …In one particular escapade, …The guerrillas swooped down on the [British] column and freed the entire lot of Americans, an incident which made the 'Swamp Fox,' instantly famous.[4]

This short paragraph reflects the many reasons for Marion's success, as discussed in virtually any history of partisan-guerrilla warfare in the Revolutionary War in South Carolina. The reasons can be organized into several themes: 1) his proficient use of civilian "ragtag" or non-professional soldiers; 2) few combatants; 3) his classic use of guerrilla tactics such as surprise attack, ambush, and raid; 4) his proficiency despite the lack of sufficient ammunition; 5) his ability to outwit regular or professional soldiery, and, 6) the extreme mobility of those he led in battle. In short, his success is attributed to his understanding and use of guerrilla combat tactics—tactics still taught by the U.S. Department of Defense.[5]

There are, however, two additional and closely related themes of Marion's success that are part and parcel of partisan-guerrilla doctrine: 1) the need for partisan guerillas to have a secure base for supplies, training, and rest, and 2) their need for strong support from the civilian population.

"Marion thus demonstrated an understanding that the true objective of guerrilla war is not the enemy army but the support of the population."[6] The nature of this relationship—between the guerrilla-partisan and the civilian population—remains underexamined.[7]

This book attempts to shed additional light on this relationship using the archaeological concepts of community, landscape, and memory. It focuses on Marion and a specific Whig[8] community, the neighborhood located in and around Snow's Island, South Carolina (Figure 1.1).

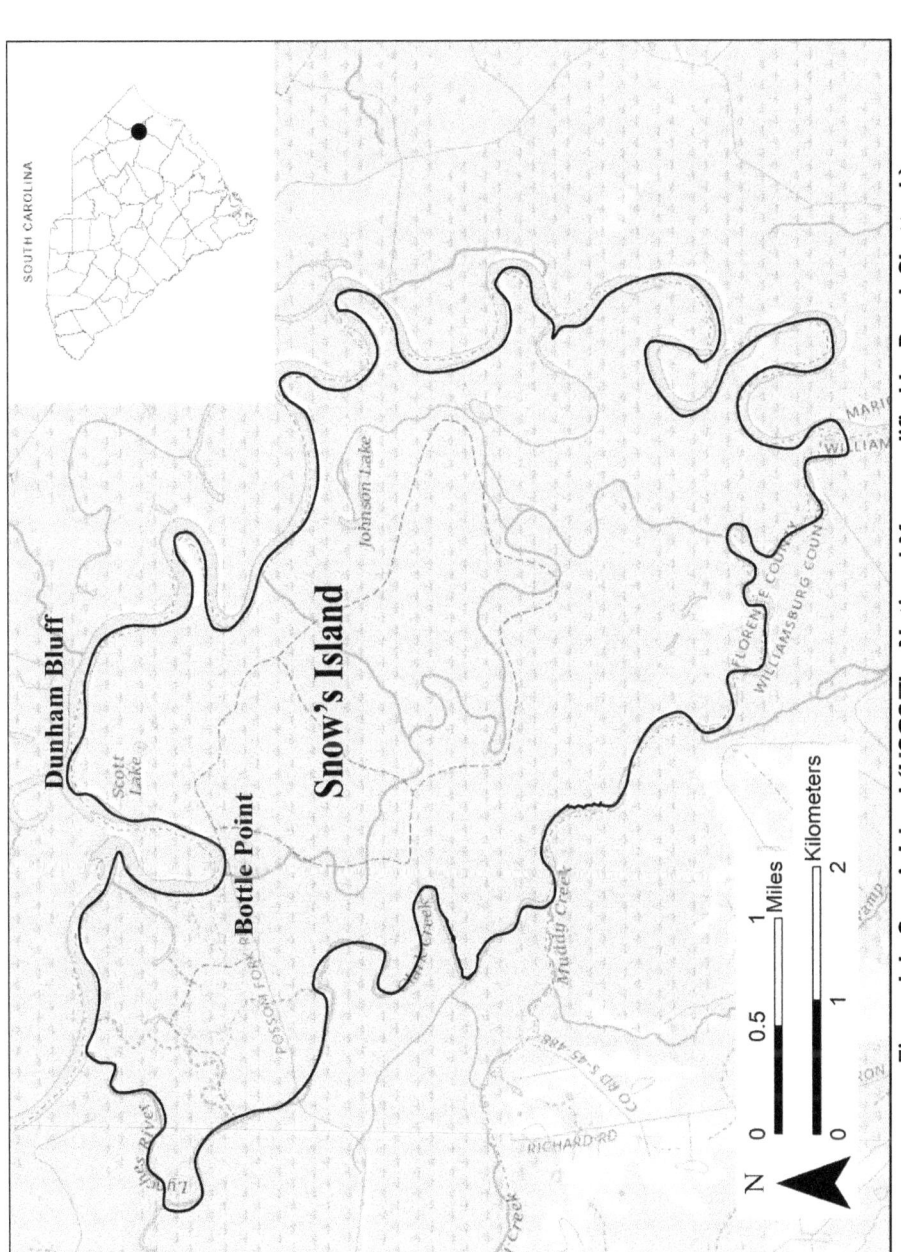

Figure 1.1. Snow's Island (USGS The National Map, modified by Brock Shattuck)

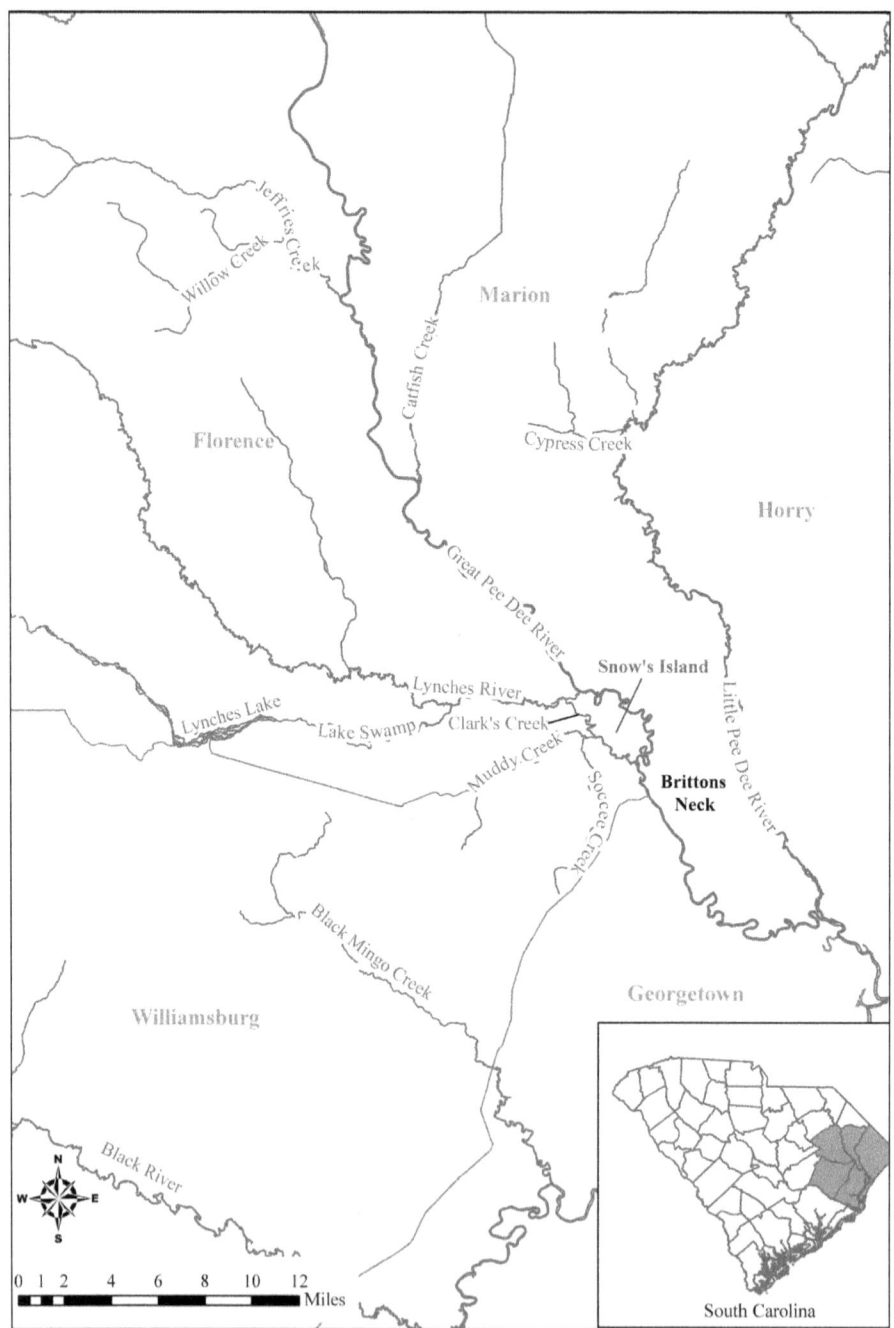

Figure 1.2. Greater Snow's Island community region (Tamara S. Wilson)

SNOW'S ISLAND

Today, Snow's Island consists of high land and swamp surrounded by three rivers or creeks. Lynches River (formerly Creek) flows downstream into the Pee Dee to form the northwestern boundary.[9] The Pee Dee winds east and south to form the northern and eastern boundaries; about one half mile up from the confluence of Lynches Creek, Clark's Creek branches off from Lynches and winds southeast to the Pee Dee (Figure 1.1). The entire island is nearly three miles from northwest to southeast, and two miles across.

Marion was supposed to have camped somewhere on this "inland" island. The Snow's Island region that was dominated by his partisans is a much larger area, however, consisting of the inhabitants of Snow's Island, Britton's Neck (to the east and south), the lands upstream from the confluence of Lynches Creek on both the Pee Dee River and Lynches Creek, and the lands directly west (Figure 1.2).

The exact borders of this community will emerge as a result of analysis of the historic record in Chapters 3 and 4.

Snow's Island was the location of Marion's legendary "camp of repose" during his partisan career (August 1780 to April 1781).[10] John Tierney notes, "His [Marion's] camps, including 'Snow's Island' and 'Peyre's Plantation,' were established deep within the South Carolina swamps."[11] Compatriot Lieutenant Colonel Henry Lee wrote after the war of the importance of Snow's Island to Marion's success: "Fertile in stratagem, he struck unperceived; and retiring to those hidden retreats selected by himself, in the morasses of [the] Pee Dee and Black River, he placed his corps not only out of the reach of his foe, but often out of the discovery of his friends."[12] The population surrounding this camp, was a *partisan community*. Its members not only supported Marion logistically but also served in the partisan ranks. As such, the Snow's Island community was part of a larger Whig *community of resistance*.

FRANCIS MARION'S EARLY HISTORY

Francis Marion was born in 1732 to Gabriel and Esther Marion of Goatfield Plantation, St. John's Parish, Berkeley County, South Carolina.[13] Very little of Marion's youth in the years before the Revolution is known and, of what is known, only that related in the writing of his first biographers, Peter Horry through Mason Locke Weems, and William Dobein James.[14] Neither source is particularly reliable.

Marion came from a family of Huguenots who settled along the Santee River in the late 17th century and became middling planters. His family moved to Winyah Bay, near Georgetown, South Carolina, and Weems tells the story that, when Marion was in his teens, he decided to go to sea. Returning from the West Indies, Marion's ship was rammed by a whale and after six days in a lifeboat, most of the crew made landfall.

That would be his last voyage. He returned to plantation life and in 1750 assumed management of the family plantation after his father died. His four brothers and one sister had married.[15]

Then, in 1756, Marion and his brothers joined the colonial militia, but his more formal military experience really began when he was a lieutenant in Captain William Moultrie's militia company in the 1761 expedition against the Cherokees. (Tradition suggests that his knowledge of guerrilla tactics began there as well.) Near Echoe, North Carolina, Marion was given the dubious honor of clearing a mountain pass lined with Cherokees in the van of the Lieutenant Colonel James Grant's army. He charged his men through the Indian ambush, clearing the way for the rest of the army.

After the expedition, Marion returned to farming and, in 1773, purchased a plantation at Pond Bluff along the Santee River, four miles below Eutaw Springs, South Carolina (the plantation house was inundated to create Lake Marion). By the beginning of the American Revolution, Marion was a well-respected member of plantation society and was elected a delegate to South Carolina's First Provincial Congress.[16]

Because he would come to be known primarily for his success as a partisan, historians tend to underestimate the importance of Francis Marion's long experience as a regular officer. From 1775, when he was selected a captain in Colonel William Moultrie's 2nd South Carolina Regiment of Infantry, until the fall of Charleston in May 1780, Marion worked his way up through the officer corps, developing skills in conventional warfare along the way. Eventually, he reached the rank of lieutenant colonel in the Continental Army (and not as a mere militia officer) and was given command of the 2nd South Carolina Regiment. As he rose through the ranks, Marion held several independent commands. He was in command at Fort Dorchester in 1775 and commanded the heavy guns on the left side of Fort Sullivan during Britain's first attempt to take Charleston in 1776. He also led the regiment in an attack against Spring Hill redoubt in the failed 1779 siege of British-occupied Savannah, Georgia. After the Americans retreated to Charleston, Marion was left with three regiments at Sheldon, South Carolina, with orders to watch the British

In the spring of 1780, the British moved north to capture Charleston. The story goes that Marion was attending a dinner party on Tradd St. in Charleston. The host locked the doors to keep the drinking going long into the night. Marion, however, was supposedly a teetotaler.[17] He decided to escape the party and jumped out of a second-story window, breaking his ankle.[18]

As the troops surrounded Charleston in May 1780, Marion and all other supernumerary officers were sent out of town. Charleston surrendered on 12 May 1780 and the British lost no time in fanning out across South Carolina. By the summer of 1780, the British were confident they had control of the colony, but one year later, their fortunes had been reversed—in no small part due to Francis Marion.

His partisan campaign began in August 1780, at a time when the state of South Carolina was without a sitting government, which meant he had no legal authority over the men who came and went into his camp. In fact, Marion's partisans were not formally reorganized as militia until the end of December 1780, when then-Governor John Rutledge commissioned him as a brigadier general in the South Carolina militia and gave him military authority over the South Carolina Lowcountry east of the Santee, Wateree, and Catawba rivers. It was then that he formally organized a militia brigade.[19]

This is not to imply that Marion's partisans were inexperienced. Military historian Clyde Ferguson asserts that "Marion became a famous partisan by leading out those militiamen who were prepared to and who already knew how to fight."[20] Some had been Continental soldiers (regular army). Many had served in the militia, either earlier in the war and/or during the campaigns against the Cherokees in the 1760s.

In short, by the fall of 1780, Marion's partisans were a mixture of regular and militia soldiers and a few slaves. Because of this, many Marion historians describe his men using the terms militia, partisans, or guerillas interchangeably. They are not wrong to do so, but I prefer the term partisans as his men were not full-time warriors. During the American Revolution, members of a militia served a term of anywhere from a few weeks to a few months and then returned to civilian life.

This caused Marion no end of grief. During the siege of Fort Motte, South Carolina (May 1781), Marion was so distraught with the militia's practice of melting away from the ranks just when needed that he threatened to resign and travel north to offer his services in that theatre.[21]

While Marion never made good on his threat, he did forge a strong relationship with the Continental Army. Scholars of the American Revolution agree that Marion's major contribution to the winning of the war was his cooperation with General Nathanael Greene's conventional Continental Army in 1781 and 1782.[22] This collaboration also aided the partisans, who needed lead to make ammunition, which was supplied largely through a conventional chain of supply.

During Marion's partisan period—roughly August 1780 to April 1781—he was usually on his own, and his ability to operate successfully without formal logistical support is considered one of his most amazing talents.

> The ability of Marion's forces to continue and even intensify operations without official logistical support must be deemed one of the great accomplishments in the history of military operations.[23]

Some attribute this accomplishment to Marion's success in combat, which provided captured supplies. But while the victory at the Black Mingo skirmish and the capture of Forts Watson and Motte included the capture of critical military supplies (arms, horses, and ammunition), these victories did not provide food to any great extent, nor was victory so routine as to provide a steady source of provisions and fodder. As will be demonstrated, I submit herein that Marion's success was due to his development of and reliance on a partisan community.

MARION'S TACTICS

Did Marion learn from the tactics of the Cherokee during the Cherokee campaigns? Many scholars believe so but, however he acquired them, historians have often compared Marion's skills in guerrilla warfare to those described by Mao Tse-tung.

Mao saw partisan warfare as a stage in the evolution of warfare in general—from partisan warfare to mobile warfare and eventually to regular warfare using standing armies while maintaining the offense.[24] He summarized guerrilla warfare in this way:

> The enemy advances, we retreat, the enemy camps, we harass; the enemy tires, we attack; the enemy retreats, we pursue.[25]

Stage one is partisan warfare: the general population is engaged in guerrilla tactics. Stage two is guerrilla warfare: professional trained soldiery is engaged in guerrilla tactics. Both partisan and guerrilla warfare are defensive. To eventually achieve victory, however, there must be a transition to offensive conventional warfare.[26]

Mao also understood that success in partisan war requires not only cooperation with conventional forces but the support of a sympathetic civilian population. This population provides a base of operation—a place to hide, rest, refit, and recruit. A "support base," as defined by him, is "an area, strategically located, in which the guerillas can carry out their duties of training, self-preservation and development."[27] Mao crudely noted the necessity of such bases: "a base area [was] as necessary as the human buttocks. After exhausting activity, you need it to rest on."[28]

To Mao, almost any isolated or rugged landscape could be useful as a base camp.

> Geography is the guerrilla's ally, as much as it is the invader's enemy. Guerrillas know the land by heart; it is their home. They hide in the native mountains, swamps, jungles, farmlands, or urban sprawl, places where an outsider would seldom dare go.[29]

Mao also states that it is the civilian population that provides food and other supplies for guerrillas, and a stable base of operation. In a compilation of his basic tactics, Mao described the perfect base camp:

> The problem is not merely one of resting and marshalling troops. We require a place that can also be used for conserving ammunition and food and for receiving and looking after wounded and sick soldiers....As soon as we are the objects of the enemy's pursuit and attack, we withdraw there, and secretly hide, so as to await an opportunity to act or to begin resisting the enemy again.

Discussing the location of such a hiding place Mao wrote that:

> A hiding place where we can rest for a long time may conveniently be found deep in the forest, in a thatched hut near a marsh, in a cave under the ground or in a mountainside, on a lonely farm, or in a small and secluded hamlet. Because of the sympathy it enjoys, a small guerrilla unit normally has no difficulty at all in finding a regular hiding place.

Mao warned:

> Sometimes such hiding places also serve as storehouses for military equipment, powder, and provisions, and also for receiving wounded and sick soldiers. More often, a separate secret location in the vicinity of the hiding place is selected for each type of storehouse because there

are people continually going in and out of a hiding place and it can very easily be discovered by the enemy.

Again, Mao sees such a hiding place as integrated into the population.[30] While not using the word "community," the concept is embedded in this quote:

> The more individuals there are among the people who support the guerrillas, so that the guerrilla unit can also maintain a communications network among the people, the easier it is for the guerrilla unit to find a hiding place. There are times when, in order to evade the enemy's pursuit and attack, and find a good place to hide, a given guerrilla unit must be split up, each of its members being obliged to find a way to hide himself in one of the houses of the local population. In such circumstances, the local population is the only hope of salvation of the members of the guerrilla unit.

Mao is supposed to have noted that the guerrilla must be like the fish in the sea, that is, to be able to swim among the local population and blend in.[31] Finally, Mao discusses the problem of provision:

> In places where the local population is hostile to the guerrillas, there is no alternative to foraging backed by force, but one should send reliable people from among the detachment, in order to guard against pillaging. When the guerrilla unit does not fear discovery, it can send out a special small unit to forage for food, to collect contributions of food, or to demand food supplies from the local authorities.

Although he noted the close relationship between the guerrilla and the population, Mao was suspect of both civilians and guerrillas. He was vigilant about what he labeled "localism" when guerrilla commanders, "because of their isolation, became 'frequently preoccupied with local considerations to the neglect of the general interest.'"[32] To Mao, guerrillas were professionals, not civilians acting in a military capacity, because he too was concerned that guerrillas would focus on the needs of the population to a point that their combat efficiency would suffer.

As will be seen, Marion's most successful tactics at Snow's Island were similar to the dictums to which Mao would later subscribe. And when they were violated, Marion paid the price.[33]

From August 1780 to April 1781, the Whig families and households on and around Snow's Island were a partisan community—in anthropological terms, a community of resistance—that Francis Marion exploited in sustaining his "partisan war." The community fit the bill on virtually all counts—as a base camp in a rugged area for Marion's guerrilla fighters, and as a safe space where they would retreat, replenish their supplies, find food and care for wounded soldiers, and hide when necessary, blending into the general population. They were far more than just a location on a map.

Through the 19th century, Francis Marion held a mythical presence in the national narrative of American independence. Snow's Island, his Sherwood Forest, was part of that narrative and may be viewed as a landscape of memory.

Endnotes for Chapter 1

1 Simms 1844; Griffith 1978:7.
2 Among those who have pronounced Marion one of the finest guerilla leaders are: Stovall (1971); Laqueur (1976:19); Weller (1977); Griffith (1978); Dederer (1983); Pancake (1985:110); Fitz-Simons (1995); Joes (1996); (2000); Keithly (2001:36); and Tierney (2006:42-43). The five standard biographies are: James (1821); Simms (1844); Horry and Weems (1891); Bass (1959); and Rankin (1973). A selection of others include: Moore (1845); Frost (1847); Lossing (1858); Hartley (1866); Stokes (1926); Epstein and Epstein (1956); Holbrook (1959); Gerson (1967); and Boddie (2000). The most recent is Oller (2016). Oller adeptly incorporates a lot of modern scholarship since Rankin and is among the best. Among those who compare Marion to Mao are Griffith (1978:5-7), and Dederer (1983).
3 General Lord Charles Cornwallis in Rankin 1973:115.
4 Tierney 2006:42. Some historians are not impressed by Tierney's scholarship on guerrilla warfare, and admittedly his book is an overview, not an academic treatise, however, for our purposes here he is suited just fine.
5 Wilson 2001.
6 Waghelstein 1995:152. See Fitz-Simons 1995 and Joes 1996 who also have discussed this relationship.
7 Rayburn Stovall's 1971 Master's thesis, "Francis Marion: 1780-1782" (Stovall 1971) and Laurent St. Georges' 1988 Master's Thesis, "Population Control and Guerrilla Warfare" (St. Georges 1988) are notable exceptions. Stovall demonstrates Marion's logistical skills as a District Commander. St. Georges' thesis focuses on Continental Army Commander General Nathanael Greene's use of propaganda and political organization with only a brief mention of partisan leaders like Marion or General Thomas Sumter.
8 Whigs were Americans in favor of independence during the American Revolution. The more modern term may be rebels, or patriots.
9 Note that Lynches River was known as Lynches Creek at the time of the American Revolution and even as late as 1825 (Mills 1825). From this point on it will be referred to as Creek.
10 The beginning of Marion's partisan career is easily established as the date he took command of the Williamsburg militia at Witherspoon's Ferry, 17 August 1780. The end date is less clear. I have chosen 13 or 14 April 1781 as the day in which Colonel Henry Lee joined Marion; shortly thereafter General Nathanael Greene returned to South Carolina (Marion to Greene, 21 April 1781, Greene Papers-William Clements Library [herein GP-WCL]). Lee and Marion would attack Forts Watson and Motte and from this point, the Americans were on the strategic offensive. The insightful Rayburn Stovall places Marion's transition from guerrilla to conventional officer as 28 May 1781, the date Marion occupied Georgetown (Stovall 1971:5). Both dates are defendable.
11 Tierney 2006:42.
12 Lee 1998:174.
13 Rankin 1973:3.
14 Marion's first, and unfortunate, biography was written by Reverend Mason Weems, who wrote the first biography of George Washington. Weems took a manuscript by Peter Horry, one of Marion's officers, and rewrote it into what can be only described as a romance (Horry and Weems 1809). Historians of Francis Marion have had to deal with the result ever since. I am using the 1891 edition of this work as the only 1809 edition I can access is in the Caroliniana Library and is rare. Page numbers are slightly off from the original as a result of different typesets. Also, the chapter heading of chapter IV of the first edition is repeated twice and thus chapter numbers are repeated. There are a few other typographical changes between editions, and later editions include illustrations, but they are remarkably the same text. William Dobein James wrote the second biography (1821). He was a young boy in Marion's Brigade, but his biography also has serious flaws, most importantly having to do with the chronology of events in Marion's life. Much more on the mythology of Francis Marion through the eyes of Weems is discussed in Chapter 9.

15 Rankin 1973:4-5.
16 See Rankin 1973, Chapter 1, and Bass 1959, Chapter 1.
17 His drink was water mixed with vinegar according to tradition. Harry Holbert Turney–High, a professor in the Department of Anthropology at the University of South Carolina in the 1950s, wrote in his classic *Primitive War,* that Thomas Sumter was unintelligent and "drank whiskey in quantity" while "Marion, though, was brilliant, even if he thought vinegar was the proper beverage of the fighting man" (Turney-High 1971:256). I suspect this is an exaggeration. There are indications in the primary records of Marion being issued rum during the encampment at Fort Johnson. Perhaps he gave it away.
18 Bass 1959:30; Rankin 1973:45.
19 Rankin 1973:147; Smith 2006a:679-680.
20 Ferguson 1979:240.
21 Smith et al. 2007:32.
22 Turney-High 1971:261; Dederer 1983.
23 Keithly 2001:50.
24 Weigley 1970:16.
25 Dederer 1983:14-15.
26 Dederer 1983:8-9.
27 Mao Tse-tung 1978:96. This use of Mao's military theory of guerilla warfare is not intended to champion his Marxist theory or his history of persecution.
28 Dederer 1983:44.
29 Tierney 2006:17.
30 Quotes from Mao in Schram 1966:115-116.
31 Quote from Schram 1966:116; fish allegory from Turney-High 1971:263.
32 Dederer 1983:38.
33 Schram 1966:116-117. I have not been able to establish a verifiable link that Mao Tse-tung had studied Marion's tactics. Obviously, Marion came first, so that when I compare Marion to Mao I am not implying that Marion learned guerrilla warfare from Mao or, Mao's likely textbook, the writings of Sun Tzu.

CHAPTER 2

AN ARCHAEOLOGICAL PERSPECTIVE

In the United States, archaeology is a subdiscipline of anthropology. Anthropology is the study of humanity—its evolutionary origins, its cultures, its languages, its biological development, past and present. Archaeologists are anthropologists who study past cultures using evidence in the form of artifacts, architecture, sites, and features found in the ground.

Archaeologists specialize in different times and eras of the past and one specialty is Historical Archaeology. An historical archaeologist studies people who lived after Europeans arrived in the Americas. We historical archaeologists not only use artifacts and sites to study this period but also the documents written by those people who used the artifacts and occupied the sites.

I am an historical archaeologist who has specialized further in the study of the American Revolution. Because historical archaeology developed as a specialized discipline within anthropology, historical archaeologists look at the past through the theories of anthropology rather than those of historians. That's why this book offers a different perspective, an archaeological perspective, on the military career of Francis Marion and the people who supported him.

When studying the past, archaeologists generally follow a standard process to have confidence that at the end of their work, their conclusions make sense and are defendable. We review what is known to date, and then formulate a question or questions (hypotheses), decide how we will go about gathering data to answer the questions (methods), gather the data (excavation, documentary research, recordation, identification of the artifacts), analyze the data (laboratory work), and then, from this total exercise, come to a conclusion or two.

This chapter describes the theory and methods used in my study of Francis Marion's partisan community from an anthropological-archaeological perspective. After considerable study of Marion's use of Snow's Island, I came to believe that there was a *community of resistance* in and around the island at the time of the American Revolution. I define a *community of resistance* as a localized population acting in concert against a common enemy. I say in *concert*, rather than in *cooperation*, because community membership may be coerced or negotiated. Communities of resistance may be pre-existing communities transformed by warfare and the struggle for liberation, or communities created because of that struggle.[1]

One type of community of resistance is a partisan community. A partisan community is a community consisting of non-combatant civilians and full time and part time warriors engaging in guerrilla warfare. From an anthropological standpoint, the people living around Snow's Island at the time of the American Revolution serve as an example of a partisan Whig community under the leadership of General Francis Marion and is the focus of this book.

ARCHAEOLOGICAL CONCEPTS OF COMMUNITY

Many archaeologists before me have studied prehistoric and historic communities and have shaped my own thinking about Francis Marion's Snow's Island community.[2] Anthropologist George Murdock and his colleagues in the 1940s and 1950s laid the foundation of archaeological community research. Murdock defined community as "the maximal group of persons who normally reside together in face-to-face association."[3] Murdock noted that the community provided an individual a better chance of survival because a group could share labor, resources, and security. Murdock recognized a community as a "universal" social group, the other being the family. Colleagues Conrad Arensberg and Solon Kimball declared that community was "a master institution or master social system; a key to society; and a model, indeed perhaps the most important model, of culture." Murdock, Arensberg, and Kimball believed that a community was defined by several elemental characteristics, including shared territory (and environment), interpersonal relationships (kinship), and social control (government and religion). More recently, anthropologists Jason Yaeger and Marcello Canuto summarized this definition of community as "a co-residential collection of individuals or households characterized by day-to-day interaction, shared experiences, and common culture." In a mobile society, for instance one of gatherers and hunters, the community was called a band. Indeed, the Snow's Island partisan community described here is like a band society with Francis Marion as their chief. Thus, a community is a bounded place, either past or present, in which families (households) clustered.

This perspective fits the partisan community or community of resistance, which incorporates both warriors and civilians within a particular geographical space, which in this case comprises the region in and around Snow's Island. Further, for Murdock and others, communities were defined by other communities.

> Within each community one finds the economic, political, religious, social, even familial activities which create cohesion among its members, and which also extend to or include those of other communities.[4]

As will be seen, the Snow's Island Whig community was surrounded by enemy Loyalist communities.

Murdock's notion of community fits well for an archaeologist digging in the dirt. It was especially fruitful in the popular settlement studies of the 1960s and 1970s and still works today.[5] It's not a perfect fit, however. Archaeologist K.C. Chang, for instance, recognized that a community was a social group that "is archaeologically most definable, but its definability is clearly not self-evident, as it generally is for example in social anthropology." Chang defined archaeological settlements as "the physical locale or cluster of locales where the members of a community lived, ensured their subsistence, and pursued their social functions in a delineable time period."[6]

Still, Chang's devotion to Murdock's definition of community provided a workable, if not perfect, theory for attempting to understand social relations of prehistoric and protohistoric sites and site clusters in the American Southwest. Single sites were often domestic sites or households and clusters of these sites were considered evidence of face-to-face interaction of several households, called villages or communities. Archaeologist William Lipe termed such clusters "first-order, face-to-face" communities. They were small enough for face-to-face interaction and "physically co-present."[7]

Archaeologist V. Kent Flannery, who studied Mesoamerican villages in south Mexico and western Guatemala dating to around 1500 to 500 B.C. recognized communities consisted of layers of sites at the house, household cluster, village-community, and catchment level. Significantly, he saw that the archaeological manifestation of a community would include more than just a cluster of households and included other functional types of sites like cemeteries and plazas. The Snow's Island partisan community described herein, for instance, also includes not only domestic sites but also ferries, military camps, and fortifications.

Flannery's "catchment area" concept is insightful and pertinent to understanding the Snow's Island partisan community as well. A catchment area is a region of resource exploitation surrounding a community, or "the zone of resources, both wild and domestic, that occur within a reasonable walking distance of a given village." Notably, the farther one moves away from the village, the "less it is likely to be exploited…since energy consumed in movement to and from the site will tend to cancel out that derived from the resource." Eventually, a resource is simply too far away to make it economically rewarding. At that distance, it is reasonable to assume that a community has found its natural boundary. The boundary of the Snow's Island community was probably also defined by the boundaries of adjacent Loyalist communities who were at war with the people of Snow's Island.

Prior to the war, the Snow's Island community was not a village but, instead, was a dispersed rural farming community. Archaeologist William Adams described such a community in early 20th-century Silcott, Washington. Adams noted that the community could "be delineated on the basis of interaction spheres, that is, on the frequency and depth of interpersonal relationships between neighbors. These borders are sharply defined, both socially and geographically."

I found a similar situation at Bay Springs, Mississippi, a dispersed rural 20th-century community I examined in the 1980s, in which church membership defined community as strongly as locale. Community households interacted more with fellow church members than with geographically proximate households down or across the road. I expect that this is the case for the colonial community around Snow's Island also, and that war changed the way that community interacted because of its resistance to an outside force.[8]

COMMUNITY AND LANDSCAPE

Obviously, I am tying the concept of community to a locality on the physical landscape—in this case the Snow's Island region. Archaeologists, geographers, and historians all have recognized the importance of the landscape.[9] As used herein, landscapes are seen the product of culture (community) and the results of a community transforming physical spaces into useful and meaningful places. Thus, the landscape is the arena for community activities. Landscape archaeology involves "evaluation of the dynamic, interdependent relationships that people maintain with the physical, social, and cultural dimensions of their environment across space and over time."[10]

Landscape is especially pertinent to the archaeology of military sites. Indeed, throughout history, military strategy and tactics were informed by the landscape and technology of the time. The idea that maneuver, fortification, and campsite choices are not only affected by landscape, but also *transform* landscape, is well established in the archaeological literature. For instance, archaeologists have examined how medieval battlefields were "chosen" based on landscape features. My own work at Civil War fortifications across Beaufort and Jasper Counties, South Carolina, used GPS data to reveal the tactical landscape constructed by Confederate military planners early in the war, while others have examined the archaeology and landscape of Civil War campgrounds. In this study of the partisan community of Snow's Island, I intend to reveal the landscape of a community of resistance from the historical and archaeological record.[11]

Further demonstrating the integral nature of archaeological community and landscape theory, both have physical (natural) and imagined perspectives that add to our understanding of communities. Humans perceive landscape as a practical problem to overcome and as the arena for resource exploitation, but also as symbolic. Social groups can be both on the landscape and part of the landscape. This is wonderfully demonstrated by Veronica Strang's study of differing perspectives of the landscape in Kowanyama, North Queensland. Strang looked at the contrasting ways that aboriginals and white Australian cattle farmers viewed, interacted with, and valued the landscape.

For aboriginals, the landscape is never "wholly divorced from emotional and spiritual interaction." The landscape is full of mythology and is not only their cosmos but also their cosmology. People are *in* and *part of* the landscape. In contrast, Strang saw that white cattle farmers that came from a largely European intellectual tradition saw the landscape as an enemy to be conquered and tamed, much like our own American frontier.[12] Western people do, however, impose meaning on landscape and on the act of taming the landscape. Evidence exists to support the conclusion that Snow's Island served Americans after the American Revolution similarly and became a landscape full of symbolic meaning that shaped how Americans remembered (and forgot) their past.

OTHER PERSPECTIVES OF PARTISAN COMMUNITIES

As far as I know, this is the first archaeological study of a partisan community. At least one historian, Lindley Butler, has paid a little attention to Loyalist communities on the British side of the war. He specifically focused on the Loyalist partisan community led by David Fanning in North Carolina. Fanning was the British equivalent of Francis Marion, and Butler's study described how Fanning's partisans relied on community networking much like Marion in South Carolina.[13]

Similarly, cultural anthropologists and social historians of Latin America have written extensively on local communities and modern guerrilla movements.[14] These studies demonstrate some common links between partisan communities of the past and guerrillas of the present. In Latin American revolutionary movements, guerrillas often hid at base camps resembling Snow's Island (although in mountainous regions) and came down from the mountains for supplies and recruitment provided by village communities.

Dirk Kruijt studied three guerrilla organizations—the Farabundo Martí National Liberation Front, the Sandinista National Liberation Front, and the Guatemalan National Revolutionary Unity. He noted that they all depended on the "local population as a vital source of material and moral support and as a reservoir of popular militias that served as allies of the guerrilla cause."[15]

In a comparative study of guerrilla movements and revolution in Latin America, sociologist Timothy Wickham-Crowley did not identify partisan communities by name but did find that peasant support was a "crucial determinant of the failure or success of rural guerrilla movements." Likewise, anthropologist Orin Starn described how the Peruvian guerrilla movement called Shining Path was organized by urban intellectuals who recruited university and high school students of rural origin who "fanned across the countryside during the 1970s to begin underground organizing, and then took up arms in the 1980s." As will be seen, these guerrillas operated much like Marion's partisan community:

> But the young women and men of the Shining Path know the hidden trails of the mountains, how to survive the cold nights, how to dodge army patrols, how to blend with the civilian population and regroup when the security forces withdraw. The guerrillas, in short, frequently have a double status in the peasant communities of Ayacucho. They are part 'insiders' and 'outsiders.'[16]

Latin American guerrilla movements seem to be part and parcel of modern Latin America, and Latin American anthropologists continue to debate whether such movements are or are not "detrimental to the rural base communities supporting them." Niels Barmeyer argued that for the village of San Emiliano, settled in the 1950s in the Las Canadas/Selva Lacandona region of Chiapas, Mexico, "getting involved with a guerrilla movement… [the village] has been able to put itself in a position that is in many ways better than before." Barmeyer demonstrated how the village supported the guerrillas with its social infrastructure, including decision-making, religious support, and food. The community provided fighters and financed weapons, much like Marion's partisan community. The guerrilla movement in turn provided a military option that strengthened the villager's position in negotiations with the weak government and landed elites. Democratic decision making as a result of guerrilla-community cooperation empowered villagers. Meanwhile, the counter-insurgency efforts by the Mexican government against the guerrillas required infrastructural support to the rural areas including roads and health facilities that improved living conditions. These examples demonstrate the importance of strong connections between civilian populations and successful guerrilla movements.[17]

While archaeologists have ignored the partisan experience, they have used community concepts in the examination of resistance movements. Kenneth E. Sassaman compared Eastern European Gypsies, Old Order Amish, and Archaic Hunter-Gatherers finding that there are "cross-cultural regularities found among traditions of resistance." He found that in all three cases, persistent resistance was maintained through geographic separation and ideological separation, through tradition. In this study, a similar result is seen in that the Snow's Island community was not only geographically isolated by rivers and swamps, but the community members retained the pre-colonial traditional social structure while acting as partisans or supporting partisans.[18]

Archaeologist Robert Preucel's study offers another example of a political or war-informed community very similar to the Snow's Island partisan community. Preucel examined 17th century Pueblo Indians in the Southwest at Kotyiti, New Mexico. Preucel asserted that community formation included the "mobilization of social identities for political purposes" and examined how Pueblo leaders "manufactured" an ethnic consciousness through resistance to draw disparate native villages together to oppose the Spaniards. In his example, group identity and resistance to outside forces was the glue that held the community together. His work is the only known example of an archaeological study such as the one proposed in this book and is the inspiration for my concept of a community of resistance.[19]

A THEORETICAL STATEMENT

The above discussion has provided a theoretical backdrop upon which to frame my concept of a community of resistance, as exemplified by the Snow's Island partisan community. I have argued that community is a useful and viable concept in archaeology, visualized as a social group with shared interests located in space and as imagined by diverse peoples who share common interests.

In the following chapters, I will demonstrate that a general community of resistance formed during the American Revolution. As a community of resistance, it emerged across South Carolina—from the initial statement of independence in 1776, through British occupation of the state after the fall of Charleston, South Carolina, in May of 1780, and until the Treaty of Paris in 1783.

Within this larger Whig community of resistance were enclaves of socially defined and physically bounded communities of resistance, one of which was Francis Marion's Snow's Island partisan community. These communities were the Murdockian settlements of face-to-face interaction, cooperation or negotiation, and clustering—or Lipe's "first-order, face-to-face" communities.[20]

When speaking of a partisan community in the next chapters, I am referring to the people and families living around Snow's Island, supporting Marion and enlisting in his ranks. When speaking of the Snow's Island community region, I am referring to the geographical space within which these families lived. Sometimes these two definitions will cross over. The context of the sentence, however, should make it clear as to whether I am referring to the region, the people, or both.

The archaeological manifestation of this community should be a cluster of archaeological sites and landscape features. As I demonstrate, even the natural boundaries of Snow's Island, a high ground swamp surrounded by rivers and creeks, was a place (landscape) and a people, both of which spread beyond the physical boundaries of these water bodies.

REMEMBERING FRANCIS MARION AND SNOW'S ISLAND

In the preface to this book, I noted that our modern memory, admiration, and commemoration of Francis Marion has been greatly influenced by his early biographers, Mason Locke Weems, William Dobein James, and William Gilmore Simms. These biographers had different perspectives and agendas when it came to be relating strictly facts versus storytelling and nation building. As a result, I have long been interested in deconstructing their myths from the raw facts of the military career of Marion. As it happened, Marion, the larger Whig community of resistance, and the Snow's Island partisan community were props in 19th-century nation building—sometimes referred to as the imagined nation.[21]

Marion became a nationally recognized hero during the transformation of the British colonies into an independent republic. Although he was revered locally, his national image was largely the result of the Reverend Mason Weems's biographical adaptation of a manuscript by Colonel Peter Horry, who

Sketch of Mason Locke Weems ("Parson" Weems)

Colonel Peter Horry in Uniform
Image courtesy of the
USC Caroliniana Library

was one of Marion's officers. Marion's fame spread across the eastern United States as America moved west after the American Revolution. He became part of the American narrative, and veterans of his brigade drew together as part of that narrative.

Along with Marion's fame, Snow's Island grew in importance. Within this imagined community, Snow's Island was revered as sacred ground. It is as much a traditional cultural place as Valley Forge, and as mythical as Robin Hood's Sherwood Forest. Therefore, in a slight divergence from my focus on Snow's Island community, I devote one chapter of this book (Chapter 9) to a detailed examination of the myths surrounding the island and Marion's memory as the "Swamp Fox."

METHODS

In order to examine the Snow's Island partisan community, I use a multidisciplinary approach, which includes the use and interpretation of historic documents, analysis of archaeological survey and excavations, and landscape analysis. To focus my examination, I seek the answer to the following questions:

1. How was the colonial population around Snow's Island transformed into a community of resistance as a result of revolution? How was it maintained by Francis Marion as a distinct partisan community?
2. What is the archaeological manifestation of the partisan community?
3. How was the partisan community and Snow's Island redefined in 19th century memory?
4. What can the Snow's Island partisan community tell us about communities of resistance?

Chapters 3 and 4 of this book paint the social landscape of the late 18th century around Snow's Island with a focus on the Britton's Neck region just prior to the American Revolution. After all, in order to study the partisan community, I must establish that a community existed! I briefly provide an overview of the development of that community.

The heart of Chapter 4 is a list of families in the Snow's Island region. This includes a discussion of the kinship, social, landholding, and business connections between these families—and any other evidence of community connections.

Generally, the idea is to establish a representative sample of who lived (or owned land) in the Snow's Island community region just prior to and during the American Revolution. Plats, deeds, genealogy, and other colonial records assist to define community membership.

Chapter 5 describes what happened to these families, and the changes that occurred in the community during the early war years from 1776 to the fall of Charleston in May 1780.

Chapters 6 and 7 present a military history of Marion's partisan career from August 1780 to the middle of April 1781, with a focus on the interaction between Marion and the Snow's Island partisan community. This book only summarizes Marion's military career from then until Marion's dismissal of his troops at Wadboo Plantation in December 1782.

During this latter period, Marion's role in the revolution and military tactics became increasingly conventional as he cooperated with General Nathanael Greene and the Continental Army. Snow's Island was largely abandoned as a guerilla camp although the people of Snow's Island continued their support of the larger revolution. How they continued their support of both Marion and Greene becomes the focus of this section of the book.

The history in these chapters relies on military correspondence, eyewitness accounts, pension applications, audited accounts, stub indents, militia rosters, and even traditional local histories. This historical data builds the case for the transformation of the pre-Revolutionary community into Marion's partisan community.[22] I also discuss evidence of those who did not join Marion and their fate.

I use the same historical data to examine the relationship between Marion and the community *after* April 1781, presenting a series of audited accounts as evidence of the supplies provided to Marion by the community. I also discuss what actions Marion took to maintain the community and what happened to the community after the base camp(s) on the island were destroyed by the British at the end of March 1781.

Chapter 8 examines the archaeological landscape of the partisan community that was created by Marion's occupation and use of the region in and around Snow's Island. The archaeological sites discussed in this chapter are those linked to the historical record and pinpoint known landscape features (place names, roads, ferry crossings, probable campsites). This analysis provides insights into the archaeological manifestation of a partisan community and a perspective on the partisan use of the landscape.

Most of the sites are only briefly described in Chapter 8 as I am demonstrating the larger or regional partisan landscape. The exception is site 38MA207. A documented Marion campsite, it provides the first opportunity for us to explicitly examine a partisan camp. For this reason, I provide additional details.

Chapter 9 may be considered a bonus chapter, as it examines the re-imagined post-war legends of Francis Marion and Snow's Island during the 19th century. In this chapter, we delve into the first Marion biography by Horry and Weems and its influence on nation building, the legend of Francis Marion as the Swamp Fox, and Snow's Island as a landscape of memory.[23]

Finally, Chapter 10 returns to a more anthropological discussion of partisan communities and communities of resistance and summarizes the previous chapters, providing some conclusions about them.

WEAKNESSES OF THE METHODS

Archaeologists seek to reveal the past as accurately as possible. Nevertheless, it behooves us to recognize that the complete story can never be told, nor can the past be completely revealed. This examination of the Snow's Island partisan community relies heavily on historical and archaeological data and therefore possesses all the usual weaknesses inherent in cases where incomplete data exists. As usual, the historical record of the war is incomplete and biased towards the winners.

For example, the Civil War caused the loss of many Southern colonial documents. At the regional level, historic records pertaining to this area of the state, like memoirs, deeds, plats, and wills are woefully vague and rare. My attempts to construct a complete and accurate cadastral map of the Snow's Island region convinced me that it is not possible.

Some plats can be pinpointed to a specific location, especially when they are located along the larger rivers, but many simply float in space because the land descriptions have no modern reference points and no other landowners shown around them.

In addition, the genealogy contained herein is tangled with generations of descendants with the same names—due to low regional populations, marriage among cousins was not unusual. On the other hand, marriage between neighbors was equally common, which serves to demonstrate the interconnectedness of community members in face-to-face relationships.

Although the audited accounts provide insightful links within the partisan community, these resources must be used with great care. It cannot automatically be assumed, for instance, that those who provided provisions to Marion in the Snow's Island region did so voluntarily or even supported the American cause. Around 1780, many citizens in the middle colonies refused certificates unless pressured and, as Quartermaster General Timothy Pickering stated, it was useless to refuse since the soldiery "had the force."[24]

This does not mean, however, that the audited accounts are useless. Historian E. James Ferguson notes, "Not all certificates represented forced collections. Many patriots gave their goods willingly." Furthermore, in December 1780, General Greene issued orders to General Daniel Morgan to conduct independent operations in the upstate of South Carolina. At that time, he was ordered to give receipts to "all such as are friends to the independence of America," implying that no known Loyalists would be given receipts. It is reasonable to assume, then, that those who provided supplies signed petitions against the Loyalists (see Chapters 5, 6 and 7), and served under Marion, probably providing those supplies freely or without much persuasion, and supporting the American cause.

It is also likely that, given the fact that there was no sitting South Carolina government during the partisan period (August 1780 to April 1781), Marion might have chosen not to issue certificates to Loyalists. If so, this probably changed around April 1781. At that time, General Greene, anxious to gain the public's support, warned General Thomas Sumter (a partisan commander in the upstate of South Carolina) to provide certificates. "But indeed any horses, or any other kind of property whether taken from Whig or Tory, certificates ought to be given, that justice may be done to the inhabitants hereafter; and if any discrimination is necessary with the people, Government may make it when the certificates are presented for payment." These examples are the sort of issues that require judicious use of the accounts, but do not negate their usefulness.[25]

Pension accounts also must be used with care and skepticism. Written as much as thirty to forty years after the war, memories fade and as I argue in some cases, memories were *created* (see Chapter 9). I have looked at a number of these accounts by pensioners and it is obvious that, even though many were illiterate, by the 1830s they had some familiarity with the early written histories and used these histories to assist their memories.

Major battles like Cowpens, Camden, and Eutaw Springs were traumatic events and show up regularly (sometimes out of order chronologically) while skirmishes are scrambled and confused with others. Snow's Island is mentioned often, but one must wonder (and it is argued herein) that part of this is because it was already a landscape of memory by the 1830s (see Chapter 9). As veterans will agree, the common soldier often has little idea where he is at any one time over the course of a campaign. Officers may have a better idea simply because it was their duty to know where they were.

Finally, pensioners needed to state under whom they served, when, and where, in order to prove they deserved a pension. Obviously, some individuals would have been tempted to enhance their resumes. Nevertheless, I believe that with critical evaluation, judicious and skeptical examination of the record, and crosschecking between multiple resources, much of the above can be overcome—at least sufficiently enough to establish the historical record of the partisan community.

Likewise, the archaeological data must be critically analyzed. As noted, no archaeologist has found the Snow's Island camp. We do not know what such a camp would look like in the archaeological record since no full excavation of a partisan camp has been undertaken and, consequently, we do not have an accurate representation of the archaeological features and artifacts that would uniquely identify remains of a partisan occupation.

Also, Francis Marion and his partisans rarely camped in a pristine location devoid of previous or contemporary occupations. Close examination of the historical record and the archaeological survey level work conducted by the author on a number of Marion sites supports the contention that Marion usually camped at plantations, ferry crossings, mills, or the houses of supporters, such that the partisan occupation of a typical camp site is mixed with other occupations.[26]

There has been, prior to work at 38MA207, the danger of circular argumentation, e.g., The archaeological remains of a partisan camp *should* look like A. We have found a site containing A. Therefore, the site is a partisan camp. Historic references to 38MA207 strongly support this location as a campsite, and therefore the analysis of this site is our first indication of what archaeological features and artifacts constitute a partisan camp. In the future, other partisan camps will be compared to 38MA207 with the hope of better clarifying this archaeological signature.

Analysis of what the 18th-century landscape looked like *prior* to the American Revolution is also important. This entails discussing landscape history in order to detect where changes occurred as a result of warfare. This section includes a brief review of the dynamic hydrology of the Great Pee Dee River. Since my first attempts to search Snow's Island in the 1990s, there has been at least one major change in the Pee Dee riverbed near Snow's Island, which created a new nearly isolated oxbow lake. Other changes that have occurred since 1780 must also be addressed and identified, perhaps leading to a more precise idea of where the remains of Marion's Snow's Island camp might be located.

Again, however, historic documents describing the region are extremely rare, and so may be our ability to accomplish the above.

Even so, while all the inherent problems and biases within the data are evident and can affect the results of examination, awareness of those problems and biases can assist in the fine tuning of any conclusions drawn.

Endnotes for Chapter 2

1 Here resistance is defined as "an underground organization engaged in a struggle for national liberation in a country under military or totalitarian occupation" (American Heritage Dictionary 1982:1052).

2 Because "community" has such wide application in anthropology and sociology, including a vast number of theoretical and ideological perspectives, I believe it is beneficial to the reader to state how it is not used. There is a large body of literature having to do with modern community studies, found especially within the discipline of sociology but not exclusively (see for example Suttles 1972 for a study of urban communities). These studies are not relevant to this discussion, nor are community health studies. There is also a body of archaeological literature devoted to the interaction of archaeology and archaeologists with modern communities. They focus on how scientists interact with and involve nonscientists in their studies (Greer et al. 2002). Still another community research area concerns the ethics and interpretation of anthropology and archaeology vis a vis the modern community (Holtorf 2005). Likewise, these studies do nothing to advance the study of community and communities from an archaeological perspective.

3 Murdock et al. 1945:29-30; Murdock 1949.

4 Arensberg and Kimball 1965:ix, 4-5; Murdock et al. 1945:79-80; Yaeger and Canuto 2000:2; Lawrence Babits 2009, pers. comm.

5 Ascher 1968; Chang 1968; Rouse 1968; Hole and Heizer 1973.

6 Chang 1968:3.

7 Lipe 1970; Varien 1999:19-23. Of course, for academia it can all become so much more complicated. What I term "Murdockian" influenced community studies have been more recently critiqued by archaeologists recognizing weaknesses and problems in attempting to integrate socio-cultural concepts of community with archaeological correlates. One of the serious weaknesses in any attempt to define community via archaeology is the possibility of the observer (the archaeologist) imposing community on a cluster of sites regardless of the actual social interaction among the occupants of the sites during the sites' occupancy (Isbell 2000; Hegmon 2002). That is, if there is a cluster of archaeological sites within a region, archaeologists, especially prehistoric archaeologists, assume that the sites were a "face-to-face" community (Isbell 2000; Hegmon 2002:277). In fact, "in the early part of this century, when site-based research dominated archaeology, archaeologists generally equated community and site" (Yaeger and Canuto 2000:3). Indeed, even Murdock and his colleagues noted that multiple human interactions might occur across a region which might involve multiple communities. Joyce Marcus makes the same point adding that "An immediate problem is the lack of fit between any society's definition of 'community' and the physical remains left for archaeologists to study" (Marcus 2000:231). She notes from her studies of complex societies in the Andes that members of a community might be defined as those claiming descent from a common ancestor, even though its members were from different villages. Archaeologists tend to use "community" to "refer to a cluster of artifacts and ruined structures that exist in space" (Marcus 2000:239). Archaeologists Mark Varien and James Potter (2008) claim a solution for historical archaeologists, and that is the historic documents. They point out in their studies of protohistoric and historic sites in the Southwest that they have the tools to sort sites chronologically (a historic record, for instance). If the sites are occupied more or less contemporarily, and they cluster, it is logical to assume that there was some human interaction between individuals inhabiting the various sites. As will be seen in this study, both history and archaeology confirm contemporariness of the sites and people along with the interpersonal economic and kin structures of the sites' (communities') occupants.

8 Flannery 1976:91; Peterson and Drennan 2005; Adams 1977:26; Smith et al. 1982.

9 The first use and definition of the term landscape originated with cultural geographer Carl Sauer in his "landmark" 1925 essay, The Morphology of Landscape (Sauer 1963:315-350). Sauer stated that: "The cultural landscape is fashioned from a natural landscape by a cultural group. Culture is the agent, the natural area is the medium, the cultural landscape is the result. Under the influence of a given culture, itself changing through time, the landscape undergoes development, passing through phases, and probably reaching ultimately the end of its cycle, of development. With the introduction of a different—that is alien—culture, a rejuvenation of the cultural landscape sets in,

or a new landscape is superimposed on the remnants of an older one" (Sauer 1963:343). Sauer's concept of culture was much more narrowly confined than culture as viewed by an archaeologist today. Nevertheless, I would argue that Sauer's definition remains current today among many archaeologists including the author.

10 Casey 2008; Anschuetz et al. 2001:157.

11 Babits 1982; Haecker and Mauck 1997; Smith et al. 2003:14-30; Geier, Orr, and Reeves 2006; Carman and Carman 2007:39-49; Smith et al. 2003.

12 Strang 1999:208, 216.

13 Butler 1994:147-157.

14 Anthropologists have studied warfare since its earliest foundation as a discipline and the literature is voluminous (Otterbein 1999; Simons 1999). Any attempt to encapsulate anthropological studies of war and warfare are doomed to failure—especially when war, conflict, and violence are considered nearly synonymous. R. Brain Ferguson attempted to compile a bibliography of "substantial anthropological discussions of war (including archaeology) in 1987, [and] we quit around 1,500 citations, because there was no end" (Ferguson 2006:475). Suffice to say that anthropologists have looked at warfare from multiple anthropological perspectives and subdisciplines. A few examples include prehistoric archaeology (Arkush and Allen 2006), cultural anthropology (Otterbein 2009), biological and biocultural anthropology (Dawson 1999; Leatherman 2005), ecological anthropology (Ember 1982), evolutionary theory and origins (Otterbein 2004; Thayer 2004), indigenous warfare (Ferguson and Whitehead 1992; Chacon and Mendoza 2007), ethnicity (Eller 1999), militarism (Ben-Ari 1998), and nationalism (Shaw and Wong 1989). Most of these studies are not directly relevant to my interest in partisan communities and communities of resistance, except in the area of guerrilla warfare, insurgency, and counterinsurgency discussed in this chapter. As mentioned in the first chapter, the University of South Carolina's own Harry Holbert Turney-High, wrote one of the classic books on primitive war (Turney-High 1971). Turney-High discussed guerrilla warfare in the final chapter of his second edition, specifically labeling Francis Marion and Thomas Sumter as guerrilla warriors, distinguished from terrorists and primitive warriors. Guerrillas have a "grudging recognition in the law of war" (Turney-High 1971:260). Interestingly, Turney-High states that the distinction between primitive war and "true (or civilized) war" as discussed in his book is the "invention of the civilian as separate from fighting forces" (Turney-High 1971:262). This would seemingly place partisans within the primitive war category according to Turney-High, however, what he means is that in primitive war, women, children, old men, are all considered enemies for elimination. Partisans and guerrillas and indeed all types of warriors in modern warfare may kill or injure civilians during warfare, but the category of "noncombatant" is usually recognized and not a direct target (Turney-High 1971:262). This brings us to modern counterinsurgency studies. Anna Simons notes, war is a "fraught" subject (Simons 1999:74) and the history of anthropologists assisting the United States Department of Defense in this area is controversial and confrontational (McFate 2005). Recently, for instance, anthropologist Roberto J. Gonzalez lambasted anthropologists contributing to the U.S. Army's new counterinsurgency manual FM 3-24 (Gonzalez 2007).

15 Kruijt 2008:93-94.

16 Wickham-Crowley 1992:51; Starn 1991:71.

17 Barmeyer 2003:122.

18 Sassaman 2001:219. His use of the term resistance meant "action in opposition to structure, the opposite of compliance."

19 Preucel 2000: 58-77.

20 Lipe 1970; Lipe 1992:3.

21 Benedict Anderson 1991.

22 During the American Revolution, a credit system was imposed whereby officers would give certificates to citizens providing provisions and service in the militia to the American forces. Starting on 22 March, 1783, "interest-bearing certificates called indents were issued in payment of these accounts" by the Auditor General's Office (Wates 1955:v). Stubs to the indents were retained by the government, which summarized the information contained in the indent. A voluminous collection

of audited accounts, indents, and stubs survive at the South Carolina Department of Archives and History. Many of the stub entries have been published by A.S. Salley and Wylma Wates (see published primary sources in References). The data provided on these accounts were rarely been used by historians until recently. During and after the revolution, the United States government provided three types of pensions for veterans and their dependents. A disability or invalid pension was provided to injuries obtained in the line of duty. Service pensions were provided to veterans who served a term of service, and widows' pensions were provided to women whose husbands had been killed or could have applied for a service pension. Numerous legislative acts from 1776 to 1869 authorized pensions and clarified how pensions were obtained. The last major pension act was passed on 7 June 1832 and was quite expansive, allowing full pay for life to any Continental line soldier, state trooper, volunteer, or militia veteran who served for two years. Even veterans with less than two years service could get a pension, just not at full pay. Furthermore, the veteran's widow or children could receive payment from "the last payment until the date of death of a pensioner" (National Archives 1974). The last act authorized payment to widows of veterans who had served only 14 days. Until recently, the records of applications for pensions by Revolutionary War veterans were virtually ignored by most historians. Today these pensions are diligently being searched by historians for new insights into battles (Babits 1998; Babits and Howard 2009). The internet has allowed genealogists to share their ancestor's applications and avocational historians have transcribed hundreds of applications and placed them on-line (Southern Campaigns of the American Revolution 2010). The National Archives, which holds the original files in Record Group 15, Records of the Veterans Administration, has also allowed the web history source Footnote.com (2010) to scan nearly 80,000 applications, providing contemporary historians of the war with a name searchable resource that may revolutionize primary source research. Furthermore, summaries of some of the South Carolina pensions have been published (Moss 1983).

23 Marion historians have often trod the tangled trail of Marion mythology first blazed by the Horry-Weems romance. Where I hope to contribute is to analyze both the trail and the trail makers from an anthropological perspective and in the guise of the landscapes of memory (Shackel 2001).

24 Ferguson 1961:60, 64; Showman and Conrad 1991:xii.

25 Ferguson 1961:63; Greene to Morgan, 16 December 1780, GP, Volume VI:590; Greene to Sumter, 15 April 1781, GP, Vol. VIII:101.

26 Smith 2008a.

CHAPTER 3
THE SETTLEMENT OF THE SNOW'S ISLAND COMMUNITY

Before the American Revolution, a dispersed rural colonial settlement existed on and around Snow's Island. At the beginning of the Revolution, this community became a community of resistance consisting of Whigs in rebellion against British rule. This chapter describes the development of the colonial community that became Marion's partisan community beginning in August 1780. This history of regional settlement around Snow's Island includes the southern Marion District (consisting at that time of Britton's Neck and the area north of Lynches Creek), the eastern Williamsburg District, and the extreme northern portion of Georgetown District (Figure 1.2).

THE SNOW'S ISLAND REGIONAL LANDSCAPE

As noted in Chapter 2, the Snow's Island community-region was both a place and a people. The geographical center of this Snow's Island community-region is Snow's Island itself, delimited by the surrounding waters of Lynches (north boundary) and Clark's Creek (western and southern boundary) and the Pee Dee River (northern and eastern boundary) (Figure 3.1). This center was neither a geographical nor political center prior to the war, but became a focal point as a result of Marion's use of it as a base camp for his partisans. The region is loosely defined within a 15- to 20-mile radius of Snow's Island (Figure 1.2). The core families of this resistance were those living on Britton's Neck across the Pee Dee River east of Snow's Island and those along Lynches Creek (Figure 3.1).

Beyond the core, many other Whig families in the region were connected through political and social relations to the Britton's Neck families and supported or fought for Marion during the Revolution. Generally, this outer region consisted of families who settled along and south of Jeffries and Catfish Creek, two branches of the Pee Dee River (Figure 3.1, facing). Somewhere along Catfish Creek there were also several Loyalist families.

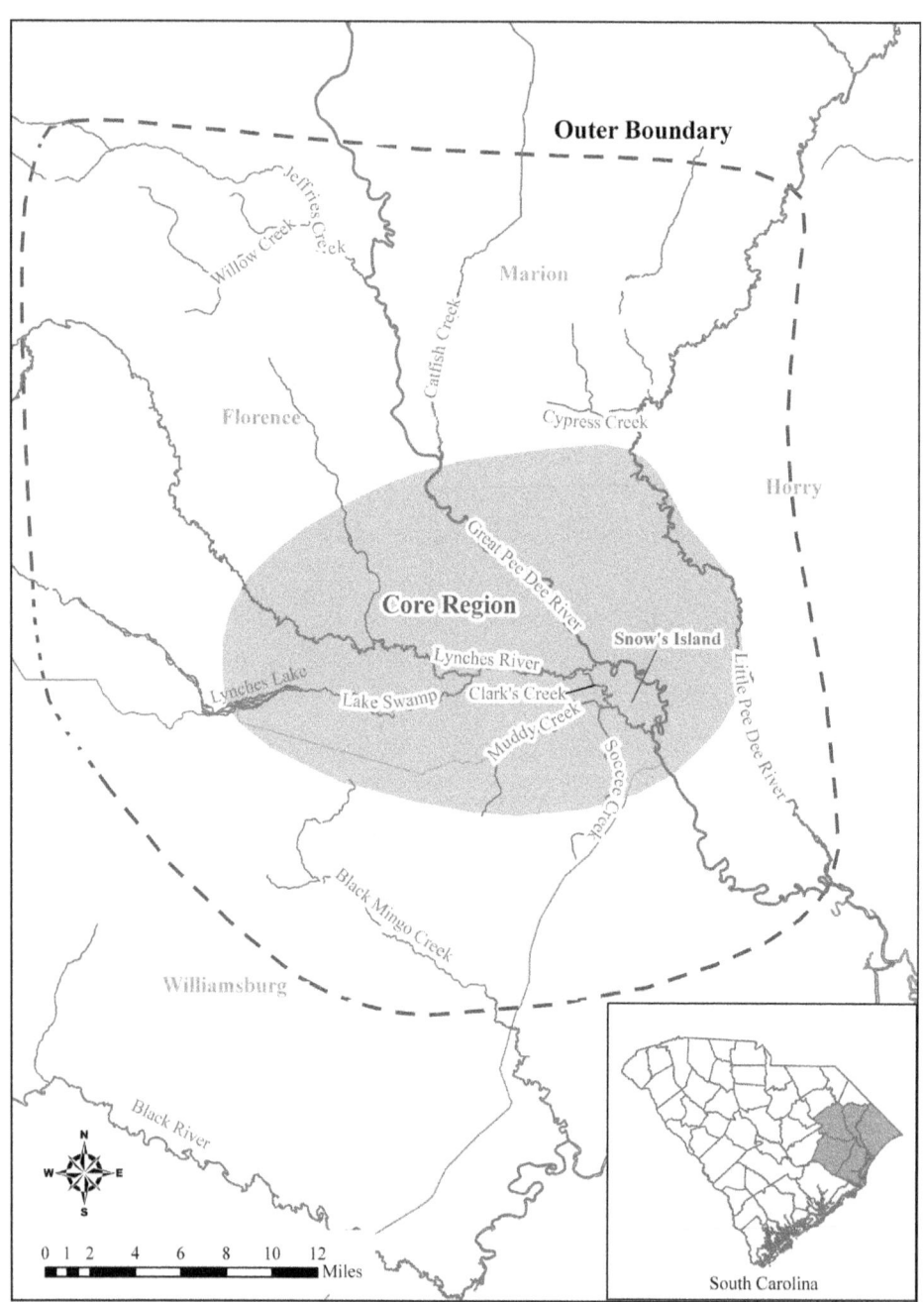

Figure 3.1. Snow's Island community core and outer regions (T.S. Wilson)

The southern edge of the region is defined as the confluence of the Great Pee Dee and the Little Pee Dee at Britton's Neck and in Williamsburg Township along Black Mingo Creek as far upstream as Indiantown. The western edge is not sharply defined, as many, if not most, Williamsburg Township residents were strong Whigs.

The eastern extent of the region is somewhere along Little Pee Dee. Determining how far upstream the region extends is problematic, but the history of Marion's use of the region (see Chapters 6 and 7) will demonstrate that an approximate line is modern U.S. 501 at Galivants Ferry. Beyond that, to the North Carolina line and east to the coast, most South Carolinians leaned Loyalist and they remained so throughout the war. There was at least one exception, however, and that family will be identified below.

The northwestern border is also vague, but strong supporters of Francis Marion included the Nettles family, living just south of modern Florence, and the Witherspoon family west of Witherspoon's Ferry. This included lower Lynches Creek and Lynches Lake. Notably, Loyalist sentiments ran strong along upper Lynches Creek.

No doubt the physical landscape of the Snow's Island region was significantly different from that seen today, but to what degree is difficult to know because the Pee Dee River has changed its channel since then. For instance, since 1993, when I first began research on Snow's Island, Bottle Point, a great bend in the river at Snow's Island, has been cut off and the old riverbed is practically an oxbow lake with only a small opening to the Pee Dee at the north end. This will close soon if it has not already.

An 18th-century plat of Snow's Island indicates that Old River Lake at Bottle Point was an active branch of the Pee Dee at that time, cutting off the high ground on Snow's Island as a separate smaller island (Figure 3.2). Other changes to the river channel since the American Revolution are unknown, but these two examples serve to assure that there were others.

The land has also changed. Nineteenth-century cotton farming, repeated 19th- and 20th-century logging, and upstream damming of the Pee Dee have all contributed to changing not only the river channel but dynamic landscape and vegetative change. Eighteenth- and 19th-century descriptions of the colonial landscape for the greater Williamsburg-Marion County region are sparse—nearly nonexistent for the smaller Snow's Island and Britton's Neck region.[1] What *is* known is that it was a region of swamps and swales.

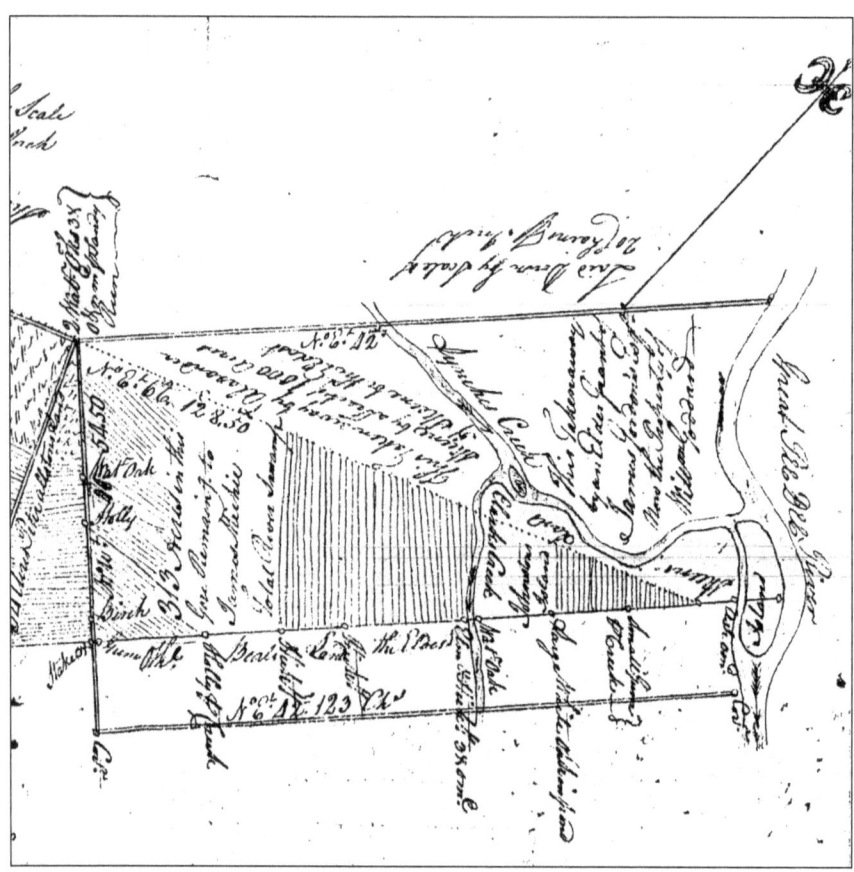

Figure 3.2. Detail of 1783 plat of James Michie's forfeited estate (SCDAH, S126102:334, 166)

The key to understanding the historic settlement of the Snow's Island region is the (Great) Pee Dee River drainage, which includes the Pee Dee, Little Pee Dee, Lumber River, Clark's Creek, Lynches Creek, downstream Black Mingo Creek, Black River, and finally the Waccamaw River (Figure 3.3). The Great Pee Dee River system drains the eastern quarter of South Carolina, running 197 miles from the North Carolina line downstream to the Atlantic Ocean.

But the Pee Dee extends even farther into North Carolina (called the Yadkin River from Badin Lake, North Carolina, northward) and indeed some headwaters of the drainage begin in Virginia. The mouth of Lynches Creek, where Snow's Island lies, is about 63 river-miles upstream from Georgetown and 30 miles north of the confluence of the Little and Big Pee Dee Rivers. By land, the mouth is about 52 miles north of Georgetown.[2]

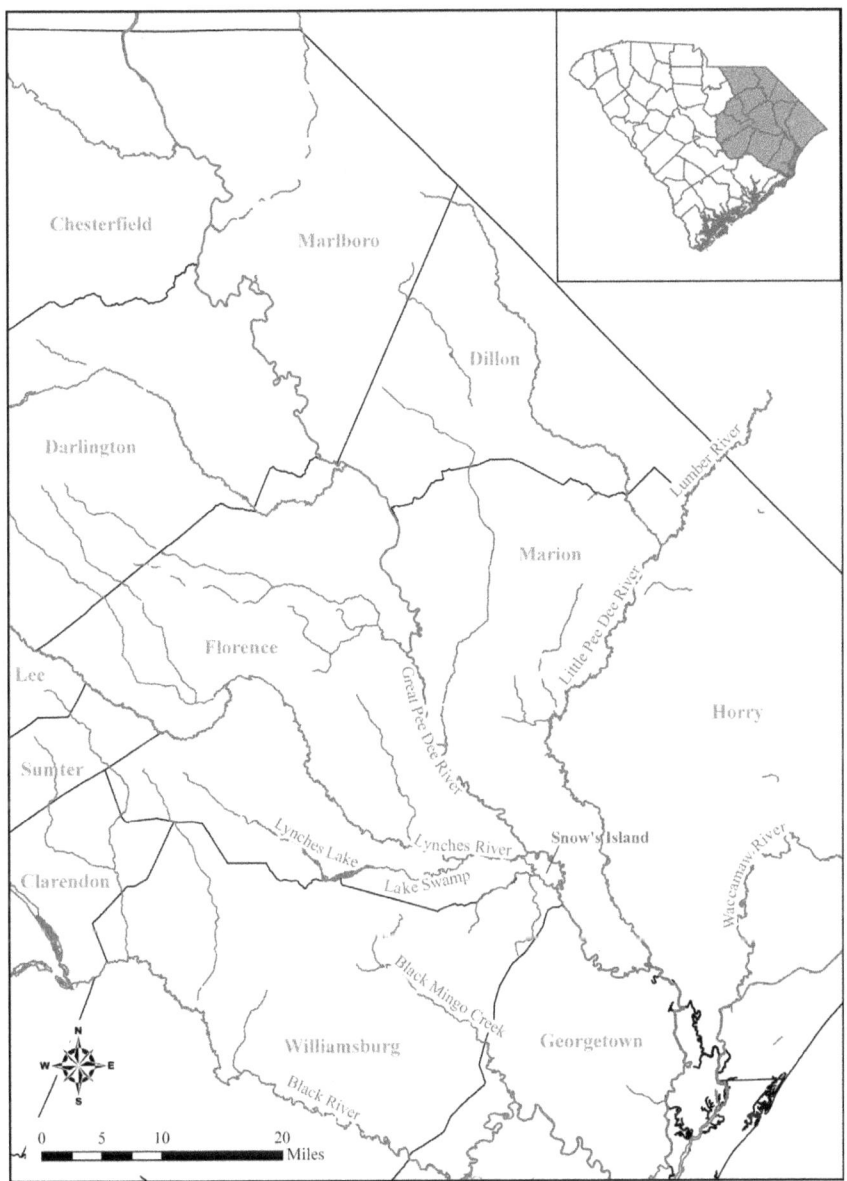

Figure 3.3. Greater Pee Dee River drainage in South Carolina (T.S. Wilson)

Today, the Snow's Island region is mostly within Marion County, that is, everything east of the Pee Dee River. West of the river are now Florence and Williamsburg counties, but Florence County was not established until 1888. Prior to that, the land north of Lynches was also part of Marion County.

Marion County is in the middle coastal plain and topographically characterized by broad and level sandy lands with gentle slopes, except near the major streams. Along the Pee Dee and Little Pee Dee, broad floodplains are subject to annual and frequent flooding. Both river channels have wandered within these floodplains over geologic time and today there are numerous oxbow lakes that were once the main channels. Archaeologist James Michie noted in a study of the Congaree River that oxbow lakes can fill and disappear within 150 years and two such cases have already been discussed with relation to Snow's Island. Creeks, swales, and ponds are also frequent in the region.

Swamps are ubiquitous but not continuous as the swamp floodplains also contain elevated sand ridges. These sand ridges are either the result of flood deposits or relict marine formations and can rise five to as much as 25 feet above the surrounding marshes, creating dramatic landscapes. Much of this land near the rivers was artificially drained after the Revolution in order to make it usable farmland.[3]

Along the Pee Dee and Little Pee Dee Rivers, soils are characterized as having poorly-drained mucky surfaces with underlying loamy subsoils. Adjacent highland soils are sandy and poorly drained. Only toward the north and east of modern highway 378 are there any well-drained soils.

Antebellum engineer Robert Mills, who published his famous *Mills' Atlas* in 1825 and his *Statistics of South Carolina* in 1826, described the swamplands as "of the richest soil" and that there was also "good clay" for making brick. "Great quantities of waste land, both upland and swamp, are to be found in this district. They are, however, good for cattle ranges." The forests at that time consisted of long leaf pine in the uplands, with hardwoods like cypress, oak, and hickory along the river bottoms.[4]

Perhaps attempting to lure immigrants, Mills described the climate as pleasant the whole year round. But eventually, even Mills had to admit that the swamps are the "principal sources" of disease and he lamented that not enough draining was being done to reclaim them. At that time, the streams were full of shad and herring in season, along with trout, bream, and perch. Deer, wild turkey, and common birds were noted. Alligators, poisonous snakes, and wolves threatened unwary settlers, and except for the wolves, still do. Nearly 72% of Marion County is woodland today, as it was then, but the timber industry has pulled out the long leaf pine and cypress and replaced these trees with quick growing slash pine for wood pulp.

Much of Marion County is still as rural as it was at the time of the American Revolution. The only urban area is the county seat Marion with a population of 7,042 and Mullins with a population of 5,029 (2000). Overall, those 19th century depictions of Marion's camp settings within large, moss-covered trees were probably not over romanticized, although cleared open farmlands on the highlands near swamps were also common in the colonial period.[5]

Williamsburg County to the west of Marion is and was much the same in terms of its landscape, especially near Snow's Island. The surface is level to gently undulating with a sand ridge east of Kingstree extending northeast toward Lynches Creek. Carolina bays are abundant and there are numerous floodplains including the Santee, Black River, and Black Mingo Creek drainages. South of Kingstree, the Black River twists and turns within a wide floodplain much like the Pee Dee. The Santee has an even broader floodplain, but there are also steep bluffs which reach 30 feet above it.

The northeastern section of the county, adjacent to Snow's Island, includes Lake Swamp, which drains into Lynches Creek. Muddy Creek and Soccee Swamp together empty into Clark's Creek at a low swamp that meets Snow's Island (Figure 3.1).

But even Muddy Creek has a high bluff line. Soils, at modern Hemingway, South Carolina and near Clark's Creek, contain both loam and clay, and are, at best, moderately drained. The little section directly west of Snow's Island at Johnsonville and Snow's Island itself are now in Florence County. According to the county soil map, all the soils are "frequently flooded." Mills described Williamsburg District as sandy with clay subsoils and rich swamp land.

All the major rivers were navigable at the time except Black Mingo Creek, which Mills reported as being obstructed. The mouth of Lynches Creek was also obstructed (see below).[6]

Sometime prior to 1826 though, Black Mingo Creek was navigable by sloops; this most likely included the Revolutionary period. The forests in Williamsburg County were, as in Marion County, full of long leaf pine away from the streams, with tupelo, cypress, ash, and beech in the swamps. Hickory and oak were found along the river bluffs. The same varieties of fish along the Pee Dee were found in the Williamsburg streams at that time, except herring and shad. Likewise, the fauna was the same as in Marion County.[7]

Snow's Island itself, being the "lair of the fox," was often described by Marion biographers. Peter Horry and Mason Locke Weems wrote that it was "a most romantic spot…Nature had guarded it, nearly all around, with deep waters and inaccessible marshes." William Dobein James described it as "high river swamp." Further, "In places, there were open cultivated lands on the island; but it was much covered by thick woods and cane brakes."[8]

Beyond these romantic sketches there are few descriptions of the island before it was logged. One exception is a letter written in 1868 by Snow's Island landowner A.W. Dozier. He described the island as "…the cultivable portion very fertile, and the whole well timbered—oak, gum, cottonwood, cypress, etc."[9]

The picture painted is that the Snow's Island landscape consisted of low land, much of it forested swamp and poorly drained. But this picture is incomplete. I have driven and walked the area around Snow's Island and the micro-topography is much more dramatic. On Snow's Island itself, the land is indeed swampy toward the south, but toward the north and along the Pee Dee riverbanks there are dramatic bluffs, especially when the Pee Dee River water level is low.

During the summer, the Pee Dee can be as much as 20 to 30 feet below the tops of the riverbanks, while during the winter, the water can rise and overflow the banks on both sides of at places like Dunham's Bluff. Indeed, in 2010, the Pee Dee overflowed its banks there, cancelling archaeological field work I had planned for January and February.

Across Lynches Creek to the north of Snow's Island is another high bluff. The topographic map indicates that Snow's Island is only 14 feet above sea level on the south end, while at Lynches Creek it is as high as 24 feet.

Meanwhile across Snow's Island to the north, the land rises to as much as 40 feet above sea level. This sharp relief certainly existed during the colonial period, but there is no record of how it affected the civilians and partisans around and on Snow's Island. Despite the seasonal fluctuations and this dramatic topography, Marion seemingly crossed the Pee Dee at will. Only once during his stay on Snow's Island does he mention that the Pee Dee was so high that he might have to move upstream to Port's Ferry.[10]

The Pee Dee was the main artery for colonial settlement of the region (Figure 3.3). The earliest settlers came up the Pee Dee, established homesteads and floated their products downstream to the Georgetown market. Although full of obstructions during the American Revolution, it was navigable for boats drawing four feet of water as high upstream as Long Bluff.[11] Lynches Creek, on the other hand, was probably full of obstructions along its length and totally obstructed at its mouth and was not likely useful as a means of transportation at that time.

After the war, the State of South Carolina let several contracts to survey Lynches Creek. The result of the surveys was the state's decision to cut a channel from Lynches to Clark's Creek rather than clear the nearly three miles of obstructions from its mouth upstream. This effort would allow river traffic from the Pee Dee to Lynches via Clark's Creek. The state may have attempted to clear Lynches because Robert Mills noted that Lynches was navigable its whole course in 1826, but today it is again obstructed at the mouth by logs and other debris.[12]

Within the Snow's Island region, there are numerous landmarks critical to understanding the settlement, landscape, and community. Many became important strategic points during the American Revolution. A more detailed analysis of these landscape features is provided in Chapter 8, but they are identified here.

Among the most important factors were the ferries that controlled the transportation network around Snow's Island (Figure 3.4). These included four core area ferries —Witherspoon's Ferry on Lynches Creek, Potato Bed Ferry on the Little Pee Dee, Britton's Ferry just south of Snow's Island, and Port's Ferry. During the colonial period ferries were chartered by the colonial government and provisions for standard operation were mandated. One key provision was that a person could be fined £50 for operating a ferry within ten miles of a previously chartered ferry. This gave the ferry operator some protection from competition, enabling the operation to be economically viable. The result was that licensed ferries were at least ten miles apart.[13]

Britton's Ferry was the first in the region, chartered in 1749 according to Marion biographer Robert Bass. I have found no record of that charter; however, it was obviously a ferry long before the American Revolution as it shows up on Mouzon's 1775 and Cook's 1773 maps (Figures 3.5 and 3.6). As will be seen, the Brittons were a dominant Snow's Island community family at the time of the American Revolution.

Port's Ferry was chartered to Frances Port in 1778, the widow of Thomas Port. The Ports were a prominent family in the Snow's Island community.

Witherspoon's Ferry is depicted on Mouzon's and Cook's maps of South Carolina (Figure 3.6). The Witherspoons also played an important role in the Snow's Island partisan community.

Another important crossing onto Britton's Neck was Potato Bed Ferry on the Little Pee Dee. Bass states that it was chartered by Richard Woodberry. Woodberry has always been considered as among Marion's warriors, although the primary sources are scant on his participation. These four ferries channeled access and travel across the Snow's Island community region.

Other ferries and crossings in the region include Burch's Ferry, fourteen miles up the Great Pee Dee from Port's Ferry and at the northern extent of the

Snow's Island community. I could find no record of it being chartered as a ferry until 1790, however it most assuredly was used as a crossing during the war.[14]

The historic record mentions several important spots along the Pee Dee from Britton's Ferry. On Britton's Neck, a road running out of the swamp from Britton's Ferry came to high ground at a location known as Hickory Hill, where it intersected a road known today as Woodberry Road. The Britton's Ferry road continued northeast to Potato Bed Ferry, approximately where U.S. 378

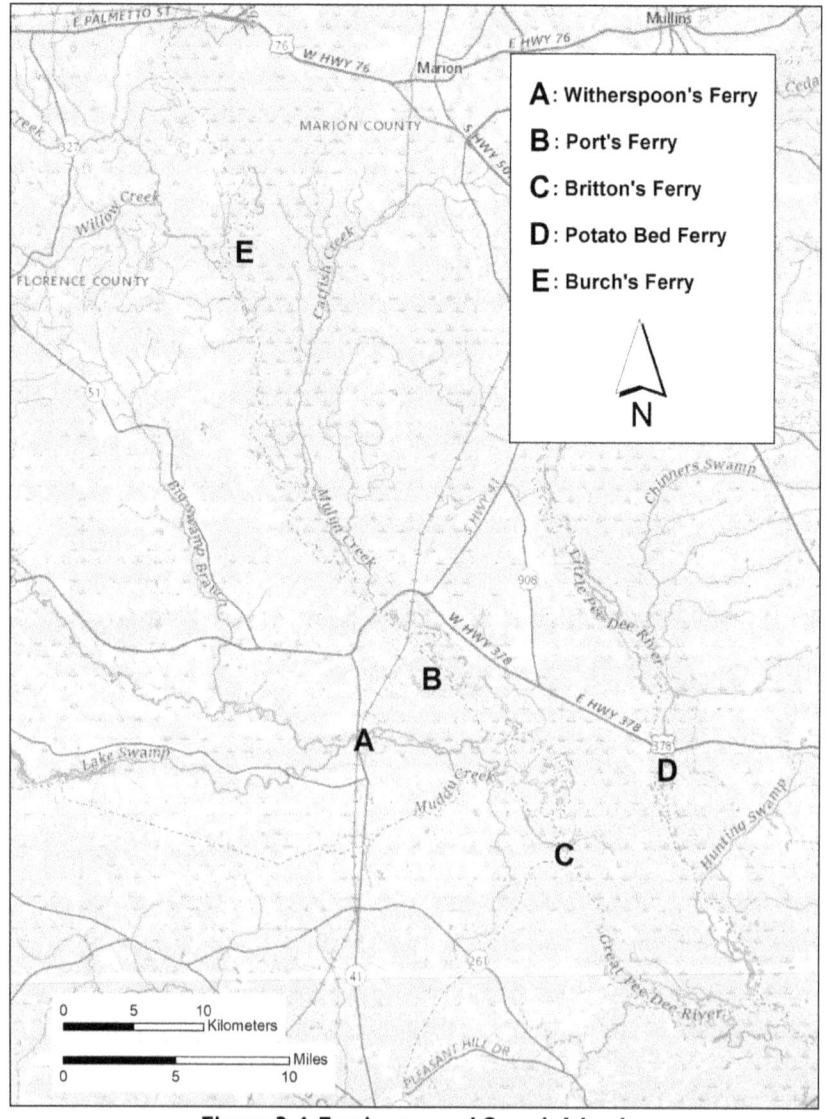

Figure 3.4. Ferries around Snow's Island
(USGS The National Map, modified by Brock Shattuck)

crosses the Little Pee Dee today. Up the Woodberry road from Hickory Hill was the house of Widow Jenkins, who plays a prominent role in our story. Approximately a mile farther north was Rae's Causeway and Hill (Figure 3.7).

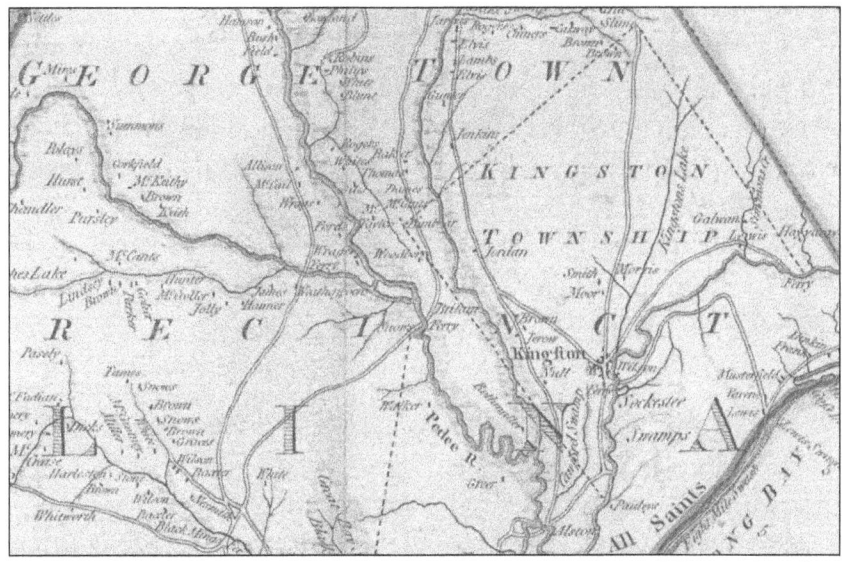

Figure 3.5. Detail of Henry Mouzon's 1775 map of North and South Carolina depicting Snow's Island and environs (S.C. Department of Archives and History)

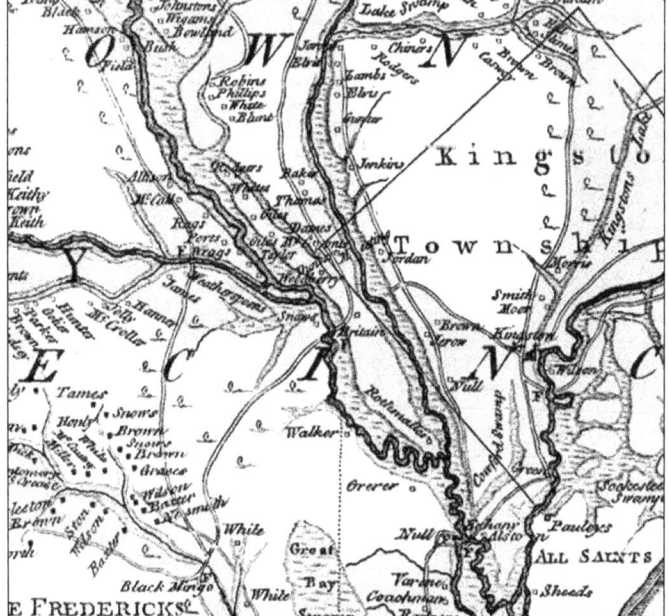

Figure 3.6. Detail of James Cook's 1773 Map of the Province of South Carolina depicting Snow's Island and environs

Above Britton's Ferry was Dunham's Bluff (Figures 1.1, 3.7, 3.8). Just south of Dunham's is a small stream that drains into the Pee Dee called Lone Pine Lake Run (Figure 3.8). Just north of Dunham's are two oxbows called Big and Little Ben Port lakes, and upstream of them is Balloon Lake, for the Bellune family (Figures 1.1, 3.8). The ridge of land running above Dunham's and continuing north was once known as Goddard's Ridge (for the Goddard family; Figure 3.8). Across the river on Snow's Island are three lakes, Johnson, Scott's, and Old River (Figures 1.2, 3.8). As mentioned previously, Old River Lake was not cut off during the American Revolution and created an island of its own.[15]

Continuing north, the next important landmark is the mouth of Lynches Creek. This location marks the northern point of Snow's Island. Port's Ferry is about three miles up the Pee Dee from the mouth of Lynches Creek (Figures 3.7, 3.8). On the east side of the Pee Dee at Port's Ferry are two lakes.

The names of these lakes have changed since the colonial period. The northernmost lake is labeled Graves [on other maps, Greaves] Lake on the 1943 (revised 1946) USGS topographic map, but was known as Dog Lake at the time of the Revolution (Figure 3.8). The lake to the southeast of Graves on that same 1943 map (Figure 3.8) was called Welsh Lake at the time of the Revolution.[16] Somewhere between Port's and Burch's Ferry on the west bank of the Pee Dee is Giles Bluff and above that Witherspoon's Bluff (Figure 3.7).[17] Around a mile north of Highway 378 is the mouth of Catfish Creek. About six miles above the mouth of Catfish is Jeffries Creek. Jeffries Creek runs northwest from the Pee Dee and its branches include Willow Creek and Middle Swamp (Figure 1.2). Just south of the mouth of Jeffries was Burch's Ferry (Figure 3.7). The west bank of the Pee Dee is a high bluff and the east is low and swampy. Above the swamps on the east side is high ground known as the Warhees (or Wahee) (Figure 3.7).

DEVELOPMENT OF THE COLONIAL COMMUNITY

Settlement in the Snow's Island region progressed at a slower rate than in the rest of the greater Pee Dee drainage. Initial settlement in South Carolina (1670-1730s), was primarily around Charleston and adjacent coastal areas. From this beachhead, settlement spread up the Ashley and Cooper Rivers, then along the coast around Georgetown and up the Santee to Williamsburg District.

In 1731, Governor Robert Johnson instituted a township system to encourage white settlement in the backcountry, thereby providing a buffer to Native American attacks near Charleston and the possibility of a successful slave revolt. Ten 20,000-acre townships were proposed with each township having a central town. To settle these townships, prospective settlers were

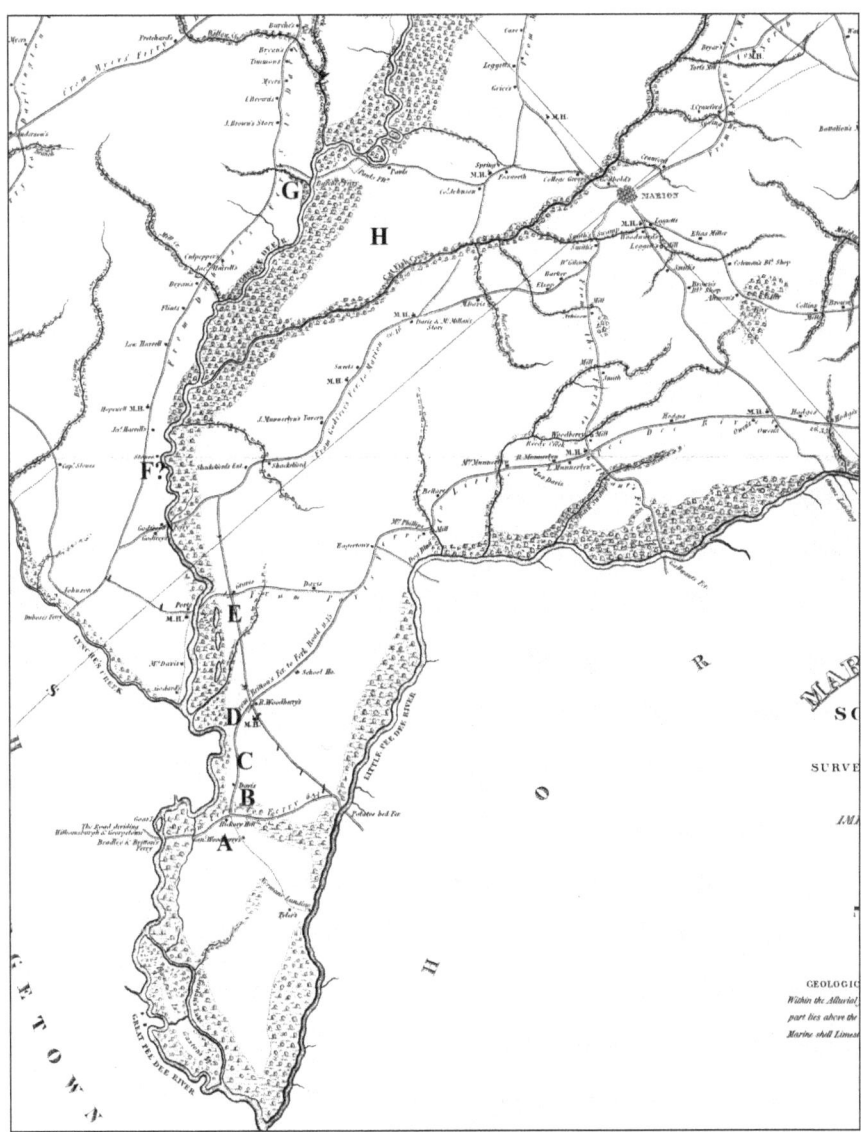

Figure 3.7. Britton's Neck and lower Marion District from *Mills' Atlas* (1825) depicting various place names in the Snow's Island region. A=Hickory Hill and road from Britton's Ferry to Potato Bed Ferry, B= Widow Jenkins home, C= Rae's causeway, D=Dunham's Bluff, E=Port's Ferry, Graves [Greaves] and Dog Lakes, F= Approximate location of Giles Bluff, G=Burch's Ferry and Mill, H=Warhee Neck (Wahee). (Bass-Canady Correspondence).

offered passage to South Carolina and provisions. Land and town lots did not have to be paid off for ten years.

The settlement of these townships went through phases of expansion from an initial burst in the first decade to slow growth in the 1740s to another expansion as immigrants arrived not only from Europe but also from the northern colonies down backcountry trails. Two townships informed settlement of the Snow's Island region. The first was Williamsburg Township, west of Snow's Island. The second was Queensborough on the Pee Dee.[18]

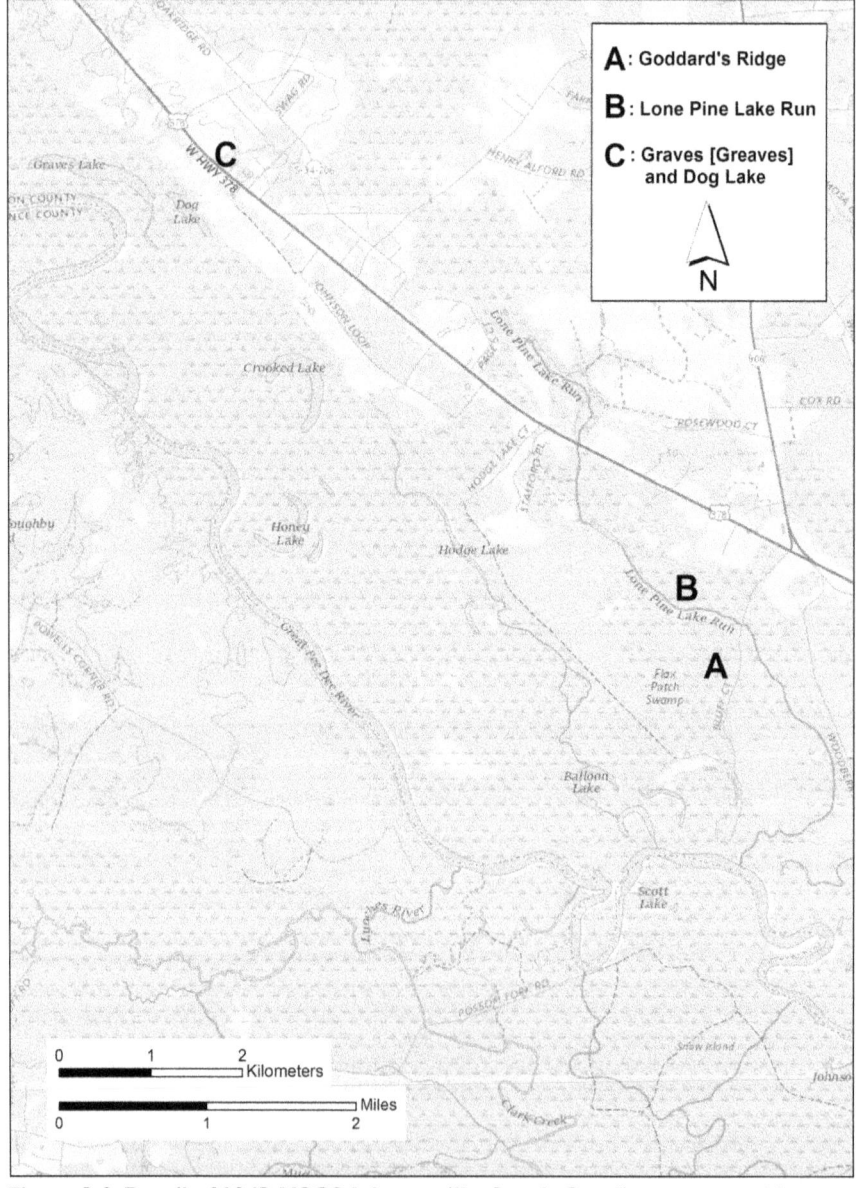

Figure 3.8. Detail of 1943 USGS Johnsonville, South Carolina, topographic map, 15 minute quadrangle, revised 1946

Williamsburg Township was centered on the Black River and was settled largely by Scots-Irish Protestants. Among the earliest families were men who became famous as followers of Francis Marion, including Witherspoon, Ervin, Goddard, and James.[19] Although much of the land was swamp, settlement of Williamsburg Township was successful as measured by the number of settlers. By 1737, there might have been as many as 500 white inhabitants, with the population concentrated around Kingstree.[20] Large tracts of Williamsburg also were purchased by nonresidents as plantations, especially the best lands along the Santee River south of Kingstree. Cattle raising and rough rice were the first crops, but Williamsburg colonists soon found indigo to be a lucrative cash crop.

Indigo production required intensive labor and as the years went by more and more slaves were brought into the township. By 1760, Williamsburg was considered a "social unit of unusual strength and vigor" according to historian Robert Meriwether. Community members were soon bound by marriage, a "National Adherence," and by their Williamsburg Presbyterian Church.[21] Despite evidence that some early residents migrated north to better lands, Meriwether declared it to be Governor Johnson's most successful township: "They were a Scotch Puritan community set down in a more easy-going English plantation province. Their high standards of conduct and education, their social compactness and their remarkable vigor were valuable aids to South Carolina progress."[22] These same characteristics would eventually contribute to a cohesive partisan community during the American Revolution.

In contrast to Williamsburg, Queensborough was a failure. In fact, it was so unsuccessful it faded into obscurity and its exact location is somewhat obscure today.[23] Faden's 1780 map (Figure 3.9), appears to be the most accurate depiction of its location, with the town of Queensborough platted just north of Port's Ferry along the north bank of the Pee Dee. Meanwhile, Faden also includes a larger area called Queensborough Parish (township) with its southeastern corner resting at the confluence of Clark's Creek with the Pee Dee—the area known as Snow's Island.

Historian Harvey Cook provides more information. The north and south borders of Queensborough plat were set at 45° northeast and southwest across the Pee Dee. The southern line was below the mouth of Lynches Creek and the eastern side was up against the Little Pee Dee. The western line included Lynches Creek. The northern line was above the mouth of Catfish Creek but below Jeffries Creek.

This description corresponds to Faden's "Parish" except that Faden does not show it extending east of the Pee Dee. Cook explains that the eastern portion was transferred to the Welsh Tract laid out in 1736.[24] Regardless, it is clear that the Britton's Neck region was known for a while as Queensborough Township. For instance, Thomas Port's 1755 plat for Dunham's Buff was recorded as being in Queensborough Township.

The township's lack of success as a settlement was due to its landscape: a "region of many and wide swamps, ill adapted as a whole to any but large plantations."[25] The better agricultural land was farther north up the Pee Dee, but in the 1730s, that land was too far away from Charleston for the authorities to consider chartering a new township.

Meanwhile, in Charleston, it appeared that settlement of the region was proceeding apace. So, in 1734, when James Gordon tried to settle one hundred families in Queensborough, the Commons House refused to assist him because they felt settlement of that part of the backcountry was going fine without government encouragement. But they were wrong. The earlier land purchasers were not settlers but speculators who bought large tracts of land with little intent to settle.

Snow's Island serves as an example. From the 1730s up to the beginning of the American Revolution, Snow's Island land was continually purchased and traded. A few families settled, but most were speculators who purchased the land but did not occupy it.

In 1735, 1,000 acres of the northern part of Snow's Island was purchased by Othniel Beale. A year later, James Gordon purchased 400 acres in the southern part of the island. Following that year, the eponymous William Clark (Clark's Creek) purchased another 450 acres. Beale sold his acreage to Elisha Screven around 1757. When Screven died, his land was divided between his sons. The land remained in family ownership until Ben Screven sold two southern tracts to James Snow, except for a square 1/8 acre where Samuel Screven was buried.[26] Elisha Screven Jr. owned the northern part and sold his 560 acres to Archibald Johnston in 1762. Archibald also bought 300 acres of land across Lynches Creek from Snow's Island. That land was formerly owned by James Gordon. Archibald died intestate and his property became the property of Andrew, his son, who sold both the Snow's Island tract and a tract across from Snow's to Joseph Alston, who sold them to Francis Goddard, who willed them to William Goddard in June 1777.[27]

In addition to the land inherited from his father, Andrew Johnston also purchased 321 acres of land between Beale and Clark in 1758. With

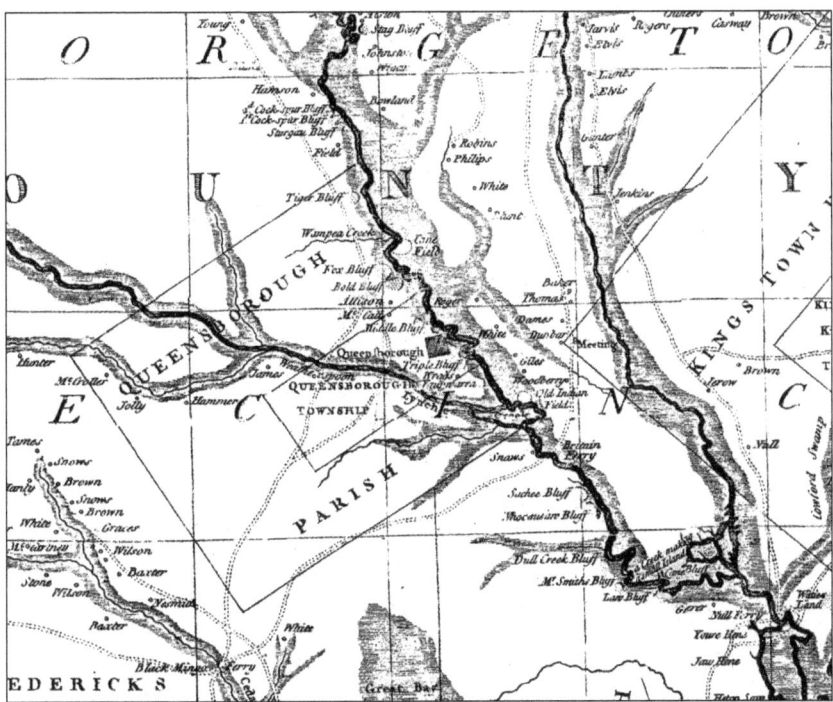

Figure 3.9. Detail of John Stuart-William Faden's 1780 Map of South Carolina depicting Queensborough (S.C. Department of Archives and History).

the Johnston family owning much of northern Snow's Island by the 1760s, the island became known as Johnston's [or Johnson's] Island. During the Revolutionary War, the island acquired a new name—Snow's Island.

The Snows of Snow's Island arrived in the 1760s. William purchased 200 acres on the extreme southern end of the island between the Pee Dee and Clark's Creek in 1763 and James Snow purchased 100 acres along Clark's Creek in 1768. William would add additional acreage through other purchases during the 1740s and 1760s. Names such as Francis and John Avant, William Green, and Josias Garnier Dupree also appear but these lands were eventually purchased by the Snows and Goddards—and by William Britton, a family name that figures prominently in this story.[28]

As noted, many of these individuals were probably not residents, although they might well have been absentee landlords with operating plantations. James Gordon, for instance, who tried to settle Queensborough, was a merchant in Georgetown and owned a large plantation along the Pee Dee near the town where he usually resided. Elisha Screven owned many tracts in Craven County including large plantations along the Sampit and Black Rivers. Screven sold some of his Sampit River land to create Georgetown. Othniel Beale was a provincial officer who lived in Charleston and had a residence in Georgetown. Both Archibald and Andrew Johnston were speculators and Georgetown merchants.[29] Of the Screvens, Samuel probably lived on Snow's Island, as he was buried there.

Then there was James Michie.[30] Michie at some time acquired land on the northern part of the island that was also claimed by the Screvens. During his life he was a prominent Charleston lawyer owning some 12,163 acres of land, which he probably purchased for speculation.[31] Michie died in 1760, leaving his estate and this land to his daughter. After the American Revolution, Hugh Giles was tasked by Georgetown Commissioners in 1783 to sort out Michie's land on the northern part of the island as part of Michie's estate.[32] The plat indicates several overlapping tracts of land, which were also owned at that time by William Goddard, Alexander Skeen, Othniel Beale, and Peter Allston (Figure 3.2).

In summary, many early 18th century landowners were speculators or absentee owners. On the other hand, the Snows, Goddards, Brittons, and Allstons were more likely residents along with an unknown number of slaves who lived on their lands and the plantations of absentee landlords.

Among those who did settle Queensborough, many did not stay long. In the late 1730s, several Pennsylvania Welsh families were induced by petition to come to South Carolina and settle on 10,000 acres in Queensborough Township, probably near Catfish Creek. They quickly saw its shortcomings as farmland and moved farther upstream along an eight-mile-wide swath of land that went all the way to the South Carolina border, with the main settlement near modern Society Hill, South Carolina. This more fertile land came to be called the Welsh Tract and it was quickly populated by Welsh, Scots, and after 1755, by many Germans.

Meriwether estimated that as many as 4,300 whites and 500 slaves had settled along the Welsh Tract and Queensborough by 1757. Some 3,000 whites and 300 slaves settled within Welsh Tract proper and the remainder located downstream. Like the Williamsburg inhabitants, they started first with deer skins and cattle, then they began to cultivate flax and hemp. Indigo soon became a lucrative crop.[33]

Once indigo became profitable, Queensborough Township became more attractive (around the 1740s) and settlement increased but it was still sparsely settled in comparison to the Welsh Tract and Williamsburg. While these settlers got their supplies from Georgetown, they sent their indigo overland to Charleston.

Generally, the early settlers located along the sandy highlands overlooking the floodplains of the major rivers. There they turned loose their hogs and cattle to roam in the swamps and planted indigo nearby. Marion historian W.W. Sellers described the settlement of lower Marion including Britton's Neck:

> Luxurious bodies of reeds were in the swamps and low grounds of the three rivers [Pee Dee, Little Pee Dee, Lumber River], and in the inland swamps and bays of the county; the uncleared uplands everywhere covered with a heavy annual crop of nutritious grass in summer for cattle to browse upon; the swamps, and especially the river swamps, teeming with acorns, and the pine woods bearing every year quantities of mast—pure mast. … All he [the settler] had to do was to watch and attend to his stocks of cattle and hogs, and feed them just enough to keep them gentle.

The result was that:

> We suppose stock raising was the business of most of the early settlers of the county, and especially in that part of Marion County called Britton's Neck. The settlers down in that region became wealthy, and outstripped the upper end of the county for near a hundred years in the pursuit and accumulation of wealth.[34]

Indeed, the "land was found to be fine for farming and unsurpassed for grazing purposes. Getting a living was so easy that not one fifteenth part of the land was cleared in the first generation or two except where the more energetic increased their slave forces." Cattle and swine were keys to the early settlement of South Carolina and the Pee Dee Drainage. "All of the Pee Dee basin was a magnificent stock range. … The meat used everywhere and in all seasons was pork and bacon … to be fattened by a feed of Indian corn in the last month. Much of it was exported. Bacon became the staple food of the farmer and of his servants, as corn became the most important cereal for man and beast." Thus ironically, although a comparatively isolated region between Georgetown and the Cheraws, Snow's Island community members became wealthy by the time of the American Revolution. As will be seen, the region provided Marion's partisans and General Greene's Continental Army with hundreds of head of cattle.[35]

As settlement increased, settlers found that Charleston, where civil courts and other government functions were located, was just too far away. In the 1750s, the inhabitants petitioned the colonial legislature to divide the northern part of Craven County from the mouth of Lynches Creek northward into a separate county so as to have a more central court system to hear complaints and bring felons to justice. It was becoming a "Place of Refuge for many evil-disposed People…Horse Stealers…Felons…[and] others cohabiting with their Neighbors Wives."[36]

Nothing was done by the legislature and the problem worsened. Settlement increased and, by the 1760s, the entire backcountry became infested with outlaws. Near anarchy reigned. Along the Pee Dee and Congaree settlers began to take matters in their own hands. These vigilantes became known as Regulators, led by prominent men in the communities, but membership consisted of a broad cross section of backcountry inhabitants including yeoman farmers and merchants.[37] Perhaps as many as 2,500 to 3,000 citizens in St. David's (Welsh Tract) and St. Mark (Catawba-Wateree Rivers) Parishes were among those who joined the Regulators.[38] Outlaws were rounded up and subjected to vigilante trials and flogging. Meanwhile, excesses by the Regulators created an anti-regulatory movement that spurred a near civil war.

In 1768, the provincial government finally acted. In the Pee Dee region, St. David's Parish was established with a system of courts and representation.[39] A study of 118 of the Regulators identified several men in the Welsh Tract above the Snow's Island community but none within the Snow's Island region. At least two served under Marion (Morris Murphy, George Hicks) and many served in the war under other officers.[40]

This was the scene in the Snow's Island region prior to the American Revolution. The people living in and around Snow's Island were widely dispersed throughout the region, but as will be demonstrated, had established a rural community with churches, plantations, ferries, taverns, mills, and a market connection to Charleston and Georgetown. Indigo, cattle, and pigs were the prominent commodities.

There were no large towns and very few villages like Kingstree, but the people were interconnected through religion, marriage, and common interests. The next chapter demonstrates those connections.

Endnotes for Chapter 3

1 It is necessary for understanding what follows to have some background into the tangled political division of the landscape prior to, during, and after the revolution; all of which make plat, marriage, and deed research difficult. At the time of the Revolution, the Snow's Island region was mostly in Georgetown District, with the northern part in Cheraw District. The exact dividing line was around Catfish Creek. But land records usually refer to the area as part of an extensive early political division called Craven County, established as early as 1682, and including all land in South Carolina north and northeast of Awendaw Creek (Stauffer 1994:6). As settlement progressed, parishes were established by the Anglican Church for elections and courts, and much of the Snow's Island region was in Prince Frederick Parish, established 1734. In 1768, the upcountry above Black Creek became St. David's Parish (Meriwether 1974:97-98). After the Revolution, Marion (1800), Horry (1801), and Williamsburg (1804) Districts were cut out of Georgetown District (Stauffer 1994:13). These borders remained relatively stable until the establishment of Florence in 1888. Snow's Island itself was in Queensborough Township, Prince Frederick Parish, Craven County during the American Revolution. Afterward it was in Williamsburg County until 1888 when it became part of Florence. All the land across from Snow's Island on Britton's Neck, and to the north across Lynches Creek was in Marion County from 1800 until the formation of Florence County

2 Kovacik and Winberry 1987:27; Linder 2000:ix; Cook 1926:57; Civil and Military Engineer of the State of South Carolina 1818:A-9.

3 Sellers 1902:15; Michie 1980:2.

4 Pitts et al. 1974a:General Soil Map; Mills 1826:623, 625, 628; Barry 1980:123.

5 Mills 1826:625-626; Pitts et al. 1974a:1; United States Census Bureau 2000.

6 Ward et al. 1989:2; Michie 1980:3; Ward et al. 1989: Pitts et al. 1974b, General Soil Map:7; Mills 1826:766-767.

7 Mills 1826:768.

8 Horry and Weems 1809:189; James 1821:67.

9 A.W. Dozier to R, 1868, Smith Collection, SCIAA.

10 Marion to Greene, 18 January 1781, Francis Marion Papers, South Caroliniana Library, University of South Carolina, hereafter SCL-USC.

11 Civil and Military Engineer of the State of South Carolina 1818:A-8.

12 Superintendent of Public Works 1825:417; Mills 1826:624.

13 Salo 2009:59.

14 Bass 1977:19; Smith 2008a:31; Daryl Young 2007.

15 Bass in Bass-Canady Correspondence.

16 Dickerson 2005.

17 Tuomey 1848:136, 240; Today, north of Port's Ferry is a modern boat landing that was once a ferry called Alison's Ferry. This ferry replaced Port's sometime in the 19th century. Where modern Highway 378 crosses the Great Pee Dee River was another ferry, called Godfrey's. Neither Alison's nor Godfrey's ferries were officially in operation during the Revolution.

18 Kovacik and Winberry 1987:79; Meriwether 1974:19, 25.

19 Boddie 1923:10.

20 Petty 1943:39; Meriwether 1974:80.

21 Meriwether 1974:84; Even before they arrived in South Carolina, the Witherspoon, Fleming, and James families were related in both blood and marriage (Meriwether 1974:84).

22 Meriwether 1974:85. Quote from Meriwether 1974:86.

23 Some sources place its southern boundary north of the confluence of Lynches and the Pee Dee (Kovacik and Winberry 1974:79, citing Petty 1943). Others place it far north of the mouth of Lynches (Lewis 2007).

24 Cook 1926:58. See also Meriwether 1974:89.
25 Meriwether 1974:89.
26 Terry Lipscomb circa 1974. It's not known who Samuel was. A Samuel Screven is recorded as being the brother of Elisha at a Wikitree genealogist website. That Samuel, however, is buried in Berkeley, South Carolina. / https://www.wikitree.com/wiki/Screven-6, accessed 15 June 2020.
27 Historian Terry Lipscomb's excellent research regarding colonial landownership of Snow's Island is undated, but is circa 1974. This date is the latest date on the Snow's Island National Register form.
28 Terry Lipscomb circa 1974.
29 Rogers 1970:35, 52, 104; Linder and Thacker 2001:300, 402, 404, 433.
30 Not the archaeologist.
31 Edgar and Bailey 1977:452-453; Coker 1987:438-341. This demonstrates the complexity of attempting a complete cadastral map of Snow's Island region and Snow's Island itself.
32 South Carolina Department of Archives and History [herein SCDAH], S126102:334.
33 Petty 1943:40; Meriwether 1974:92-93, 94.
34 Sellers 1902:29-31.
35 Quotes from Cook 1926:60, 74-75.
36 Lipscomb and Olsberg 1977:163.
37 Linder 2000:67.
38 Brown 1963:113.
39 The formation of St. David's Parish is important in that the new parish's southern boundary was a line running from a point along Lynches Creek northeast to North Carolina. It crossed the Pee Dee a little above the mouth of Black Creek (Meriwether 1974:98). During the Revolution, the Prince Frederick militia companies to the south (or the Snow's Island community) and St. David's militia companies north of the line belonged to the same regiment, making sorting out Snow's Island community members all the more difficult.
40 Brown 1963:112, 124-125; Moss 1983:443-444, 712.

CHAPTER 4
THE PRE-REVOLUTIONARY SNOW'S ISLAND COMMUNITY

By the beginning of the American Revolution, the speculators were largely gone, and a dispersed rural community had formed in the Snow's Island region. Most of the Snow's Island community families who became the partisan community settled on the island, on Britton's Neck, along southern Lynches Creek and Lynches Lake west of the island, and up the Pee Dee on both sides of this wide river.

This chapter presents summaries of a selection of families, confirmed by historic records, who were living in the Snow's Island region at the time. First discussed are several of what I consider core families, documented to be living near and/or on Snow's Island, mostly on Britton's Neck and Lynches Creek near Snow's Island, and usually in the geographic core region (Figure 4.1). They became stalwart Whigs and were closely connected through marriage, land purchases, civil disputes, and friendships. Many of these families included pre-war community leaders in their church and local government.

A second tier of families are examined next with less detail. These families usually resided beyond the geographical core but still within the wider Snow's Island region (Figure 4.2). A few are found within the Snow's Island core, but they were not intimately connected to the core families. Nevertheless, these too would be included among Marion's partisans. Many were living in Williamsburg Township and play a part in this story.

A third tier consists of individuals or families documented as living in the greater Snow's Island region, but the exact location of their homesteads or properties are obscure and they seem to have fewer social connections to families in the other tiers. The involvement of many of the second- and third-tier families with the core community is unknown.

It is impossible to demonstrate all the complex social connections in this community, but the following examples show that the core region was a tight community prior to and during the American Revolution and that families in the other tiers were also important to the community.

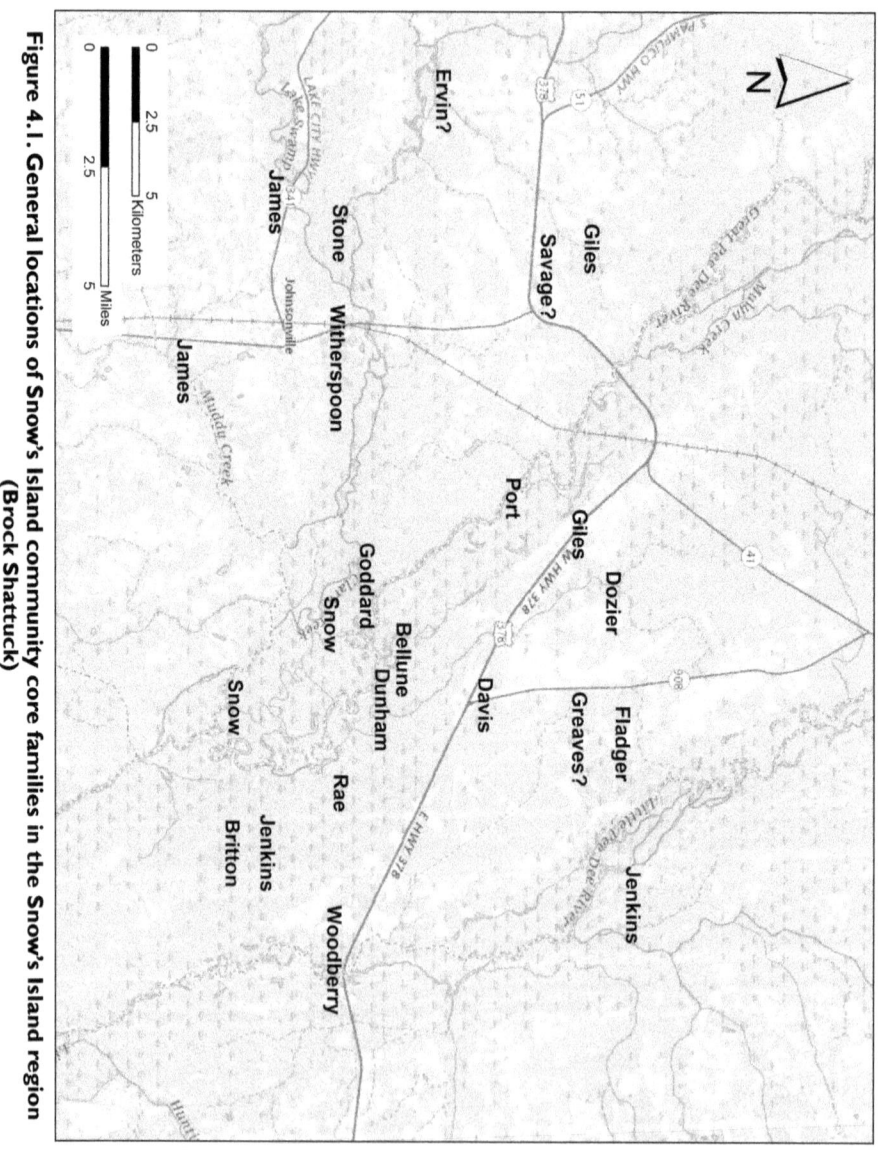

Figure 4.1. General locations of Snow's Island community core families in the Snow's Island region (Brock Shattuck)

The Pre-Revolutionary Snow's Island Community | 57

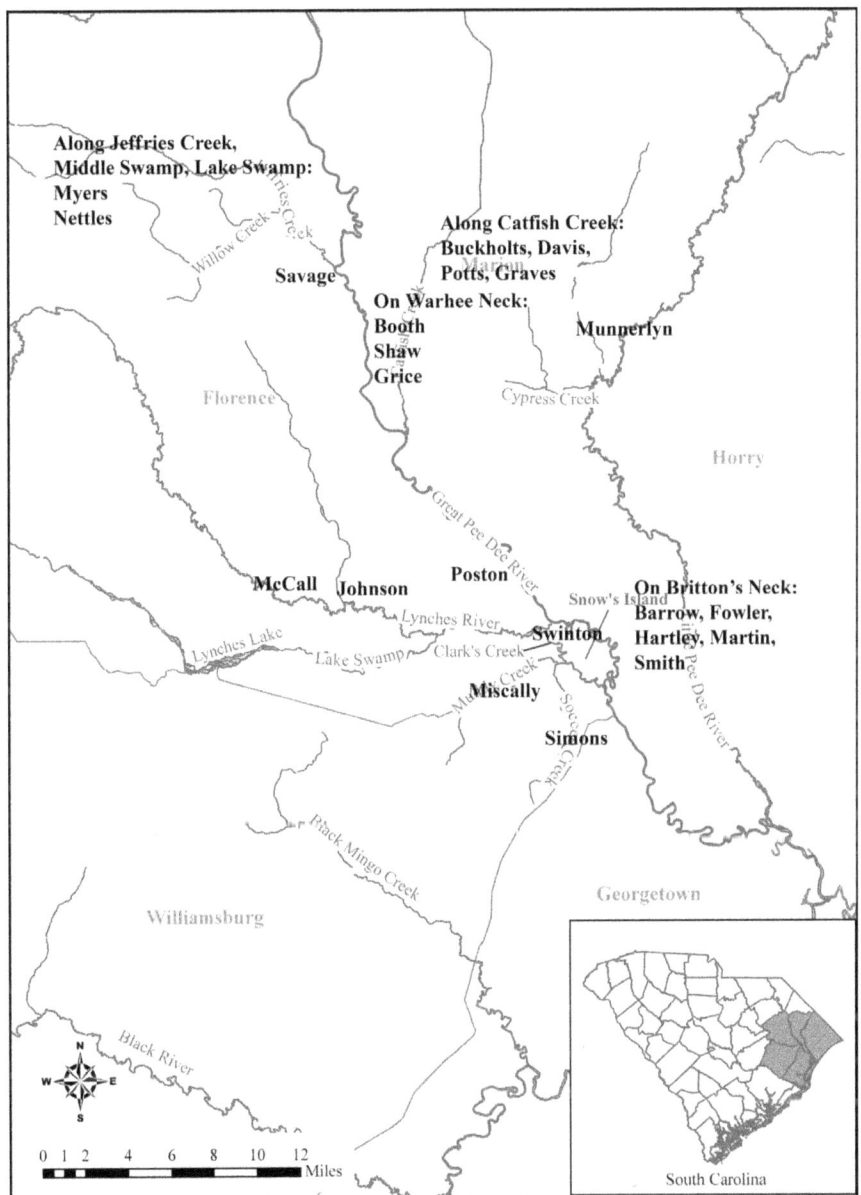

Figure 4.2. General locations of Snow's Island second tier families (T.S. Wilson)

The purpose of this chapter is not to provide an in-depth genealogical analysis. Rather, my goal is to provide enough information to establish that they were: 1) present in the region during the American Revolution, 2) tied to other regional families through marriage, kinship or business relations, and 3) were supporters of Francis Marion.

Some surnames and individuals are mentioned at what may seem to be random points, but their names will appear again either in this chapter or the next. Readers with no interest in the genealogical connections between Marion's partisans may wish to skip this chapter, while those with a strong interest in the "men who rode with Marion," will find information and citations that may assist them in their own family research.

CORE FAMILIES

Britton. The peninsula defined by the Great Pee Dee and Little Pee Dee became known as Britton's Neck.[1] Some of the earliest settlers on Britton's Neck were the Britton brothers—Timothy, Francis, Phillip, Moses, and Daniel—who settled between the Little Pee Dee and Great Pee Dee in the 1730s (Figures 4.1, 4.3). No better example of the development of the Snow's Island community can be found than the Brittons. For this reason, I provide a little more detail on this family than many others.

The founding father, Francis Britton Sr. (d. 1731), settled near Charleston in the late 17th century and sired 11 children. Son Daniel came to the neck first but was soon followed by his brothers. Daniel went into the cattle and tanning business. Philip (d. 1749) settled nearby in the Blue River Swamp area and married Jane Goddard, daughter of the first Francis Goddard (see Goddards below). Timothy (d.1750) also settled nearby and married Jane's sister Mary Goddard. Moses (d. 1750) married Hester Jolley. There were Jolleys [Jolly] on Britton's Neck, and along Lynches Lake (Figure 3.9), but further information on her kin is not known.

Francis Britton Jr. (II) married Ann Hyrne (not part of a Britton's Neck family) and established Britton's Ferry in 1747. Britton's Ferry became a critical ferry during the Revolution. Another son, Joseph Britton, did not purchase land on the neck but, as the last surviving brother, inherited his brothers' land.[2]

Francis Britton Sr. (I) also had two daughters. Hanna Britton married a Ray or Rae, another Snow's Island community family (Figure 4.1). Hanna either followed her brothers onto the neck or her husband was already friends with the Brittons and moved with them to the neck. The other daughter

The Pre-Revolutionary Snow's Island Community | 59

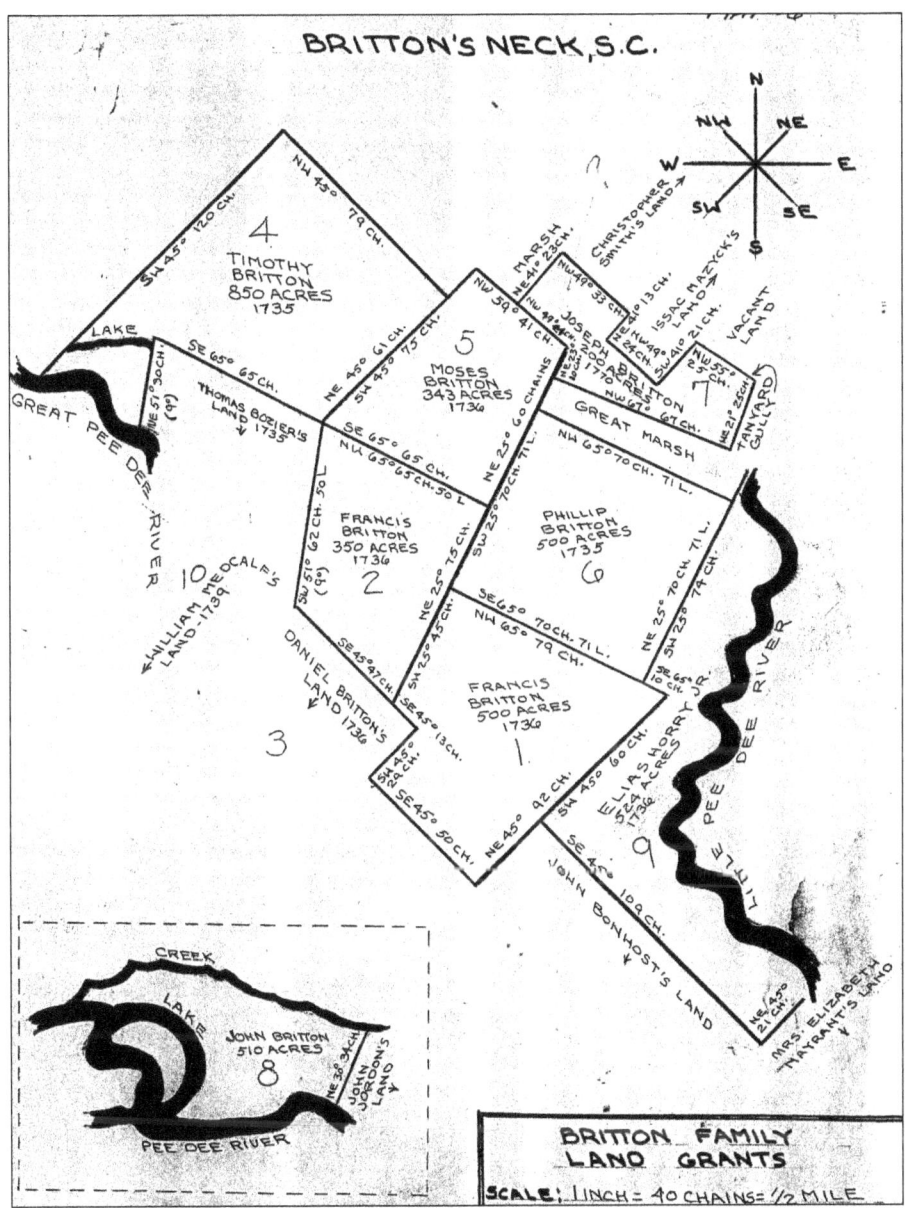

Figure 4.3. Mrs. Phyllis Canady's cadastral map of Britton families on Britton's Neck (Bass-Canady Correspondence, permission, Deryl Young and Marion County Historical Center, Marion County, South Carolina)

Sarah Britton, married Michael Mixan (Mixon). Mixons settled above the neck between Catfish and Little Pee Dee. A Michael Mixon (probably Sarah's husband) owned property on Lynches Creek.[3]

Thus, by the 1760s, numerous Brittons had settled the neck region and had established community ties through marriage. Most of those mentioned above were already dead by the beginning of the American Revolution. The grandchildren of Francis Britton (I) comprised the revolutionary generation and their first names were in most cases the same as their fathers, uncles and cousins. Many others died in childhood.[4]

Two Philip Brittons lived in the region and were cousins. Both were dead by 1790. One was the son of Timothy and Mary Goddard Britton. The other was the son of Joseph.[5]

Another son of Timothy and Mary was named William (another case where there may have been two). William purchased land farther upstream in Queensborough Township near a place called Spring Swamp. It's location cannot be verified, although today there is a Spring Swamp on the east side of the Little Pee Dee across from Britton's Neck.

Daniel Britton was most likely the son of Moses Britton. Daniel married a woman named Mary and purchased his own land along the Pee Dee River, and probably inherited other land. He died during the war around 1781 or 1782, after which his wife married Benjamin Davis, another prominent Snow's Island partisan family member.

Francis Britton (III) was the son of Francis (II) and died during the American Revolution (1780). Either Francis II or III was named as "Overseer of the Poor" along with community members Thomas Goddard and John Ervan (probably Ervin). This was likely Francis III because Francis III became tax inquirer in 1766 and served as justice of the peace for Prince Frederick Parish. He was a member of the Prince Frederick Church, but joined Indiantown Presbyterian Church by 1787. Francis married Ann Goddard (see below) and purchased land adjacent to Joseph Britton. Further tying the Brittons to the Goddards, he was one of the executors of Francis Goddard's (II) will. Henry Britton, another son of Francis (II), died prior to 1785. He is mentioned here because traditional family history states that Henry was born at Hickory Hill on Britton's Neck (Figure 3.7).[6]

There may be four more Brittons of the Revolutionary War generation, but their records are so vague that there is not much to say about them. In any case, all were children of Joseph Britton. One, Thomas Britton, moved across the Pee Dee to land between the Pee Dee and Black Mingo Creek and became a Marion partisan. The other three were Moses, Joseph, and John.[7]

There were several William Brittons, one born in 1750 to Timothy and Mary Goddard Britton. Several land grants for a William Britton were granted, both before and after the war, for land in Queensborough Township and on the Little Pee Dee. One William Britton died in 1800, and in his will, he named William Bellune and Richard Woodberry as friends. Both gentlemen will be discussed below. In Britton's will, Snow's Island community members Stephen Britton, John Greaves, and Elizabeth Greaves were named as purchasers, and William Snow was present during William Britton's dying illness.[8]

Finally, another Britton of interest is Stephen Britton. Stephen's connection to the rest of the Britton's Neck Brittons is not clear. He was born in 1765 and died in 1810 and was only 11 at the beginning of the war, but there was also a Stephen Britton in the Craven County militia, who had land in Marion and Georgetown after the war.[9]

Bellune [*Balloon, Bullen*]. The Bellunes are an example of a Snow's Island community family that cannot be tied to the landscape prior to the Revolution through plat research. Nevertheless, evidence is strong that they were in the Britton's Neck region, clearly near Port's Ferry, and perhaps just west of Dunham's Bluff where Balloon Lake is located (Figures 3.8 and 4.1). Marion biographer Robert Bass was convinced this lake was originally spelled Bellune Lake and I would have to agree.[10]

William Bellune was the most prominent Bellune in the historic record. William, was born in 1755, died in 1839, and married Frances Rebecca "Part." Most likely her last name was actually Port, for William Balloon was named in Frances Port's will.[11] William was also named as a "trusty friend" in Andrew Farwell Johnson's will and lived at that time at Marion Courthouse.[12] William signed three important petitions in 1776, 1783, and 1814 that link him to the Britton's Neck region (see below).[13] William also witnessed a deed for Daniel Davis on Cypress Creek Bay, Great Pee Dee in 1810.[14]

Two other Bellunes, John and Francis, signed the 1783 petition of Upper St. George inhabitants unhappy with the pardons being offered Loyalists after the Revolution.[15] A Francis Billum was listed, along with William Goddard, in the 1790 Williamsburg County census and owned 70 slaves. Indicating a long presence in the neighborhood, James C. Gilpha and William Bellune were named in a Bill for Partition versus R. Woodberry in 1843.[16] It is assumed this William is a descendant of the Revolutionary War Bellunes.

Davis. It is abundantly clear that there were several Davises in the region during the American Revolution but sorting them out is problematic. For instance, three Benjamin Davises signed the 1783 petition.[17] Historian W.W. Sellers stated that the Davises came to Britton's Neck around 1735 and were among the region's first settlers along with the Britton, Graves [Greaves], Fladger, Tyler, and Giles families.[18] They settled near the "Old Neck" church, which was near the modern-day entrance to Woodberry Road off U.S. 378 (Figure 4.1).[19] Robert Bass stated that the Davises were Welsh and came as part of the Pennsylvania Welsh migration to Queensborough.[20]

The three Benjamin Davises at the time of the American Revolution appear to be father, son, and grandson. One Benjamin Davis signed a 1776 Craven County militia pension. Benjamin Davis Sr. and Benjamin Davis Jr. signed the 1814 petition for reestablishing a ferry at Port's Ferry. Benjamin Davis Jr. later became a leading citizen and was elected to serve in the Ninth (1791) General Assembly and is likely the Benjamin Davis who acquired 660 acres on the northeast side of the Pee Dee and 500 acres on Bakers Swamp, a branch of Catfish Creek (Figure 4.2) between 1792 and 1801. Given the plethora of Benjamin Davises in the region, little more can be stated with any assurance.[21]

One of the Benjamin Davises, however, was closely tied to the Port family (see Port family below Port), along with Joseph, William, and Henry Davis, which led to legal judgments after the war. Another Benjamin Davis, probably Ben Sr., wrote his will in 1802, in which it is indicated that the Davises intermarried. Ben's daughter Mary married William Davis. Daughter Elizabeth married Henry Davis Jr. This Ben had two other daughters, Hannah and Frances, a son, Nimrod, and a wife Hannah.[22] The will was witnessed by Robert and Ann Dunnam (see below). Another daughter of a Benjamin Davis married John Dozier, who later married a Giles.[23]

Joseph Davis signed all three petitions—the Craven County 1776 petition, the 1783 Prince George petition, and the 1814 petition for reestablishing Port's Ferry. In the latter he was named as the person to run the ferry, clearly placing him as living nearby. Joseph Davis's children requested a pension after the war in his name. In the application, they state that Joseph volunteered at Port's Ferry, along with Benjamin Davis, Benjamin Munnerlyn, Francis Goddard, Jonathan Collins, and Moses King.[24] Joseph signed a Presentment concerning the location of courts in Georgetown District in 1794.[25] Also of note in the pension was that his daughter Maria married a Fladger (see below).

Of William and Henry Davis, there is not much evidence. A William Davis was a captain in Colonel George Gabriel Powell's St. David's Regiment and a William Davis served in Colonel Hicks's regiment in 1777. As noted, William signed the 1776 petition and he and William Jr. both signed the 1783 petition, so it is obvious they lived in the Snow's Island region. Henry signed the 1776 militia petition and the 1783 petition.

A Lieutenant Henry Davis is listed in Colonel Powell's 1775 regiment and there is evidence that this Henry, who said he would be 79 in 1828, was the brother of Joseph Davis. Henry Jr., presumably his son, signed the 1814 Port's Ferry petition. Likewise did Abraham, Daniel, John, and Thomas Davis.[26]

Francis Davis is well fixed in the region. His pension application indicated he was born in Britton's Neck in 1756, and as noted, he was in William Davis's militia company at the beginning of the war.[27]

Besides the above, there was also a David Davis. David was a lieutenant in Powell's regiment and, along with Miles Davis, was a signer of the 1776 militia petition. Again, it cannot be assumed that all the signers of the 1776 petition lived in the Snow's Island region since many of the unit's men lived in the Cheraw District above Black and Jeffries Creeks. Nevertheless, it is well established that Davises lived on the upper part of the neck prior to the war and perhaps at least one or two lived at the location indicated on colonial maps by Mouzon, Cook, and Faden (Davis or Davies) (Figures 3.5, 3.6, 3.9) and *Mills' Atlas* (Figure 3.7). There are numerous judgments in the Marion County Equity Rolls for the above Davises, however, sorting through them is not necessary here as it is established that the Davises were an important Snow's Island family. Additional information is supplied in the Port family discussion.[28]

Dozier [*Dozer*]. John Dozier (1741-1807) was born in Virginia and moved to South Carolina by 1768 where he was appointed deputy surveyor. His name is on multiple properties bought and sold prior to the Revolution. In 1800, he owned as many as 42 slaves. After the war he served in the 11th and 12th General Assemblies (1794-1795, 1796-1797) and as a delegate to the state constitutional convention. He married Elizabeth Giles, daughter of Robert Giles, according to historians Bailey and Cooper, but the Giles family website states that she was Abraham Giles's daughter. They had a son, Leonard Dozier, in 1771. Leonard eventually was the administrator of Abraham Britton's estate along with Frankey Britton (perhaps his wife) in 1800. John Dozier's second wife was Ann Davis, daughter of a Benjamin Davis and widow of Abraham Giles Jr.[29]

John Dozier was a captain in the St. David's Parish Regiment and signed the 1776 petition. He also signed the 1776 Protestant petition, placing him at

Britton's Neck. According to his will, he lived on land purchased from Joseph Brown (in 1808), but owned 1,601 acres of land at Lone Pine Lake Swamp (Figure 4.1) which he purchased from Samuel Wragg's 2,000 acres of land from Hugh Giles (see below), and 450 acres of land from Gavin Witherspoon (see below). John Dunnam (see below) witnessed Dozier's will.[30]

Dunnam *[Dunham]*. The Dunnams are associated with the Dunham's Bluff archaeological site (Chapter 8) across from Snow's Island (Figures 1.1, 4.1 and Chapter 5). John Dunnam (1694-1727) seems to have been the first Dunnam in South Carolina. His male children were John (b. 1714), Ebenezer (b. after 1722), and Robert (1726-1790). These three migrated up the Pee Dee and settled on Britton's Neck. Robert's wife, Susan Burne, had a brother named Andrew who came to Britton's Neck along with the three Dunnam brothers. Reverend Evan Pugh noted in his diary that on 2 November 1762 he "Went from home to Britain Neck loged at Mr. Dunhams."[31]

Thomas Port (see below) originally owned 300 acres of land at Dunham's Bluff and 36 acres of that land or land adjacent to it was granted to Ebenezer Dunnam in 1775 (Figure 4.4). Genealogist James T. Dunnam believes Robert Dunnam (Dunham) died at his home on Dunham's Bluff and is buried there.[32]

John Dunnam Jr's children were John Peter (b. 1739/40), Ebenezer (b. 1745), and Jacob (1750-1798). John's brother, Ebenezer, married Frances Commander in 1745 (whose mother was a Screven) and had only one child, Ebenezer Jr. Robert Dunnam (Dunham) had several children, Robert Commander (1760-1813), Elizabeth (1748-1818), Joseph (b. 1754), Ann (b. 1758), Thomas (1768-1820), Susan (1753-1825), and Hanna (1764-1812).

The marriages of Robert Dunham's children (Elizabeth, Ann, Susan, Robert Commander, and Hanna) demonstrate the complex connections between Snow's Island community families. Elizabeth married Jonah Woodbury [Woodberry] son of John Woodbury (see below) and Margaret Collins. Ann married John Peter Port, son of Thomas Port (see below). Susan married William Davis Sr. (see above), son of Benjamin Davis and Rachel Port (see below). Robert Commander married Mary Ann Davis, who was Benjamin Davis and Rachel Port's daughter. Hanna married Benjamin Davis Jr. another son of Ben and Rachel. Further generations of Dunnams continue these connections but, as they emerge into the 19th century, they will not be discussed here.[33]

What is clear is that there were several male Dunnams of the right age to have participated in the American Revolution and as will be seen, they were ardent supporters of the cause. Ebenezer and Ebenezer Jr. signed the 1776 and 1783 petitions.[34] John signed the 1776 petition and John Jr. signed the 1776 petition. Robert signed both.

After the war, several Dunnams migrated west to the Mississippi Territory. Robert Commander Dunnam was one of them. Out west, Robert Commander named Samuel Ervin his executor and "trusty friend" in his will. Colonel John Ervin had a son named Samuel and this may well be him (see below). Their friendship demonstrates the continuing ties of the Snow's Island community after the war.[35]

There is no record of John Dunnam having land in the neck at the time of the American Revolution, but it is likely that he was residing in the neighborhood. He did obtain land in Marion District after the war. He also hired himself out as an overseer in 1808 to neighbor Stephen Shackelford to manage Shackelford's crop and 20 slaves. John's audited account also indicated his presence in the neighborhood.[36]

As mentioned, Robert Dunnam's brother-in-law was Andrew Burne. There is no record of an Andrew Burne owning land in the Marion County region. In fact, other than an audited account shared with Robert, there is no other record of Andrew. He was probably living with the Dunnams, who were faithful followers of Marion, at the time of the Revolution.

Ervin. Another family difficult to locate precisely on the landscape are the Ervins. Three Ervins played significant roles in the Snow's Island story and just to make it interesting, two of them are named Hugh; the other was John Ervin.

The Ervin family settled in Williamsburg Township in the 1730s. John Ervin (1754-1810) was born on his father's (John Sr.) plantation on Cedar Swamp (southwest of Kingstree) in 1754. After the war he acquired land on the Great and Little Pee Dee Rivers, and along Lynches Creek. He must have had land there prior to the war, however, since he joined the Britton's Neck militia and eventually became the commander of the Neck's regiment. He was also a founding member of the Aimwell Presbyterian Church, which was established between 1770 and 1780.

This church was located "ten miles above the junction of Lynches Creek" and many members were supporters of Francis Marion. Ervin married Jane Witherspoon in 1775 and thereby became the brother-in-law of Gavin and John Witherspoon (see Witherspoons). Jane died in 1790 and John Ervin married his cousin, Margret Ervin, daughter of Hugh Ervin. He held several civic offices after the war.[37]

John's father-in-law through that second marriage was Hugh Ervin Sr. (d. 1785), who was also his uncle. Hugh Sr. married Elizabeth James. He purchased land in Pudding Swamp, along Black River and Lynches Creek prior to the war. One tract of 150 acres surveyed in 1763 was bisected by Lynches Creek. He was active at the beginning of the war, serving as a member of the Second and Third General Assembly and was a trustee of the Indiantown Presbyterian Church. During the war, Hugh became a colonel under Francis Marion.[38]

Hugh's son, Hugh Jr., (1759-1817) was also old enough at the time of the war to participate as a captain under Francis Marion. At the time of his birth, his father also lived on Cedar Swamp. Sometime in the 1780s, he migrated to Lynches Creek, within the Snow's Island community. It is possible that the tract of land along Lynches Creek assigned to his father (above) was actually Hugh Jr.'s land or it was land his father gave to him.

Hugh married another Witherspoon, Elizabeth, in 1783. Thus, at the close of the war, John and Hugh Jr.'s brothers-in-law were John, Gavin, and Robert Witherspoon, the latter operated Witherspoon's Ferry. All were founding members of the Aimwell Presbyterian Church between 1770 and 1780. As Howe concludes, "These families [Ervins and Witherspoons] were living on the Pedee in the Revolutionary war and took an active part in it." In other words, they were community leaders. Hugh Ervin Jr.'s son, James (1778-1838) married Gavin's daughter in 1805.[39]

Fladger. The first Fladger in the region was Robert, who settled around 1734. The Fladgers are named as one of the early Britton's Neck families by Gregg and Cook. Robert's property was along the Little Pee Dee and Giles Bay (just north of Potato Bed Ferry on Britton's Neck) (Figure 4.1). He was named on the 1740 Jury List for Prince Frederick Parish. He married an Elizabeth Lewis. Genealogist Jo Church Dickerson makes a strong case that, when he died in 1741, Fladger's widow then married Abraham Giles (I). Her name is seen in the records as Elizabeth Fletcher, but Dickerson believes this was really Elizabeth Fladger. If so, then Hugh Giles was the half-brother of Charles Fladger, son of Robert and Elizabeth. Giles played a significant role in the Snow's Island community.[40]

Not a lot is known about Charles Fladger. He had land on the Pee Dee in the 1770s adjacent to Hugh Giles. He married a cousin, Elizabeth Keene. She was the daughter of Ann Lewis Keen[e]. Charles is on the Jury lists for 1778-79 and 1783, but he died shortly after the war. He signed the 1776

Craven County militia petition, the 1776 Protestant petition, and the 1783 petition. His son was named Hugh Giles Fladger, another hint of the connection between the Fladgers and the Giles. Hugh Giles was identified in the complex Port case (see Davis and Ports), named as purchaser, or as "sworn before," leading to the belief that he was a judge or justice of the peace after the war.[41]

There was also a Henry Fladger who signed the 1783 petition against the Loyalists. According to Sellers, he was the son of Hugh Fladger, who was the first Fladger in the region, rather than Robert. However, Henry does not show up in any jury lists. He platted 375 acres on Barn Ridge along the Little Pee Dee River in 1790 after the war. In that plat, Henry Davis, Hugh Fladger, and Robert Giles were also named. Sellers goes on to state that Henry served under Marion during the Revolution.[42]

Giles. There were three male Giles in the community prior to the American Revolution and all became active Snow's Island community partisans. They were Abraham (?), Hugh Giles (1750-1802) and Abraham Giles (II) (ca. 1750-ca. 1790). Abraham Giles (I) was probably the first Giles in South Carolina and was the father of Hugh and Abraham (II). Historian Victor Stanley mentions a Robert Giles who he claims was the father of Abraham, Hugh, and a John Giles. Genealogist Jo Dickerson, however, has not found a connection between Robert and the others.

Abraham settled along Black River and Black Mingo between 1700 and 1736 (Figure 3.9). Abraham Giles (I) was platted land on the Pee Dee River at Dog Lake near Port's Ferry in 1754 (Figure 4.1) (see also Figures 3.5, 3.6, 3.9 for various Giles homesteads). A Carolina bay northeast of Dunham's Bluff has been called Giles Bay since at least 1771, according to a plat of land for John Rae (see below). Jo Church Dickerson believes that this bay was not named for Abraham but for a Giles Holiday, absentee landowner.[43]

Abraham married Elizabeth "Fletcher" in 1747 (but see above, "Fladger") and had, besides Hugh and Abram (II), two daughters Elizabeth and Ann.[44] Elizabeth (II) married John Dozier [Dozer]. Reverend Evan Pugh noted in his diary that he "got to Giles Married Dozer & Came back to Tilmon Kolbs" on 22 January 1771. Abraham Giles died sometime before 1771 and Hugh was named Executor of his will.[45]

Abram or Abraham Giles (II) married Ann Davis but had no children. He died around 1787 and his widow married John Dozier, whose first wife died in 1791. Abraham is probably the "Abram" who signed the 1776 Craven

County militia petition, the 1776 Protestant petition, and the 1783 petition against the Loyalists. In his audited account (see Chapter 5), he is called Abraham also.[46]

Hugh Giles (1750-1802) was named overseer for Prince Frederick Parish in 1776. He rose from a lieutenant in the Prince Frederick militia to colonel by 1780. Hugh acquired land south of Abraham (Sr.) and eventually "became one of the great landholders on Peedee River." He was also a surveyor prior to the war and his name appears in numerous land transactions in and around Snow's Island. In other words, he knew Snow's Island very well. He was also a prominent member of the community before the Revolution and helped transform the community into a partisan community during the war. He was elected a member of the Second General Assembly (1776-1778) and, after the war, represented Prince Frederick Parish in the Sixth General Assembly. He was a justice of the peace, road commissioner, delegate to the state constitution, and numerous other posts. He adjudicated pension and audited accounts for veterans after the Revolutionary War. Originally, the town of Marion Court House was named Gilesborough in his honor.[47]

Hugh married Sarah Ball on 4 February 1772. The Reverend Evan Pugh married Hugh and Sarah as he had John Dozier.

There is a depression on Britton's Neck near the Jenkins' house (see below) called Ball Slough, which Robert Bass believed was named for the Ball family. For such a prominent person, Giles was surprisingly free of kin in the region, but as stated, his name appears often in surveys and after the Revolution, as a juror or witness for his veterans.[48]

Prior to the war, Hugh owned quite a bit of property in the Snow's Island region, especially land near Port's Ferry, but a 1778 tax list indicates that he resided across the river [west] on Deep Creek.[49] This creek today is west of Port's Ferry (Figure 4.1). A river bluff above the Pee Dee was called Giles Bluff in this area and was probably named for him.

Hugh had several children including three sons, Hugh (II), Robert, and, of course, another Abraham. Since Abram (II) had died by 1787, it is assumed that Abraham (III) was the Abraham who administrated Hugh Sr.'s estate in 1803 along with Leonard Dozer [Dozier]. Abraham was also involved in a suit with Mary Davis in 1804.[50]

Goddard. The Goddards are intimately tied to Snow's Island as Robert Bass asserts that Francis Marion's Snow's Island camp was at William Goddard's Plantation (Figure 4.1). Like the Davises and Brittons, there were multiple Francis and William Goddards and the Goddard genealogy is even more convoluted than that of the Brittons. The following is the best that I can determine.

Francis (I) was a vintner in Charleston who settled in Williamsburg Township before 1737. Besides plantation land, he owned two lots in Kingstree in 1739. According to a hand-written note in the Bass-Canady Correspondence, Francis died in 1746. He had two sons, Francis (II) and William Goddard, and three daughters, Mary, Jane, and Frances. Mary Goddard married Timothy Britton (1743) and Jane married Phillip Britton.[51]

Francis (II) was named a church overseer for Prince Frederick Parish in 1761. Francis (II) married Anne Snow, the sister of George and James Snow, a daughter of Nathanael Snow Jr. Francis (I) owned land on the northern end of Snow's Island that was eventually purchased by Francis Goddard (II) and then willed to his son William (II) in 1777. A deed to Hugh Thompson for 500 acres along Lynches Creek, just across Snow's Island from Clark's Creek, indicates that his land bordered Frances Goddard's land. This female form of Francis (Frances) could be a misspelling and perhaps should be Francis Goddard. Terry Lipscomb's research seems to imply that.[52]

William Goddard (I) married Elizabeth Britton, daughter of Joseph Britton, sometime before 1757. They had one son, Francis Goddard (III) born in 1757. William (I) died in 1757 and Elizabeth then married Samuel Jenkins, who died around 1780 of consumption. Elizabeth had seven children by Jenkins.[53]

William Goddard (II), son of Francis Goddard (II) signed the 1783 petition against the Loyalists. As noted, he inherited land on the north end of Snow's Island from his father, where Marion supposedly camped.[54] His ownership is confirmed by the James Michie plat (Figure 3.2) and he also owned land across Lynches Creek north of Snow's Island. His house is depicted on *Mills' Atlas* and is thought to be archaeological site 38FL282 (see Chapter 8).

Francis Goddard (III), the son of William Goddard (I), died in battle in 1781 (see Chapter 7). Francis (III) also inherited land on Britton's Neck from his uncle Francis Goddard (II).[55] The ridge of land from Port's Ferry to Dunham's Bluff was known as Goddard's Ridge to Marion biographer Robert Bass, who grew up on Britton's Neck (Figure 3.8).

Francis Goddard (III) signed the 1776 Craven County militia petition and the 1776 Protestant petition. Francis III was Reverend James Jenkins's older half-brother. Francis III was a bachelor and he moved the family "down in the neck" during the war for safety. They settled on Francis Goddard's property about a mile or less down the road from John Rae's. In summary, the Goddards owned the northern end of Snow's Island and the land across Lynches Creek from Snow's Island during the Revolutionary War.[56]

Greaves [*Graves*]. Another Britton's Neck family living close to the Brittons was the Greaves family. Today Greaves Lake near Port's Ferry is a reminder of the family's presence. The father of the Greaves family in America was probably Joseph Greaves (I), born in England between 1710 and 1720, and who was living in Prince Frederick Parish by 1743, as indicated by marriage records (he married Rebecca Bennett). Their children, most born in the 1740s, were of the Revolutionary War generation and included Joseph (II) (b. 1744), Elizabeth (b. 1745), John (b. 1746), Francis (1747), and two others—Mary and James (b. ?). It is not conclusive that Joseph was the father of these children, but it is logical to conclude so.

Joseph Greaves was listed on the Jury List of 1767; Francis, John, and Joseph are found on the 1783 Jury List. Joseph and John are found on the 1778-79 Jury Lists. Joseph, Francis, and John are also found in the 1790 census for Georgetown.[57]

Joseph Greaves (II) (1744-1790-1810) is the most prominent of the family. He married Elizabeth Evans and their children included a Joseph (III), Bennett, Francis, and Mary Ann, all born between 1777 and 1786. Joseph was made a lieutenant in Colonel Powell's St. David's Parish militia and was later a Captain under Hugh Giles. Joseph signed the 1776 Craven County militia petition, the 1776 Protestant petition, and the 1783 protest against Loyalists. Joseph Greaves (II) settled near Port's Ferry on 600 acres of land, probably around the time it was platted in 1768 (Figures 3.7 and 4.1). In 1773, Joseph was named in a judgment roll, owing Francis Goddard £500. He is on the 1767 and 1783 Jury Lists for the region.[58]

John Greaves [Graves] was platted 150 acres on Britton's Neck shortly after the war in 1784. This land, or another 150-acre tract under his name, was on Giles Bay (Figure 4.1). He is on the 1783 Jury List for Georgetown. The executors of John's will were Francis, William H., and Bennett Greaves. The latter was a signer of the Port's Ferry petition. Francis and Bennett are named as nephews of John Greaves, and William H. was his son. William Bellune, Benjamin Davis Sr., Joseph Greaves, and Joseph Davis are all named as appraisers in an 1808 suit.[59]

Francis Greaves signed the 1783 petition against the Loyalists and the 1814 Port's Ferry petition. He is named in various judgments after the war. He is also on the 1783 Jury List.[60]

James Graves settled on Catfish Creek at the northern end of the Snow's Island region in 1758 (Figure 4.2). There was also a Robert Graves who settled "on the neck" in 1771.⁶¹

James. The James family was one of the first to settle in Williamsburg and married early into the Witherspoon family (see below). By the time of the American Revolution, there were James families spread widely through Williamsburg Township. According to William Boddie, William James was one of a party of 40 Scots-Irish Protestants who settled around Kingstree in 1732. A 19th-century history by the Reverend James Wallace adds that William James was Welsh and went first to Scotland, where he married the daughter (Elizabeth) of John Witherspoon and joined the migration to South Carolina via Ireland. William and Elizabeth had four children—Mary, Janet, John, and William (II). Both William and Elizabeth were dead by 1750 from an epidemic that also killed David Witherspoon. William James also had a brother, John James, who was among the original settlers. Family tradition has distinguished this James as John James of Ox Swamp.⁶²

By the time of the American Revolution the following James were in the community: Gavin James, William D. James, Nathaniel James, David James, James James, Robert James, and two John James, one "of the lake" and the other called Major James. All played roles as Whigs in the American Revolution.⁶³

The documents on the James family are conflicting and, after some attempt to sort them, I am resigned to present this information as the best I can sort it—some of the information, therefore, may be incorrect. Still, the connections are of interest in the examination of the Snow's Island community.

John James (1732-1791), son of William, was a captain prior to the war. At the beginning of the war, the Williamsburg community turned to him as their militia leader and they voted him a major. His sons were William Dobein James and yet another John James (see below). James (I) was one of the founders of the Indiantown Presbyterian Church around 1760. This church was a hotbed of Whig resistance during the war.⁶⁴

John James (II) (1757-1825) was the son of John James, which indicates that his grandfather was the original Williamsburg William James. He owned some 1,496 acres including land near Muddy Creek and was one of the Snow's Island core community members (Figures 3.5, 3.6, 3.9, and 4.1). In fact, I believe he might be the one known as John James "of the lake" or "of Lynches Lake" in the literature, distinguishing him from John James the Major. His grandfather, William, was also known as living on the "lake." John

James (II) married Mary Ervin and was the brother-in-law of John Ervin and Robert Witherspoon. He was a Captain during the American Revolution and afterwards served Williamsburg in the 10th and 13th General Assemblies (1792-1794, 1798-1799) and in numerous civil positions. One of these was superintendent for opening navigation of Lynches and Clark's Creek in 1778. Like nearly all the Jameses, he was active in the Indiantown Presbyterian Church.[65]

John James's (II) brother William Dobein James (1764-1830) wrote one of the early biographies of Francis Marion and did as much as anyone to enhance Marion's reputation and memory (see Chapter 9). William Dobein James was a young man during the war, and was living with his father before the war. Sick during the fall of 1980, young William turned to Gavin and Robert Witherspoon to provide information about Marion that fall. In other words, he was not an eyewitness to most of Marion's partisan period. William served in the 10th General Assembly (1792-1794) and numerous civic positions after the war, including as a judge in the Court of General Sessions. Unfortunately, due to insobriety, he was impeached in 1827.

To add to the confusion, the historical sketch of the Indiantown Presbyterian Church notes that "The James brothers of the Lake, cousins of the Major, were Marion's trusted scouts. Their names were James, John, William, Robert, and Gavin."[66]

In summary, the Jameses are an example of another family that became strong supporters and leaders in the partisan community during the American Revolution.

Jenkins. Much of the Jenkins family history comes from the autobiography of the Reverend James Jenkins. The patriarch of the Britton's Neck Jenkins family was Samuel Jenkins, who married Elizabeth Britton (the widow of William Goddard). They had seven children, but three died young. The surviving children, who were of the Revolutionary War generation, consisted of Samuel (II), Britton, and James. Samuel (I) was killed in 1780.[67]

James was born in 1764 on the north side of the Pee Dee, but Samuel moved first to Georgetown and then back to Britton's Neck and settled near Port's Ferry. From James, it is known that he had an uncle James Jenkins and a cousin named John Jenkins. James's half-brother was Francis Goddard, who took charge of the Jenkins family after Samuel's death. In 1778, Goddard was already the head of the family, and moved them down near the Brittons (Figure 4.1). At this location, the boyhood home of Francis Marion biographer Robert

Bass, would occur several Revolutionary War incidents that have made it into the lore.

James was a friend of Loftis Munnerlyn who witnessed James's pension application and audited account. Samuel and Samuel Jr. both signed the 1776 Craven County petition. A Samuel Jenkins was named a Petit juror for Prince George Parish in 1778-1779.[68]

Two other Jenkins assisted Francis Marion—Thomas and Joseph Jenkins. It is not clear if they lived in the Snow's Island community region as they are both listed on the 1778-1779 Jury Lists for Prince George. Thomas had several hundred acres on the northeast side of the Little Pee Dee at Big Swamp and Chinner's Swamp (Figure 4.1). While this area became a strong Loyalist region, Thomas provided large amounts of provisions to the Whigs.[69]

Munnerlyn. The Munnerlyns were a large family that was active in the service of Francis Marion. They lived generally along the Little Pee Dee north east of Snow's Island and, for the purposes of this study, on the eastern edge of the Snow's Island region, but not within the core (Figure 4.2). They are included here because of their intimate connections to the core families around Britton's Neck both before and after the war.

James Munnerlyn (ca. 1700 to ca. 1800) was the patriarch and had seven children. The Munnerlyn children included William (1745-ca. 1790), James (II) (1748-ca. 1818), P. Benjamin (ca. 1750-1800), John (1751-1821), Loftis (1753-1843), Francis (1765-1784?), and Alma (1750-1773). No Munnerlyn land plats prior to the American Revolution appear in the South Carolina State Archives. There are no Munnerlyns listed on the jury lists for Prince Frederick either.

However, an 1817 deed of land to Thomas Munnerlyn from Benjamin Munnerlyn for 936 acres includes within it a 350-acre grant to James Munnerlyn dated 1769. This must describe the family landholdings, supported by Loftis Munnerlyn in his Revolutionary War pension application, where he stated he was in the Battle of Blue Savannah "near where this deponent lives." Furthermore, his post-war home is depicted on *Mills' Atlas* along Reedy Creek, beside B. Munnerlyn's home (Figure 3.7).[70]

As a result, not much is known about the Munnerlyns prior to the war. Benjamin did not marry until after the war and then to Ann Batchelor, whose name is not well-known among the community. James's wife is unknown. Loftis (sometimes Loftus) married Rachel Collins and a Jonathan Collins joined with Benjamin Munnerlyn at Port's Ferry to go to war.[71] It is possible that Jonathan and Rachel were related, perhaps as siblings. If so, that is likely how Benjamin became acquainted with Rachel. A Collins also lived adjacent to the Munnerlyns.

Francis Munnerlyn was only a teenager during the war and family tradition has it that he was killed by Loyalists at his home, but his death is sometimes dated to 1784. John Munnerlyn married Sarah Keen, another Marion District name. In the settlement of his estate, known community members Hugh Flager [probably Fladger] and Henry Davis were named.

Much more on the Munnerlyn family history in Marion County appears in records during and after the war. Whereas their war-time exploits will be discussed further in later chapters, historical records show that James, John, and Loftis all signed the 1783 petition against the Loyalists and that Benjamin signed the 1814 petition for the reestablishment of Port's Ferry. Loftis filed a detailed pension and audited account for a pension after the war, and Colonel James Ervin was his attorney.[72]

Port. The Ports are a Snow's Island community family well fixed on the landscape. Thomas Port (d. 1777?) was residing in Prince Frederick Parish by 1760. He purchased nearly 4,000 acres of land along the Pee Dee River, including land on both sides of what became Port's Ferry just north of the mouth of Lynches Creek. He became a leading citizen in the parish and St. David's Parish. In fact, he was named as a commissioner in St. David's Parish in 1768.

Thomas was captain of the Pee Dee militia in the Cherokee War and served in the First and Second Provincial Congresses and the First General Assembly. In 1755, Port purchased 550 acres across from Snow's Island that included Dunham's Bluff. In 1759 he acquired another 36 acres, which were transferred to Ebenezer Dunnam in 1775 (Figure 4.4). He was named a captain in the militia in 1775.

Thomas Port married Frances Hinson. Historians Bailey and Cooper stated that the Ports had one child named Rachel who married Benjamin Davis (see Davis). However, she is not mentioned in any Port papers and may be Thomas's sister instead. When Thomas Port first established his ferry is unknown, but it must have been prior to the war. The first known charter to Port's Ferry was to his wife Frances in 1778.[73]

Thomas Port wrote his will in 1776, however, it was not proved. Thomas left all his estate to Joseph, Benjamin, William, and Henry Davis "and others his nephews and neices [sic] after the death of his wife Frances." Frances died sometime before 1812. In her will she left her estate to several individuals.[74]

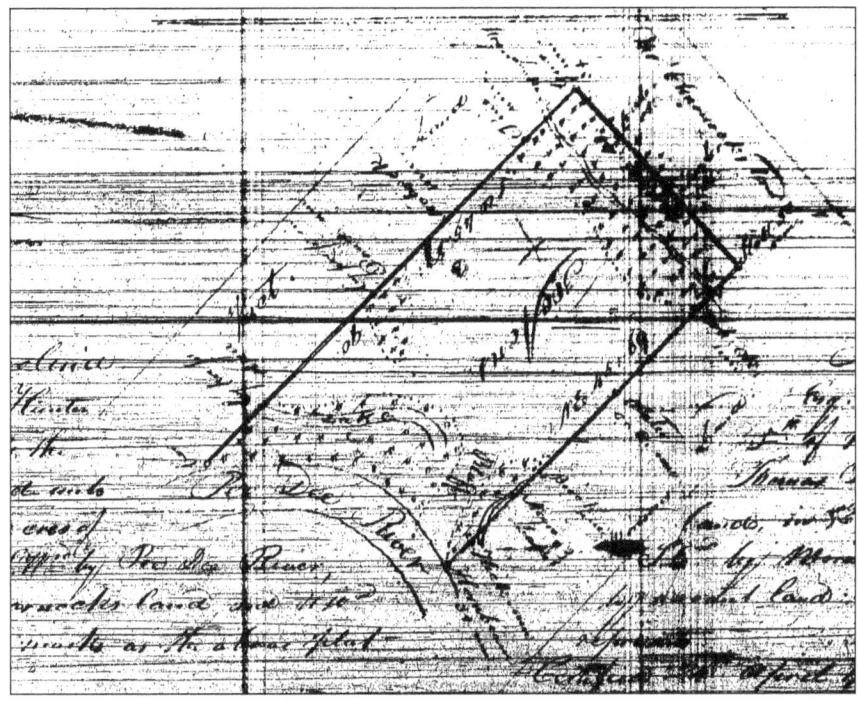

Figure 4.4. Plat of Thomas Port's 336 acres and Dunham's Bluff (SCDAH, S213184:6,68)

Sorting out these two wills must have become a nightmare for many Snow's Island community members and resulted in a suit between the Humphries and the Davises. Frances left the land around Port's Ferry to Mary Port Snow, the daughter of Thomas Humphries. Frances Port's other land was to be divided between the children of Thomas Humphries, including Elizabeth Witherspoon Humphries, if Frances died without issue. Frances also named Hugh James Alison, John Balloon Alison, William Green Balloon, "old William Balloon," Nancy Davis (wife of Benjamin Davis), and Thomas Port Davis (son of Benjamin) to inherit various slaves and property. Her will was witnessed by John Portell (Postell?). The lawsuit is not as important here as the appearance in the judgment of a multitude of Snow's Island family names: Alison, Balloon, Davis, Port, Postell, Snow, and Witherspoon.[75]

The community connections go even deeper. Another suit filed in 1813, Joseph Davis versus Samuel Snow, named even more Snow's Island community residents.[76] The names in this suit included Davis (Joseph, Benjamin, William, and Henry), William H. Greaves, James Alison, Port (Peter, Joseph, John and James), Richard Godfrey, Thomas Perkins, Bennett Greaves, and witnesses

William Bellune, Sarah Munnerlyn, Ann Dozer, and Thomas Harley among others. It is not known if these suits were hostile or simply the legal means of resolving an inheritance problem. In any case, after the war, a legal suit engaged much of the Snow's Island core community members.[77]

Thomas Port's nephews included Benjamin, Peter, Joseph, and John. There were two eastern shore landings at Port's Ferry, a normal one and another needed during high water (Figures 3.4, 3.7, 3.8, 4.1). Benjamin Port ran the ferry.[78] Not much is known about the Ports during the American Revolution, however, Thomas, Benjamin, Peter and Joseph signed the Craven County militia petition in 1776. Peter also signed the 1776 Protestant petition. Benjamin and Benjamin Jr. signed the 1783 petition denouncing Loyalist pardons. This evidence confirms their presence in the Snow's Island region during the war, but exactly where on the landscape is not clear. In one final example of the interconnections of the Snow's Island community, Frances was called to testify in court regarding the will of John Witherspoon in 1804.[79] In any case, they were active Marion partisans (see Chapter 6 and 7).

Rae [*Rea*]. John Rae lived in the neck on 200 acres of land just up the road (north) from the Brittons and adjacent to Giles Bay (Figure 4.1).[80] The land was platted in 1771. His land probably straddled the road from Britton's Neck northward as a low portion of that road (now Woodberry Road) is known locally as Rae's Causeway and the adjacent hill is known as Rae's Hill. The British camped there in 1781.

Mrs. Phyllis B. Canady, genealogist of the Britton family, believed that John was the son of Hanna Britton Rae, the sister of the Britton brothers (see above) and her husband was William Rae, who had a 400-acre grant of land amidst the Britton family. Philip Britton (d. 1749) left property to John Rae, his nephew, so there is some corroboration there. There was also a connection between John Rae and William G. Bellune, possibly through marriage. In a Bill of Foreclosure between George W. Woodberry and Henry L. Williams in 1838, the land in question was allotted to William G. Bellune in John Rae's estate, deceased. The description of the property indicates it was the same land Rae obtained in 1771, being adjacent to Greaves land and along the Great Pee Dee.[81]

John Rae, Edmund, and William Ray (probably Jr.) signed the 1776 Craven County militia petition. John Rae also signed the 1776 Protestant petition and the 1783 petition. There is no other information about the Rae/Ray's except for their support of the Whig cause.

Savage. Nathan Savage is well known as the soldier who Marion biographer Wiliam Dobein James indicates slung rosin onto the roof of Rebecca Motte's house during siege of her house in May 1781. Savage acquired as much as 4,578 acres between the Pee Dee and Lynches Creek north of Snow's Island during his lifetime; a 1786 tax return indicates that he owned 1,350 acres at that time. Despite his ownership of all this land, it is not clear exactly where he lived during the Revolution. Gregg places Nathan's house at that time at the mouth of Lynches Creek. According to an 1841 land dispute, he acquired land near Godfrey's Ferry just north of the old Port's Ferry in 1786, 1787, and 1791, but there is no record of his having land there prior to the war (see Poston family below).[82]

It is also possible that he had land just south of Jeffries Creek during the 1780s and moved south afterward. In 1778, Nathan joined the St. David's Learning Society implying the possibility of a residence farther upstream the Pee Dee than near Poston, South Carolina.[83]

Nathan signed the 1776 Craven County militia petition. He also attended the state constitutional convention. After the war, he represented Prince Frederick in the Sixth General Assembly. Nathan's wife was Penina or Penninah. Penina died around 1810 and her estate appraisers included Richard Godfrey, Austin Stone, Francis Greaves, and Robert Ervin among others.[84]

Snow. The Snows, for whom Snow's Island is named, came fairly late to eastern Williamsburg Township. Although they were prolific across the township during the colonial period, they are not well represented today. Dr. Nathaniel Snow was the first Snow to come to South Carolina around 1696 or 1697. The Revolutionary War Snows were probably the sons and daughters of Nathaniel Snow Jr. (1747-1752) (or d. 1760 according to William Boddie) and were named Mary, John, Nathaniel (III), George, Ann, William, and James. His daughter Ann married Francis Goddard (II) (see above).

The Snows settled in Williamsburg Township in Prince Frederick Parish in the 1760s, especially along the Black River. The name Snow appears on both the 1775 Mouzon map and 1773 Cook map of South Carolina where it appears on the west bank of the Pee Dee at Britton's Ferry and twice along a branch of Black Mingo Creek (Figures 3.5, 3.6, 3.9, 4.1). One of those depicted on Black Mingo is George Snow (Figures 3.5, 3.6, 3.9). The Snows of the Snow's Island community included James, William, George, Hannah, and Nathaniel (II or III).[85]

James Snow (1730-1793) owned land on the western side of Snow's Island along Clark's Creek. He was married to Hannah; both assisted Francis Marion (see Chapters 6 and 7). In 1786, he, William Goddard, Austin Stone, and John James were named commissioners. Interestingly, sometime before 1790 he freed his 77 slaves and re-hired them under indenture. According to William Boddie, this experiment cost him "much of his property and was not regarded with favor by the community."[86]

There may have been two William Snows living at the time of the Revolution. One owned property around Georgetown. It is possible he was the same William Snow who owned property on the southern end of Snow's Island, but it might not be the same individual. One William was the son of William and Mary Snow, born 1748. The other was the son of a Nathaniel Snow (probably senior) and thus the brother of Nathaniel (II). The son of William and Mary appears to be the one who owned land on Snow's Island. One William Snow, also probably the Snow's Island William, was an ardent believer, being a vestryman from 1770-1773, and church warden (1774-1776) for Prince Frederick. He was elected to the Provincial Congress in 1775. He was also a member of the Second General Assembly (1776-1778). Having land on the southern part of Snow's Island, it is no surprise that he was a commissioner for opening of navigation of Lynches and Clark's Creek in 1778.

William Snow sold some of his property on Snow's Island to William Britton in 1775. He was a witness for William Britton's will. He left 650 acres of Snow's Island property to his son Samuel in his own will.[87]

George Snow does not appear in historic documents very much, but he did have land on Muddy Creek west of Snow's Island. His property was adjacent to land owned by Moses Britton. George was listed in the 1767 and 1778-1779 Jury Lists for Prince Frederick Parish.[88]

Stone. Austin Stone (1748-1818) lived west of Snow's Island along Lynches Creek. His father was Philip Stone of Virginia; it is not clear how Austin got to South Carolina as his father was born and died in Virginia, and the family website states that Austin was born in Marion County.[89]

Austin married Elizabeth Singletary. They had eleven children. Five were born during the American Revolution (1775-1783), evidence of the advantages of being in the militia and able to get home on occasion. Austin had 800 acres lying in the fork of Lynches Lake and Lynches Creek. There is a Singleton Swamp, a branch of Lynches Lake that may have connection with his wife

(Singleton-Singletary), at least 100 additional acres on Lynches Creek, and another 450 acres in nearby Marion County.

The Austin Stone family was listed in the 1790 Williamsburg County Census as including six males, five females and no slaves. In 1786, he was listed on a petition for opening navigation on Lynches Creek. In 1791, he and William Goddard were named to a board for improving navigation on lower Lynches Creek. In an 1810 estate settlement for Peniah Savage, wife of Nathan Savage (above), Austin was named, along with Francis Greaves, Loveless Gasque, Robert Ervin, and Richard Godfrey. Finally, Austin signed over his compensation for militia duty in Colonel Giles's company to William Goddard after the war, possibly to pay a debt.[90]

Witherspoon [*Witherspoone, Weatherspoon*]. The Witherspoons were among the first Scots-Irish Protestant families of Williamsburg Township and, by the American Revolution, were spread widely across the township as depicted on the Mouzon, Cook, and Faden's maps (Figures 3.5, 3.6, 3.9). The entire family is an example of a prominent family prior to the war who became strong supporters of the rebellion. A separate study could be done on these strong Whigs who joined the Williamsburg militia and fought under Marion.

John Witherspoon was the founding father in South Carolina, who arrived from Ireland in the 1730s. He was among the families that settled around Kingstree circa 1734.[91]

Within the Snow's Island community were three Witherspoon brothers, John, Gavin, and Robert, two of whom settled along Lynches Creek. As mentioned previously, the brothers were also the brothers-in-law of Hugh and John Ervin. John Witherspoon (1742-1802) was the son of another Gavin Witherspoon (1748-1773) and Jane James.[92] John inherited land on Lynches Creek west of Snow's Island. When his brother, Robert, died, he was vested with Witherspoon's Ferry, a site that became a strategic position during the Revolution.

John was also among those former members of the Indiantown Presbyterian Church (including brother Gavin and Hugh and John Ervin [see above]) who moved to Lynches Creek and established Aimwell Church. The church was located around ten miles above the mouth of Lynches Creek and at the northern extent of the Snow's Island community. In his will, John donated the 634 acres of land at Witherspoon's Ferry (inherited from his brother Robert) to the Aimwell Church. In doing so, he named his friends Samuel Ervin, John D. Witherspoon, and Robert Ervin trustees of the property. He also allowed

William Johnston, who was leasing the lands, to continue to do so as long as he conducted himself with "propriety."[93]

When the Revolution began in 1775, John was on the committee to execute the Continental Association in Prince Frederick. He joined the Britton's Neck regiment as a private and by the end of the war he had risen to a captaincy. He signed the 1776 Craven County militia petition and Gregg has him listed as an ensign in Captain Thomas Port's volunteers. His wife, Mary Conn, may have been the daughter of Thomas Conn, who lived up the Pee Dee and who was named along with John in a judgment in 1788.[94]

The second brother, Robert Witherspoon (1745-1787), operated Witherspoon's Ferry during the Revolution. He served as a private in the war and signed the 1776 Craven County militia petition. After the war, he represented Prince Frederick in the Sixth General Assembly (1785-1786). He married Mary James, but they had no children.

Two other Robert Witherspoons are recorded during the colonial period. One was born in 1728 and lived near Ox Swamp. His home may be depicted on 1825 *Mills' Atlas* although he died in 1788. Bailey and Cooper believe this particular Robert was not the one who served in the legislature. The third Robert died in 1818, and as far as I can tell, is not closely related to the Robert Witherspoon on Lynches Creek although he was probably distantly connected.[95]

Brother number three, Gavin Witherspoon (1748-1834), accompanied his brothers north but it appears he did not settle on Lynches Creek. Instead, he moved north to Hewson's Creek, the small branch where it is believed Burch's Mill was located (see Chapter 8). If so, then he may have been the one who first decided to establish the Aimwell Church. He also had land on the other side of the Pee Dee and is listed as being in Liberty County (now Marion) in 1786 after the war.[96]

Gavin was a private who signed the 1776 Craven militia petition and rose to a captaincy under Marion. After the war, he represented Marion District in the Tenth General Assembly (1792-1794) and served as justice of the peace, road commissioner and commissioner tasked with improving navigation along the Pee Dee. There was probably another Gavin, or Gaven, Witherspoon in Williamsburg County. The evidence for this is that both Gavin and John are listed on the 1778-1779 Jury Lists with the words "of Pee Dee" after their names.[97]

As mentioned, Witherspoons were spread across Williamsburg Township and all appear to have been Whigs, but not necessarily within the region defined as the Snow's Island community. One of these was David Witherspoon who was probably living along the Black River south of Snow's Island at the time of the Revolution. He was at least the second David, the first having arrived along with the earliest families in the 1730s. The David Witherspoon living at the time of the American Revolution died of his wounds in 1792. He is included herein for his role in assisting the troops on Snow's Island.[98]

Woodberry [*Woodbury*]. It would be a gap in this study to leave out Richard Woodberry, who was a local hero of the American Revolution. The Woodberrys were a Britton's Neck family who rose to prominence after the war and included a general during the War of 1812. Richard, who married Elizabeth Britton, signed the 1776 Craven militia petition and the 1783 petition protesting Loyalists. His name is also on the 1814 petition. However, this may well be his namesake and son Richard (II).

All of Richard's land was platted after the war so it is not confirmed that he was on the neck at the time of the war. However, I believe he owned land at Potato Bed Ferry and operated the ferry there at the time of the war. Marion mentions in a letter written in October 1780 that he crossed the Little Pee Dee at "Woodberry's."[99]

SECOND TIER FAMILIES

Besides the core families, there were a number of families in the wider region that also supported Marion during the war, but were not as closely connected to the Britton's Neck-Lynches Creek-Snow's Island core described above—or data about their connections are less evident. Even so, I chose to include them because they played roles in the partisan career of Francis Marion at Snow's Island (see Chapters 6 and 7). In some cases, they settled (or purchased land) just before the beginning of the war, and thus had not established connections to other families when the war began. Also, while some settled within the geographical core region, others settled in two enclaves along Jeffries Creek and Catfish Creek.

In placing a family in this second-tier list I am not implying secondary social status in the community—just that their connections are not as complex or interwoven within the community as the families above.

Buckholts, Buckholtes. The Buckholts arrived in the mid-18th century and settled on Catfish Creek at the northern end of the Snow's Island region (Figure 4.2). There were three Buckholts: Abraham, Jacob, and Peter. Abraham became a justice of the peace in 1756 and was a major in the militia in 1775.

Jacob was listed on the 1744 Jury List for Prince Frederick Parish. Abraham and Peter were listed on the 1778-1779 Jury Lists.[100]

Peter Buckholts acquired two property tracts, of 200 and 300 acres, on Catfish Creek in 1764. He signed the 1776 Protestant petition and served under Marion. After the war, he moved to Georgia and it appears from genealogical websites for the Buckholts that many other family members moved out of South Carolina in the early 19th century. Jacob, for instance, mortgaged his property for $60.00 to Samuel Thompson in 1820, but the debt remained unpaid as of 1829.[101]

McCall. George McCall was born on Lynches Creek on 10 September 1760, according to his pension application (Figure 4.2). His father may have been Charles McCall who had 250 acres of land platted in 1764. George was a young man at the time of the American Revolution. He moved to Darlington District after the war.[102]

Miscally [*McKelly; Mizcally*] In 1766, Hugh Miscally was platted 100 acres on Muddy Creek (Figure 4.2). This creek ran into Clark's Creek at Snow's Island and thus his land was near Snow's Island in Williamsburg Township.

Not much is known about Hugh Miscally. It is known that he and his wife, Mary, purchased four slaves from the Jordan family who lived along the Santee, but there are no known marriages between the Miscallys and other Snow's Island community members. This may be significant because Hugh became a Loyalist during the Revolution and played a different, but profound, role in the story of Snow's Island. Despite his loyalism, Mary apparently remained in the area as she was listed in the 1790 Williamsburg Census as having three male members of the household—possibly sons—and 16 slaves.[103]

Myers. At the extreme north end of what I define as the Snow's Island community region is a stream draining into the Great Pee Dee called Jeffries Creek. Along this creek and its tributary Middle Swamp, and along Lynches Creek, at Sparrow Swamp and Lake Swamp, were several settlers who, like the core Snow's Island community, intermarried and entered business relationships with community members. Two of the more prominent families were the Myers (Figure 4.2) and Nettles families (see below). The patriarch of the Myers family was John Myers (d. 1771), whose sons, George (1739/40-1789), Daniel (1745-1803), and John (b. 1765) served and supported Marion. John originally bought land along the Pee Dee before moving to Jeffries Creek in 1756

George Myers married a Nancy Bass. Both families moved to the Middle Swamp region. George's daughter Mary married Samuel Burris after the war in 1789, and Samuel served under Marion.[104] Other members of the Bass family married into the Nettles family.

Nettles. The Nettles, originally a Virginia family, settled on Jeffries Creek, Lynches Creek, and Middle Swamp at the extreme northwestern corner of what is defined as the Snow's Island community region (Figure 4.2). As with the Britton, Witherspoon, and James families, there were multiple George, Robert, and Joseph Nettles, all names of men who served under Marion. Interestingly, however, not one seems to have signed the 1776 Craven County militia petition or any other petitions. There were also Nettles in Williamsburg County, including Joseph and Robert, who are listed in Boddie's history.[105]

Poston. The land immediately northwest of Port's Ferry and north of Witherspoon's Ferry is known today as Poston (Figure 4.1, Figure 4.5, Figure 4.6). This area may have been known by that name as early as 1815. A map originally surveyed in 1815 depicts Poston, however, the map was "improved" in 1882 so it is not known if the improvement included new place names (Figure 4.5). Today, Postons are found throughout Marion and Williamsburg Counties.[106]

The Postons time of arrival in the Snow's Island community is not clear but they were there during the war. It is believed that John Poston came from Pennsylvania to Marion County around 1766. He was born in 1755 and died between 1821 and 1830. John, John Jr., and Joseph Poston signed the 1776 Craven County militia petition, and John served as a private in Hugh Giles and John Ervin's regiment, with Joseph Greaves company, meaning they had to be in the region and therefore quite likely living near the modern post stop of Poston. Perhaps John Jr. and Joseph were the young sons of the John who came to South Carolina, and although living around Port's Ferry at the time of the war, did not own title to the land.[107] There is no known land platted to Postons in Marion until after the war. No Postons appear in the jury lists for Prince Frederick Parish.

Potts. Thomas Potts (d. 1760) was one of the early Williamsburg Township settlers of the 1730s and a member of the Indiantown Presbyterian Church. He had a son, Thomas (II), and four daughters, Mary, Ann, Elizabeth (married a Swinton), and Margaret (married another Potts).[108]

Thomas (II) inherited land from his father along Black River but also owned land on the Pee Dee River and Catfish and Potato Creeks (Figure 4.2). He was active early in the war, serving on the committee to enforce the Continental Association in 1775. He served in the 5th Regiment of the South Carolina Continental Line until 1778 and afterward joined Marion and was a captain. Boddie also says he was a surgeon for Marion.

After the war, Thomas (II) represented the Williamsburg District in the 11th General Assembly.[109] This implies that his residence was on Black River; he is listed in the 1790 census for that county, but represents an example of someone who also owned property surrounding the Snow's Island community region. I expect there were many other landowners, like Potts, who owned land in both districts.

As an interesting aside, William Potts was a witness to the pension application of Reddin McCoy. McCoy lived in Sumter District but in his will, he states that his son-in-law was William Potts. William testified of seeing Reddin separately at his father's house when Marion camped there, and at the Snow's Island camp, which he [William] had visited. It has not been established that William was the son of Thomas Potts (II), however, William mentions that Benjamin Screven's home was about two miles from his father's, and Benjamin owned 150 acres adjacent to Thomas Potts on Black River.[110]

Shaw. Revolutionary War veteran William Shaw lived to be over 100 years old, having been born in 1759, and, according to Gregg, was interviewed by Gregg in 1859. William signed the 1776 Craven County militia petition and was a witness to Benjamin Munnerlyn's audited account and Jonathan Collins's pension application. It is not exactly clear where William lived but it appears from judgments of Thomas Wiggins estate adjoining Shaw's property that Shaw lived on the Warhee Neck (Figure 4.2) (east side of Pee Dee near Catfish Creek).[111]

Simons. Shadrach [*Shade, Shadrack*] Simons (1758 -1801) lived near the Great Pee Dee on Soccee Swamp south of Snow's Island on property bounded by William Snow's property (Figure 4.2). The plat of land for this site is dated 1791, so I can't confirm that he was in that area prior to the war. He also had some 6,681 acres in Georgetown and his father, John, was taken prisoner and died in Charleston in October 1780.

Shade was a captain in Colonel John Baxter's regiment. After the war, Shade represented Williamsburg District in the 12th General Assembly (1796-

The Pre-Revolutionary Snow's Island Community | 85

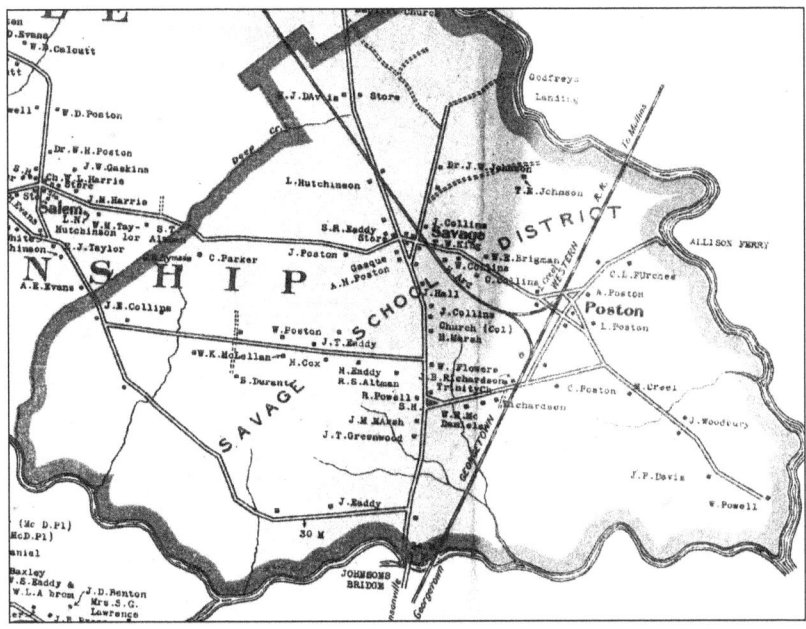

Figures 4.5. Detail of 1913 Florence County school district map
S.C. Department of Archives and History)

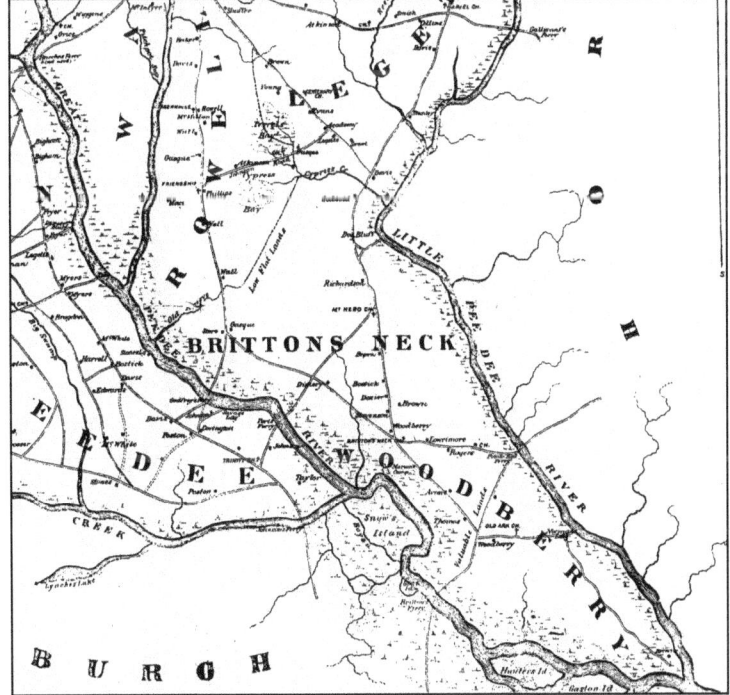

Figure 4.6. Detail of Marion County map, surveyed by Harlee, 1815,

1797). In December 1783, he married Mary Bellune, but after her death in childbirth, he married Elizabeth Britton in 1785. She was the widow of Henry Britton, not the "Widow Jenkins" described elsewhere.

After the war, William Goddard signed over the indents of Francis Goddard to Shade Simons as part of a business contract, possibly having to do with the settlement of Francis's estate. Daniel and Francis Britton witnessed that document.[112]

Swinton. The Swintons are included here although their plantation was on the Pee Dee near Georgetown, South Carolina. Hugh and Alexander were the sons of William Swinton who came to American from Scotland as a Royal Surveyor and actually laid out the town of Georgetown. Alexander and Hugh were defrauded out of much of their father's estate upon his death. They recovered well and later owned land in Williamsburg Township and on Catfish Creek in Marion County. Alexander was made an overseer in the Prince Frederick church in 1766.[113]

Hugh was born in 1737. He had several tracts of land along the Pee Dee, and oddly, a 75-acre tract on Snow's Island platted in 1769, hence his inclusion here (Figure 4.2). This land later became Francis Goddard's land, but no record of that transaction survives.[114]

THIRD TIER FAMILIES

Table 4.1 lists Marion District residents who assisted Francis Marion during the war or were members of his brigade. They were selected because they appear to have lived within the Snow's Island region but where exactly is unknown. Little other information is known about them (Figure 4.2).

No doubt other families not represented here lived in the region and on Britton's Neck and supported Francis Marion. This chapter serves only to provide a documented geographical and genealogical sample of the Snow's Island community.

Table 4.1. Snow's Island Third-Tier Community Members

Family/Individual	Location/Source	Family/Individual	Location/Source
Barrow, James	1776 Britton's Neck Protestant Petition, AA2116	Perkins, Lewis	Pension R8114, A.A. 5897
Dawsey, Fowler	1776 Britton's Neck Protestant Petition, 1776 Craven Petition, named in B. Munnerlyn A.A. W8479	Booth, John	On Pee Dee near Warhees, Pension W25258
Fletcher, John	Pension S45841	Gasque, Robert & John	A.A. 2718A, 2719 Indent T 202
Hartley, William	1776 Britton's Neck Protestant Petition, 1783 Loyalist Petition	Johnson, James	Lake Swamp, A.A. 4068
Martin, James	1776 Britton's Neck Protestant Petition, 1776 Craven Petition	Grice, Thomas	Warhee Neck, (land plat SCDAH, S213184 9:36; Pension R4301)
Port, Peter	1776 Britton's Neck Protestant Petition, 1776 Craven Petition	Collins, Jonathan	? Marion District, Pension, S18771
Rice, John	Pension R8747	Jesse Wiggins	Near Great Pee Dee, Pension R11502
Smith, Jessy	1776 Britton's Neck Protestant Petition, 1776 Craven Petition	Tyler, Samuel & John	AA7984, 7983 witnessed by Robert Dunnam

Endnotes for Chapter 4

1 Cook 1926:58-59. Mrs. Phyllis Canady did an extensive genealogy of the Britton family. Canady noted that "Most everything that has been written about the Britton family of South Carolina is incorrect" (Canady 2001:24), meaning the traditional histories like Alexander Gregg (1925). As she has minutely cited primary source material for many of her assertions I have confidence in her overall research and cite her extensively. Her research consisted of several bound manuscripts not consistently numbered, therefore the page numbering system used in the citations is mine.

2 Canady 2001:4-8.

3 Canady 2001:10.

4 This same problem exacerbates the problem of sorting out Snow's Island community families in the discussion that follows. I am deeply beholden to many genealogists who are far better able to keep straight several generations of Snow's Island community members than I. Readers with an interest in the genealogy of Marion's partisans should note the citations in this chapter. They contain a wealth of information not used herein. Those members of the Britton family who moved away from the Snow's Island region are not mentioned.

5 Canady 2001:13-14.

6 Bailey and Cooper 1981:92; Canady 2001:16, 20, 24.

7 Canady 2001:27-29.

8 Canady 2001:14-15; Utley et al. 1985:56. Lucille Utley and several of her colleagues transcribed Marion County Judgment Rolls, Equity Rolls, Probate Records, and Deeds. These have been bound by the Three Rivers Historical Society of Hemmingway, South Carolina, and are sold to genealogists. I have chosen to cite the primary sources by Utley's bound transcriptions. This is not only for ease of citation, but to recognize her work and not to give the reader the false impression that I have painstakingly poured through county archives to find these primary sources on my own. Remember, my primary purpose is not genealogy but demonstrating community.

9 Canady 2001:44.

10 Ashford 1982:2.

11 Moss 1983:62; Frances Port, Will, Book 1:75, Estate Packet Roll 645, SCDAH, S108093:17, 621.

12 Andrew Farwell Johnson, Will, 7 September 1812, Book 1:278; Estate Packet Roll 404, SCDAH, S108093:17,824.

13 There are four petitions that help establish the residence of Snow's Island community members. The first was a 1776 petition signed by the Upper Craven County regiment of militia protesting being stationed at Cheraw Hill, while another regiment was in Charleston assisting in its defense against the British. At that time there was no Loyalist threat and petitioners believed the post could be defended with two sergeants and 25 privates (S213089:5,24). An unknown number of the 366 (or 566) men lived above Jeffries and Catfish Creek so their signatures alone do not confirm that they lived in the Snow's Island region. The second petition was also signed in 1776 by Britton's Neck Protestants for the Disestablishment of the Protestant Episcopal Church (S165015:1776,1). The third was a 1783 petition of Prince George Parish residents protesting the pardon of Loyalists after the war. The names include residents of Britton's Neck and surrounding region (S165015:1783,134). The final petition, dated 1814, was a petition of residents on both sides of Port's Ferry for reestablishment of the ferry (S165015 1814:59). These four petitions, used in conjunction with other sources, helped greatly to identify members of the Snow's Island community. All four are cited extensively in this chapter.

14 Utley and Sutcliffe 1997:26.

15 SCDAH, S165015:1783,134. Prince George was south of Prince Frederick Parish however, the names of other residents (William Goddard, Benjamin Port, and the Davises) on the petition clearly indicate that at that time the "Upper" region included Britton's Neck.

16 Utley 1981: 3.

17 SCDAH, S165015:1783,134.

18. Sellers 1902:448.
19. See also Figures 3.5, 3.6, 3.9. They all depict a "Davies" or "Daves" that may be Davis.
20. Bass in Bass-Canady Correspondence.
21. SCDAH, S213089:5,24; SCDAH, S165015:1814,59; Bailey 1984:146.
22. Benjamin Davis Will, 1802 Will Book1:27, SCDAH, S108093:17,566.
23. John Dozier [Dozer] Will, January 25, 1808, Will Book 1:45, SCDAH, S108093:17,589.
24. Joseph Davis Pension, S10534. Federal pensions can be found at www.fold3.com and South Carolina state and federal pensions (for South Carolina) are available at the South Carolina Department of Archives and History listed under the pension number.
25. SCDAH, S213190 32:246.
26. Gregg 1925:245; Francis Davis, Pension, S8290; Utley 1981:19; SCDAH, S165015 1814:59.
27. Francis Davis Pension S8290.
28. Gregg 1925:245; Utley 1981.
29. Bailey and Cooper 1981:193-194; Pringle 1916:47; Utley et al. 2005:58.
30. John Dozier Will, Will Book 1:43, SCDAH, S108093:17,589.
31. Rudosill 1993:14. Reverend Evan Pugh was a Baptist minister presiding at Cashaway Baptist Church in Society Hill, South Carolina. Although not a resident, he ministered to those in the Snow's Island area and traveled up and down the Pee Dee. He was friends of both Tories and Whigs, and his diaries are an excellent source of information about life along the Pee Dee during the American Revolution.
32. Dunnam 2010a; Dunnam 2010b; Rudisill 1993:14; Smith 2008a:10; SC Deed Abstracts 4R0:270-273, SCDAH, S213184:6,68 and S213184:7,96.
33. Dunnam 2010a.
34. One of the Ebenezers was listed among purchasers of "Negroes" as part of the settlement of James Keen's estate in 1801. This suit provides another excellent example of the interrelated families of the Snow's Island community (Utley et al. 1985:257). Bondsmen for this suit were Joseph Davis, John Munnerlyn, William Bellune, and James Davis. Appraisers include Stephen Britton, William Bellune, and Joseph Greaves. Besides Ebenezer Dunnam, other purchasers included Joseph Greaves, Timothy Britton, William Bellune, John Munnerlyn, Richard Godfrey, Joseph Munnerlyn, Joseph Davis, and Jason Munnerlyn.
35. Dunnam 2010b; Ervin 1978:219, 226.
36. Utley et al. 2005:188.
37. Bailey and Cooper 1981:218-219; Ervin 1978:220-221; Howe 1870:413.
38. Bailey and Cooper 1981:217; SCDAH, S213184:8,151.
39. Bailey 1984:190-191; Bailey and Cooper 1981:218; Ervin 1978:221; Howe 1870:413.
40. Dickerson 2005:4-5; Gregg 1925:69; Cook 1926:59; Warren 1977:55.
41. Dickerson 2005:3-4; SCDAH, S213019:19,67; SCDAH, S111001:10,40; Warren 1977:55; Utley and Smith 1985a:18,39,128.
42. Sellers 1902:491; SCDAH, S213190:34,406.
43. Dickerson 2005:3, 6; Boddie 1923:25; Stanley 1938:32; SCDAH, S213184:20, 42; SCDAH, S213184 6:181.
44. Pringle 1916:56; Bass and Davis, July 13, 1980, Bass-Canady Correspondence; Jo Church Dickerson 2005:2. Reverend Alexander Gregg believed that Hugh was the son of Robert Giles (Gregg 1925:70). I'm inclined to go with Bass and Jo Church Dickerson, who state that he was not (Dickerson 2005:2). Furthermore, Dickerson believes that Abraham Giles in fact married Elizabeth Fladger, a widow whose first husband was Charles Fladger.
45. Blankenstein and Blankenstein 2010; Rudisill 1993:104; Bailey and Cooper 1981:263; Jervey 1943:176.
46. Dickerson 2005:3.

47 Pringle 1916:217; Bass Tour Notes in Bass-Canady Correspondence ; Bailey and Cooper 1981:263-263. Hugh Giles is really the unsung hero of Marion County history who led the district Whigs before Marion arrived in 1780. His legacy was overshadowed by Marion, and the integration of these militia within Marion's brigade.
48 Rudisill 1993:118; Bass-Canady Correspondence.
49 Dickerson 2005:3.
50 Utley et al. 2005:79-80; Utley et al. 2005:149.
51 Bass 1959:104; Lipscomb circa 1974:2; Boddie 1923:25, 143; Bass in Bass-Canady Correspondence; Francis Goddard, Charleston Will Book ,1740-1747:324.
52 Pringle 1916:168; Lipscomb circa 1974:2; Charleston Will Book Volume 8, 1776-1784; SCDAH, S213184:20,322.
53 Jenkins 1842:7, 18; Bass in Bass-Canady Correspondence; Canady 2001:25.
54 Charleston Will Book 18:1776-1784.
55 Charleston Will Book Volume 8:1776-1784. This will is another example of the close family relationships within the Snow's Island community. The will names William Goddard (II), Francis (II) his son, and Francis Goddard (III), his nephew. At one point, the will even called Francis, "Francis Francis Goddard." The will also names three daughters. One is named Frances. The land Francis II gives to William was formerly purchased from John Dunnam. Francis's (II) will provides Mrs. Francis[es] Port £50 per year to take care of his young daughter Francis[es]. Francis (II) gives only £100 to his wife Ann Snow for a suit of mourning clothing. The executors of the will were Francis and Daniel Britton, and it was witnessed by James Snow, Natt Snow, and William Britton.
56 Bass in Bass-Canady Correspondence; Jenkins 1842:17.
57 Graves 2010; Warren 1977:62; Hendrick and Lindsay 1975:30, 33, 34.
58 Graves 2010; Gregg 1925:245; SCDAH, S136002:099a,329a.
59 SCDAH, S213190:9, 355; SCDAH, S213190:21,1; Warren 1977:62; Utley et al. 1985:196; Utley and Dalrymple 2002:52.
60 Warren 1977:62.
61 Stanley 1938:31.
62 Boddie 1923:10, 11, 21; Wallace 1856:26; Cooper 2007:7.
63 James 1821; Boddie 1923:116.
64 Howe 1870:407, 412.
65 Bailey 1984:308; Howe 1870:407, 412.
66 James 1821:vi; Bailey 1984:312; Cooper 2007:18.
67 Jenkins 1842:18.
68 Jenkins 1842:8; SCDAH, S213184:11,34; James Jenkins Pension S18054; Jenkins 1842:17; SCDAH, S18054, Audited Account [henceforth A.A.] 4018a; Hendrick and Lindsay 1975:34.
69 Hendrick and Lindsay 1975:30,34; SCDAH, S213184:17;245, Items 1 and 2.
70 Munnerlyn 2010; Utley and Sutcliffe 1997:80; L. Munnerlyn Pension S18136; *Mills'* 1825.
71 Collins Pension S18771.
72 L. Munnerlyn A.A. 5399
73 Bailey and Cooper 1981:572; Utley 1981:20; Smith 2008a:31; Gregg 1925:164-165; Bailey and Cooper 1981:572; Moss 1983:779; SCDAH, S213184 6:68; S372001:4RO,270; Deryl Young 22 August 2006, pers. Comm.
74 Utley and Smith 1985a:17; The following individuals, a who's who of the Snow's Island families, were named as heirs in Frances Port's will: Mary Port Snow, children of Thomas Humphries, Elizabeth Witherspoon Humphries, Hugh James Alison, John Balloon Alison, James Alison (son of Francis Alison), Frances Rebecca Alison (daughter of Francis Alison), William Green Balloon, Nancy Davis (wife of Benjamin Davis), Thomas Port Davis (son of Benjamin Davis), John Calhoun Davis, Margaret Davis, wife of William Davis, William Balloon, and John, Nancy, and Benjamin Godfrey (children of Rebecca Godfrey and Rachel Graves) (S108093:17,621).

75 SCDAH, S108093 17:621.
76 Joseph Davis filed on behalf of many nieces and nephews of Thomas Port against Samuel Snow and Thomas Humphries who had taken possession of Port's lands on both sides of the Pee Dee at Port's Ferry (Utley 1981:19-20).
77 Utley et al. 2005:175-176.
78 Deryl Young and Tres Hyman 2008, pers. Comm.
79 Utley 1981:20; Utley and Smith 1985a:117.
80 SCDAH, S213184:20,42. A Reverend John Rae was the first minister of the Williamsburg Presbyterian Church and was a well-known figure in Williamsburg's colonial history. He died in 1760 and left no children. I found no connection between the two, but the possibility exists (Boddie 1923:81).
81 Robert Bass to Elizabeth T. Davis, 27 November 1974, Bass-Canady Correspondence; Rae-Ray, 24 January 1972, Bass-Canady Correspondence; Jenkins 1842:27; Boddie 1923:75; Utley 1981:85.
82 James 1821:120; Bailey and Cooper 1981:635; Gregg 1925:303; Utley 1981:104-105; Utley et al. 2005:13-14.
83 Gregg 1925:282.
84 Bailey and Cooper 1981:635; Utley 1981:107; Utley and Smith 1985a:52.
85 Boddie 1923:80; Dedication Speech, Bass-Canady Correspondence; Lipscomb circa 1974:2; George Snow A.A. 7194.
86 Gregg 1925:446; Boddie 1923:248.
87 Bailey and Cooper 1981:680; Boddie 1923:92; Lipscomb circa 1974:3; SCDAH, S108093:14,74; SCDAH, S108093:17,548.
88 SCDAH, S213184:18,55; S213184:13,343; Hendrick and Lindsay 1975:30; Warren 1977:113.
89 Stone 2010.
90 Austin Stone, Will, Book 1:118, SCDAH, S108093:17,666; Boddie 1923:168; Gregg 1925:46, 453; Utley and Smith 1985:52; Stone A.A. 7420.
91 Montgomery 1835:1.
92 Bailey and Cooper 1981:783.
93 Howe 1870:413. SCDAH, S108093 1:29. Another source states that they founded Hopewell Presbyterian Church instead of Aimwell (Wallace 1856:36). An 1822 map depicts the Hopewell Meeting House about ten miles above the mouth of Lynches Creek where Wallace says it was located (Wilson map, 1822). Howe puts Hopewell twenty miles farther north (Howe 18/0:413). Both Howe and Wallace agree that, whatever the church was named, it was near Jeffries Creek. For John's will see SCDAH, S108093:1,29.
94 Bailey and Cooper 1981:784; Gregg 1925:246; SCDAH, S1366002:136a,120a.
95 Bailey and Cooper 1981:784; Bailey and Cooper 1981:785; Hartman 2005:185-186.
96 SCDAH, S213184:21,362; Bailey 1984:609.
97 Bailey 1984:609; Hartman 2005:183-184; Hendrick and Lindsay 1975:38.
98 Boddie 1923:11,17,18; D. Witherspoon A.A. 8639.
99 Richard Woodberry Will Book 1:244; SCDAH, S108093:17,790; Marion to Gates, 4 October 1780, State Records of North Carolina [henceforth SRNC], Volume 14:665.
100 Gregg 1925:76, 120, 284; Warren 1977:36; Hendrick and Lindsay 1975:30, 33, 34.
101 SCDAH, S111001:6,301; S111001:6,37; Utley et al. 2005:88.
102 McCall Pension R6598; SCDAH, S213184:7,437; George McCall, Will, Estate Book 8:490, SCDAH, S108093:7,786.
103 SCDAH, S213184:9,114; SCDAH, S213003:2Q,126; 1790 Federal Census.
104 Myers 2007:12, 19, 29.
105 Myers 2007:141; Boddie 1923:117.

106 Harlee 1815-Bethea 1882 Map of Marion County.
107 Landers and Poston circa 1965:8; A.A. 6057.
108 Boddie 1923:25, 57, 80.
109 Bailey and Cooper 1981:579; Boddie 1923:131.
110 Reddin McCoy S7198; Reddin McCoy Will, Will Book D2:78, SCDAH, S108093:26,351; SCDAH, S213184:19,376.
111 Gregg 1925:404; Munnerlyn A.A. W8479; Collins Pension S18771; Utley and Smith 1985a:132.
112 Shadrack Bible 2010; SCDAH, S213212:1,259; Bailey 1984:517; Canady 2001:21; F. Goddard A.A. 2916a.
113 Maybin and Foxworth 1957:9; Rogers 1970:134; SCDAH, S213184:21,240; Pringle 1916:188.
114 SCDAH, S213184:11,110.

CHAPTER 5

THE WAR BEGINS

This chapter discusses the formation of a Whig community out of those living around Snow's Island. The purpose is not to rehash the early part of the war, but to present the evidence of the initial formation of a community of resistance, which became Marion's partisan community.

Five years prior to the arrival of Francis Marion, the residents within the Snow's Island community chose sides in the rebellion against Britain. In other words, the Snow's Island partisan community was already formed when Marion arrived at Witherspoon's Ferry on 17 August 1780 to take command of the Williamsburg militia. Combining with the Britton's Neck militia, these two regiments made up the core of Marion's Brigade later in the war.

Years of disputes between England and the individual colonies over taxation continued until the colonies began to resist in a united fashion. In 1774, the first Continental Congresses met in Philadelphia. As part of their business, they adopted a continental association "pledging Americans to embargo most trade with Great Britain" and "declaring their opposition to British policy." A year later, South Carolina Whigs met in Charleston on 11 January 1775 as the Provincial Congress. The Provincial Congress approved the resolutions of the Continental Congress, including the adoption of the Continental Association. John James, Hugh Giles, John Witherspoon, Thomas Potts, Francis Britton, and William Snow, from Prince Frederick Parish, were all members of the association. These men were from established families in and around Snow's Island and became the initial instigators of Whig opposition in the community.[1]

Even at this early date, pockets of rebellion and loyalism were emerging in South Carolina, along with some who wished to remain neutral. The Charleston Whigs sent a party to the backcountry hoping to find converts, but Loyalists in the Saxe Gotha region rejected their proposals—as did those around Thicketty Creek and Ninety Six. Some who resisted or called themselves "Nonassociators" were arrested and their homes destroyed.[2]

Around Snow's Island, Whig sentiments were strong, possibly augmented by suppression of Loyalist sentiments. One Whig community organizer was ferry owner Thomas Port, who was elected to represent the residents around Snow's Island in the Provincial Congress. John James later joined him.

When news of the battle of Lexington and Concord in Massachusetts (19 April 1775) arrived in South Carolina, the Snow's Island community was already poised to act. Port wrote the First Council of Safety on 21 July that he had "summonsed the male inhabitants of sd District to Assemble together to Choose there [sic] officers to teach them the Military Discipline and make them usefull if Called on to March Against our Enemies." He described the district as "on the south wst side of pee dee River, and on the north Est side of Linches Crick, from the mouth of sd Linches Crick up to willow Crick, all Inclusive." This description fits the land just across Lynches Creek north of Snow's Island. Port further noted that the inhabitants "Cheerfully Obayed" and "did me the Honnour unnemously to Chose me there Capt, Mr Hugh Giles, first Leut, Mr Thos Potts second Leut." Finally he adds as a *nota bene* that "I have the pleasure to inform you that Every man of the above Districts that has Assembled together has signed the Association without one Desenting Voice." This region did not include Britton's Neck, but as I have noted, Francis Britton was elected to the Association.[3]

On 15 September 1775, Royal Governor William Campbell officially dissolved the Commons House and left South Carolina. The following day, Nonassociators signed a treaty with the Whigs at Ninety Six, South Carolina, in which they agreed to remain neutral and the Whigs agreed not to act against them. By that time, Thomas Port's volunteers had become part of St. David's Parish Regiment. Among the regiment were 1st Lieutenant Daniel Britton and Ensign John Witherspoon, along with the Britton's Neck volunteer corps under Captain John Dozier, 1st Lieutenant Henry Britton, and 2nd Lieutenant Joseph Graves.[4]

Despite the treaty, bloodshed between Loyalists and Whigs occurred there on 19 November at Ninety Six. After that encounter and a December campaign against Tories on the Reedy River, much backcountry Loyalist opposition was suppressed.

In March 1776, South Carolina drafted a state constitution and created a General Assembly. But help was on the way for the Loyalists. The previous fall, the British, believing there was strong support for them in the southern colonies, had begun to formulate plans to come to their rescue. On 1 June, a British fleet arrived off Charleston Harbor, and on the 28th, with a combined land and sea attack, the British forces attempted to capture an American fort built on Sullivan's Island. Fort Sullivan had been built by the Whigs in February because they had become wary of a British invasion of South Carolina. The attempt failed, resulting in a great victory for the Americans.[5]

On that day, Major Francis Marion was in charge of the left wing inside Fort Sullivan. Among his men were several residents of the Snow's Island community. When the British fleet arrived, a call had gone out for volunteers, and among those mustering at Port's Ferry were Joseph Davis, Benjamin Davis, Francis Goddard, and Jonathan Collins, all under the command of Lieutenant Benjamin Munnerlyn, and Captain Shade [Shadrack] Simons. They had marched to rendezvous with others at Dunham's Bluff, and then continued to Charleston, where they reported to Marion. One Snow's Island community member, David Witherspoon, was wounded in the battle, and rendered "incapable of gaining a Livelyhood." He still rendered service to Marion, providing food and forage throughout the war, as he lived until 19 August 1792.[6]

In spite of their failed attack, the British remained off Charleston until August, which lent hope to South Carolina Loyalists. Also, in the upstate, Cherokees and Loyalists dressed as Native Americans raided Whigs. In response, the Whigs mounted a major attack against the Cherokee villages in upper South Carolina and North Carolina, and effectively neutralized Indian opposition for the remainder of the war.[7]

On 2 August 1776, news of the Declaration of Independence arrived in South Carolina. The Declaration ended hope of reconciliation between England and America and kept Whig leaders in South Carolina active and their forces in the field.

During 1776, some 2,000 South Carolinians enlisted as Continentals or state troops but as the next year unfolded—without a major British presence—enthusiasm for military duty diminished. To counteract this, the South Carolina General Assembly ordered "undesirables" into active duty and attempted to attract volunteers by offering cash and land. In 1778, they became desperate enough to allow one-third of the militia to be made up of slaves, although a move by Colonel John Laurens to arm slaves was thoroughly defeated in the General Assembly. Still, South Carolina Continentals remained at their stations in Charleston and one former plantation owner, Francis Marion, began to rise through the ranks.[8]

Many Snow's Island residents were also losing their enthusiasm for militia duty. Having been formed as part of the St. David's Upper Craven County militia, they had been stranded at Cheraw Hill through the fall of

1776, ostensibly to guard the armory there. Meanwhile, another regiment was detached to Charleston to assist in the fight against the British.[9] Angered that their presence at Cheraw Hill not only was causing them to lose their crops, but was also a waste of their time when two sergeants and 25 men could effectively guard the armory, they gathered together and signed a petition protesting their condition.

Among the signers were Snow's Island community members: John Barrow, William Bellune, James Britton, Daniel Britton, Joseph Britton, Stephen Britton, William Britton, Benjamin Davis, Joseph Davis, Fowler Dawsey, John Dozier, Ebenezer Dunnam, Ebenezer Dunnam Jr., John Dunnam, Robert Dunnam, Charles Fladger, Abram Giles, Hugh Giles, Francis Goddard, Benjamin Graves, James Graves, Joseph Greaves, Gavin James, Benjamin Port, Peter Port, Thomas Port, John Poston, John Poston Jr., Joseph Poston, John Rae, Edmund Ray, William Ray, Nathan Savage, William Shaw, Jessy Smith, Gavin Witherspoon, and John Witherspoon. There were either 366 or 566 individuals who signed the petition (the first number is not clear on the original) and there may have been many others in the Snow's Island region who signed it, many who probably lived above Jeffries Creek and were Cheraw residents.[10]

The year 1777 was relatively quiet as far as outright conflict goes; however, Whigs continued to harass those with Loyalist leanings. Early in the year, the new rebel government passed a banishment act, requiring Loyalists to leave the state. Many did, while others joined the Continental ranks in Charleston. Perhaps to persuade neutral and Loyalist-leaning residents in the Snow's Island region to join the cause, Captain Thomas Potts provided rations for a sergeant and several privates to "recruit" militia men for the Whigs.

In 1778, an act was passed requiring all males age sixteen and older to sign another oath of allegiance and those who refused were to be denied the right to vote or conduct business. Despite these measures, when the British turned their strategic attention back to the southern states, there were plenty of Loyalists who had remained in the state and awaited their opportunity for revenge. Among those were an estimated 3,800 men who stood ready to assemble along the Congaree, Pee Dee, and Enoree Rivers.

There were more Loyalists along the Little Pee Dee near the Snow's Island region, which may be the reason that around this time, Francis Goddard moved his mother and half-brother from his house along the Pee Dee downstream and into the safety of Britton's Neck on Britton property. There, they were "in the midst of a neighborhood of hot Whigs and warm friends of their country."[11]

During the summer of 1778, the militias were called out and, through 1779, remained active. Francis Davis, for instance, served under Hugh Giles for a peaceful three-month tour while the company was stationed at Orangeburg. George McCall was drafted and served at Seewee Bay under Captain Daniel Dubose, as did Loftus Munnerlyn. On 7 December, Nathan Savage joined and served until the 28th of February 1779. He had served in 1776, and served tours from that time until December 1782, eventually totaling 550 days under Giles and Marion. He also supplied sundries and two steers to the militia. The Jenkins brothers also joined at this time. Samuel was only 13 but continued with Colonel Horry and Marion throughout the war, returning home only when he needed clothes.[12]

With the militias called out of the region, civilians in the Snow's Island community began to be threatened by the Loyalists from along the upper Little Pee Dee. The Reverend James Jenkins recorded his cousin's move to Britton's Neck:

> But there was a body of Tories over Little Pee Dee, who were becoming very troublesome, constantly committing depreciations on their neighbours; in consequence of this, my cousin John Jenkins, being the only Whig in that settlement, feeling his life to be constantly in jeopardy, took refuge in the Neck.[13]

The Loyalists "came down on a plundering expedition, and scoured out the settlement" including the Jenkins home. These raids were probably cyclical, depending on the strategic situation in the colony. For instance, Jenkins states that the neighborhood was "never much infested with Tories," but then clarifies that he was in service at Britton's Neck, "between the Great and Little Pedee rivers which was the only Whig neighborhood on the North side of Great Pedee in that section of the Country we were stationed there principally to protect the Whig Citizens …from the invasions of the Tories."[14]

In December 1778, after a stalled northern campaign, the British returned to the southern colonies, believing that the South was still inhabited by large number of loyal families who would take arms once they provided a regular army to support them. Their southern strategy was to capture Savannah, Georgia, and then march northward to take Charleston and regain the southern colonies. Some 3,000 British regulars, German Hessians, and Provincials arrived and easily defeated the American guard at Savannah on 29 December 1778. Having established a base at Savannah, the British moved north toward Charleston and up the Savannah River in a series of probing actions. One long probe by

British General Augustine Prévost nearly reached Charleston but turned back to Savannah. In September 1779, a French fleet arrived, and the Americans turned to the offense, marching to Savannah in an attempt to take back the city. From 16 September to 8 October, the Americans, with support of the French, conducted classic 18th-century siege operations against the well-fortified British. Then the Americans and French launched an attack against one of the stronger defenses called the Spring Hill redoubt. Francis Marion was the commander of the American spearhead. Although they reached the fort's parapet and planted a flag, they were soon overwhelmed and pushed back. In Marion's ranks were Jonathan Collins and Benjamin Munnerlyn. Munnerlyn had joined in 1776 and was wounded in the leg. The repulse disheartened the French, who left on the 20th. The combined force had lost some 824 casualties. The Americans were forced back to Charleston, with Marion remaining behind to command a rear guard near Sheldon Church, South Carolina.[15]

It did not take long for the British to resume the offensive. On 11 February 1780, Sir Henry Clinton, now in charge of the British effort, landed on Seabrook Island and marched toward Charleston and the Americans there chose to remain behind their defenses. By the end of March, the British had trapped the Americans in Charleston, with British forces closing inland escape routes and a British fleet closing the harbor.

Marion, having broken or twisted his ankle and thus ineffective, was ordered to leave town on April 13. Exactly what he did between then and July 1780, when he joined the American forces at Hillsborough, North Carolina, is not well established but it is reasonable to assume that he first returned to his plantation, and then when Charleston fell, began a painful journey northward to Hillsborough, North Carolina, with a few fellow refugees.[16]

Among the militia serving near Charleston at this time was the Britton's Neck regiment under Colonel Hugh Giles. In one company, commanded by Joseph Graves, was William Bellune who served from 28 March to the 22 May, and John Tyler who served from 1 March to 22 May. John Greaves, Loftis Munnerlyn, and John Booth were also there. According to draftee Peter Buckholts, they camped at Lynches Causeway on the Santee River until Charleston fell, then returned to Georgetown and were discharged on 19 May. Colonel John Ervin may have supplied them out of his own plantation, as on 16 May he provided 16 bushels of corn. Gavin Witherspoon also may have supplied them with 200 corn blades back in February. Finally, Robert Dunnam and his brother-in-law, Andrew Burn, either supplied the American army with 65 head of hogs and 61 sheep or were employed to drive these livestock in March and April 1780.[17]

At the first of April, Sir Henry Clinton began formal siege operations against the Americans trapped in Charleston. Meanwhile, Colonel Banastre Tarleton and Lord Charles Cornwallis, British officers who would play a major role in the British struggle, began operations in the region surrounding Charleston, blocking outlying American reinforcements from entering the city.

Besides Marion, South Carolina Governor John Rutledge and a few members of his council also left the city on April 13. Snow's Island resident Francis Davis claimed that he was among the party to guard Rutledge's escape. The city was closed to escape the next day. However, George McCall was able to escape by way of Haddrell's Point. On 12 May, American commander Major General Benjamin Lincoln surrendered the city, 3,400 Continental soldiers, 1,000 Continental and South Carolina sailors, and some 2,000 militia. South Carolina was back in British control.[18]

After the fall of Charleston, the British fanned out across South Carolina taking and fortifying the backcountry towns of Ninety-Six, Camden, Cheraw, and Georgetown, South Carolina, and Augusta, Georgia. The general feeling across South Carolina was that the rebellion was soon to be over. Scattered American units across the colony that had not been taken in Charleston disbanded and members returned to their homes. John Booth and Loftis Munnerlyn's company marched to Camden and disbanded. John Greaves suffered additional loss in that his black horse was impressed by Lieutenant Colonel William Washington's Light Dragoons. Lewis Perkins was captured in Charleston but paroled home. Jonathan Collins was also captured but was kept in prison for 18 months.[19]

Not every Whig militia or regular soldier was ready to surrender, however. In the Snow's Island region, a revived resistance movement was quickly forming under Hugh Giles. Daniel Horry's dragoons, for instance, received eight bushels of corn, and two bushels of peas from Hugh Giles on 25 May. That same day, Elias Smoot (?) received from Benjamin Port one pound of gunpowder by order of Giles.[20] By the end of July, Giles was in contact with the new American commander of the Southern army, General Horatio Gates, the hero of Saratoga. Gates wrote Giles at the end of July, "you will give the fullest assurances, in my Name, to the Friends of the United States of America, that a powerful Army is marching to their protection."[21]

Meanwhile, Britain was taking actions that, over the next few months, would eventually snatch defeat from the jaws of victory. After the fall of

Charleston, the British paroled adult males except Continental soldiers. Under the terms of the parole, former rebels were to return home and not be further molested. This gesture was warmly received. As Colonel Robert Gray observed,

> [T]he Whigs & Tories seemed to vie with each other in giving proof of the sincerity of their submission & a most profound calm succeeded.[22]

But then the British issued a proclamation that former rebels would have to swear allegiance to the Crown—and be ready to "maintain and defend the same against all other persons whatsoever." This translated into taking up arms against their neighbors. Then, to compound their mistake, the British began to confiscate the estates of leading Whigs. Adding more provocation, the British took horses, cattle, and provisions from American plantations and Whigs were stripped of their political power while others in favor with the British were promoted.[23]

Another problem arose with the Loyalists who had not left the state, voluntarily or with some encouragement, prior to 1780. They had laid low or fought small skirmishes with the Whigs in the backcountry since 1777, but now, with the British in control of all the major towns, they came alive and began a campaign against those who had previously persecuted them.

The British did little to stop them. The combination of inept British policy and Loyalist harassment needed only an additional spark to ignite a partisan war, and the arrival of a new Continental Army led by Horatio Gates was just what was needed.

Who accompanied Gates?

Francis Marion.

Horatio Gates

Endnotes for Chapter 5

1 Weir 1970:55; Piecuch 2008:17; Wallace 1951:256; Rogers 1970:115.
2 Edgar 1998:223.
3 Rogers 1970:110; Boddie 1923:92; Salley 1900:128-129.
4 Edgar 1998:223, 225; Piecuch 2008:53; Lumpkin 1981:1; Gregg 1925:245-246.
5 Edgar 1998:226-227; Piecuch 2008:87-88; Lumpkin 1981:14-15.
6 Bass 1959:16; Joseph Davis Pension, S10534; D. Witherspoon A.A. 8689. As will be seen, Benjamin and Joseph Davis and Francis Goddard, signed the Craven County Petition that fall at Cheraw Hill, South Carolina. It is possible that the militia was dismissed after the Battle of Sullivan's Island and they returned home, or the time frame is mistaken in the pension account applied for by his children after his death. On the other hand, Joseph Davis' signed audited account indicates that he joined "into the service of his country immediately upon the commencement of the American Revolutionary war and continued his service until the end of the war except for very short periods" (Joseph Davis A.A. 1802). This is unfortunately the kind of ambiguity one must deal with when using the pension and audited accounts, including the fact that the Marion District Joseph Davis' audited account also includes the records of a Joseph Davis who served in Captain Calhoun's company at Ninety Six.
7 Edgar 2008:229.
8 Edgar 2008:231.
9 John Booth of Warhees was one of the men in the other regiment that went to Charleston (Booth Pension W25258).
10 SCDAH, S213089:5,24.
11 Piecuch 2008:94-95, 98; Potts A.A. 6071; Jenkins 1842:17.
12 Francis Davis Pension S8290; McCall Pension R6598; L. Munnerlyn A.A. 5399; Savage A.A. 6786; Savage Stub Indent [henceforth S.I.] P505; S. Jenkins A.A. 40211/2.
13 Jenkins 1842:17.
14 Jenkins 1842:17; J. Jenkins Pension S18054.
15 Edgar 1998:231; Lumpkin 1981:29; Bellesiles 2006:1036-1040; B. Munnerlyn Pension W8479; Collins Pension S18771.
16 Edgar 1998:233; Lumpkin 1981:47; Rankin 1973:45.
17 Bellune A.A. 430; Greaves A.A. 3057; Tyler A.A. 7983; Buckholts Pension R1465; Booth Pension W25258; Greaves S.I. Y763, A.A. 3056; L. Munnerlyn A.A. 5399; J. Ervin A.A. 2237; G. Witherspoon, A.A. 8690; Dunnam and Burn A.A. 2099.
18 Borick 2006:192-194; Edgar 1998:233; Francis Davis Pension S890; McCall Pension R6598.
19 Booth Pension W25258; L. Munnerlyn A.A. 5399; Greaves A.A. 3056; Perkins Pension R8114; Collins also claims he was at the skirmish at Blue Savannah, which occurred only four months later (Collins S18771).
20 H. Giles A.A. 2817; B. Port A.A. 6030.
21 General Horatio Gates to Colonel Hugh Giles, 29 July, 1780, Gates Papers.
22 Gray 1910:140. Colonel Robert Gray was a Provincial officer in the South Carolina Rangers from Cheraw District. He wrote his "observations" on the war around the spring of 1782 and is full of insights into the people around the Cheraws – Pee Dee region.
23 Proclamation quoted in Edgar 1998:233; Gray 1910:141.

CHAPTER 6

MARION AND THE PARTISANS: 17 AUGUST 1780 TO 13 APRIL 1781

This chapter relates the history of Francis Marion's use of, interaction with, and management of the Snow's Island partisan community. It details the period between 17 August 1780, when Marion took command of the Williamsburg militia, and 13 April 1781, shortly after the British had destroyed the Snow's Island camp. During this time, Francis Marion was usually on his own, acting in the strategic defense. I have divided this discussion into three periods: 1) 17 August to 3 December; 2) 4 December to January 31; and 3) 1 February to 13 April.

During the first period, Francis Marion and his partisans were without regular army support and largely alone in the Lowcountry as true partisans (Figures 6.1 and 6.2). It ends with the arrival of General Greene and the third Continental Army of the South.[1]

During the second period, Marion made his most intensive use of Snow's Island as a winter camp and was physically present on (or near) the island. Lieutenant Colonel Lee was detached to join Marion at the end of this period and together they attempted to capture British-held Georgetown, South Carolina. It ends when General Greene recalled Lee to rejoin him in North Carolina.

During the third period, the American Continental Army began a long retreat through North Carolina, chased by the British, in what historians have called the "Race to the Dan [River]." Marion was again without support in South Carolina and was in a period of extreme danger, as the remaining British forces in South Carolina were able to consolidate, attack Snow's Island, and destroy Marion's camp and depot. It ends with Greene's return to South Carolina.

17 AUGUST 1780 TO 3 DECEMBER 1780

On Thursday, 17 August 1780, Francis Marion was reacquainted with the Snow's Island community when he, Peter Horry, and around 10 others arrived at Witherspoon's Ferry, South Carolina, to take command of the Williamsburg militia (Figures 3.4, 3.5, 3.6).[2]

After the fall of Charleston on 12 May 1780, Marion made his way north to Hillsborough, North Carolina, and joined the Continental Army, which was temporarily under the command of Major General Johann de Kalb. From there, De Kalb sent Marion and a small band of South Carolina refugees to guard Cole's Bridge along the Pee Dee in North Carolina.[3] Shortly afterward, Major General Gates took command of the army and Marion joined Gates on his march into South Carolina. In one of the most revealing descriptions of what would be Marion's partisans for the next several months, Colonel Otho Holland Williams noted that:

> Colonel Marion, a gentleman of South Carolina, had been with the army a few days, attended by a very few followers; distinguished by small black leather caps and the wretchedness of their attire; their number did not exceed twenty men and boys, some white, some black, and all mounted, but most of them miserably equipped.[4]

Marion remained with the Continental Army until they arrived at Rugeley's Mill, north of British-occupied Camden, South Carolina. Then, the day before Gates decided to move closer to Camden, Marion was ordered south to take charge of the Williamsburg militia and destroy all river transportation along the Santee River, thereby blocking the British in Camden from retreating to Charleston.[5]

Early the following morning, while the Americans were marching toward Camden, they unexpectedly met Lord Charles Cornwallis and the British Army marching north to surprise them. Dawn on 16 August revealed two large armies facing-off in an open forest to begin the Battle of Camden. Marion and his men heard the cannon fire from the battle as they marched south to Witherspoon's Ferry.[6]

At Witherspoon's Ferry on Lynches Creek, four miles upstream from the northwest corner of Snow's Island, Major John James and around 200 men waited. The ferry had been a rendezvous earlier in the war and would become a well-used crossing point for Marion throughout the rest of the war. It is possible that Colonel Hugh Giles, with the Britton's Neck militia, was there as well. It is more likely that Giles did not join Marion until a few days later.

Marion quickly split his new command and ordered three companies under Peter Horry south to the lower Santee River. There, Horry was to destroy all the ferry and plantation boats from the mouth of the Santee upstream to Lenud's Ferry and collect lead shot for Marion's partisans (Figure 6.1). Marion, probably still organizing the militia, waited a few days before proceeding to the Santee on the same mission. Marion passed through Kingstree (Figure 6.1) with 70 men[7] on the 22nd and probably collected Horry's ammunition, proceeded to Murray's Ferry on the Santee River (Figure 6.2), and chased away the British guard on the 23rd. Then he moved upstream to Nelson's Ferry (Figure 6.2), near modern day Eutawville, South Carolina.

At Nelson's on the 24th, Marion heard that a British detachment was escorting 150 American prisoners who had been captured at the Battle of Camden to Charleston. He attacked the escort the next day at Great Savannah (Figure 6.2), recaptured the prisoners, and was quickly on the road back to Witherspoon's Ferry, arriving by the 26th. In the skirmish, Benjamin Munnerlyn received his second wound, this time in the shoulder.[8]

With the loss of a second Continental Army under Gates (the first being lost in the surrender of Charleston), Marion was now a partisan alone in the Lowcountry of South Carolina. Loyalist Robert Gray recorded that a "Universal panic seized the rebels after the battle of Camden."[9] It certainly affected Marion's partisans, for half of his 70 men left him within two hours of his victory at Great Savannah and most of the rescued Continentals deserted. Marion immediately went into a defensive mode, consolidating forces and turning to the Snow's Island community for support.[10]

Writing from Witherspoon's, Marion informed Horry of Gates's defeat and ordered him to immediately gather up what men and supplies he could and join him on Britton's Neck, where he was going to "encamp." Traveling with the troops were probably two cattle from Gavin Witherspoon whom Giles receipted on the 24th. On the 29th Marion took "post" on the north side of Port's Ferry to wait for Horry.[11]

On 3 September, Marion learned some 200 Loyalist militiamen, under the command of Major Micajah Ganey, were marching toward him from the Loyalist community along the Little Pee Dee northeast of Britton's Neck. Marion hesitated, but the five Munnerlyn brothers convinced him to attack in hopes of rescuing their father, who had been robbed and was being held prisoner by the Loyalists.

Marion marched that night with his entire command of 53 men and attacked the Loyalist camp, dispersing them. The Munnerlyns' father was

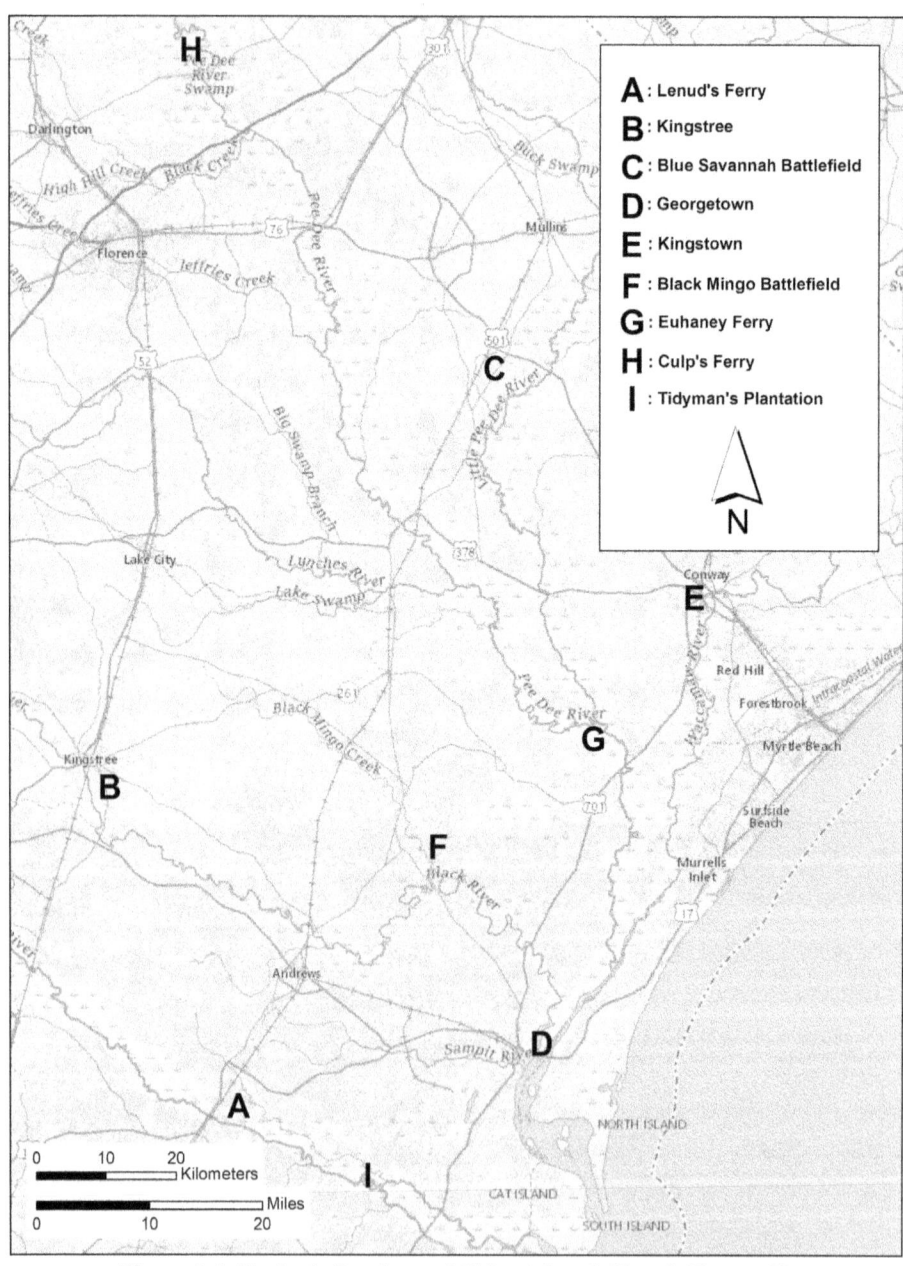

Figure 6.1. Marion's Battles and Skirmishes 1 (Brock Shattuck)

rescued in the skirmish. Learning that this was just a detachment, he moved three miles farther to the main body where he set up an ambush and "put them to flight (though they had 200 men) when they got into a swamp, impassable to all but Tories." These actions became known as the Blue Savannah skirmish (Figure 6.1).[12]

Returning to Port's Ferry, Marion began the construction of a redoubt on the Britton's Neck side at Welsh (now Dog) Lake 5 September 1780 (Figure 3.7). It was here that Colonel Giles and the Britton's Neck militia joined Marion. Perhaps Marion came to Giles and convinced him to consolidate forces. George McCall wrote that "Marion came to us…we then crossed the River at Ports Ferry and commenced to build a redoubt." Giles had been in camp at Giles Bluff (Figure 3.7).[13]

At Welsh Lake, Giles provided his own militia and Marion with sixty bushels of corn, 22 ¾ (pounds?) of iron, and other items.[14] Marion sent Major James across the Pee Dee River and Lynches Creek to Williamsburg to gather intelligence.

While they were encamped at the redoubt, more men drifted in to join Marion. John Booth was one. Thomas Grice may have been another, but he had joined Marion by September.[15]

Two days later, 7 September 1780, Marion followed James with 100 men, leaving 50 at the Port's Ferry redoubt. He had learned that a combined force of British regulars and Loyalist militia were in Williamsburg Township burning the homes of his partisans. At Indiantown, Marion joined James, who had learned from a prisoner that the enemy numbered 200 and that 200 more were on their way and that their objective was to not only burn Whig houses but also find and destroy Marion's command. Furthermore, the British had occupied Georgetown (Figure 6.1). Marion turned around immediately and returned to the Port's Ferry redoubt.

The next day, the intelligence was worse. A detachment of British and Loyalists, under Major James Wemyss, had crossed or was about to cross Lynches Creek at Witherspoon's Ferry, putting them only a few miles west of Marion. A detachment of British from Georgetown had crossed Black River (to Marion's south) and were heading toward him. And, the Loyalists along the Little Pee Dee were reconsolidating. Marion and the Snow's Island community were being threatened from three sides. Marion may not have known, but a force was also marching toward him from Camden, South Carolina.[16]

Partisans usually disperse when threatened by stronger forces and Marion followed that pattern. Marion and about 60 warriors made for North

Carolina; the rest, including many who had lost their homes, melted into the forests and swamps to find their families. On the way, Marion passed Thomas Pott's home and he and his father joined Marion. William Potts, thirteen, was left at home.[17]

Marion's remnants camped at White Marsh, North Carolina (another swamp). Based on various sources, Marion's only probable escape route would have been down Britton's Neck, crossing the Little Pee Dee at either Potato Bed Ferry or Woodbury's landing (downstream), up through Kingston (now Conway, Figure 6.1), stopping at Ami's Mill along Drowning Creek (Lumber River), and then turning north to White Marsh, thereby circumventing the Loyalists on the Little Pee Dee. He would use that route to return at the end of September.

While Marion's partisans were on the march, British Major Wemyss was unintentionally doing his best to ensure that the population around Snow's Island, if reluctant in the past to support Marion, would from this point on remain staunch Whigs. "Under the guidance of [Major John] Harrison's Tories, Wemyss and his Myrmidons burned a swath fifteen miles wide along the seventy-mile route from Kingstree to Cheraw."[18] Wemyss wrote Lord Cornwallis that the region was aflame in rebellion. "Every Inhabitant has been or is concerned in the Rebellion & most of them very deeply. Wherever I have gone the Houses were deserted by the Men, even their Negroes & Effects were in general carried away." He adds as a post script that "I forgot to tell your Lordship, that I have burnt & laid waste about 50 Houses & Plantations, mostly belonging to People who have either broke their Paroles or Oath of Allegiance, & are now in Arms against us." Wemyss' route would have taken him from Indiantown (where he burnt the Presbyterian Church), north across Lynches, up the river road along the west side of the Pee Dee to Long Bluff and then to Cheraw. Many Snow's Island community members lost their homes. Those known are John James, John Frierson, and Nathan Savage, but many more would have been burnt within this 15-mile-wide swath.[19]

When Marion stopped at Ami's Mill, he sent Major James back to the Snow's Island region to gather intelligence. James returned with the news of Wemyss' raid and that the partisan community was enraged.

Early historian David Ramsay noted that Wemyss' destruction of the Snow's Island region "had a contrary effect from what was expected. Revenge and despair co-operated with patriotism to make these ruined men keep the field. The devouring flames sent on defenseless habitations by blind rage and brutal policy, increased not only the zeal, but the number of his [Marion's] followers." Wemyss turned out to be Marion's best recruiter.[20]

On Sunday evening, 24 September, Marion mounted up his partisans and returned to South Carolina. Traveling first to Kingston (now Conway) (Figure 6.1) he crossed the Little Pee Dee at "Woodbury's" [probably Richard Woodberry's Potato Bed Ferry] onto Britton's Neck.[21] Exactly what he did there between the 25th and 28th is unknown. Reading his letter report in conjunction with James's account, he crossed the Pee Dee and met James's father with more men "near Lynches Creek." Given these points of reference, it is probable that Marion, after a journey of 60 miles to Kingston, and another 10 to 12 to Woodberry's, rested his horses either at Woodberry's, or at the Port's Ferry redoubt. He then crossed the Pee Dee at Port's Ferry and Lynches at Witherspoon's Ferry. There he learned a British and Loyalist force was camped at Dollard's Tavern on the south bank of Sheppard's Ferry on Black Mingo Creek, "fifteen miles below" (Figure 6.1).[22]

That night, Marion's force galloped to Black Mingo Creek crossed on a bridge about a mile above (upstream) of Sheppard's Ferry. The noise of the horse's hooves on the wooden bridge alerted the British who formed a line in a clearing opposite the tavern. Marion and his men came on at a gallop, but when they approached Dollard's Tavern, Marion divided his force into three detachments: one detachment consisting of mounted officers attacked directly ahead, another consisting of two companies of dismounted men attacked on the right, and a third detachment of cavalry attacked on the left. At thirty yards, Marion's men fired. The Loyalists took the fire, returned two fires and then seeing themselves being flanked, dispersed into the Black Mingo swamp.[23]

Casualties were probably few. No two sources agree. Marion stated he lost Captain Logan and one other man. A lieutenant and six privates were wounded. The Loyalists lost at least three on the field. Some were wounded and Marion took 13 prisoners. Marion was told that there were several more dead found in the woods. Importantly, Marion captured the Loyalists' baggage and horses. The *South Carolina American General Gazette* reported two Loyalists killed, seven wounded, and ten prisoners, with Marion suffering two killed, eight wounded.[24]

The British were at first appalled by the attack and temporarily abandoned Georgetown. But later they concluded that the militia "behaved with a good deal of spirit."[25] James wrote that the casualties were as much as a third of both commands, killed and wounded. William Boddie claimed massive numbers of men and casualties in the skirmish and literally miles of trench work constructed prior to the battle by the Loyalists, but this simply cannot be. Marion left the battlefield quickly and, as usual after victories as much as defeats, many of his men dispersed home while Marion retreated across the Pee Dee at Britton's Ferry and on to Ami's Mill on the Lumber River.[26]

In the attack, John Booth received a minor wound in the stomach, the bullet having been deflected by his cartridge box. William Shaw was wounded when a musket ball creased the top of his head.[27] Snow's Island partisans also included George McCall, Redden McCoy, and Benjamin Munnerlyn.

The next day Marion returned to North Carolina and camped, probably at Ami's Mill. This trip required crossing the Pee Dee at Britton's Ferry onto Britton's Neck and then the Little Pee Dee at Woodberry's. Marion had wanted to attack another detachment on the Black River, but so many men, including those of the Snow's Island community, wanted to return home and learn the fate of their homes, that he was forced back to North Carolina. James notes that when Marion dismissed those who wanted to go home, "he appointed them to meet him at Snow's Island." By this time, Marion would have been very familiar with Britton's Neck and the Snow's Island region.[28]

Marion felt compelled to admit to Gates that American partisans had responded to Wemyss' actions with their own atrocities.

> I am Sorry to Acquaint you that Captn. Murphy's Party have burnt a Great number of houses on Little Peedee, & intend to go on in that Abominable work, which I am Apprehensive may be Laid to me; but, I assure you, there is not one house Burnt by my Orders, or by any of my People. It is what I detest to Distress poor Women & Children."[29]

Captain Maurice Murphy was another militia officer who was not attached to Marion at that time. Marion had no authority over him since there was no American government in South Carolina. But only a few days later, Marion laments that one of his own, a Snow's Island community member and partisan officer, had joined in the practice.

> I am Sorry to inform You that Colo. [Hugh] Ervin has adopted the Burning of houses & Captn. Murphy still pursues it. I think it will be the Greatest hurt to our Interest. The former was with me a Little While, but has separated as I would not permit him to Burn any houses.[30]

From the British perspective, the Pee Dee and Snow's Island community was becoming a focal point of rebellion. North of the Snow's Island region, Loyalist officer Lieutenant Colonel Robert Gray of the Cheraw militia wrote of the problems along the Pee Dee:

> The second rebellion had been so general in this district, that at least three fourths of the inhabitants upon this river [Pee Dee] had taken active parts in it, and in this number must be included almost every person of influence & popularity here...
>
> The only well affected part of the district, exclusive of the inhabitants on Black and Lynch's creek, lies on little PeeDee [illegible] the frontier toward North Carolina.[31]

Gray goes on in this letter to express his opinion on how to suppress the rebels in the region. He believed that 100 mounted regulars and 300 militia men were necessary at Cheraw along with Major Harrison's Corps. With a strong post at Cheraw, there would be enough men to scout the region and, most critically for the Snow's Island community, "secure the different ferries on Pee Dee [Port's and Britton's] betwixt this and the George Town District." Gray goes even further in his letter to describe the strategic importance of Port's and Witherspoon's Ferry and the Snow's Island region.

> Port's Ferry is near the confluence of Lynch's Creek with Peedee and a detachment of twenty men from the post established there would be sufficient to keep possession of Witherspoon's ferry over that Creek, it not being above four miles distant and is a pass of the last importance as it entirely commands the communication to the south side of this river betwixt the two regiments, that creek not being passable for Twenty four miles above that place.[32]

Gray's analysis of the landscape and political situation within the Snow's Island region was spot on. Had Cornwallis acted upon his advice, Francis Marion's use of the Snow's Island region as a base camp and depot and the people as a support population would have been thwarted. Luckily—for Marion, the Snow's Island community and the American cause—Gray was ignored. Historians have commented that the regular officers in the British military looked down on the Loyalist militia. Perhaps here is an example of that arrogance.[33]

On 8 October, Marion was on the move again, this time in a daring, or perhaps foolhardy, attack on Georgetown.[34] From a "Mr. Gime's," sixty-five miles from Georgetown, he journeyed all night to the port city and attacked at noon the next day. The British wisely held up in a redoubt and refused battle. Marion, without artillery, could only parade through town and then retreat over the Black River to somewhere on the Little Pee Dee where he was camped by 15 October. The route would have probably taken him across the Pee Dee and onto Britton's Neck. In what would become a familiar complaint against his fellow partisans, Marion lamented their fickle nature.

> I have never yet had more than Seventy men to Act with me, & some times they Leave me to twenty or thirty &, it is with Great Difficulty I can again recruit. I wish I had some Authority to punish those who Leave me, for many who had fought with me I am Oblige to fight against.[35]

Sometime after the 15th, Marion was back in the Snow's Island region. Perhaps he was there because, as James had stated, it was where he had said he would meet the partisans who had left to check the fate of their families. Biographer Robert Bass has him stationed at Port's Ferry but provides no primary reference.

Still, it is possible, since a local resident, Abram Giles, provided 19 bushels of corn, 182 wt fodder, 72 lbs of beef, and 32 lbs of bread or wheat to John Nelson's militia on 19 October. The traditional story is that over the next week, while waiting for the militia to return to him (read Snow's Island partisan community), Marion discussed the merits of retreating north to join the Continentals in North Carolina. Hugh Horry talked him out of it and eventually as many as 150 partisans returned. From the British perspective, the Pee Dee was "totally in the enemy's possession; and indeed, they make inroads into the very banks of the Santee." To keep them in check, the British commandant in Charleston, Colonel Nisbet Balfour, believed that a post should be established at Cheraw or Kingstree.[36]

On 24 October, Marion gained intelligence of a British detachment at the forks of the Black River. Crossing the Pee Dee and Lynches Creek (no doubt at Port's and Witherspoon's Ferries) he marched west through Williamsburg Township and the next night attacked the camp at Tearcoat Swamp (Figure 6.2). This success provided Marion and his partisans with as many as 80 horses, saddles, and arms.[37] He also sent a detachment to chase and capture the British commander, Lieutenant Colonel Samuel Tynes. He was back on Lynches Creek by Saturday, 4 November 1780, no doubt camping at Witherspoon's Ferry. By that time, Colonel Giles had returned from illness, and 200 men also returned, no doubt including many Snow's Island partisans.[38]

Marion became optimistic that his forces might soon double. If so, he planned to tackle Georgetown again. The British apparently and unknowingly agreed with this assessment. On 1 November, the British commander in Charleston estimated that the various rebel parties "betwixt the Pedee, and Santee…exceed[ed] thousand." On the 17th, Lord Rawdon (British commander in Camden) wrote Cornwallis that Marion's men were "accurately counted, & amounted to 400." That same day, Colonel Balfour wrote Cornwallis that Marion's complement at Georgetown amounted to 500.[39]

Whatever the actual size of Marion's reinforcement, he went on the offense the next day. His objective was to return to the Santee River ferries and attempt to intercept British traffic from Charleston to Camden and Winnsboro, South Carolina. Once along the Santee, he learned that the infamous British Legion Commander Lt. Colonel Tarleton and his cavalry were at Richardson's Plantation, 16 miles north of Nelson's Ferry (Figure 6.2). Tarleton had made a sweep from Camden south to Richardson's, burning Whig houses and destroying the seasonal corn crop.

Marion marched at night to attack Tarleton, but upon a reconnaissance of the plantation, he found that Tarleton had nearly 400 men and two artillery pieces. Marion could not face these odds and withdrew toward Benbow's Ferry (Figure 6.2) located along the Black River ten miles north of Kingstree, South Carolina.[40] Tarleton's intelligence was equally alert, and he came after Marion. On 8 November, Tarleton chased Marion through the swamps and bogs near modern day Manning, South Carolina.

Marion arrived at the Benbow's Ferry, crossed and waited for Tarleton. His position would have been a strong one had he faced Tarleton, but after a seven-hour chase, the British commander turned back to burn more Whig houses and destroy the corn crop along the Santee, and then marched north to Camden, burning more houses in the high hills of the Santee.[41]

Tarleton's unsuccessful chase of Marion produced mixed reactions among the British command structure. Tarleton believed that "Nothing will serve these People but Fire & Sword." Cornwallis was not impressed. Writing Tarleton the very day he was chasing Marion through the swamps, Cornwallis said, "I am not sanguine as to your Operations in that County. The Enemy, I believe, is in no great Force, & Marrion is cautious and vigilant." Balfour, however, was unimpressed with Tarleton's efforts for opposite reasons. He thought Marion's exploits were concerning, writing Cornwallis that "Marions movement I beg Tarleton may be remembered of—it is no Joke to us." [42]

Obsessed with Georgetown, Marion turned again to attack the town, having heard that it was lightly garrisoned. But his intelligence failed him this time. Georgetown had been reinforced by an additional 200 Loyalists. The British came out and "Scrimaged" with Marion and he drove them back

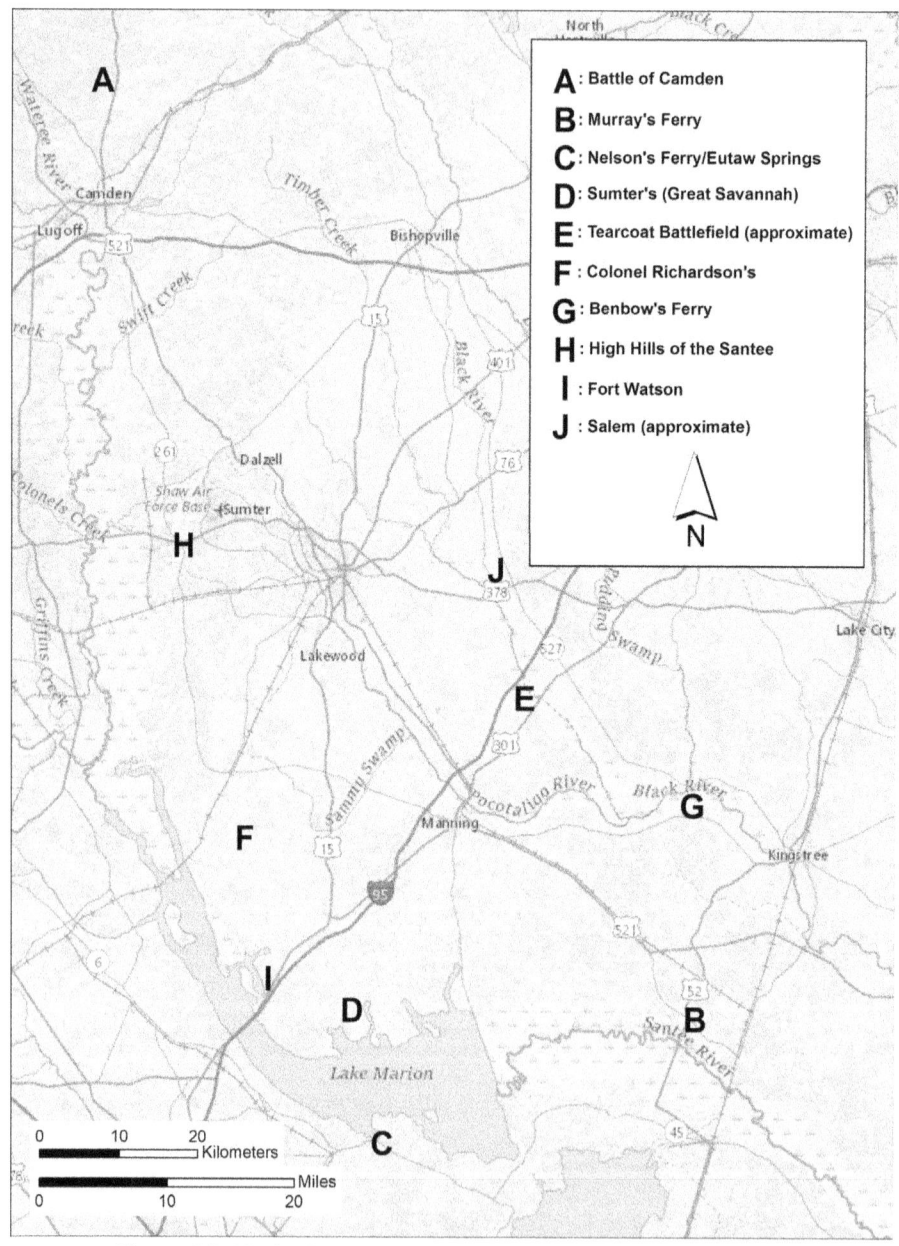

Figure 6.2. Marion's Battles and Skirmishes 2 (Brock Shattuck)

into the town. Once again, the British hid in their redoubt and waited him out. And, once again, Marion, short on ammunition and having no artillery, was forced to retreat to Black Mingo on the 17th and then to Britton's Ferry on the 21st.[43]

Although Tarleton failed to disperse Marion, his presence in the Lowcountry may have influenced the region's fickle Whigs. They had not turned out in the numbers that Marion wanted and he was still short of men. In any case, Lord Cornwallis decided that the time was right to take the war to Marion and debated whether a British presence at Kingstree would pressure Marion's partisans further. Although Cornwallis ultimately decided that it would be too dangerous, Colonel Balfour in Charleston ordered Major Robert McLeroth to take post at Kingstree and then, since they were so close, to take command of Parks [no doubt Port's] and Britton's ferries, which would effectively control two strategic points within the Snow's Island community.[44]

Balfour's letter reporting his decision to Cornwallis reveals that, from the British perspective, the Snow's Island community was full of families sympathetic to the British cause, only waiting the opportunity of "quitting Marion":

> By letters from C. Cassells [Lt. Col. James Cassels] I am pressed in the strongest manner, to give only an opening for his people, and our friends, upon the Little Pedee [,] thos on the banks of great Pedee, on the frontiers of N Carolina as well as those on Lynches Creek to come in to him, all which can be effected, by taking possession of Parks [no doubt Port's] and Brittons ferry, upon Lynches Creek & the lower part of the Pedee which forks [i.e., Britton's Neck] he means to defend with his Militia, if once given to him. He assures me, of many offers, made him from that Country, of their desire, of quitting Marion (whom they all looke upon only as a plunderer) and joining us.[45]

Later in that same letter, Balfour informed Cornwallis that Marion's retreat had given them an opportunity toward "turning the scale."

Whether or not there actually was a large measure of Loyalism in the Snow's Island community is unknown but morale in the community was at a low point. On 21 and 22 November, Marion wrote two letters to General Gates from "PeeDee" and "PeeDee Britton Ferry."[46] Having returned to his friends within the Snow's Island community, Marion wrote of his frustration with his warriors and their commitment to the Whig cause—no doubt including some living within the Snow's Island community. Enclosing in his letter of the 22nd a list of men under his command (not found), he wrote "it is not often I have so many thou I have had more, the People here is not to be depended on for I seldom have the same set a fortnight, & untill the Grand Army is on the Banks of the Santee, it will be the same." Marion clearly stated the reason for the lack of support:

> Many of the people has Left me & gone over to the Enemy, for they think that we have no Army coming on, & have been Deceived. As we hear nothing from you a Great while, I hope to have a line from you in what manner to Act, & some Assurance to the people of Support.[47]

While Marion raged against the poor turnout among the community, a few core Snow's Island community members were consolidating a camp on or near Snow's Island, of which Colonel Hugh Giles was probably in charge. Giles had already provided his militia company and Marion with supplies at the Port's Ferry redoubt. Now he began to gather supplies for the camp at Snow's Island. On the 24th he receipted Benjamin Port for "bullets" to be sent to "the Public Camp Johnstons Island" by Thomas Potts. This is the first historic record indicating a camp on Snow's Island.[48]

Joseph Jenkins also provided a four-year-old "steer." In fact, although Bass and others have traditionally stated that the Jenkins brothers were the ones who showed Marion the benefits of camping on Snow's Island, it was quite possibly Giles who led Marion to the highland swamp base camp. A surveyor before the war, Giles knew the island as well as the Jenkins brothers, and perhaps better.

Before Marion arrived on the Snow's Island scene, Giles had arranged for corn to be ground for Gates's army and had been gathering cattle for Gates "in the fork of Pee Dee & Lynches Creek" where he had "collected his regiment." Giles was still gathering cattle as late as 16 August, the day before Marion arrived at Witherspoon's Ferry. On that day, Giles "impressed" a steer from Nathan Savage. Giles was probably referring to his camp at Giles Bluff, but also could have been referring to the Snow's Island camp where he asked Benjamin Port to deliver the lead shot. If so, there had been a camp on the island since August 1780.[49]

Meanwhile, on the 29th, the Charleston newspaper published a list of people whose estates had been seized by the British, including Francis Marion, and Peter and Hugh Horry.[50]

4 DECEMBER 1780 TO 31 JANUARY 1781

As it turned out, Colonel McLeroth did *not* invade the Snow's Island community, but instead retreated to the Santee River. By this time, Marion's reputation had grown and it was the consensus of the British commanders—Cornwallis in Winnsboro, Lord Rawdon in Camden, and Balfour in Charleston—that it was better to leave Marion on the Pee Dee than risk another regiment against him.[51] Besides, they had a more pressing issue to deal with at the beginning of December.

The second day of December 1780 may be considered a turning point in the Revolutionary War in the South. It was on this day that Major General Greene arrived in Charlotte, North Carolina to take command of the Continental Army of the South. Greene found the remnants of Gates's command in a deplorable condition—nearly naked, starving, and with little logistical infrastructure. In a series of letters to famous personages such as Governor Abner Nash of North Carolina, Thomas Jefferson, George Washington, and Henry Knox, Greene lamented "the Shadow of an Army in the midst of Distress."[52] Yet the busy commander took time to introduce himself to Marion, probably with the intent to gain control of the Whigs in South Carolina. In his introductory letter he encouraged Marion in keeping up a partisan warfare:

> I have not the Honor of your Acquaintance but am no Stranger to your Character and merit. Your Services in the lower Part of South Carolina in aiding the Forces and preventing the Enemy from extending their Limits have been very important and it is my earnest Desire that you continue where you are untill further Advice from me....
>
> I like your Plan of frequently shifting your Ground. It frequently prevents a Surprize and perhaps a total Loss of your Party. Untill a more permanent Army can be collected than is in the Field at present we must endeavor to keep up a Partizan War and preserve the Tide of Sentiment among the People as much as possible in our Favour.[53]

While praising Marion and recognizing the importance of partisan warfare, Greene was a realist and recognized the nature and weaknesses of partisan warfare, militias, and partisan communities. In a letter to Samuel Huntington, President of the Continental Congress, Greene painted an unflattering picture of the partisan community, and, no doubt, he was including those in the Snow's Island region. He described Sumter and Marion's militia as of two types:

...composed of men whose cases are desperate being driven from their dwellings, and others allured by the hopes of plunder. The first are the best of Citizens and the best of Soldiers, the last are the dregs of the community and can be kept no longer than there is a prospect of gain. With this force upon such a loose constitution and in such a wretched state we shall have it in our power to carry on nothing but a kind of fugitive war.[54]

General Nathanael Greene

It was around late November-early December that Marion began to view the partisan camp on Snow's Island as his base of operations, although I believe it is clear that Colonel Giles was consolidating a camp there by at least mid-November, if not sooner. On 6 December, Marion wrote Gates (not knowing that Greene had replaced him four days prior) from "Linches Creek Near PD." This was exactly two weeks after he had written from Britton's Ferry, clearly demonstrating that he had been within the Snow's Island community region during that whole time, during which he was most likely consolidating his forces and the community. He was likely doing so from Snow's Island or even Dunham's Bluff.[55]

It was not in Marion's character, however, to be anywhere too long and he was soon on the move again, maneuvering west of Snow's Island along the Santee and northward to the High Hills of the Santee.

On 13 December, Marion caught up with Major McLeroth near the High Hills and again "skirmaged" with his forces. Sometime after this action, Marion moved to the Santee, prevented British reinforcements from crossing the river at Nelson's Ferry, and burnt a riverboat. After these actions, he retreated to Black River (probably to Benbow's Ferry), leaving small parties to harass the British along the Santee and in the High Hills. During these actions, the British were convinced that he had as many as 600 men under his command. In fact, Marion complained that if he only had 100 Continentals, "I should be able to do much more ... the militia ... act with Diffidence."[56]

Marion remained on the Black River for another two days, and then returned to the Santee to gather intelligence on British movements. Finding a strengthened force at Nelson's Ferry, and hearing that British reinforcements were on their way to Georgetown, he retreated to Indiantown, in Williamsburg District, closer to his base on Snow's Island. He wrote to Greene: "Emagining the Enemy had an Intention to cut my retreat off from Peedee, is the reason I have retreated from Santee."[57] Marion heard that the British were planning to establish a post at nearby Kingstree, however, he dismissed this intelligence because of a lack of food resources in the region.

Marion's 27 December letter to Greene is critical to understanding his mind regarding the Snow's Island community region. First, at this time, Marion clearly saw the Snow's Island region as his central base of operation. A quick glance at the map indicates that if the British in Georgetown moved north, it would "cut off" his "retreat" to the safety of the Pee Dee, or Snow's Island community. Second, the region just west of Snow's Island, around Indiantown and Kingstree, was comparatively lacking in food and forage in comparison to other areas. So it was that the region was both a base of operation and an area of resource exploitation or central place.

The next day Marion was back in the Snow's Island region and probably on Snow's Island itself. In a letter written from the "Mouth of Linches Creek, Peedee," Marion repeats his fear of the British reinforcement of Georgetown and its threat to his camp there.

> The Enemy reported they Intended an Attack on a Small post I had here which is the reason of my retreat to this place. Shoud they Attempt it I hope my Situation will give me an Advantage. I shall remain here a few days to rest my horses, when I will again, Advance to Black River.[58]

Strategically, the British were concentrated in Camden, Nelson's Ferry, and Georgetown. Marion's northern flank was covered by Greene, who had taken up winter camp along the east bank of the Pee Dee River north of Cheraw, South Carolina. From the Snow's Island community, Marion sent out patrols to Georgetown and to the Santee to gather intelligence and harass the British.

At the end of December, activities around Snow's Island increased. From 19 December to 6 January 1781, William Snow provided Marion 12 steers and two calves for "Camp Snow's Island." On the 29th, the Snow's Island camp received 173 bushels of corn. On 1 January 1781, James Snow provided Marion's warriors with eight cattle at "Camp Snow's Island" (Figure 6.3).[59]

For the next three weeks, during a wet but mild winter, Francis Marion would be on (or near) the island organizing his brigade.[60] From there, patrols and spies sallied forth to gather intelligence about the movements of the British in Georgetown and westward toward the Santee. Around Snow's Island, men were camped in detachments, which allowed them to both forage locally and guard entry points into the community and camp.[61]

According to biographer Robert Bass, one detachment was across the river at Dunham's Bluff. Bass believes that Marion ordered Colonel John Ervin to "throw up a small redoubt on the lower side" of the bluff." Bass's source for this is Reverend James Jenkins's 1842 reminiscence, which stated that the redoubt was "thrown up on the east side of Great Pee Dee, by order of Colonel Irvin" and Bass assumed that the order came from John Ervin.[62] The redoubt was manned by a detachment of Captain John Dozier's Britton's Neck militia.[63]

The other source is the audited account of Loftis Munnerlyn. Munnerlyn records that Marion sent 30 men to his father's house and removed his father and mother "in the vicinity of the redoubt which is situated on the right bank of Pee Dee river opposite Snow's Island." Furthermore, Munnerlyn remained in service at Marion's camp "being the only place of safety."[64]

Thomas Grice found out the hard way that the best place to be that winter was at one of Marion's camps. On a furlough home from Snow's Island, he was captured by Loyalists who kept him prisoner until he told them how many men Marion had.[65]

Meanwhile, Marion worked to fortify the community against possible attack and to consolidate his authority over those living in the area by gathering supplies from the surrounding countryside and bringing them to Snow's Island. Writing his adjutant, John Postell, Marion made it clear that the region south of Snow's Island was to be scoured and sealed against an attack from Georgetown.

> You will proceed with a party down Black River, from Black Mingo to the Mouth of Pedee, and come up to this place [Snow's Island]; you will take all boats and them to camp; put some men to see them safe; you will take every horse, to whomsoever he may belong, whether friend or foe. You will take all arms and ammunition for the use of our service. You will forbid all persons from carrying any grains, stock or any sort of provisions to Georgetown, or where the enemy may get them, on pain of being held as traitors and enemies to the Americans. All persons who will not join you will take prisoners and bring to me. You will return as soon as possible... N.B. You will bring up as much rice and salt in the boats as possible.[66]

Postwar reminiscences soften Marion's apparently harsh orders concerning the treatment of the community. For instance, eyewitness Colonel Horry (through Weems) paints a picture of community cohesion and support.

> For this purpose he always kept a snug hiding-place in reserve for us; which was Snow's Island, a most romantic spot, and admirably fitted to our use. Nature had guarded it, nearly all around, with deep waters and inaccessible marshes; and the neighboring gentlemen were all rich, and hearty whigs, who acted by us the double part of generous stewards and faithful spies, so that, while there, we lived at once in safety and plenty.[67]

William Dobein James, a youth fighting in Marion's brigade, may or may not have been present at the camp, but elaborated considerably on Marion's efforts to secure Snow's Island.[68]

> At and near Snow's Island, Gen. Marion secured what boats he wanted; and burnt those more remote. To prevent the approach of an enemy, he fell upon a plan of insulating as much as possible the country

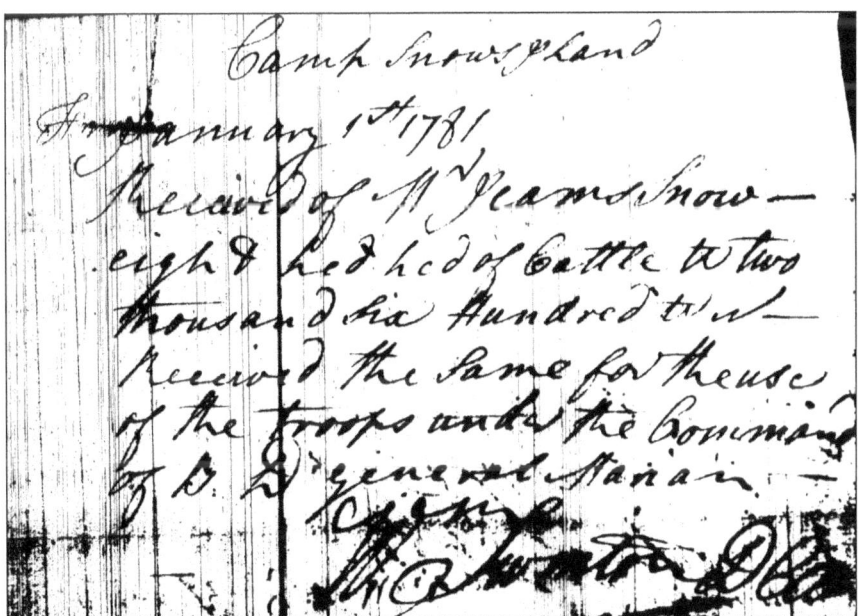

Figure 6.3. William Snow's receipt for cattle requisitioned for the men at Marion's Snow's Island camp (A.A. 7197, SCDAH)

under his command. For this purpose he broke down bridges, and felled trees across causeways and difficult passes. As there was no market in that day, and the vicinity of a road was dangerous, the inhabitants aided him much in this design … .

Colonel P. Horry and Maj. John Postell…were posted, the first on Waccamaw creek, the second on the neck between Black and Pedee rivers, with orders [repeating the orders to Postell above]. Thus martial law was fully established, and, for self defense, never was it more necessary.[69]

James painted a picture of a rough, lean time, the men surviving on beef and sweet potatoes.

During this period men were but badly clothed in homespun, which afforded little warmth. They slept in the open air, according to their means, either with or without a blanket. They had nothing but water to drink. They fed chiefly upon sweet potatoes, either with or without fresh beef. …but all sighed for salt! for salt! that first article of necessity for the human race….As soon as Gen. Marion could collect a sufficient quantity of this desirable article at Snow's Island, he distributed it out in quantities, not exceeding a bushel to each whig family; and thus endeared himself the more to his followers.[70]

James may have exaggerated the lack of provisions; on the day he was promoted to Brigadier General of the militia, Marion wrote to Greene that he was "oblige[d] to keep so many of my men in Detachments to prevent stock being drove off, that I have been Oblige[d] to call on Col. Kolb for part of his regiment which I expect dayley." This may be interpreted in different ways. Perhaps he dispersed his men as a better means to find food. Or he was gathering so much beef that it was necessary to disperse them to find enough forage. Marion wrote that his chronic ammunition shortage "prevents me from moving from this Place & Expose me to danger shoud the Enemy advance." Regarding the salt issue: "I have heard of 150 bushels salt on Waccoma…I have sent a party to Bring It off & hope it will arrive today." Whether poorly fed or well fed, Marion was definitely concerned about other logistical needs: "My people are remarkable healthy notwithstanding they are without tents or any Rum. They have had neither this five Months, past." His few Continentals needed clothing: "I coud wish a dozen suits of Cloaths & as many Blankets coud be procured."[71]

Writing from Lynches Creek (probably at Snow's Island) the following week, Marion repeats that he is scouring the countryside and rivers around Georgetown to deny the British subsistence and to gather supplies for both his and Greene's army, a typical and effective tactic to starve the enemy. "All the boats on Waccomay & lower part of Peedee River will be brought up, with what rice Lay near the Enemy," he wrote, and "the Cattle will be drove at a distance from them" True to his goals, Marion sent Peter Horry and 40 men to the Waccamaw River to collect boats and drive off cattle.[72]

There Horry met up and engaged a British detachment. This action alarmed Marion, who worried that the British might be attempting to link up with a Loyalist unit along the North Carolina border. That would not only threaten Marion's eastern flank but more importantly give the British possession of the countryside from Georgetown to North Carolina, including all the bountiful plantations along the Waccamaw River "which contains a Great quantity of provisions of all kind."[73]

Marion's letter of 14 January provides more clues as to the relationship between himself and the Snow's Island community. Marion wrote to General Greene at that time that he "shoud" march his whole force to attack the Loyalists along the North Carolina border, but to do so, he would have to draw in all his detachments, "which would leave fifty miles Open to the Enemy, and the Inhabitants finding their property & familys Exposed will Desert me almost to a man." Thus, Marion's plans were directly informed by the need for community security and that required a military presence in the region. In that same letter, Marion laments the lack of cooperation from Colonel Abel Kolb, who, if he could be coerced to join Marion, would give him the flexibility to attack the British along the Waccamaw.[74]

Marion's movements were also stymied by the rainy weather. In a letter to Greene on 18 January, Marion wrote from Snow's Island that "The river is so high I am [o]blige to remove a few miles near Mrs Ports Ferry on the South of Peedee where I shall remain a few d[a]ys."[75] The next day he had not moved to Mrs. Port's, but he writes from "Goddard's Plantation," which, if he was at the main plantation house, was higher ground than Snow's Island (see Chapter 8). There he ordered Captain Postell to gather the rice boats and send them up the Pee Dee to Euhaney Ferry where it was to be stored (Figure 6.1).[76] Postell was also to gather up 50 slaves for the boats "as belong to those persons who may be with the enemy, or from those estates which the enemy think forfeited....taking care not to distress any family, but taking them where they can be best spared."[77]

The rain kept the Pee Dee River high, preventing Marion from shipping rice upstream to General Greene. The high water also may have caused him to disperse his troops even more widely, for he notes to Greene that he is forming magazines in two places "North of Peedee." Perhaps one of these depots is the camp and redoubt at Dunham's Bluff across from Snow's Island (see Chapter 8).[78]

During Marion's third week on the island, he got two pieces of good news, both on the 23rd of January. First, Marion learned from Greene that American General Morgan had soundly defeated British Lieutenant Colonel Tarleton at the Battle of Cowpens in upstate South Carolina.[79] Such news would help Marion keep his fickle partisans in the ranks. Eventually this victory would have negative strategic implications for Marion, however, as Greene would be forced into North Carolina when British Lord Cornwallis, angry about the defeat, decided to go after Morgan. In the next few months, Marion would again find himself on his own against the British in the Lowcountry of South Carolina. The second piece of good news was that Lieutenant Colonel Lee, with his 2nd Partisan Corps, had been detached to join Marion and arrived that same day.

Lee's command was the 18th-century equivalent of a combined arms unit, consisting of both mounted and dismounted light troops. Marion's own morale must have skyrocketed. Lee's force was just what Marion needed: a highly mobile and well-disciplined professional unit.

General Daniel Morgan

Greene's initial purpose was for Lee and Marion to capture Fort Watson, a recently built fort on the Santee River (Figure 6.2). If that could be accomplished, then Greene would consider sending a large unit south of the Santee to break the supply line between Charleston and Camden and give Cornwallis something to ponder. But Marion knew that the post at Wright's Bluff was well protected and he doubted it could be surprised. Instead, Lee and Marion decided to go after Marion's old nemesis, British troops at the post at Georgetown.[80]

Marion and Lee's plan was tactical genius, but too complex for forces that had not served together. From Snow's Island, Marion and Lee's infantry (about 90 men) got on flat boats and drifted quickly downstream where they arrived at the mouth of the Pee Dee and hid on a small island nearby.

Meanwhile, Marion called in Postell to join him at Kingstree. With Lee's cavalry and Marion's mounted militia they rode for Georgetown. The plan was for the infantry to attack the town from the river and the mounted troops to arrive immediately afterward and support the attack. Unfortunately, the infantry attacked prematurely and did not directly go for the redoubt. Instead, they attacked less critical targets. Although the British were surprised and the commandant was captured, the British wisely did as they had over the past fall whenever Marion showed up—simply retired to their redoubt and brick houses. This time they waited until dawn broke, and as the sun came up, they were about to catch the exposed Americans in a crossfire when Marion recognized the situation and withdrew.[81]

Lieutenant Colonel Henry Lee

Marion and Lee retreated to Murray's Ferry on the Santee. Lee, warned by Greene that he needed to be prepared to be recalled, moved back to the Snow's Island community region and was camped at Port's Ferry by the 27th. On the 31st, Lee and his 150 dragoons crossed over to Benjamin Port's land.

While there, Lee was active in exploiting the Snow's Island community's resources especially around Port's Ferry. Joseph Greaves, who lived nearby, provided Lee's cavalry with 2500 bundles of fodder, 26 bushels of corn, 612 more bundles of fodder, leather, and 36 wt of pork. Gavin Witherspoon provided "Col. Lee's Legion" with 10 bushels of corn, 300 bundles of fodder, 90 lbs of pork, and 90 lbs of flour. Abram Giles provided 28 bushels of corn, 2500 wt of fodder, 100 wt of rice. Francis Port added 10 bushels of corn on the 31st and 316 wt of Pork, 30 wt of beef, 40 bushels of corn, 1000 wt of fodder. Lee probably also was involved in the acquisition of 58 head of hogs from Hugh Ervin for General Greene's army on 1 February.[82]

Although Greene pressed Lieutenant Colonel Lee to join him, Lee waited a few days for his cavalry to return before moving northward. On 3 February, he was still waiting for his cavalry at Culp's Ferry north of the Snow's Island community (Figure 6.1). Apparently, Lee was reluctant to leave Marion, partially because people south of the Santee were wavering in their support of the cause, which was likely due to a lack of Continental forces in South Carolina.

Greene however, had no choice. After the Battle of Cowpens, an enraged Lord Cornwallis had decided to march north into North Carolina to cut off Daniel Morgan's retreating detachment from Greene's main force. Morgan eluded Cornwallis, but Cornwallis went for broke. He burned his own wagons to increase his speed and chased Greene across North Carolina in a desperate attempt to bring him to formal battle. This campaign became known as the "Race to the Dan[River]."[83]

Marion moved to the Santee, camped at Cordes' Plantation (not depicted), and dispatched two detachments of 30 men each across the Santee on the 29th to harass the British.[84] With Greene turning toward North Carolina and Lee reluctantly following, Marion was again left to hold the South Carolina Lowcountry. About this time, according to Robert Gray, the South Carolina population was consolidating into large regions of Loyalist and Whig communities.

> All the loyal inhabitants at Ninety-Six district being about one half & living partly betwixt Broad & Saluda rivers, commonly called the Dutch Fork, & in other places of that district, all the inhabitants of Orangeburg District from a few miles to the Southward of Santee to the Saltketchers, being almost unanimous in favor of Government where the friendly parts of this province on the South side of the Santee, the rest were enemies.[85]

1 FEBRUARY TO 13 APRIL 1781

For a moment, Marion was enthused about a report from Major James Postell that the inhabitants on the west side of the Santee were "disposed to join us." That was quickly replaced with the reality of seeing his militia again melting away. Lee had been right; the Whig communities and partisans were alarmed at Greene's move into North Carolina. At the forks of the Black River, Marion wrote that he was attempting to rally them, but "all my Indeavours has proved fruitless." With only 200 men, Marion informed Huger that he would retreat to Lagre's Plantation north of Lynches Creek (not depicted). Meanwhile, two fellow partisans, Colonels William Clay Snipes and another named Baker brought in Georgians to the Lowcountry, and Marion lamented that they would only "plunder the Inhabitants, which will make more Enemys [sic]."[86]

But Marion had more to worry about than Snipes and Baker. He was in the process of retreating to Lagre's because Francis Lord Rawdon was after him, as described in a letter from Rawdon to Cornwallis:

I am just returned from my excursion after Marion. I find that his numbers did not much exceed three hundred, all mounted. By forced marches we got below him but he got off, tho' narrowly, across Scape Whore [Scape Ore swamp]. We forced him over Lynches Creek & should have driven him across Pedee had not news of a Corps advancing against Ninety Six recalled me.[87]

Once again, Marion was lucky. He escaped Rawdon, as he had Tarleton back in the fall. The American force threatening British outposts on the west side of the Santee and Congaree Rivers was that of Brigadier General Sumter. Sumter's maneuvers the previous fall had caused the British to recall Tarleton from the heels of Marion. Ironically, although they were most likely unintentional, Sumter's maneuvers had saved Marion again.

It was, in fact, a double irony. When Governor Rutledge promoted Marion to general at the end of December 1780, he had placed all South Carolina militia under Sumter. This had not been a problem while Greene was present in South Carolina and in overall command because Sumter and Marion were engaged in separate districts. Now with Greene gone, Sumter was technically in charge of all South Carolina forces, including Francis Marion and his Snow's Island partisans, and Marion was no Sumter enthusiast.

Greene broke the news to Marion on 11 February, requesting that Marion "Communicate & Concert" with Sumter. Meanwhile, Sumter had gone on the offense and attacked the British outposts on the western side of the Congaree and Santee Rivers and his raids on Forts Granby and Belleville had drawn Rawdon away. Sumter then crossed the Santee and attacked a foraging party from the newly built Fort Watson that Greene had wanted Lee and Marion to tackle earlier.[88]

After being chased by Rawdon, Marion ended up on Jeffries Creek (Figure 1.2), about 20 miles upstream of Snow's Island and at the periphery of the Snow's Island community.[89] Sumter, with the British closing in, wrote Marion on the 20th, requesting that he move westward toward the Santee to draw off Rawdon's forces.[90]

Marion complied, but in comparison with his lightning strikes of 1780, he dawdled. His orderly book records his headquarters as being at Jeffries Creek from 16 February to the 21st ("Jeffry's Creek" and Burch's Plantation)[91] before he began a slow march south toward Snow's Island.

Colonel Horry, probably with a detachment, arrived on Snow's Island by the 22nd. Marion (or at least his headquarters detachment) camped at Huges [Hughes] Plantation that same day. On the 23rd, Marion arrived at

Joseph Glover's Plantation along the Pee Dee River between Georgetown and Britton's Neck. The next day, he was either once again at "Peedee" or still at Glover's. In other words, Marion hugged the west side of the Pee Dee River from the 16th to the 23rd rather than heading westward and turning toward Sumter. Three days later, Marion arrived on the Black River and camped at Green's Plantation (not depicted). It was that day that Marion finally answered Sumter's request, noting, with what might be read as surprise, that "you Desire I should make a Junction with you." In that same answer, Marion let Sumter know that the British were at the High Hills of the Santee in force and that his partisans were too weak to support Sumter. He added that he would attempt to move as close as possible and harass foraging parties.[92]

Although it might be inferred that Marion was avoiding Sumter, it is possible that despite his attitude toward Sumter, he really was doing all he could. The British knew that Marion had fewer than 300 men and that their presence in the area "prevented ...[him] from attempting to interfere" with their pursuit of Sumter. Either way, by 6 March, Sumter had escaped British pursuit and was on his way back to the Upcountry and Marion remained on the Black River, camping at Green's and nearby Salem (Figure 6.2).[93]

With Sumter running northward and Greene and Cornwallis in North Carolina, the time was right for Lord Rawdon, who had received fresh reinforcements, to focus entirely on Francis Marion and the Snow's Island community. Unlike in the fall of 1780, the British were free of distractions and Lord Rawdon took advantage of the situation immediately. Now began a brilliant, but ultimately unsuccessful defensive campaign by Marion, known by some as the "Bridges Campaign."[94]

Earlier that winter, Colonel John Tadwell Watson arrived in South Carolina with a battalion of Provincial Light Infantry. Colonel Balfour sent him to the Santee with orders that he was to have a detached command, as Watson noted, to "protect the communications of the Santee River to Camden and to cover the Eastern District of the Province. ... that the eastern part of the Province was my front, that I was to consider Camden on my left, and Georgetown on my right flanks ... and to communicate with Lord Rawdon." Thus, Marion became Watson's problem. Watson had constructed Fort Watson on an Indian mound (now on the Santee Wildlife Refuge) (Figure 6.2). This was the fort that Greene had wanted Marion and Lee to attack. Sumter had attacked one of Watson's foraging parties but now that he was out of the way, Watson was ordered by Lord Rawdon to find Marion and "press him to the utmost."[95]

Watson set out about 5 March with around 500 men consisting of his own Provincial Light Infantry, Major Harrison's South Carolina mounted Rangers, Loyalist volunteers under Colonel Henry Richbourg, a detachment of the 64th Regiment of Foot, and critically, two 3-pounder cannons.

Marion moved to the Santee River on 3 March and camped near the home of Kintey—Cantey's Plantation. Moving forward to meet Watson, he set up an ambush at a causeway through Wiboo Swamp on 6 March (Figure 6.4). Watson's scouts spotted Marion's men and the two forces looked across the causeway at each other until Watson ordered his mounted Loyalists forward. Marion responded by ordering Peter Horry's mounted troops forward. After a brief clash, both sides retired. Then both sides formed on opposite banks and opened fire.

Watson had the advantage of artillery and pushed back Marion's troops. He followed with another cavalry charge, which Marion parried with another of his own. Again, both sides retreated, and then Watson sent his infantry down the causeway. Seeing the infantry charge, Marion withdrew to Cordes' Plantation farther down the river road, still along the Santee.[96]

The next day, Watson reformed and moved down the "Lower Road" and camped at Blakely House. By 9 March he had reached Cantey's Plantation, was harassed by Marion, and again encamped.

On what was likely the next day, Watson was again on the move and reached Mount Hope Swamp to find that the bridge had been destroyed by Marion's men. Across the morass, Hugh Horry and William McCrotty's riflemen were stationed to delay the crossing. Watson used his cannon to disperse them.

Marion continued down the road toward Murray's Ferry (on the Santee) thinking Watson would follow. But instead, Watson turned north for the Lower Bridge on the Black River towards Kingstree. By turning north, Marion was in danger of being cut off from the Snow's Island community and base camp. But that wasn't the end of the danger. If the British could coordinate efforts from Charleston, Georgetown, and Kingstree, they would have Marion trapped against the sea.[97]

Marion acted quickly, sending McCrotty's riflemen and John James, with about 70 men, to the north side of the Lower Bridge. They crossed at a ford downstream. When Watson arrived, he found the bridge partially destroyed and all of Marion's force arrayed against him.

Marion held the lower swampy side of the river and Watson the high ground, yet despite the fact that the high ground is usually the best tactical position, Marion had the advantage. Watson again brought forward his

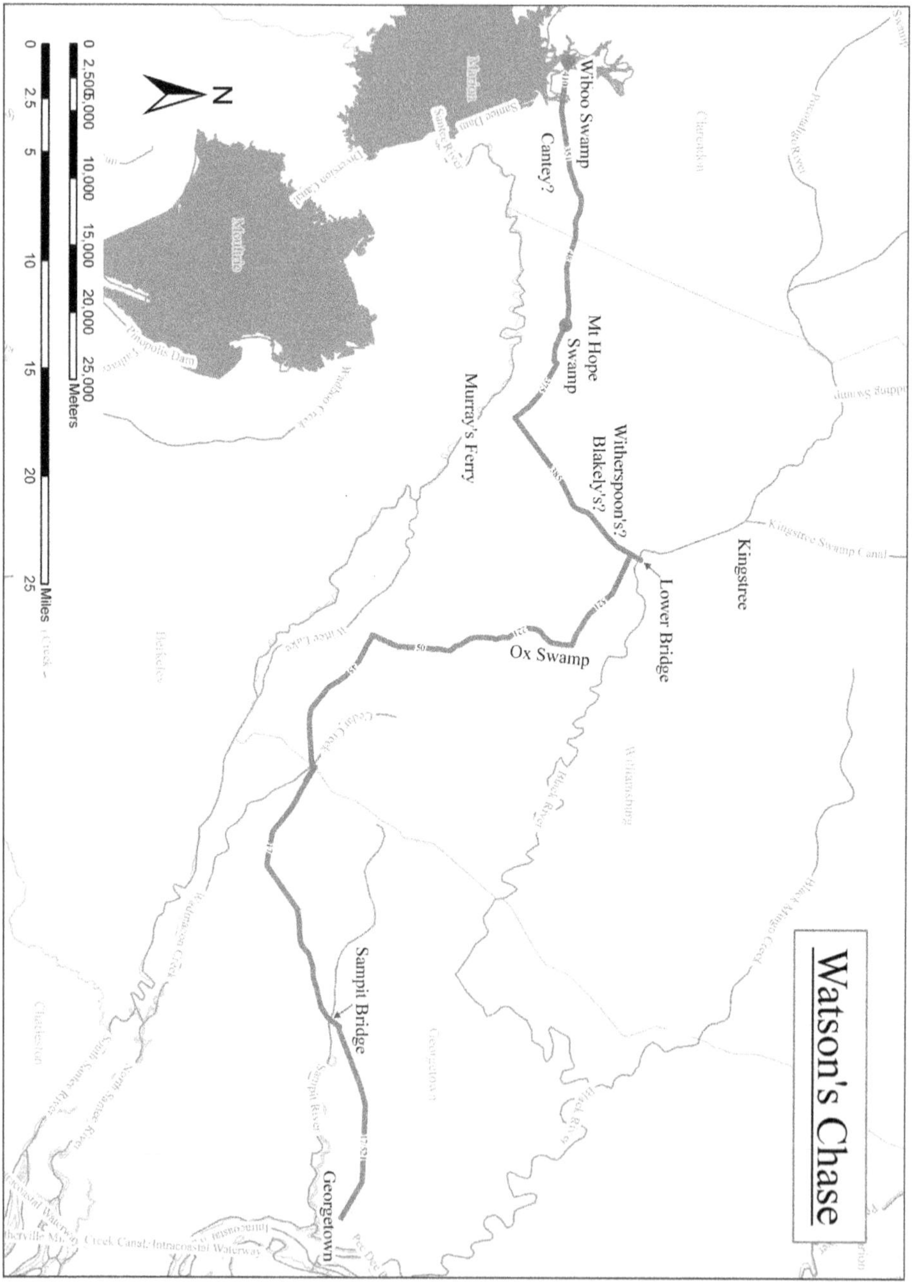

130 | *Francis Marion and the Snow's Island Community*

Figure 6.4. Watson's march toward Snow's Island (T.S. Wilson)

artillery, but this time, the artillerymen could not depress their guns low enough to do Marion any harm. Meanwhile, Marion's riflemen picked off the artillerymen.

Watson next tried the ford downstream that Marion had used to cross to the north bank and was again stopped by rifle fire. He abandoned the crossing and camped at Witherspoon's Plantation "a mile above the bridge." Marion supposedly moved to "General's island" a mile downstream from the ford and sent a detachment across the river to continue harassing the British colonel. On 15 March, Watson moved to Blakely's (possibly a different Blakely's from the previous one) and sent a letter to Marion requesting that four of his wounded be allowed to pass on to Georgetown for care. Marion agreed.[98]

By this time, Marion's harassment had battered the British considerably. Unable to force a crossing, Watson had no choice but to press forward along the southern bank of the Black River. Sometime after 16 March, he was back on the move, with the apparent intent of crossing downstream at Potato Bed Ferry and going north to Snow's Island. But at Ox Swamp, he found that a detachment of Marion's command had once more beaten him there and destroyed the bridge.

Meanwhile, Marion had followed Watson and was now behind him. At this point, Watson must have decided that he had better abandon his march to Snow's Island and get to the safety of Georgetown. He turned right (south) to get back on the Santee River Road.

Now the march became a rout. Marion's forces kept up a harassing fire on the rear of Watson's column. And, once again, when Watson arrived at the Sampit River bridge, the last river crossing to Georgetown, he found a partially destroyed bridge and Marion's mounted riflemen across the stream.

Watson, although desperate, did not panic. He sent his light infantry across the river to engage the riflemen and then turned his attention to Marion's main force, which was coming up behind. Watson's artillery fired canister down the road checking the attack. Marion's riflemen on Watson's front gave way and Watson was finally able to proceed across the Sampit. He camped at Trapier's Plantation near Georgetown on 21 March and presumably arrived in Georgetown the following day.[99]

Despite a brilliant campaign, however, Marion failed to stop the British from getting to Snow's Island. Shortly after the battle at the Sampit Bridge, he learned that the Snow's Island camp had been destroyed by another British detachment. Unbeknownst to him, Colonel Welbore Ellis Doyle, guided by Snow's Island community resident Hugh Miscally,[100] had marched with the Volunteers of Ireland across Lynches and Jeffries Creek and down to Snow's Island.[101] There, he had found the camp guarded only by Colonel Ervin and a few sick and wounded soldiers. Doyle destroyed the camp and Marion's supplies. It is assumed that among those supplies were 960 lbs of pork, 65 bushels of corn, and 500 wt of corn blades just arrived from David Witherspoon's Plantation on 15 March.[102]

Few primary sources provide any details about Doyle's raid.[103] The Loyalist Charleston *Royal Gazette* reported on 4 April that:

> Marion's repository of stores and plunder, on Snow's Island, was a few days since destroyed by a detachment of his Majesty's forces under Lieut. Colonel Doyle. Colonel Doyle then sent the light company of the Volunteers of Ireland to destroy a flat on Lynches Creek, which they effected, though opposed by a considerable body of the enemy."[104]

The Savannah Loyalist newspaper also recorded the story, adding the details that seven of Marion's men were killed and 15 taken prisoner.[105]

Despite the destruction at Snow's Island, British correspondence was focused on a much more significant event. On 15 March, a large battle had occurred between Lord Cornwallis and General Greene at Guilford Court House, North Carolina, and they offer little insight on the skirmish at Snow's Island. Colonel Balfour mentioned Doyle's raid with a simple communication: "By letter just received from Lord Rawdon I find that Lt. Col. Doyle has got at Marrions baggage on Snows Island, and destroy'd it completely—It is now the time to chase these gentry from the country, if a little exertion is made."[106]

William Dobein James stated only:

> In the mean time, Col. Doyle, an active, enterprising officer, had driven Col. Ervin, who commanded only a weak force, from Snow's Island. But before retreating he had Marion's arms, stores and ammunition thrown into Lynch's creek. This, at the crisis, was a most serious loss.[107]

Biographers Horry and Weems do not mention Doyle's destruction of Marion's camp, nor does Marion mention it in any of his correspondence. (His Orderly Book is confusing and will be discussed further below.)

Another early postwar account related to Snow's Island, somewhat peripheral to the combat, is that of British Cornet Thomas Merritt (sometimes Merrit). Accounts of Cornet Merritt on Snow's Island are told in Reverend James Jenkins's memoir of the Revolution, and British Colonel John Simcoe's memoir of his experience with the Queen's Rangers.

At the beginning of March 1781, Merritt was sent to Marion's Snow's Island camp under a flag of truce to deliver a letter. From Georgetown, he crossed onto Britton's Neck at Britton's Ferry and made his way north to the Widow Jenkins's home. There the two had an angry exchange and Merritt proceeded to Ervin's redoubt [Dunham's Bluff] where "he was taken prisoner and confined in Wm. Goddard's house until the British relieved him." He was taken prisoner in response to the British taking John Postell.[108]

Jenkins's account matches that mentioned in a letter from British Colonel Saunders published in Simcoe's memoir many years later. In that account, Merritt was jammed into a small cabin with twenty other prisoners. When the camp was "alarmed" by "a party of British having come into that neighborhood [Snow's Island]," Merritt led an escape to a river "at some distance" (Pee Dee, no doubt), where they found a rice boat and proceeded downstream to Georgetown and safety. The British were quite happy about Merritt's return and he was offered a lieutenancy.[109]

That is the extent of what are and what might be considered primary sources about the skirmish at Snow's Island. Secondary sources are also lean on hard, verifiable, facts. Both 20th century Marion biographers Robert Bass and Hugh Rankin get most of the details of the skirmish from 19th century biographer William Gilmore Simms, which has been summarized above.[110]

As mentioned in the newspaper account of the skirmish on Snow's Island, Doyle or a detachment of his, quickly seized Witherspoon's Ferry at Lynch's Creek after destroying Marion's camp. According to James, Marion heard Doyle was at Witherspoon's and sent mounted riflemen ahead of his main body who found Doyle's troops scuttling the ferry boat. They fired across the river at the British, who returned fire and then retreated north. Marion arrived shortly afterward.

With the boat sunk and the river swollen, Marion marched upstream five miles before finding a place to cross, which he did (famously swimming his horses). He pursued all day and the next morning but could not catch Doyle.[111]

Doyle's seeming cowardly retreat is explained by yet another recall from Colonel Rawdon in Camden. Doyle had received orders to return immediately—Cornwallis was moving north and American General Greene was returning to South Carolina.[112]

Marion, however, did not know that. By 1 April, Marion had gone as far upstream as Burch's Plantation or Mill (Figure 3.7) in pursuit of Doyle.[113] There, quite possibly in anger, Marion proclaimed that anyone who he drafted and refused to join would have their names published as "Enem[ies] to the

State." Furthermore, their property could be seized and given to "friends of America."[114]

Marion probably waited a few days to see the effect of his orders and then boldly crossed to the eastern side of the Pee Dee and by 12 April was camped at Alston's Plantation along Warhee (Wahee) Neck (Figure 4.2).[115] James stated that the crossing was the result of Marion's learning that Colonel Watson had rested, refitted, and was on the march toward him from Georgetown.

The intelligence was correct. Watson's march north from Georgetown followed a direct route through the Snow's Island community. His original plan had been to travel up the west side of the Pee Dee as had Wemyss in the fall of 1780, "in order to cross thro' the heart of the Country which shewed the strongest marks of disaffection" but he was happily surprised to receive a "deputation from the Inhabitants of the little Pedee." These Loyalists told him that if he would cross the Pee Dee on the east side, they would assemble and join him. Crossing onto Britton's Neck at the ferry (Figures 3.5, 3.6), he marched north and arrived at the Widow Jenkins's home on 7 April.[116] Reverend Jenkins, a boy at the time, watched the British at a safe distance. His cousin John, who was a scout for Colonel Horry, also appeared. The British chased after James, but John waited while James mounted the horse behind him. Together they made off into the swamp, where James hid until Watson left. Watson raided the house, killed seven head of cattle and destroyed the garden. Then Watson encountered the redoubtable widow, another argument ensued, and Watson decided to move up the road and camp at John Rae's Plantation (Figure 4.1).[117]

Watson marched north past Snow's Island and camped along Catfish Creek at Hickory Grove around the 12th or 13th. He would have passed very close to the camp and redoubt at Dunham's Bluff and thus was quite accurate when he said he crossed through the heart of disaffection. According to Jenkins, his men were "blowing their bugles as they went." Evincing the porous nature of the community, Jenkins said that the Little Pee Dee Loyalists were good to their word: "The day after we cross'd at Brittains Ferry near two hundred of the Pedee Militia join'd us at James Davis's." These were Major Micajah Ganey's Loyalists from the Little Pee Dee. Some might have been from nearby Cypress Creek (see below).[118]

Once again, Marion was about to be rescued by serendipitous events beyond his control. When Watson arrived along Catfish Creek, he camped only a few miles away from Marion. Although Marion apparently crossed the Pee Dee to face Watson, it was a reckless move

Marion's condition was as desperate as it ever had been. The Snow's Island depot had been destroyed, the Snow's Island community had been invaded, and the people were likely scattered into the swamps. He had no more than two rounds of ammunition per man.[119] Watson's intelligence was that Marion was out of salt and ammunition, and that he was desperate for gunpowder and food.[120] Furthermore, Watson had learned of Marion's proclamation for the people to either join him or be "branded enemies." Watson wisely used that proclamation to take the high ground and declare peaceful intentions. He, in turn, proclaimed that "whereas Marion insisted upon their turning out in arms—we only desired them to stay at home, & cultivate their Lands, & that every man found at home might rely upon protection." The result was that Marion's partisan force dropped to 150 men and was "daily diminishing."[121] Marion could not possibly attack the combined forces of Watson's regulars and Ganey's Loyalist militia and had no choice but to re-cross the Pee Dee or, as he discussed with his officers, possibly retreat to North Carolina essentially abandoning his loyal Snow's Island community.

Then, Captain James Conyers, a Continental flag officer, arrived in Marion's camp with news that Colonel Lee and his Partisan Corps were behind him. In addition, Nathanael Greene and the Continental Army were marching back to South Carolina. Marion quickly recrossed the Pee Dee to Burch's Mill and plantation.[122]

Endnotes for Chapter 6

1 Marion kept his partisans dispersed widely across the landscape and he often detached small parties on independent raids and ambushes. Since I focus on the partisans around Snow's Island and not a detailed military history of Marion's partisan warfare, not all these actions are described, unless they provide further examples of the Snow's Island community's wartime activities.

2 Salley 1937:127; Bass 1959:40. William Dobein James recorded that Marion arrived at Witherspoon's Ferry on 10 or 12 August (James 1821:46). However, it is clear from Peter Horry, who was with Marion at the time, that they were still with General Horatio Gates on the 10th. Dates, numbers of men, and combat casualties recorded by historians and even eyewitnesses of the Revolution are notoriously inconsistent. Generally, I will lean toward accounts written as soon after the event as possible by eyewitnesses or participants, except where there are obvious errors. I say reacquainted with the community because Marion and Horry traveled through the Pee Dee region during their attempt to recruit men to their regiment in 1775 (Horry and Weems 1898:29).

3 De Kalb to Major General Caswell, 10 July 1780, de Kalb Papers; Salley 1959:121.

4 Williams 1822:488.

5 According to James, sometime between 3 August and 16 August, Williamsburg militia officers sent a messenger either to Gates or Marion requesting a Continental commander and that Governor Rutledge commissioned Marion to take command (James 1821:44). Otho Williams states that Marion "at his own insistence" requested to be detached and sent to the lowcountry for intelligence purposes (Williams 1822:488). I believe both are correct, because there is some intriguing evidence that Marion's detachment to the Pee Dee militia was prearranged. A letter written by Gilbert Johnston "for Susannah," dated 8 March 1790 includes this mysterious passage "Marion two Horrys & Francis Huger met Folsom and Giles my house. All chose Marion bar[?] Folsom" (Gilbert Johnstone Papers, SCL). Gilbert Johnstone owned a plantation on the Waccamaw River, and raised a battalion of light horse, serving in the N.C. Rangers under Colonel Ebenezer Folsome (and later under Marion). He also contributed supplies to Marion during the war. The two Horry's are Peter and Hugh, who, of course served under Marion. Francis Huger was a captain in the 2nd South Carolina Regiment. Hugh Giles has been mentioned before. My interpretation is that this meeting took place during Marion and Horry's journey north into North Carolina after the fall of Charleston. It is logical that Marion's route north would have gone through the Waccamaw area. I believe all met at Johnston's house and discussed who would lead the militia once a second Continental Army came south. Marion was the logical choice as a Lieutenant Colonel. Folsome, obviously disagreed, perhaps because he too was a Colonel (Gilbert Johnstone to Susannah Gilbert Johnstone Papers, SCL; Powell 1975).

Horry states that they were ordered south to destroy boats along the Santee thereby blocking the British escape route from Camden (Salley 1937:127). The latter is supported by Marion's orders to Horry on 17 August 1780.

6 Legg et al. 2005; Salley 1959:121.

7 The British thought he had 150 (Cornwallis to Cruger, 27 August 1780, Cornwallis Papers [henceforth CP], P.R.O. 30/11/79:39-40).

8 Lewis Perkins Pension R8114; James 1821:44; Marion to Horry, 17 August 1780, Gibbes 1853;12, Vol. 1:11; Marion to Gates, 29 August 1780, Gates Papers, Sparks Collection; Hamilton to Cornwallis, n.d. CP, P.R.O. 30/11/63:74; B. Munnerlyn Pension W8479.

9 Gray 1910:142.

10 Marion wrote Gates that all 150 Continentals came with him to Port's Ferry but they were "much dissatisfied" (Marion to Gates, 29 August 1780, Gates Papers, Harvard). Cornwallis reported that 85 refused to go with Marion and continued to Charleston; William Dobein James says that all but three deserted Marion on the ride back to the Snow's Island region (Cornwallis to Cruger, 27 August 1780, CP, P.R.O. 30/11/79:39-40; James 1821:55). Certainly some Continentals did follow Marion to camp as he wrote Gates 15 September 1780 that some were on their way to Wilmington, North Carolina, and Colonel James Reid wrote General Jethro Sumner confirming that 57 had arrived (Read to Sumner, 12 September 1780, SRNC 14:771; Marion to Gates, 15 September 1780, SRNC

11 Marion to Horry, 27 August 1780, Gibbes 1853:11; G. Witherspoon A.A. 8690; Marion to Gates, 29 August 1780, Sparks Collection. Its possible that this camp was at Dunham's bluff.

12 L. Munnerlyn Pension S18136; Rankin 1973:71; Marion to Gates, 15 September 1780, SRNC, Vol. 14:617. For such a small affair, many Snow's Island community partisans claim to have been involved. Besides the Munnerlyn brothers were Francis Davis (Davis Pension S8290), Jonathan Collins (Collins Pension S18771), George McCall (McCall Pension R6598), and William Shaw (Shaw Pension S19078). A non-resident Jesse Wiggins (Wiggins Pension R11502) also claims to have been there. Loftus Munnerlyn's pension account is a wealth of information but some of it is quite confusing. Most critical is that he states that "his father's house was unroofed by the tories and Genl. Marion sent a group of thirty men who removed Declarant's father and mother who were aged in the vicinity of the redoubt which is situated on the right bank of the Pee Dee river opposite Snow's Island" (L. Munnerlyn Pension S18136). In a later application, he states that his father "was recovered when the Tories were fired upon ran to Marion's company" (L. Munnerlyn Pension S18136). This latter action was in the context of the skirmish of Blue Savannah. The issue is that while the former account is a powerful primary source confirming the camp and redoubt at Dunham's Bluff (Chapter 8), other sources indicate that the redoubt was not constructed until 1781 (Jenkins 1842:18,29). Based on Hugh Giles' audited account, there likely was a redoubt at Port's Ferry also (Giles A.A. 2817). Marion to Gates 15 September, 1780, SRNC; McCall Pension R6598; Colonel Hugh Giles A.A. 2817.

13 Marion to Gates 15 September, 1780, SRNC; McCall Pension R6598; Colonel Hugh Giles A.A. 2817.

14 The last item is unreadable on the audited account but appears to be "2 quires of paper." While at Giles Bluff his Britton's Neck regiment had feasted on 60 bushels of corn from his own corn crop (H. Giles A.A. 2817).

15 Booth Pension W25258; Grice Pension R4301.

16 Bass 1959:52.

17 Marion to Gates, 15 September 1780, SRNC, Vol. 14:617-618. Marion may not have left for North Carolina until around the 12th. On that day, Charles Fladger provided forage to the militia (Fladger A.A. 2414). Marion passing by Potts home found in Redden McCoy Pension S7198.

18 Bass 1959:57.

19 Wemyss to Cornwallis, CP, P.R.O. 30/11/64:91-92; Gregg 1925:303,584. General Henry William Harrington wrote General Gates 17 September 1780 that Wemyss or one of his detachments crossed the Pee Dee at Britton's Ferry on Sunday 10 Sept 1780 and recrossed on Tuesday "& plunder, burn & destroy every thing in their way" (Harrington to Gates, 17 September 1780, SRNC Vol. 14:651-653). If so, two days on the neck would have given him an opportunity to burn many more Snow's Island partisan community homes.

20 James 1821:58; Ramsay 1785:177.

21 Marion to Gates, 4 October 1780, SRNC, Vol. 14:665.

22 James 1821:58.

23 Marion to Gates, 4 October 1780, SRNC, Vol. 14:665.

24 *South Carolina American General Gazette* 11 October 1780.

25 Balfour to Cornwallis, 5 October 1780, P.R.O. 30/11/3.

26 James 1821:59; Boddie 2000:98-99.

27 James 1821:58; Smith 2008a:40; Booth Pension W25258; Shaw Pension S19078; George McCall (McCall Pension R6598); Redden McCoy (McCoy Pension S7198); and Benjamin Munnerlyn (B. Munnerlyn Pension W8479).

28 Marion to Gates, 4 October 1780, SRNC, Vol. 14:665; James 1821:60.

29 Marion to Gates, 4 October 1780, SRNC, Vol. 14:665.

30 Marion to Gates, 15 October 1780, SRNC, Vol. 14:622.

31 Gray to Cornwallis, 30 September 1780, CP, P.R.O. 30/11/64:130-131.

32 Ibid.

33 Piecuch 2008:190-195.

34 Marion's actions here are questionable. Certainly, it was foolhardy to attack a fortified position like Georgetown with only 70 men. The British had at least that many, two howitzers, and a redoubt to hide behind, plus a galley in the harbor (Rankin 1973:91). Even if he took Georgetown, he could not have held it. Perhaps the move was a shrewd attempt to keep his partisans together and morale high. Meanwhile, Gates and North Carolina militia officer, General Henry Harrington, had been writing Marion to join Harrington in an attack against Wemyss at Cheraw (Harrington to Gates, 25 September 1780, SRNC Vol. 14; Gates to Marion, 11 October 1780, Gates Papers, Reel 12:697; Harrington to Gates, 15 October 1780, SRNC Vol. 14:697).

35 Marion to Gates, 15 October 1780, SRNC, Vol. 14:621. One of those men who joined him shortly before his attack on Georgetown was Peter Buckholts. Buckholts would remain with Marion until being discharged at Wadboo Plantation in 1782 (Buckholts Pension R1465). More typical of the partisan-militia pattern of service was exemplified by Snow's Island community stalwarts like Gavin James, Hugh Swinton, and John Witherspoon. Gavin joined Colonel McDonald's company on 5 August 1780 and served to 12 May 1781. He returned on the 23 July and served until 23 August. Again, he rejoined the command from 23 September to 23 October, the 23 November to 23 December, then, in 1782, he served two terms as a sergeant 2? March 1782, 28 days, and 27 June, 20 days (G. James A.A. 3991). Hugh Swinton's service began on 30 November 1780 for 121 days. Then he served 15 days from 10 to 25 February 1781, 70 days from 19 March to 5 June 1781, 30 days 5 January 1782 to 5 February, and 40 days from 5 November 1782 (Swinton A.A. 7589). John Witherspoon service consisted of four "tours": 1 December 1780 to 25 February 1781, 7 March to 28 March, 1 April to 28 June, and 15 July to 31 August (J. Witherspoon A.A. 8692). For Marion, planning and executing a campaign strategy was pure frustration, with men coming and going constantly. Yet these men not only served but also provided provisions and fodder. Swinton even loaned the state cash in 1780 (Swinton S.I. K56).

36 James 1821:60; Bass 1959:75; Abram Giles A.A. 2816; Marion to Gates, 4 November 1780, SRNC Vol. 14:726; Balfour to Rawdon, 26 October 1780, P.R.O. 30/11/3:289-290.

37 Smith 2008a:111; Marion to Gates, 4 November 1780, SRNC Vol. 14:726.

38 Joseph Nettles was one that returned, joining Marion on 1 November 1780 (J. Nettles A.A. 5489) along with Gavin Witherspoon (G. Witherspoon A.A. 8690). George Nettles would join a month later, on 1 December 1780 (G. Nettles A.A. 5487).

39 Colonel Nisbet Balfour to Lord Rawdon, 1 November 1780, CP, P.R.O. 30/11/4:5-6; Rawdon to Cornwallis 17 November 1780, CP, P.R.O. 30/11/4:74; Balfour to Cornwallis, 17 November 1780, CP, P.R.O. 30/11/4:76.

40 Bass 1959:80; Marion to Gates, 9 November 1780, Papers of the Continental Congress, [henceforth PCC], Item 171, M247.

41 Marion to Gates, 21 November, 1780, SRNC Vol. 14:746. It was after being led through 26 miles of swamp and bogs that Tarleton, according to, William Dobein James, uttered his famous line "Come my boys! let us go back, and we will soon find the game cock (meaning Sumter) but as for this d—d old fox, the devil himself could not catch him" (James 1821:63). Tarleton wrote Cornwallis that they "made a rapid March of 26 miles thro' Swamps, Woods & Fastnesses towards Black River without a Halt. ...I had the Mortification not to fight them but I had the Pleasure in a great Measure to disperse them" (Tarleton to Cornwallis, 11 November 1780, CP, P.R.O. 30/1/4:49). See Chapter 9 for more discussion of Tarleton's quip.

42 Lt. Col. Banastre Tarleton to Lt. Col. George Turnbull, 5 November, 1780, CP, P.R.O. 30/11/4:29-30. Cornwallis to Tarleton, 8 November 1780, CP, P.R.O. 30/11/82:12. Balfour to Cornwallis, 17 November 1780, CP, P.R.O. 30/11/4:76. But Loyalist Robert Gray agreed with Cornwallis about Marion, calling him "..timid & cautious & would risk nothing" (Gray 1910:144).

43 Marion to Brigadier General William Harrington, 17 November 1780, Gregg 1925:343; Marion to Gates, 21 November 1780, SRNC Vol. 14:746. Marion lost his nephew Gabriel Marion in one of the skirmishes (Marion to Gates, 21 November 1780, SRNC Vol. 14:746).

44 Balfour to Cornwallis, 24 November 1780, CP, P.R.O. 30/11/4:98. In capturing Port's Ferry, McLeroth also would have had to take possession of Witherspoon's Ferry.

45 Balfour to Cornwallis, 24 November, CP, P.R.O. 30/11/4:98. It appears that the notion that the Pee Dee was ripe for the taking was widespread in Charleston. A Loyalist controlled Charleston newspaper reported at this time "that about 200 of the inhabitants near Peedee River, over whom Mr. Marion and his associates for sometime past have exercised the most despotic and cruel tyranny, lately collected together in arms and fell in with a gang of banditti…" killing Colonel Murphy (*South Carolina and American General Gazette*, Vol. XXIII, 15 November 1780). If this is the same Murphy who had been burning Loyalist houses and refusing to cooperate with Marion, he was not killed.

46 Marion to Gates, 21 November 1780, SRNC Vol. 14:746; Marion to Gates, 22 November 1780, GP-WCL.

47 Marion to Gates 21 November 1780, SRNC Vol. 14:746. Marion's proclamation on 3 November 1780 to the people of Prince Frederick Parish had little effect on the Whig population. General Gates had proclaimed that paroles given to the British to not to take arms against them (British) were not to be followed. Marion restated Gates proclamation and ordered all members of Colonel McDonald's Craven County militia to join him by the 9th or face imprisonment. Part of the motivation behind the letter may have also been to better gain control over the Whigs in the community, as Marion believed that General Harrington was recruiting the region (Marion to Gates or Harrington in Bass 1959:78). In any case, Marion was publically announcing that the he was in authority over the Craven County militia (which included Colonel Giles men of the Snow's Island community). Marion also writes again of a lack of ammunition and the need of a surgeon, the lack of which not only caused a man to bleed to death but also increased his desertions as "many is Oblige to return for want of Medicines, for I have not any whatever" (Marion to Gates, 21 November 1780, SRNC, Vol. 14:747).

48 Sometime prior to the island being called "Snow's," it had been called "Johnson's Island" after the Johnson family.

49 Benjamin Port A.A. 6030; Joseph Jenkins A.A. 4020; Bass 1959:104-105; Giles to Gates, 12 August 1780, CP, P.R.O. 30/11/3:5; Savage A.A. 6786.

50 *South Carolina and American Gazette,* Vol. XXIII, 29 November 1780.

51 Bass 1959:102-103.

52 Greene to Nash, 6 December 1780, GP, Vol. VI:533.

53 Greene to Marion, 4 December 1780, GP, Vol. VI:520.

54 Greene to Huntington, PCC, Item 155, Vol. 1:471.

55 Bass 1959:104; Lipscomb circa 1974:1; Rankin 1973:126; Marion to Gates, 6 December 1780, Horatio Gates Papers, Reel 13:67. The whole problem of the camp on Snow's Island versus across from Snow's Island will be discussed in detail in Chapter 8. For now, it is assumed that Marion's "Snow's Island camp" was on Snow's Island.

56 Marion to Greene, 22 December, GP, Vol. VI:605; Rawdon to Cornwallis, 16 December 1780, CP, P.R.O. 30/11/4:167; Marion to Greene, 22 December 1780, GP, Vol. VI:605.

57 Marion to Greene, 24 December, GP, Vol. VI:608; Marion to Greene, 27 December 1780, GP-WCL, Vol. 13:29.

58 Marion to Greene, 28 December 1780, GP-WCL, Vol. 13:35.

59 William Snow A.A. 7197; James Snow A.A. 7196.

60 Winter may have been fairly mild in 1780-1781. Evan Pugh, a Baptist minister from the upper Pee Dee kept a diary from 1762 to 1801 and while he did not religiously record the weather he often noted that it was "cold" or "cloudy" or "warm." His entries for December 1780 through January 1781 record: 25 Dec "Windy day but warm," 7 January "Cloudy & Wet morning," 10 January "Wett day,"27 January "had heavy rain," 4 and February "very Worm for ye [the] Time" (Rudisill 1993:202-203). There is no doubt it was very wet that month.

61 Among Snow's Island community members who specifically mention being camped at Snow's Island in their pension applications are Peter Buckholts (Buckholts Pension R1465), Redden McCoy (McCoy Pension S7198), William Potts (in McCoy's Pension S7198), Benjamin Munnerlyn (B. Munnerlyn Pension W8479), William Shaw (Shaw Pension S19078), Lewis Perkins (Perkin Pension R8105), and Thomas Grice (Grice Pension R4301). Among Marion's partisans who were not Snow's Island

residents, but camped on the island were Thomas Irwin (Irwin Pension S31164), William Grifis (Grifis Pension R4320a), John Scott (Scott Pension S32508), John Nelson (Nelson Pension W53), John Roberts (Roberts Pension S18188), William Kendle (Kendle Pension W7978), John Might (Might Pension W4548), Richard Rawlins (Rawlins Pension S21934), and Robert Roberts (Roberts Pension S9468).

62 Bass 1959:105; Jenkins 1842:18.

63 Bass 1959:105. John Rice probably was stationed at this redoubt. He says that he was stationed for two months "at a small redoubt on Great Pee Dee" under John Munnerlyn and Colonel John Ervin. This could be the Port's Ferry redoubt or the Dunham's Bluff redoubt. Unfortunately, Rice's chronology is confusing as he says this happened in 1779 and in 1780 he rejoined Marion then went to Wadboo, which event did not occur until 1782 (Rice Pension R8747). More on this detachment and redoubt will be discussed in Chapter 8. William Fullwood stayed at Marion's camp "between great & little peedee, at a place called Brittans Neck. Here we staied perhaps two or three weeks" (Fullwood Pension S18829).

64 L. Munnerlyn A.A. 5399. Several pensioners mention that they specifically joined Marion because it was the only safe place to be from the Loyalists. Jesse White is a typical example. He lived along Jacks Creek a tributary of the Santee. In June 1780, he was taken prisoner by Loyalists and taken to a British camp. The British paroled him and he immediately ran away and joined Marion since the region he lived in was a Loyalist community. He "considered himself safe with Marion" (White Pension S32062). Munnerlyn's account indicates that the camp was not only safe for partisan warriors but also for noncombatants like Munnerlyn's father and mother. It also was safe for British deserters. John Might was born in Prussia (Hessian) and deserted to join Marion (Might Pension W4548). Others who expressed the need to be with Marion for safety include George McCall (McCall Pension R6598) and William Vaughan, who lived along the Charleston to Camden road where "Tories" were numerous (Vaughan Pension W11691).

65 Grice A.A. 4301.

66 Marion to Postell, 30 December 1780, James 1821:Appendix 13. Marion was acting on General Greene's orders to collect boats, but he also may have been acting as a result of his promotion. On 30 December, with a Continental Army back in South Carolina, Governor John Rutledge wrote that he had promoted Marion to Brigadier General in the South Carolina militia and that his command would include militia units east of Santee, Wateree, and Catawba Rivers (Bass 1959:126). The news supposedly arrived 1 January, but it would be in keeping with that promotion that he ordered the scouring of the countryside. From this point on, Marion would slowly return to conventional tactics as he built and trained his brigade, but for the next few months he would still be a guerrilla. This letter is the first one Marion wrote from "Snow's Island." James lists John Postell as a Major while Bass calls him Captain Postell (James 1821:13; Bass 1959:124).

67 Horry and Weems 1809:189.

68 In the introduction to his biography of Francis Marion, James notes that he was left in North Carolina when Marion left White Marsh and did not return to Marion until the campaign against British Colonel John Watson in March 1781, so what he knew about activities in January are secondhand. On the other hand, he may have been on the island, for he was still confined to his sick bed during that campaign as a result of smallpox (James 1821:68).

69 James 1821:69-70.

70 James 1821:71-72. Prior to the war, salt had been imported to the colonies from the Bahamas and war with England had cut the normal supply. It soon became scarce and South Carolina plantations along the coast began producing salt from the sea. Salt was essential health and was used as a meat preservative. Apparently it also was an aid to the digestion as a letter from Daniel Horry to John Gervais noted that eating beef without salt caused "disorders in their bowels" (Horry to Gervais, 15 June 1776, Moultrie Papers, South Caroliniana Library, University of South Carolina [henceforth SCL-USC]). Clearly Marion was using salt as a means of community control, distributing salt to friends and keeping it from his enemies. After the Americans controlled Georgetown in 1781, Marion became the "primary disburser of salt in South Carolina" (Stovall 1971:85). Governor Rutledge granted exemptions from the militia for those producing salt (Stovall 1971:86).

71 Marion to Greene, 1 January 1781, GP-WCL, Vol. 14:4.

72 John Potts may have been one of the people Horry impressed beef from at this time. Potts audited account indicates that on the 1? January 1781, Marion received 13 head of "stears" (John Potts A.A. 6069). He would provide peas, pork, fodder, and 3 more steers that year.

73 Marion to Greene, 9 January 1781, GP-WCL, Vol. 14:37; Marion to Greene, 14 January 1781, GP-WCL, Vol. 15:5.

74 Marion to Greene, 14 January 1781, GP-WCL, Vol. 15:5. Lest one thinks that Georgetown was all Marion had to worry about, he also had detachments along the Santee watching Nelson's Ferry. Others were skirmishing with British detachments (Marion to Greene, 18 January 1781, Francis Marion Papers, SCL-USC).

75 Marion to Greene, 18 January 1781, Francis Marion Papers, SCL-USC. He didn't have to tell Greene about the rising water. Greene wrote General Daniel Morgan that the Pee Dee upstream of Snow's Island had risen 25 feet in 30 hours that week (Greene to Morgan, 19 January 1781, GP, Vol. VII:147).

76 This ferry is just south of where the Little and Great Pee Dee Rivers converge near modern Yauhannah, South Carolina.

77 Marion to Postell, 19 January 1781, James 1821:Appendix, 14-15. Marion followed this letter with another short one to Postell, informing him that his father could keep his canoe (Marion to Postell, 19 January 1781, James 1821:15).

78 Marion to Greene, 20 January 1781, GP, Vol.VII:165; Marion to Greene, 20 January 1781, LOC-GP.

79 Greene to Marion, 23 January 1781, GP, Vol. VII:173.

80 Wright 2000:160-163. Lee immediately wrote to Greene, informing him that he [Lee] had a new "plan too long to explain." The letterhead was "Marion's Camp," which historians have interpreted as being the Snow's Island camp. It is also possible that Marion had moved to Mrs Port's at the ferry or was at Goddard's Plantation on the ridge above Snow's Island (see Chapter 8). At the end of the letter, Lee asked for a reinforcement of 60 infantry and directs them to "take post at Mr. Benjamin Ports, where he will find a party of horse. Mr. Port lives on the east side of the Peedee" (Lee to Greene, 23 January 1781, GP-WCL, Vol. 16:28). This would have been close to the redoubt built in September 1780.

81 Marion to Postell, 23 January 1781, James 1821: Appendix, 17-18; Lee to Greene 25 January 1781, GP, Vol. VII:197-198; Lee 1812:223-225; Bass 1959:136-137. After going into camp on Snow's Island, British correspondence concerning Marion's activities drops almost completely, as if he had dropped off the face of the earth. Part of this was because they were much more concerned about Daniel Morgan in the upstate. While undoubtedly there was some concern, I can only find one letter from Colonel Nisbet Balfour, the British Commandant in Charleston that mentions Marion in January. In that letter Balfour reports Marion and Lee's raids calling Lee and Marion "Two very enterprising Officers" (Balfour to Clinton, 31 January 1781, CP, P.R.O. 30/11/109:9-10). Several Snow's Island community partisans recall being in the attack against Georgetown, however, since Marion attacked the town several times before capturing it, and the pension accounts are usually vague in terms of time frame, those individuals are not listed here.

82 Lee to Greene, 27 January 1780, GP, Vol. VII:206; Benjamin Port A.A. 6030; Greaves A.A. 3057; G. Witherspoon A.A. 8690; Abram Giles A.A. 2816 (The date on this account is 7 February 1780, but must be 1781 since the provisions were for "use of Partizan Legion by Lt Colonel Lee"; Frances Port A.A. 6031; Hugh Ervin A.A. 2236a.

83 Lee to Greene, 3 February 1781, GP, Vol. VII:247.

84 Marion to John Postell, 29 January 1781, James 1821:Appendix 20-21; Marion to Greene 31 January 1781, GP, Vol. VII:230. These two raids were led by John and James Postell.

85 Gray 1910:148.

86 Marion to Greene, 2 February 1781, GP, Vol. VII:239; Marion to Brigadier General Isaac Huger, 6 February 1781, Francis Marion files, SCL-USC.

87 Rawdon to Cornwallis, 15 February 1781, CP, P.R.O. 30/11/69:23-24.

88 Greene to Marion, 11 February 1780, GP, Vol. VII:281; Rawdon to Cornwallis, 7 March 1781, CP, P.R.O. 30/11/69:12-13.

89 O'Kelley 2006:513. All brigades, regiments, and companies maintained an orderly book, which published General Orders of the day, passwords for the day, promotions and demotions, punishments and other information. Francis Marion's Orderly books exist for the period from June 1775 (2nd South Carolina) to 28 December 1779 and 15 February 1781 to 15 December 1782. The gap, of course, includes the period when Charleston fell and Marion was a partisan. Once he formed his brigade, Marion returned to keeping an orderly book. Each entry included a location for the entry, which was usually the brigade headquarters location, or at least the location of the adjutant. It was not necessarily, but usually, the location where Marion was physically present, and it is very useful for keeping track of Marion's movements when nothing else is available. The original orderly book is at the Huntington Library, San Marino, California. I have a copy of this original, but for ease of citation, I will usually cite O'Kelley's transcription (O'Kelley 2006).

90 Bass 1959:140-141.

91 There is a receipt for "84 bushels of corn" from Wm James Cooper signed by Marion 19 February 1781, at "Camp peedee river" (Libbie & Co. 1895; Francis Marion Files, SCL-USC).

92 Horry to Saunders, 22 February 1781, Saunders Papers, address "Pee Dee"; O'Kelley 2006:513-515, 517, 697; Frierson 1999:4; Linder and Thacker 2001:321; Marion to Saunders, 24 February 1781, Saunders Papers; Gibbes 1853:26-27; Marion to Sumter, 26 February 1781, Gimelson 2007. Gimelson is a website for an auction house that was selling the letter. Sometime in February 1781, Marion burned a boat owned by Thomas Potts (Potts A.A. 6071; S.I. R293). Since Pott's Plantation was somewhere along Black River and "near Pee Dee" it may have been at this time that he did so. Why he did so is not known but may have had to do with protecting a river crossing.

93 Rawdon to Cornwallis, 7 March 1781, CP, P.R.O. 30/11/69:12-15. While camped at Salem, Marion published a proclamation against looting along the Santee. According to the proclamation, there were parties not associated with his brigade who were responsible. He promised to publish the plunderers' names, after which, it would be lawful for anyone who found them to "put them to Death" without being "called to account" (O'Kelley 2006:518).

94 O'Kelley 2006:520. Much of what we know about the location of Marion during this campaign is due to a series of letters he exchanged with Watson and British commanders in Georgetown and Charleston. Marion and the Georgetown commandant Colonel John Saunders had been negotiating a prisoner exchange since 22 February. While Watson and Marion parried on the battlefield, letters flew back and forth concerning a prisoner exchange gone bad. Captain John Postell had escorted prisoners from Snow's Island to Georgetown. Unfortunately, the British recognized Postell and seized him. Postell had been paroled when Charleston fell and was under obligation to remain on his plantation. From Postell's perspective, the British had broken the terms of the parole when they had seized his plantation in January (although he had been fighting for Marion for some time prior) (Bass 1959:130). Both sides claimed that the other was violating "the laws of nations" (Marion to Watson, 7 March 1781, Gibbes 1853:30). To read the exchange between Marion and Watson see Gibbes 1853:26-38.

95 Watson, undated, Clinton Papers, Volume 232:21, WCL; Rawdon to Cornwallis, 7 March 1781, CP, P.R.O. 30/11/69:12-15.

96 Boatner 1966:677; Dornfest 1997:225; O'Kelly 2006:518-519; Rankin 1973:166; Marion to Lt. Col. Balfour, March 7th, 1781, Gibbes 1853:29.

97 Col. Watson to Marion, 7 March 1781, Gibbes 1853:29; Col. Watson to Marion, 9 March 1781, Gibbes 1853:33.

98 Rankin 1973:168; James 1821:101-102; Marion to Watson, 16 March 1781, Gibbes 1853:41.

99 Rankin 1973:173-174; Watson to Saunders, 21 March 1781, Saunders Papers.

100 There is no direct evidence that Miscally guided Colonel Doyle to Snow's Island. But I know he was a British guide and he lived just west of Snow's Island. He would have known the island and the British knew Marion's camp was somewhere on the island. Miscally paid for being a British guide with his life. He was recognized and hung for his deeds at Fort Motte when the fort was captured by Marion and Lee in May 1780 (Smith et al. 2007a:28).

101 Marion biographers usually discuss the Bridges Campaign as a two-pronged assault against Marion and the depot on Snow's Island (James 1821:98; Bass 1959:143). That is, they write that Rawdon simultaneously ordered Watson and Doyle to march for Snow's Island. The traditional interpretation is that Marion was so focused on Watson he totally missed Doyle's approach. But this explanation requires a major failure of his usual highly efficient intelligence network. Two other possibilities exist. First, give credit to the British, they kept their intentions hidden. Colonel Balfour in Charleston wrote someone, probably Colonel Saunders in Georgetown on 5 March that "As you will observe, a movement is intended against Marrion, as little intelligence as is possible should be given of the movement" (Balfour to ?, 5 March 1781, Saunders Papers). Second, in Rawdon's letter to Cornwallis on 7 March, he states that Watson is "press[ing]" Marion (see above). Much later, on the 24 March, Rawdon writes Cornwallis again, and this time states that "Lt Cols Watson & Doyle with separate Corps are now hurrying Marion" (Rawdon to Cornwallis, 24 March 1781, CP, P.R.O. 30/11/69:21-24). The most likely reason Marion did not know about Doyle was that the British did not plan a two-pronged assault. Indeed, Doyle did not set out for Snow's Island until 22 March, much later than Watson (Nase, 22 March 1781). I believe Doyle's march to Snow's Island was the result of intelligence gained from Hugh Miscally. If so, Marion's scouts would have had much less time to discover Doyle and report to Marion. We can speculate even further, that Miscally arrived in Camden during the Watson campaign and offered his guide services to Rawdon, who immediately jumped on the opportunity to sneak in the backdoor to Marion's camp.

102 Simms 1844:222; Bass 1959:156-157; David Witherspoon A.A. 8689.

103 Historians even differ on exactly when it occurred. The chronology of events of Watson's move from Blakely's Plantation until 13 April when Lee returned to South Carolina and rejoined Marion is horribly confused between the few primary sources and various secondary accounts. Unfortunately, this is not only the time period in which the Snow's Island camp was destroyed, but shortly thereafter, British Colonel Watson marched through the Snow's Island community. What follows is the best that can be sorted at this time.

104 *Royal Gazette,* 5 April 1781.

105 *The Royal Georgia Gazette*, 12 April 1781.

106 Balfour to Saunders, 2 April 1781, Saunders Papers I have made considerable effort to find Rawdon's letter to Balfour to no avail. If Balfour or Rawdon passed the news up the chain of command, no record of it is in the British Headquarters Papers, P.R.O.

107 James 1821:104.

108 Jenkins 1842: 19; Simcoe 1844; Jenkins 1842. Under the rules of war, Merritt's flag should have been honored and that includes safe passage.

109 Simcoe 1844:244-246; Balfour to Saunders, 2 April 1781, Saunders Papers.

110 Bass 1959:156-157; Rankin 1973:175-176; Simms 1844:222-223.

111 There is a tradition that a detachment of Marion's partisans chased Doyle to Willow Grove, just north of Lynchburg, South Carolina, where they fought Doyle. I am skeptical. As far as I can tell the tradition originated in a story by Colonel J.A. Rhame, entitled "The Battle of Willow Grove," published by the Daughters of the American Revolution (Rhame 1915). Rhame's account does not jive with William Dobein James or any other accounts, admittedly vague, about Doyle's raid on the Snow's Island camp. For instance, he says that the British were "found quietly in possession of the camp" and surprised by Marion. The detachment under Captains Nelson and Conyers chased Doyle to Willow Grove, where they engaged in a day long battle, only ended by nightfall. The British hid in a log fort, which the author, as a boy, used to dig out musket balls embedded in the fort walls for small shot. Rhame dates the battle to 8 March 1781, which does not fit with numerous primary sources of the British campaign against Snow's Island. John C. Parker in his *Guide to the Revolutionary War In South Carolina* (2013:309) states that it occurred on 6 April. Henry Nase's eyewitness diary, however, indicates that Doyle arrived back at Camden on 1 April, with 14 prisoners (Nase, 1 April 1781). John Oller dates the battle to 30 March (Oller 2016:30). This does not fit the timeline I have hypothesized either (see below, endnote 112). Perhaps an archaeological study could determine if this battle occurred or not.

112 James 1821:105; Bass 1959:169. The sequence of events surrounding the end of the Watson campaign, the destruction of the Snow's Island camp, and the chase of Doyle are difficult to unravel. Marion's orderly book entry for 11 March puts the headquarters at "Glover's Plant. Peedee" (O'Kelley 2006:521). The next entry is 24 March at "Peedee" (O'Kelley 2006:524). Both of these are probably Joseph Glover's Enfield Plantation along the Pee Dee near modern Plantersville, South Carolina (Linder and Thacker 2001:321). The next entry is Burch's Mill on 1 April the following week (O'Kelley 2006:525). The 1 April date seems accurate for Marion being at Burch's. Robert Bass quotes a letter from Watson saying he will be in Georgetown "this afternoon" and Bass dates the letter on 28 March, implying that the Sampit River battle did not occur until around the 27th. This date is probably incorrect. The letter is undated in Gibbes, however, in the Peter Force Papers, Library of Congress, the letter is dated the 20th. This is in sequence with the 21 March letter in Saunders that has Watson at Trapier's Plantation just outside Georgetown and across the Sampit. So the affair at the Sampit Bridge has to be around the 20th. Thus, Marion was on the move toward Snow's Island after the 21st. Most historians have placed the Snow's Island skirmish around 28 or 29 March, which I believe to be the result of their reading Evan Pugh's diary (Rudisill 1993). Evan Pugh, a minister on the upper Pee Dee, wrote in his diary on 28 March "Marion's camp taken", and on the 31st that the British were at Burch's (Rudisill 1993:205). This assumes that Pugh had instant news. More likely a few days passed before he learned of the attack. For instance, he learned of the 12 May British evacuation of Camden on 15 May. Also, Marion dispatched Peter Horry southward to make a swing around Wadboo, Goose Creek and Moncks Corner to gather intelligence on 28 March 1781. Since Horry was involved in chasing Doyle, the Snow's Island attack had to be before 28 March (Marion to Horry, 28 March 1781, Horry Collection in Peter Force Papers, LOC). The best timeline with the least conflicting data is that the Sampit Bridge battle occurred on 19 or 20 March. Doyle attacked Snow's Island sometime between the 24th and 27th, Marion crossed Lynches Creek, and Doyle retreated all before 28 March. The 11 and 24 March entries in the orderly book indicate that Marion was keeping his headquarters at Glover's Plantation while he was in the field against Watson.

113 F.M. Orderly Book, 1 April 1781, Huntington Library. At Burch's that day, Marion signed a receipt to John Dozier who gave up 117 bushels of corn for Marion's command (Dozier A.A. 2022). The following day, Frances Port added 10 bushels of corn (F. Port A.A. 6032). On the 5th, John Ervin added seven head of hogs (J. Ervin A.A. 2237).

114 F.M. Orderly Book, 1 April 1781, Huntington Library.

115 Watson to Saunders, 16 April 1781, Saunders Papers.

116 Watson to ?, undated, Clinton Papers, Vol. 232:21 WCL. James has Watson crossing the Pee Dee at Yauhannah Ferry and the Little Pee Dee at Potato Bed Ferry onto Britton's Neck (James 1821:106). This is incorrect.

117 Jenkins 1842:25.

118 Watson to Saunders, 16 April 1781, Saunders Papers; Jenkins 1842:27; James 1821:106.

119 James 1821:106.

120 Watson to Saunders, 16 April 1780, Saunders Papers.

121 Watson to ?, undated, Clinton Papers, WCL.

122 Conyers to Pierce, 21 April 1781, GP-WCL.

CHAPTER 7
MARION AND GREENE

The return of the General Nathanael Greene and his Continental Army to South Carolina and Cornwallis's march northward to Virginia marked the beginning of the end for British domination in South Carolina. From this point on, the Americans were on the offensive. Marion coordinated closely with Greene, both strategically and tactically as a regular officer. Marion's role grew, eventually controlling all of the South Carolina militia and overseeing the defense, administration, and government of a large military district that included Cheraw, Georgetown, and Charleston civilian district.[1] Marion was no longer a partisan-guerrilla, although he still made use of tactics like ambush and raid.

While these events had several profound implications, for the purposes of this book, the most important was that Marion no longer needed Snow's Island as a safe retreat for his partisans. Nevertheless, the Snow's Island community still supported Marion and a militia presence was maintained in the region under his general oversight. Marion made at least one visit to the region after April 1781.

As the British abandoned or lost their backcountry outposts and were forced to retreat to Charleston, most of the war's action was confined to the Charleston region. From this point on, the Snow's Island community experienced peace, except for a few Loyalist raids, which decreased after the Loyalists signed a truce with Marion.

This chapter summarizes Marion's maneuvers during the remainder of the war with the purpose of demonstrating how the Snow's Island community continued their support of the American cause.

14 APRIL 1781 TO JULY 1781

For a moment, the British Colonel Watson must have enjoyed feelings of victory and revenge. After being battered by Marion, he had invaded and scattered the Snow's Island Whigs. Doyle had destroyed Marion's depot, and the Loyalist militia were pouring into Watson's camp, "and of a kind too, who when collected, even by themselves not the least afraid of Marion, would restore, if not quiet at least our Supremacy in that District." Then his world quickly changed. His intelligence learned that Lee had joined Marion. Furthermore, the Whig militia in Cheraw was assembling, having heard that Greene was on the march and that, astonishingly, Lord Cornwallis "had quitted the Province." With the road west to Camden blocked and thinking that Marion and Lee were going for Georgetown again, Watson retreated southward. He took a different route on his return—instead of crossing at Britton's Ferry, he angled southeast and crossed the Little Pee Dee at Potato Bed Ferry. The fifty-mile march took him closer to friendly Loyalist communities on the other side of the Little Pee Dee, and he arrived along the Waccamaw on 19 April.[2]

As he marched southward, he experienced the frustration Marion had felt for the last year. The Loyalist militia had melted away while the Snow's Island community reformed under Marion. The Loyalists at least took Watson up on his offer for them to return to the cultivation of their lands.

Marion and Henry Lee joined forces on 14 April 1781. Reinforced, Marion left one officer north of the Snow's Island region to watch Watson and gather cattle, another to disperse the Loyalists in route to join Watson,[3] and another to go down to the lower part of South Carolina near Beaufort. With Watson in Georgetown and Greene threatening Camden, British posts along the Santee River were exposed and blocking the Santee would cut the British supply line between Charleston and Camden. When Greene ordered Lee to join Marion, he did not want them to go after Georgetown as Watson believed, but instead, attack the British posts along the Santee, including Fort Watson (Figure 6.2), which they did—Lee and Marion marched to the Santee River and surrounded Fort Watson on 15 April.[4]

Watson had built the fort on an Indian mound and it sat 23 feet above the surrounding landscape.[5] After six days, Major Hezekiah Maham of Marion's brigade suggested that they build a tower to fire down into the fort. This brilliant tactic resulted in a British surrender on 23 April.[6] The capture of Fort Watson included the capture of a large store of ammunition, which Marion would soon used to capture Fort Motte. Two days later, Greene and Rawdon clashed at Hobkirk's Hill just north of Camden. Greene retreated, but the British suffered significant casualties.⁷

It is not known what occurred in the Snow's Island region during this time, however it appears that it was being patrolled by Marion's mounted detachments. Evidence for this comes from the audited account of Major John James. On 18 April, James provided 30 horsemen (a company), 30 horse provisions, and forage. On the 20th he provided dinner for 70 men. The next day he provided dinner for 28 men and on the 24th "Supper" for 20 men. A few days later he added pork and 12 bushels of corn. It is logical to assume that this detachment was camped at his plantation in northeastern Williamsburg Township. This was not the only time that the plantation was used. James provided two meals for 20 men on 8 July and again on 16 July. He provided Colonel Horry's dragoon recruits with breakfast on 12 September 1781. Nor was he stingy in providing food and forage for various troops throughout 1781, including bacon, flour, corn, pork, rice meal, beef, bread, fodder, and potatoes.⁸

By early May, the strategic situation was desperate for the British. Rawdon had been weakened by the recent Battle of Hobkirk's Hill (Camden, South Carolina) and needed Colonel Watson to reinforce him in Camden. Lee and Marion had moved to the High Hills of the Santee, effectively blocking Watson's path to Camden. But then, Marion and Lee, looking for Watson, marched back to Fort Watson and crossed the Santee.

They just missed him. Watson had left Georgetown, crossed the Santee at Lenud's Ferry and marched to Monck's Corner. Picking up additional troops, he marched up the west side of the Santee and crossed again to the east side near the confluence of the Wateree and Congaree at the less-used Buchenham's Ferry. He joined Rawdon in Camden on May 7th.⁹

Once across the Santee, Marion and Lee decided to attack Fort Motte, another outpost like Fort Watson, that protected the British supply line, located at the confluence of the Congaree and Wateree Rivers (not depicted). This siege lasted from 6 May to 12 May.¹⁰

This time the fort was taken by fire. The Americans dug a ditch to the fort's exterior and then shot flaming arrows on the roof of the Motte house that stood in the center of the fort. William Dobein James states that it was Snow's Island community member Nathan Savage who threw a rosin ball up on the roof to start the fire,¹¹ and when the roof caught fire, the British had to surrender.

Marion suffered two deaths, Lieutenants McDonald and Cruger, but unlucky John Booth was again wounded in the leg. After the siege, three Loyalists were hung, Lieutenant Fulker, John Jackson, and as already mentioned, Snow's Island neighbor, Hugh Miscally.[12]

Meanwhile, in Camden, Rawdon decided to abandon the backcountry. By 14 May, he was safe across the Santee at Nelson's Ferry. Marion and Lee split at this point and Lee moved north to capture Fort Granby. This fort, located in modern Cayce/West Columbia, was yet another British outpost along the supply line.

During the siege of Fort Motte, Greene and South Carolina came close to losing Francis Marion. Since Greene's arrival, the commanding general had been prodding Marion to supply horses to the Continental Army. Greene, alarmed by the amount of forage needed to supply his mounted militia, but recognizing the necessity of a cavalry force to screen his infantry and provide intelligence, decided that the best thing to do was to dismount the militia and use their horses to form a regular cavalry force. As has been noted previously, Marion was constantly irritated by the militia's coming and going and his inability to keep a sizable force in the field. Many of Marion's men had again left him after Fort Watson fell and he knew that dismounting his partisans would not only exacerbate the situation, but also knew they would desert to a man. By the opening day of the siege, Marion had reached a boiling point. When he received another request for horses from Greene, he fired back:

> I acknowledge that you have repeatedly mention [sic] the want of Dragoon horses & wish it had been in my power to furnh them but it is not nor never had been….but if you think it best for the service to Dismount the Malitia now with me I will Direct Col Lee & Cap Conyers to do so, but am sertain we shall never git their service in the future. This would not give me any uneasiness as I have somtime Determin to relinquish my command in the malitia as soon as you arrived in it & I wish to do it as soon as this post is Either taken or abandoned.[13]

Marion added that it was his intent to go to Philadelphia after the siege. Greene, realizing that he had pressed Marion too far, backed off and rushed to Fort Motte.

After the siege, Marion and Greene met face to face for the first time. Whatever Greene said, Marion stayed with the militia. Perhaps Greene offered him a chance at his favorite target—Georgetown—because shortly thereafter, Marion marched to the town and, after 10 months, was finally able to report its capture on 28 May 1781.[14]

In early June, Greene moved against one of the few remaining British strongholds in the backcountry at Ninety Six, South Carolina, and Marion was ordered to move westward and join Sumter. Many Pee Dee militiamen were reluctant to leave their region to assist Sumter, but Marion left Georgetown in charge of Peter Horry and detached several units from his brigade across the Lowcountry. While he moved his mounted troops to central South Carolina, he sent Maham to the Goose Creek region to skirmish with British foragers and drive away cattle. He also sent Colonel Horry up the Pee Dee to "quell" the Loyalists there under Ganey.[15]

The Loyalists along the Little Pee Dee, Drowning Creek, and upper Cheraw had been a constant irritant to Marion and the Snow's Island community since the fall of 1780. As James noted, Marion "could not well turn his arms against him [Ganey], and the whig settlements were left exposed to his depreciations."[16] Loyalist Robert Gray noted:

> They carried on a continual predatory war against the rebels & sometimes surprised them at their musters. In short, they carried on the war against the rebels precisely as they had set the example & as the post at George Town supplied them with arms & ammunition they overawed & harassed Marion' brigade so much that he was obliged to leave the inhabitants of the Cheraw District at home to protect their properties while he could only call out the people of Williamsburg Township & the neighborhood of George Town…
>
> It may not be improper to observe here that the Rebel Militia did not at all times turn out voluntarily under their leaders, for when they were averse to an expedition they compelled them on pain of death.[17]

By this time, though, the fortunes of war dictated that the Loyalists seek another alternative than harassment. Marion, likewise, needed his strategic rear to be secured. So, when Marion ordered Horry to "quell" the Loyalists, he did not mean attack. Instead, Horry and British Loyalist Major Micajah Ganey met and negotiated a truce.

Under the terms of the truce, the Loyalists and the Snow's Island community would cease hostilities. Further, any complaint of "injuries," which would include not only violence but plundering and such, would be adjudicated by a jury consisting of both Whigs and Loyalists, and any plunder would be restored.

The agreement was to last three months. After three months, Ganey agreed to a 12-month extension of the truce, although he stated he could in no way restore any property that the British themselves had taken. It is probable that the Loyalists in northeastern South Carolina realized that the British were not likely to return to the backcountry and were wisely attempting to mitigate the likely outcome of an eventual American victory in South Carolina.

For the Snow's Island community, the truce meant that incursions by Loyalist bands were less likely and they were encouraged not to take advantage of the situation. Marion, in support of the Continental Army's logistical needs, ordered the command at Georgetown to gather salt and secure it various places along the Pee Dee, primarily to be used in preparing salted beef for the army. However, Marion probably distributed some to the Snow's Island community as he had before.[18]

Through June 1781, Greene pressed the British at Ninety Six. Hearing that Lord Rawdon was on his way with a relief force, Greene made an all-out assault on Ninety Six and was repulsed. Greene lifted the siege and Lord Rawdon relieved the fort—only to abandon it and retreat to the Charleston region. Greene chided both Sumter and Marion for failing to join him in the siege.[19]

In early July 1781, Marion sought out a British column attempting to join Lord Rawdon, who was then retreating toward Charleston. He missed the British detachment, allowing the two British forces to link up at Orangeburg, South Carolina. Greene appeared, but the British were content to stay behind the fortifications at Orangeburg. Already wearied by the Ninety Six siege, Greene decided to fall back to the High Hills of the Santee. Then Sumter came up with an idea that, perhaps had it not been proffered by Sumter, would have been a good idea.[20]

Sumter convinced Greene that, with Lee and Marion's forces, he could raid the zone around Charleston and Moncks Corner, cutting off the British in Orangeburg from those in Charleston. Historian William Gilmore Simms would label this campaign the "Raid of the Dog Days" as it took place during the hottest part of the year.[21]

Reluctantly, Marion followed Sumter's orders. The American detachments met their objectives and, as planned, met at Moncks Corner to encounter a detachment of British under the command of Colonel John Coates. Coates marched toward the safety of Charleston, but Lee caught up with the British rear guard at Quinby Bridge. Coates's main body was able to secure themselves at Shubrick's Plantation on 17 July 1781 and Marion and Lee decided that the British were too well posted in the plantation's outbuildings to attack without heavy losses.

Unfortunately, when Sumter arrived, he ordered them to charge and they did so to their regret. Exposed in an open field, Marion's men stood their ground but were cut down. Losses were exceedingly heavy and both Marion and Lee were convinced they were entirely needless.[22] Marion's men were furious, and having been reduced to 100 men, he left Sumter immediately, marching 15 miles that evening and retiring the next day to Peyre's Plantation.

AUGUST 1781 TO DECEMBER 1782

In August 1781, John Rutledge returned from a trip he had taken to Philadelphia. With the British now bottled up in Charleston, it seemed time to reestablish a sitting South Carolina government. In one of Rutledge's first official acts, he issued a proclamation against plundering Loyalist property. The proclamation essentially struck down a previous practice of General Sumter's—to recruit soldiers by offering them slaves from Loyalist plantations as a reward for service—and Sumter resigned. One year earlier, Marion had taken charge of a rabble of partisans at Witherspoon's Ferry. Now he was the commander of the entire South Carolina militia.[23]

On 22 August, Marion marched south of Charleston to aid another militia commander, Colonel William Harden. For a week, he maneuvered in the Green Pond, South Carolina, region looking for an opportunity.

Then, on 30 August, Marion set up one of the most daring ambushes of his career. At Parker's Ferry, South Carolina, he placed himself between two enemy forces, one camped at the ferry and another marching up the road to join it. A coordinated attack could have surrounded Marion and destroyed him, but instead, Marion defeated both in turn.[24]

Meanwhile, Greene marched down the western side of the Santee. At his front was a large force of British under the command of Colonel Alexander Stewart. Stewart gave ground before Greene and camped at Eutaw Springs, South Carolina (Figure 6.2). Marion and Greene joined forces at Lauren's Plantation above Eutaw Springs, and together the combined forces marched downstream. The following day, 8 September 1781, Marion found himself commanding the front line of an American force of over 2,200 men. Facing him were 1,900 British. With American regulars in support behind him, this front line, consisting of the same panic-prone partisans Marion had dealt with for a year, stood and fired 17 rounds before retiring in order. The Americans eventually were forced to retreat, but again, like at Guilford Court House, North Carolina, and Hobkirk's Hill, South Carolina, British casualties were high and not easily replaced. The Battle of Eutaw Springs was the last major engagement of the war in South Carolina. But another Snow's Island community member was lost. The Reverend Jenkins lost his cousin John.[25]

Marion returned to the Santee region after Eutaw Springs. Many militiamen returned home, as usual, after the battle. On the same day that Marion was commanding the front line at Eutaw Springs, Loyalist Major Ganey wrote Marion that all was not well in the northeastern corner of South Carolina. He was having a dispute with the notorious Colonel Murphy.[26] This Whig militia officer had gained a reputation for plundering the previous fall, and now he and Ganey were accusing each other of not living up to the terms of the truce. Murphy would not turn over a horse owned by Ganey until Ganey found and returned horses that the Loyalists had taken. Ganey also noted that other horses, "negroes and a number of cows" were also being detained.[27]

How Marion reacted is not known, but at the end of September, North Carolina Loyalists began to gather strength and their raids pushed into South Carolina, further threatening the peace in the Snow's Island community. Peter Horry marched to Lynches Lake, a branch of Lynches Creek, just west of Witherspoon's Ferry on the western edge of the Snow's Island community (Figure 4.2). There, on 20 September, he wrote General Greene that Whigs on the Pee Dee and at Long Bluff (along the Pee Dee north of Jeffries Creek) were requesting Marion's return. That same day Major James wrote Marion that some Loyalists had ridden through the heart of the Snow's Island community. "A small party came down Britton's neck, and carried off some horses; they took off all Mr. Gibson's." Furthermore, Major Ganey was being pressured to join the other Loyalists, seize prominent Whigs, and send them to Wilmington, which was still in British hands. Before any response could be made, Horry wrote that the Loyalist threat had been lessened for the moment as a result of a clash between Loyalists and Americans at Lindley Mill, North Carolina, where the Loyalists had been defeated.[28]

At the same time the South Carolina governor issued another proclamation providing a full pardon to the Loyalists if they would surrender themselves within 30 days. Ironically, they would only receive the pardon if they served six months militia duty—afterwards they could return to their homes. It was ironic because a year before, the British had offered similar terms to the Whigs and the Whigs were outraged that they had to turn on their friends and could not simply return to the peace of their homes.[29]

Events far to the north helped seal the eventual American victory in South Carolina. Lord Cornwallis surrendered his army on 20 October 1781. The war was practically over, but it would take another 14 months before the British would evacuate Charleston, and more would die on both sides.[30]

Through the fall of 1781, Marion hovered along the northern bank of the Santee, camping occasionally at Peyre's Plantation, Cantey's Plantation, and Murray's Ferry.[31] While along the Santee, he continued to send detachments towards Charleston to watch the British and harass foragers.

Typical of many late war skirmishes and actions was American Colonel Hezekiah Maham's raid on British occupied Fairlawn Plantation (Figure 7.1) in November 1781. He burned the mansion, captured those sick soldiers who could walk and sent the others to a nearby fort. The British in the fort did not try to attack, believing Maham's force was too strong.[32]

What exactly was happening within the Snow's Island community at this time is unknown. What *is* known is that throughout the two years, they

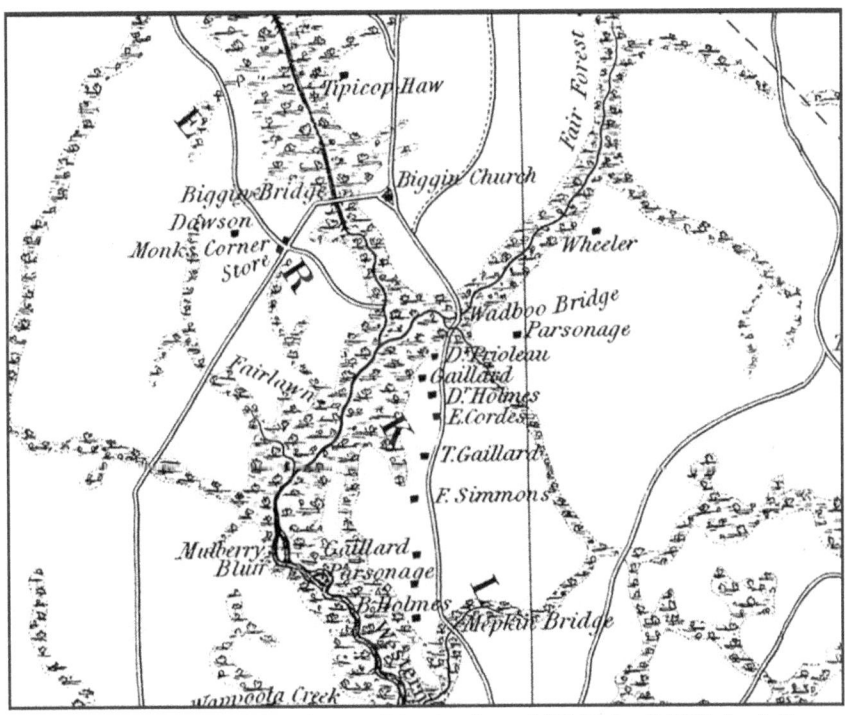

Figure 7.1. Detail of Charleston District from *Mills' Atlas* (1825) depicting location of Fairlawn, Moncks Corner, and Wadboo Plantation

continued to support the Whig cause with provisions. For example, Table 7.1 provides a short list of supplies received by Marion or Greene over the course of the period from 1780 to 1782. The exact dates of the transactions are not precisely known, except in one case.

Table 7.1. Supplies received from Snow's Island community

Name	Date	Items	Source
Thomas Potts & Hugh Thompson's estate[33]	1781 & 1782	Sundries for Continental and state use	S.I. H228
Joseph Greaves	26 Nov 1781	350 wt beef	A.A. 3057
William Snow	1781	825 wt beef	A.A. 7197
William Shaw	No date	Wagon and team	S.I. X1604
Estate of Francis Goddard	1781, 1782	Provisions and supplies militia and Continental use 20 beaves to state	S.I. 6200
	No date		S.I. C390
John Dunnam	1780	1 steer	A.A. 2098
Charles Fladger	1779, 1780, 1781, 1782	Provisions and forage for Continental and militia	S.I. P381
Robert Nettles	1781	1920 wt beef	A.A. 5490
George Nettles	1780	320 wt beef	S.S. N593
Zachariah Nettles	1780	5290 wt beef Continental use	S.I. N592

According to Loyalist Robert Gray, there was still strong Loyalist support in the backcountry. It was in this context that Robert Gray wrote that the "whole province resembled a piece of patchwork, the inhabitants of every settlement, when united in sentiment being in arms for the side they liked best & making continual inroads into one another's settlements."[34]

During that same month [November 1781], General Greene and Governor Rutledge decided it was time to restore civil government in South Carolina. They chose Jacksonboro, 35 miles outside of Charleston on the Edisto River, as the location to hold the first session.

Marion was elected to the state senate and, in mid-January 1782, took his seat, having turned over his regiment to Colonel Horry. Without his presence, an on-going dispute between two of his subordinates, Colonel Horry and Hezekiah Maham, nearly ruined Marion's brigade. The two officers had been bickering for over a year and when Marion put Horry in command, Maham rejected his authority, claiming that he was the senior officer. Horry was also worn out and wanted Marion to return to command the brigade, but Marion was unable to leave the senate. The bickering continued into February.[35]

Meanwhile, along the border, North Carolina Loyalists continued to cross the state line and intrude upon the peace between the Snow's Island community and the Little Pee Dee and upper Pee Dee Loyalists. Major Ganey again wrote Marion at the end of January about the situation. Exactly what was said is not known, as the letter is only referenced in correspondence between Horry and Marion.[36]

The problem continued through February, and by March, Thomas Burke, the North Carolina governor, wrote to John Mathews, the new South Carolina governor, complaining that Loyalists along the Little Pee Dee were using the South Carolina neutral zone as a refuge, from which they could raid North Carolina and return across the line to hide under the protection of the truce established between Ganey and Marion. Burke requested the cooperation of Marion to "take measures" to stop these "outlaws, … remorseless plunderers and murderers."[37] Mathews passed Governor Burke's letter on to Marion with the hope that Ganey was not, in fact, sheltering these Loyalists. Both governors knew that Marion and Ganey were in touch, and as they did not trust Ganey, were subtly saying to Marion that the Loyalist was his problem.

It is possible that these troubles kept the local militia in the field under Colonel Baxter. On the 10 December 1781, for instance, James Snow provided 1,590 wt beef, (8 head cattle) and on the 10th of January he provided 1,250 bushels of rough rice and 69 bushels of clean rice for the use of Marion's brigade. On the 13th the total included 700 lbs beef, 14 bushels of clean rice, and 470 of something else (unreadable) for Colonel Baxter. On the 20th or 30th, he provided 3 pecks of clean rice and a small hog for troops "on their way to camp from an outpost; being a part of Marion's Brig." The next month, on 16 February, James entertained 17 men and horses for a day and a night, providing forage. Meanwhile, Hugh Ervin provided 3 bushels of corn and 1,200 wt of pork (12 hogs) on 10 December 1781 and would add another 450 wt of pork (5 hogs) on 22 March 1782. These indicate that an active force was still in the Snow's Island region gathering cattle and keeping an eye on the Loyalists.[38]

Hostilities along the Little Pee Dee would continue; eventually Marion would have to deal with it in June. But Marion had other problems to solve first. His brigade was camped at Wambaw, South Carolina, and on 25 February 1782, they were surprised by a large detachment of British.

Marion learned that the British were on the move but arrived too late. He immediately took what men he had and went in search of them. Following a lead, he marched along the south side of the Santee downstream and eventually arrived at Tidyman's Plantation (Figure 6.1). While he and his men were resting, the British appeared and Marion, trapped against the river, had no option except to attack. But for some reason (one officer blamed Marion for giving the wrong order) his cavalry drew off instead of charging. His main line collapsed, and some were pushed into the river. Marion escaped and rallied some men, but the British thought that he had drowned.[39]

After the Tidyman's disaster, Francis Marion returned to the Santee, where he was better positioned to both watch the British in Charleston and protect Georgetown. While Georgetown was in American hands, the British were constantly threatening the town.

There had been discussions about fortifying the port town but Marion thought it could not be done, advising that Black Mingo, along Black Mingo Creek, was a safer place to keep supplies. Besides being a deep, narrow stream, it was difficult to approach by land requiring the passage of three rivers—the Santee, Pee Dee, and Waccamaw. Furthermore, Marion for the first time, paid tribute to the people there, including those near Snow's Island, saying: "around that spot is inhabited by our best Citizens, my Old first followers." This is the first time Marion publicly recognized the Snow's Island community for their support.[40]

March and April 1782 were relatively peaceful. Marion hovered along the Santee and/or Cooper Rivers watching the British. At the end of March, Marion wrote that Ganey "is Yett quiet" and had gone to North Carolina. Apparently, Ganey and Marion had been corresponding, and Ganey had promised to deal with those North Carolina Loyalists hiding along the Little Pee Dee and Drowning Creek (Lumber River). But Ganey was too weak to resist the North Carolina Loyalists under David Fanning and was coerced into taking up arms again.

Thus, Marion was ordered back to his old haunt, the Snow's Island community, to deal with Ganey—either through negotiation or battle. On 2 June 1782, Marion was once again at Witherspoon's Ferry, the place where two years ago he had taken command of the Williamsburg militia.[41] He sent Colonels Horry and Baxter, along with Major James, to find and deliver to Ganey two letters. One was a copy of a letter from the British General in Charleston to Greene, suggesting a cessation of hostilities. This was sent to suggest to Ganey that there were negotiations going on for ending the war. The second was from Marion stating that "I have marched thus far with my brigade, for the purpose of either making terms, or prosecuting the war."

Marion received orders from Governor Mathews on the 23rd of May to meet with Ganey and offer terms, namely that Ganey would lay down arms and go home. Further, Gainey would deliver all slaves, horses, and cattle "plundered from the inhabitants of this or any other State," remain at peace, and obey South Carolina laws for two or three months. He and his followers would then be called to assist the United States, for which they would receive full pardon. If they did not submit, Marion was free to obtain peace through the "force of arms." Marion was immediately on the march and camped at Burch's Mill by the next day.[42]

On 8 June, Ganey and Marion met at Burch's and signed a treaty.[43] On 9 June, Loyalists along Lynches Creek came to Burch's to surrender. By the 16th, many more had come. Those Loyalists who did not want to sign were allowed to go to Charleston to join the British but had to abandon their property.

Ganey was allowed to go to Charleston to resign his commission and return to join Marion. A few former Loyalists followed Ganey and would later join Marion as well. More Loyalists across the Pee Dee held out, so Marion marched north, crossed the Pee Dee at Mars Bluff (north of Jeffries Creek), and made a show of force, after which more Loyalists came in and surrendered.

By 8 July, Marion was back at Murray's Ferry along the Santee.[44] He left behind Colonel Baxter's Britton's Neck militia to "over Awe" those who submitted and seek out those who had not. Among those in Baxter's detachment was young James Jenkins. Jenkins does not mention being at Mars Bluff, however, he does remember camping at Rae's and at the redoubt built by Marion back in September 1780 at Port's Ferry. From there he moved up a few miles but was sent south to find some Loyalists that had taken a rice boat. John Rae joined them the 27th of June and served 31 days. Thomas Grice also volunteered again at this time and was under Colonel Baxter.[45]

With the signing of the treaty, the Snow's Island community was relatively safe from Loyalist raids. The treaty probably reduced banditti and revenge activities in the region as well. As Simms later wrote, the treaty "put an end to the domestic feuds upon the Pee Dee." Those along the Little Pee Dee, for instance, were now "new made citizens," meaning they had joined the American cause. The treaty even drew praise from some Loyalists. Marion "behaved with great good faith towards them," according to Loyalist Robert Gray. Still, the community had a military presence in the form of Baxter's militia and cowboys rounding up cattle for Nathanael Greene and Marion's forces to the south and west. As Simms noted, Baxter's militia were needed "not only with reference to the doubtful *personnel* of the country [Loyalists], but the valuable *material*, cattle and provisions, which might have been carried off to the enemy." Several audited accounts and indents indicate that Snow's Island community residents were participants during this on-going round-up of resources in 1782 (Table 7.2).[46]

That summer, Greene requisitioned 3,000 head of cattle. These cattle were primarily rounded up along the Pee Dee and Little Pee Dee by Colonel Thomas Wade just over the North Carolina border, however, some must have been from the Snow's Island community. Former Loyalists complained that cattle were being taken without their being given receipts. At that time, Marion was in Georgetown as the British had conducted a successful raid of plantations around the town, taking rice and corn. The British also gave receipts for supplies taken, so Marion was concerned that this would give the Loyalists an excuse to take up arms again.[47]

Toward the end of August, American Major Robert Forsyth toured the countryside from Georgetown to Colonel Wade's plantation in Anson County, North Carolina, near the Pee Dee River. His route would have most likely taken him through the Snow's Island region. The foraging by the militia for food and supplies was taking a toll on the Snow's Island community, as shown in a rare description of the region of the time. Forsyth noted that the "Country…could not afford me Forage for my Horses." He also reported that he had stopped at two depots, and reported they were safe. It is possible he was referring to the Snow's Island or Dunham's Bluff camp (Chapter 8). His report indicates that the region, if not Snow's Island proper, was still being used as depot for military stores and as a foraging region, and that its resources were depleted.[48]

Toward the end of August, Marion moved to Wadboo Plantation, a large plantation along the Cooper River, just south of Moncks Corner (Figure 7.1). From this location, he could keep an eye on the British.

On 29 August 1782, Marion would fight his last battle. A British foraging party appeared at Moncks Corner and learned of Marion's presence at Wadboo. Fearing that he would attack the foraging party, the British commander struck first. When Marion learned of the British presence, he arranged his men in plantation outbuildings and easily withstood a weak charge. (Some men in Marion's ranks that day were former Loyalists, including Micajah Ganey.) After the skirmish, again low on ammunition, Marion moved to St. Stephens along the Santee. By 24 September, Marion was back at Wadboo and settled in. He detached parties around Charleston, but his camp remained at Wadboo until 14 December 1782, when the British evacuated Charleston. The following day, Marion dismissed his militia and rode home to his ruined Pond Bluff

Plantation. Among the Snow's Island residents dismissed were Peter Buckholts, Redden McCoy, Thomas Grice, and John Rice.[49]

Although Marion and his militia detachment returned home, the war was still not officially over and those remaining troops in the field still had to be fed. Three days after Marion retired, his brigade receipted Hanna Snow for 1 beef of 400 wt. John Ervin provided 2.5 bushels (corn?), 5 bushels of potatoes, thirty wt of beef, and 150 (?) of fodder on 15 January 1783.[50]

Cattle were still being rounded up in the Snow's Island region at least as late as February 1783. Colonel Wade in North Carolina was still supplying hides and beef, and his foraging region was along the Pee Dee. David Davis "furnished" ¾ of "a three year old Beef" 31 March 1783.[51]

Some of Marion's militia still was in the field, and Marion eventually wrote the governor asking for the militia in Georgetown to be relieved. Finally, on 26 June 1783, General Nathanael Greene furloughed the Southern Army.

The Snow's Island community had done their part in winning the war for the Americans. Throughout the war, some had come and gone as their terms of service expired. Others had stayed with Marion either out of devotion to the cause or fear of going home lest they be attacked by Loyalists. Table 7.3 confirms this service, listing a number of Snow's Island community members who served. Their precise dates of service are not clear.

THE RESISTANCE WITHIN THE RESISTANCE

The Snow's Island partisan community was a cohesive Whig community of resistance surrounded by Loyalist enemies. The evidence presented indicates a surprising, tightly integrated community of like-minded, related families— all supporting Marion and the Whig cause. Indeed, it has been difficult to find dissent within the families named.[52]

It would be logical to assume that part of the reason it is so difficult to find Loyalists among the families in the Snow's Island community region is that the Whigs ultimately won the war and dissenters were forced from the region, the state, and the country, unable to engage in postwar community activities, including the writing of their history. In short, this is not the complete story. The existence of loyalism was stronger than the record of a few single individuals might suggest.

First, as previously discussed, there was Hugh Miscally, the Snow's Island community resident who lived along Muddy Creek, who very likely guided Colonel Doyle's detachment to Marion's Snow's Island camp. Miscally's widow Mary apparently remained in the community after the war, so she was not

Table 7.2: Supplies/Provisions from Snow's Island community, 1782

Name	Date	Items	Source
Peter Buckholts	1782	250 lbs of beef	S.I. R17
Francis Davis [1]	July 9 August 22 Sept October	?00 wt beef 600 wt beef 500 wt for Marion seven head sheep	A.A. 1785, S.I. G102
David Davis	June 14 Nov	280 lbs beef two steers to Marion's Brigade	
Francis Greaves	19 Feb 11 June 22 Sept	3 hoggs 400 wt beef 1 stear, 300 wt	A.A. 3055
George Snow	20 August	400 wt beef to garrison at Georgetown	A.A. 7194
William Snow	Nov.	beef	A.A. 7197
John Rae	19 June 22 Sept 20 Oct	60 wt pork 1 steer 1 steer	A.A. 6283a
John Witherspoon	6 June 1782(?3) ?	2 bushels corn 1 stear 2 beaves	A.A. 8692
Abram Giles	14 Nov 24 Dec	3 bushels corn 2 bushels corn, rations for 20 men	A.A. 2816
Gavin Witherspoon	22 Sept	500 and 800 wt beef to Marion	A.A. 8690
David Witherspoon	13 Feb 13 March 31 July	1 peck corn, 2 rations 240 lbs pork 800 wt beef	A.A. 8689
John Dunnam	5 June ? Oct	1 steer 1 steer	A.A. 2098
Ebenezer Dunnam (estate of Andrew Burn)	1782	3 hogs 2 hogs 1 hog	A.A. 2097 S.I. Q78, Q80
Benjamin Port	2 July	1 small steer	A.A. 6030
Thomas Grice	2 Nov. 5 Dec.	2 hoggs 10 hogs to Marion and Captain Ruduph	A.A. 3103
Austin Stone	1782	1375 wt beef and 1 bushel corn	A.A. 7420
Richard Woodberry	1782	? Continental and militia use 400 lbs beef, Green's army	S.I. 1:80, Y1373

[1] There was another Francis Davis at Ninety Six, so I have listed only the beef and sheep provided "for Gen. Marion" in September 1782.

Table 7.3: Snow's Island community partisan service

Name	Period of Service	Type	Source
Francis Bellune	?	Militia duty	S.I. F31
Francis Davis	104 days 1782-1783	Militia duty	S.I. N174
David Davis	31 days 1782	?	S.I. G100
Benjamin Davis	12 May 1780 20 Feb 1783 (?)	Lt. Militia	A.A. 1776
Austin Stone	113 days 1780-1781 92 days 1782	Britton's Neck Regiment	S.I. 1:3
William Bellune	?	Private in militia	S.I. Y688
John Poston	63 days 1780 40 days	Col. Giles Regiment Ervin's Regiment	A.A. 6057, S.I. Y922
Joseph Poston	90 days 1781	Ervin's Regiment	A.A. 6058, S.I. Y921
William Rae	"since reduction of Charleston"	?	A.A. 6278
John Rae	31 days 1782	militia	A.A. 6283a
J. Munnerlyn	245 days August 1780 to 1 August 1781 31 days 1782	As captain (plus 92 days as Lt)	A.A. 5398
B. Munnerlyn	60 days 13 Mrach 27 June 1782	As Lt.	A.A. 5397
Robert Gasque	30 days 23 Nov. 1782 30 days 22 Aug 178?	Baxter's regiment Lt for Marion	A.A. 2718a
Thomas Gasque	30 days 1782		A.A. 2719
Peter Port	67 Days	Under Marion	A.A. 4046

driven away. Then, there was James Michie. It is doubtful Mitchie was ever a resident or even stepped foot in South Carolina, but he owned land in the area prior to the war and was compensated for his loss by the British government.

Just outside the core Snow's Island community, on upper Britton's Neck, was a group of families living along Cypress Creek, a small branch from Terrell Bay that drains into the Little Pee Dee River (Figure 1.2).[53] Several names from this area are listed on the 1781-1782 pay rolls of the Loyalist Georgetown militia and the Little Pee Dee militia under the command of Colonel Robert Gray.

One of these companies was under the command of Major Micajah Ganey, whose involvement has already been discussed above. "On Catfish Creek, the Little Peedee, and the tributaries of Drowning Creek, many remained loyal to the crown. Under the leadership of Major Micajah Ganey they had formed themselves into a loyalist regiment of militia."[54] Ganey's second in command was Jesse Barefield, who was ambushed by Marion at Blue Savannah and wounded at Georgetown. (Jesse's brother Miles was killed in the war.)

Prior to the war, the Barefields lived on Drowning Creek and the Little Pee Dee. A Jesse Barefield was granted land in Colleton County after the war—it is possible that the Colleton County Barefield was the same Little Pee Dee Loyalist who moved after the war.[55]

Within Ganey's unit there were three captains, one lieutenant, one sergeant, and 15 privates. One captain was Ananias Ganey, who acquired land after the war along Catfish Creek and was most likely a relative of Micajah. He also owned land on the southwest side of Little Pee Dee adjacent to Richard Woodberry. The other two captains were Mesech Williams and Wright Wall. There were several Williams in the land records of the South Carolina State Archives whose first names were Meshick, Meshack, or Meshich and are probably the same individual or fathers and sons. These records date to the 1820s—Meschack Williams, for instance, purchased 136 acres along the Little Pee Dee in 1825.[56]

Wright Wall acquired 140 acres along Cypress Creek in 1788. A suit of letters for the estate of Wright Wall also mentions 333 acres on Cypress Creek. Gasques were named as two purchasers. The Wall family was mentioned in Sellers's history of Marion County as "extensive in name and connections" and "can be traced no farther back than to Wright Wall." Wright Wall's land records are all post-1788 at the South Carolina State Archives. A Wright Wall, most likely our man, also served in Colonel Powell's St. David's Parish militia in 1776, so it appears he changed sides—perhaps twice. An 1806 sale for the settlement of John Case's estate named Wright Wall as vendue master. Among the staunch former Whigs named in the settlement were Loftis Munnerlyn and Robert Dunnam. Wright was also involved in other settlements, so we infer that his Loyalist service was certainly not held against him after the war.[57]

Sergeant David Palmer was another Loyalist on the muster rolls. He acquired 50 acres land after the war on Cypress Creek in 1786 and in 314 acres in 1790. Palmer was obviously welcomed back, as he was named among purchasers of Robert Gasque's estate settlement in 1806. Among others named was John Munnerlyn; the suit was certified before the congregation of Friendship Meetinghouse. In 1828, Ann Philips appointed her son, William L. Philips, to settle the late David Palmer's estate. The relationship between Ann and David is not known. However, there were two Philips in the Loyalist unit under Major Ganey, privates John and William. William Philips acquired 100 acres of land in 1796 along Cypress Creek and, in the land grant, Elias Wiggens, another private, was named as having land adjacent to Williams. Wiggens's land on Cypress Creek was acquired in 1772. Elias sold that land to a David Owens in 1784, the witnesses included Wright Wall and David Palmer.[58]

James Tindall, another private in Gray's Loyalist regiment, acquired 240 acres on Cypress Creek in 1792. Another Loyalist, Joseph Hux [Hucks], had 515 acres of land along nearby Reedy Creek, but also acquired 300 acres of land on Terrell Bay, the headwaters of Cypress Creek. An indenture made in 1824 indicated that Hux's land had been acquired as early as 1778.[59]

There are others on the Loyalist list, but those listed above establish several important points. First, Loyalists lived along Cypress Creek near the Whig Britton's/Neck Snow's Island residents. Second, they had their own community connections, which at least after the war, were as tight as those of the former Whigs. Third, they were accepted after the war and connected or reconnected with the Snow's Island community through business and probably marriage. This acceptance was despite the petition signed by many Snow's Island community families protesting leniency for Loyalists.

It is possible that their acceptance into the community after the war was due to the truce signed between Ganey and Marion. Many of these men (Hux, Palmer, Tindall, and Wiggens) accompanied Ganey and Mesesh Williams as guards on the trip to Charleston after the truce was signed.[60] Most likely, they followed Ganey to Marion's camp and served at Wadboo and were among Simms's "new made citizens." I also suspect the reason that their land records postdate the Revolution is that they lost their lands during the Revolution and had to reacquire them after the war. The records mentioned above hint that many of these land acquisitions were for land occupied prior to the war.

There are a few hints in the primary source material that there was another community of resistance within the partisan community—the largely invisible community of enslaved African Americans owned by both Whigs and Loyalists alike. The complex relationship between colonial whites and African Americans was made even more problematic as a result of the war. Unfortunately, there is not enough information to deeply probe its depths within the Snow's Island community, but it is nevertheless necessary to recognize this community of resistance within the resistance.

It has been established that Marion's partisan warriors included African Americans, as Otho Williams's famous description of Marion's followers, "…some white, some black…" indicated. Of those who were in the ranks, some were servants of officers, most notably the famous "Oscar" alias "Buddy" who, according to tradition, was Marion's "slave-servant-friend." Another was Jasper Browngard, a servant of Lieutenant James Kennedy, who served in Peter Horry's cavalry. Still another was Moses Irvin who "in his youth served

Gen. Marion as a hired servant and attended him at various times during the war of the Revolution and particularly during the siege of Charleston." Moses was not a Snow's Island community member. He was captured by the British, escaped, and was given his freedom for service in the American ranks.[61]

The numbers of free African American partisans serving under Marion are unknown, but there were some. One example was Jacob Perkins who lived on the Pee Dee and served under Marion. He moved to Tennessee after the war. Likewise, George Perkins was born in Marion County and served under Marion. He likely signed the 1776 Craven County militia petition. Jim Capers was a drummer and claimed to have been under the command of Marion.[62]

But most African Americans in the Snow's Island community were field slaves rounded up from both Whig and Loyalists plantations to perform labor. For these, of course, there is little information, but the first census of 1790 provides some clues as to the possible size of the slave population in the Snow's Island community. Table 7.4 lists some of the families and individuals discussed and the number of slaves listed in that census.

Having said that, the following families had no slaves: James Snow (with 77 free persons), Peter Buckholtz, Benjamin Davis Jr., William Davis, Robert Gasque, John Gasque, Thomas Gasque, John and Stephen Ganey, James Grice, Thomas Greaves, Joseph Hux, Samuel Jenkins, Joseph-James-John Poston, Joseph Britton, Elisha Barefield, Benjamin Munnerlyn, James Munnerlyn (Jr. ?), William Shaw, Wright Wall, Michael Wall, John Tindal, Richard Woodberry, William Witherspoon, and the "widow" Wiggins. It is interesting that many former Loyalists along the Little Pee Dee had no slaves in the 1790s. This may be represented as a loss of property resulting from the war rather than an ideological or moral decision.

Although Table 7.4 is from a post-war census, it is strong evidence of a sizable slave population in the Snow's Island community prior to and during the war. These slaves were likely ordered to work on the redoubts and fulfill other labor needs. While their labor would have assisted the partisans, they may also have been a burden to Marion's mobility, security, and logistics.

For instance, when Marion had to retreat into North Carolina, were slaves brought along? If they fought in the ranks, they would have been mounted. They had to be fed and clothed and their provisions would have reduced those available for warriors and civilians. Some would have been guarded lest they attempted to escape to Georgetown. This would have reduced the effectiveness of warriors in the ranks. The logistical needs at the Snow's Island camp would have increased even further when Marion had Horry and others round up slaves to keep them from the British and Loyalists. Exactly how Marion and the community dealt with these issues is simply unknown.

There are a few hints of slave resistance within the Snow's Island community, however. The first is a curious entry in David Davis's audited account, which states that sometime in 1781 (no month or day given), Davis housed and fed five blacks for six days and three blacks for one day who were "on trial for felony."[63] The second is even more curious. Ebenezer Dunnam's audited account indicates that he was compensated for the execution of a slave named Jack, who was tried and found guilty of poisoning someone. The trial was held on 20 October 1783 at the home of Benjamin Port. Joseph Greaves, Benjamin Davis, Abraham Giles, Francis Greaves, and Anthony Sweet were the "freeholders" or members of the jury.[64] Jack was found guilty, but before the sentence of death was carried out, he was valued at £93 sterling, for which Dunnam was compensated. There is no other information about this incident; however, since it was included as part of the compensation of Dunnam's audited account one assumes, perhaps incorrectly, that it had something to do with or related to or an event during the war.

Yet another incident is related in Loftis Munnerlyn's audited account. During the taking of Georgetown, Marion rounded up local plantation slaves to dig entrenchments. One "yellow fellow" among them was identified as having provided provisions to the British, upon which Marion had him hung.[65]

Still another piece of evidence is a letter by William Snow, written from his Santee plantation on 9 September 1781. This letter indicates that, unlike his brother James, William had a more hardened attitude about his slaves. The letter is addressed to a "Mr. Rhodes" who is to bring his slaves from another location to him at Santee (probably his Snow's Island plantation, because he adds in the letter "My love to Billy Goddard"). His greatest concern was for Mr. Rhodes to be sure to "keep your mind still from black or white until you are ready to set off, or the negroes will hide out of the way" (i.e., don't signal to the slaves of the impending move).[66] Obviously, many slaves fought for the British or escaped to the British lines.[67]

Marion's attitude towards slaves and slavery is complex. He did not agree with Sumter's law of recruiting soldiers by offering them slaves from Loyalist plantations. He was compassionate toward women and children, black and white. Yet, he was a ruthless disciplinarian and, as noted above, would execute a slave who served or joined the British as a soldier.

Table 7.4: 1790 slave population by family in the Snow's Island community

Name	#	Name	#	Name	#
Baxter, John	83	Bellune, William	3	Davis, Henry	21
	36	Britton, Stephen	6	Davis, David	4
Ervin, John	29	Britton, Thomas	11	Davis, William Jr	4
Ervin, Hugh	19	Britton, Philip Jr.	5	Davis, Ben Sr.	16
Fladger, William	16	Britton, Philip estate	10	Davis, Ben	8
Goddard, William & Francis	70	Britton, Mary	30	Davis, William Sr.	48
James, John	11	Barrow, James (with two others)	34	Davis, Francis	8
Fladger, Elizabeth (with John Keen)	12	Dunnam, Jacob (and Screven estate)	115	Davis, Joseph	8
Greaves, Joseph	24	Dunnam, Ebenezer	17	Dozier, John (with two others)	33
Greaves, John	6	Dunnam, Robert	30	Port, Benjamin	9
Greaves, Francis	37	Port, Francis (e)	26	Savage, Nathan	22
Greaves, James	2	Perkins, Lewis	9	Stone, Austin	3
Giles, Hugh	10	Potts, Thomas	28	Snow, William	43
Giles, Ann	8	Potts, William	17	Tindall, James	5
Witherspoon, Elizabeth (estate of James)	21	Witherspoon, Gavin Jr.	38	Rae, John (with one other)	40
Witherspoon, Gavin	27	Witherspoon, John	3	Palmer, David	1
Witherspoon, Gavin (estate of James)	31			Simons, Shade (for himself)	63

Endnotes for Chapter 7

1 Stovall 1971:14-15. Rayburn Stovall marks Marion's conversion from guerrilla to conventional tactics after 28 May 1781 when he captured Georgetown (Stovall 1971:5, 14-15).

2 Watson to ?, undated, Clinton Papers, WCL; Watson to Saunders, 16 April and 19 April, 1781, Saunders Papers.

3 This occurred at McPherson's Plantation in Williamsburg District which Rankin places prior to the engagement at Lynches Creek. Marion does say it took place at Mr. McPherson's, but he also says he sent Hugh Horry, who was in command, across the Pee Dee to intercept the Loyalists who were intending to join Watson.

4 Marion to Greene, 21 April 1781, GP-WCL; Lee 1812:330; Marion to Greene, 21 April 1781, Huntington Library, Marion Papers.

5 The archaeological site is now within the Santee National Wildlife Refuge. University of South Carolina archaeologist Leland Ferguson excavated the site in the 1970s (Ferguson 1975).

6 This was another battle often listed in the pension or audited accounts of Marion's partisans including, Peter Buckholts (Buckholts Pension R1465), George McCall (McCall Pension R6598), Redden McCoy (McCoy Pension S7198), John Booth (A.A. 620), who was wounded again, and Samuel Jenkins (A.A. 40211/2).

7 Smith et al. 2007a:20. About this time, John Fletcher joined Baxter's command under Marion. Fletcher, a minor early in the war, had been hiding in the swamps since Gates's defeat when he and his brothers "took to the swamps." His brothers joined Marion but he remained behind "lingering round his parents not daring to shelter himself, or to build a fire in the woods to sleep by, many knights when the rain and snow were falling." He served three terms of service of 15 days, 38 days, and 70 days beginning 26 April through December 1781 (Fletcher Pension S45841; A.A. 2432).

8 James A.A. 3993.

9 Buchanan 2019:105; General Thomas Sumter to Greene, GP, Volume VIII:216-217.

10 During this time, Marion had a detachment under the command of John Munnerlyn at Black River. On 5 May, Benjamin Davis provided the detachment with 12 rations, 2 bushels of corn, and on 21 May Benjamin Davis provided the detachment with 8 rations, a bushel of corn, and 100 wt of fodder (Benjamin Davis A.A. 1776). Likewise Austin Stone furnished 375 lbs of beef (Stone A.A. 7420). Furthermore, Gavin Witherspoon provided 1050 wt of beef to General Greene's army (G. Witherspoon A.A. 8690). He would add another 380 wt on 12 July to Marion's brigade.

11 Much more likely, the house was set fire using fire arrows fired from a musket (Smith et al. 2019).

12 James 1821:120; Smith et al. 2007a:26-28. Booth Pension W25258. Booth's pension was from his widow. In his audited account he states that the wound was received at Fort Watson (A.A. 620). Others at Fort Motte were Peter Buckholts (Buckholts Pension R1465), George McCall (McCall Pension R6598), and Redden McCoy (McCoy Pension S7198).

13 Marion to Greene, 6 May 1781, GP, Volume VIII:214-215.

14 Smith et al. 2007a:33. Marion did delay for a bit at Peyre's Plantation, which in the historic literature has been known as his second Snow's Island camp. According to Bass, it was also "surrounded by creeks and morasses," and he was among "Huguenot friends and relatives, in the swamps where he and Gabriel [his brother] had fished and hunted" (Bass 1959:198).

15 Marion to Greene, 16 June 1781, GP, Vol. III:394. Benjamin Davis Jr. provided four sheep to Marion's command on this date (Benjamin Davis A.A. 1776, S.I. R74). Likewise, on the same day, Horry received 11 bushels of corn and 56 wt of bacon from Joseph Greaves (Greaves A.A. 3057). Four days earlier, Ebenezer Dunnam Jr. had a "stear" of 350 wt impressed (E. Dunnam A.A. 2096).

16 James 1821:122.

17 Gray 1910:149-150.

18 Horry and Ganey, 17 June 1781, Gibbes 1853:98; Ganey to Marion, 25 August 1781, Gibbes 1853:130; Colonel [Thomas] Wade to Greene, 4 July 1781, GP, Vol. VIII:494.

19 Bass 1959:216-218.

20 Bass 1959:224-225.
21 Lipscomb 1978:32.
22 Francis Goddard was killed in this battle (Jenkins 1842:27). Colonel John Baxter was one of the wounded according to George McCall (McCall Pension R6598). Redden McCoy (McCoy Pension S7198) and L. Munnerlyn (A.A. 539) mention this battle. Smith 2008a:71-73.
23 Bass 1959:210.
24 Smith 2008a:77-79. As has been demonstrated throughout this chapter, detachments of Marion's command were still active in the Snow's Island region. On 30 August 1781, John Rae provided a detachment of Peter Horry's command with a row boat and six [hides?] of tanned leather (J. Rae A.A. 6283a).
25 Babits 2006:344; Jenkins 1842:28. Many who rode with Marion claim to have been in this battle. Among those who are recognized as being in the Snow's Island community were Jonathan Collins (Collins Pension S18771), Samuel Jenkins (A.A. 40211/2), and Jesse Wiggins (Wiggins Pension R11502).
26 I am not sure this is the same Maurice Murphy the Marion had difficulty with, but the actions of this Murphy as reported by Ganey certainly support that idea, and there are post-war records for a Maurice Murphy at the South Carolina Department of Archives and History. As noted in Chapter 6, he had been reported as killed in Charleston newspapers.
27 Ganey to Marion, 8 September 1781, Gibbes 1853 Vol. 3:136.
28 James to Marion, 20 September 1781, Gibbes 1852, Vol. 3:171; Horry to Greene, 20 September 1781, GP, Vol. IX:379-380; Horry to Greene, 28 September 1781, GP, Vol IX:406.
29 Gibbes 1853:176.
30 Feeding the army was still a necessity and George Snow provided 1,000 wt of beef on 22 October 1781 and 2,000 wt on 27 October to General Greene's command (George Snow A.A. 7194). The receipt interestingly says that the beef was "purchased" with the certificate by the commissary general.
31 During this time David Davis provided two "stears" to "Camp Santee" 14 November 1781 (Davis A.A. 1782).
32 Smith 2008a:83-85.
33 Hugh Thompson had land just across from Snow's Island at the confluence of Lynches and Clark's Creek prior to the war. Nothing more is known about him and he probably died before or during the war.
34 Gray 1910:153.
35 Bass 1959:224, 227-229.
36 Horry to Marion, 31 January 1782, Gibbes 1853:245-246.
37 Governor Burke to Governor Rutledge, 6 March 1782, Gibbes 1853:265-266.
38 James Snow A.A. 7196, S.I. T199; Hugh Ervin A.A. 2236a.
39 Smith 2008a:91-92.
40 Marion to Greene, 8 March 1782, GP, Vol. X:463.

41 On the way there, Colonel John Ervin may have supplied him with six bushels (corn?) and six bundles of fodder (J. Ervin A.A. 2237).
42 Marion to Greene, 23 March 1782, GP, Vol. X:534; Marion to Greene, 21 May 1782, GP, Vol. XI:232; Marion to Ganey, 2 June 1782, Gibbes 1857:183; Instructions for Marion, Mathews to Marion, 21 May 1782, Gibbes 1857:176; O'Kelley 2006:571.
43 Simms states that the emissaries Marion sent to Ganey got into such a heated argument that a skirmish broke out before cooler heads prevailed (Simms 1844:312). Although the historic records are rare and vague, it would appear that Joseph Burch had established a plantation, ferry, and mill within a few hundred yards of each other along the bank of the Pee Dee River at the east end of Mill Branch Road, southeast of Florence, South Carolina. Recent excavations by the author at the probable site of Burch's Mill suggest that the treaty was signed at the planation (see Chapter 8).

44 Marion to Greene, 8 July 1782, GP, Vol. XI:412. James states that some 500 men surrendered to Marion at Bowling Green (James 1821:167).
45 James Jenkins A.A. 4018a; Jenkins 1842:29; John Rae A.A. 6283a; Thomas Grice Pension R4301.
46 Simms 1844:316; Gray 1910:156; italics in original, Simms 1844:317.
47 Forsyth to Greene, 25 August 1782, GP, Vol. XI:576; Marion to Greene, 5 August 1782, GP, Vol. XI:492; Marion to Greene, 9 August 1780, GP, Vol. XI:511.
48 Forsyth to Greene, 21 August 1782, GP, Vol. XI:566.
49 Smith 2008a:10-11; Smith 2008b:103; Buckholts Pension R1465; McCoy Pension S7198; Grice Pension R4301; and Rice Pension R8747.
50 Hanna Snow A.A. 7195; John Ervin A.A. 2237.
51 Wade to Greene, 10 February 1783, GP, Vol. 12:428; David Davis A.A. 1782; Guerard to Greene, 27 February 1783, GP, Vol. 12:482. James Johnson's audited account states that he provided a steer as late as 30 November 1783 for the garrison at Georgetown (Johnson A.A. 4068).
52 I did not conduct research in Canada to investigate the archives of Loyalists. However, I did discuss these archives with Jim Piecuch, author of a recent book on Loyalists (Piecuch 2008), who did not find much evidence for Loyalists along the Pee Dee in the Snow's Island region (James Piecuch February 2010, pers. comm.). This is supported by previous historical research on South Carolina (Calhoon 1965; Sabine 1979; Lambert 1987; Calhoon et al. 1994).
53 There are actually several Cypress Creeks in South Carolina, including those in Dillon County, Beaufort County, and Colleton County. There is also one in Georgetown County at Plantersville, South Carolina. However, from the various land postwar land records, it is evident that the Cypress Creek of interest to this study is near modern day Centenary, South Carolina. The fact that Georgetown County's Cypress Swamp could be confused with the Centenary location, is cause for caution in this discussion.
54 Rankin 1973:69.
55 Clark 1981:187-188; Rankin 1973:71,123; Bass 1959: 49, 88; SCDAH S213190:36,411.
56 SCDAH S213190:38,88; Utley et al. 2003:142; SCDAH S213190:40,109.
57 SCDAH S213190:23,112; Utley and Smith 1985a:130; Sellers 1902:432; Moss 1983:962.
58 SCDAH S213190:3,246; Utley et al. 1985:194; SCDAH S213190:26,94; Utley et al. 2003:167; Clark 1981:188; Utley et al. 2003:178.
59 SCDAH S213190:19, 30,53, 299; SCDAH S213190:26,170; Utley et al. 2003:129.
60 Clark 1981:188.
61 Williams 1822:488; Boddie 2000:3; Moss and Scoggins 2004a:36-37; Moses Irvin Petition 1836, SCDAH S165015:40.
62 Moss and Scoggins 2004a:183-184. There is no other information as to any relationship between Jacob, George, and Marion partisan Lewis Perkins.
63 David Davis A.A. 1782.
64 Dunnam A.A. 2096. Anthony Sweet lived in Britton's Neck and was intimately a part of the Snow's Island community. His land was near Cypress Creek and after the war he was involved in transactions with former Loyalists.
65 Loftus Munnerlyn A.A. 5399.
66 Snow to Rhodes, 9 September 1781, Gibbes Vol 3:140. In Chapter 4, I indicated that, according to Bailey and Cooper (1981:680), the William Snow of Santee was not the same as the William Snow of Snow's Island. However, this reference to Billy Goddard tends to indicate that they may be the same after all.
67 Moss and Scoggins 2004b.

CHAPTER 8

THE ARCHAEOLOGY AND LANDSCAPE OF THE SNOW'S ISLAND COMMUNITY

This chapter examines the material remains (sites and artifacts), of the Snow's Island partisan community. It also discusses the partisan community landscape. In previous chapters, I have used the historical documents to demonstrate that the colonial community around Snow's Island was transformed by war into a partisan community, a kind of community of resistance. What, then, is the material evidence for this partisan community? This chapter attempts to answer that question, and then makes observations about the evidence.

As I noted in the second chapter, archaeologists, especially prehistorians, look at a cluster of archaeological sites, or material culture locations, and from those sites assume a sociological community.[1] However, in historical archaeology, when additional evidence is available from the written record, archaeologists are wise to use that evidence. This is the direction used in this chapter.

Although focused on material evidence, this chapter does not rely on material evidence alone, however, especially for landscape analysis. The historic record assists in making the case for material evidence and site identity. There are also examples of locations discussed below, for which there are ample historic records pinpointing the historic site's location, but for which I have found no material evidence (artifacts, archaeological sites). Yet, the documentary evidence is so overwhelming, even if sometimes circumstantial, that to ignore the data would be senseless. In other words, both sites (historic locations) and archaeological sites are used as part of the landscape analysis. For each site discussed below, both the historical and archaeological evidence is presented.

A full in-depth archaeological discussion of each site is not necessary here or is it provided, except in the case of sites 38MA207 and 38MA165.[2] These two sites are the first known examples of 18th century partisan occupations excavated by professional archaeologists. Prior to locating 38MA207, I assumed that a partisan, by definition, would not be uniformed or armed with large numbers of standard issue military weapons. The logical assumption is then that a partisan camp site is not likely to contain many military-related artifacts, but rather mostly artifacts from a variety of weapons. This chapter offers the first opportunity to examine the material culture of the partisan. Therefore, additional details and analysis is offered.

ARCHAEOLOGICAL METHODS

A general methodology for this study was provided in Chapter 2. This section describes the archaeological methods used to locate and examine sites. The archaeological fieldwork for these sites was conducted over several seasons, widely separated in time. I have been engaged in a search for the archaeological evidence of Marion's Snow's Island camp since 1993. Field survey on and around Snow's Island using metal detectors has occurred sporadically, as time and funds permitted. The first field season in 1993 discovered sites 38FL280, 38FL281, and 38FL282. Block excavations were conducted at 38FL282 in 1993, 1994, and 2000 (Figure 8.1).

In 2006, I engaged in a large survey to discover archaeological sites associated with the career of Francis Marion on behalf of the Francis Marion Trail Commission. Again, the primary field method was to conduct metal detecting surveys at locations determined from researching historic documents. This resulted in the discovery of sites 38MA165, 38MA205, 38MA206, 38MA207, and 38MA212. Formal trench and small unit hand excavations using shovels and trowels was conducted at 38MA207 to discover if intact features were present.[3] Two additional sites, 38FL380 and 38MA55, were discovered by other archaeologists. The field methods used by these archaeologists were shovel testing and surface collecting. Methods used and objectives sought at the sites discussed below were not part of a single comprehensive program or field effort. The only shared goal for each of the efforts at these sites was to find evidence of Revolutionary War period occupations.

Metal Detecting. Once considered the pariah of archaeological methods, metal detecting has been proven to be a superior method of locating and defining military sites.[4] Military equipage of the regular soldier, including accoutrements, ammunition, buttons, badges, and weaponry, are all metal and their presence at a site assists in identifying site function and cultural association. Therefore, battlefields, usually covering a large area, can be efficiently examined using metal detectors to define combatant locations and maneuvers. Likewise, metal detectors can assist in determining activity areas within a military camp.

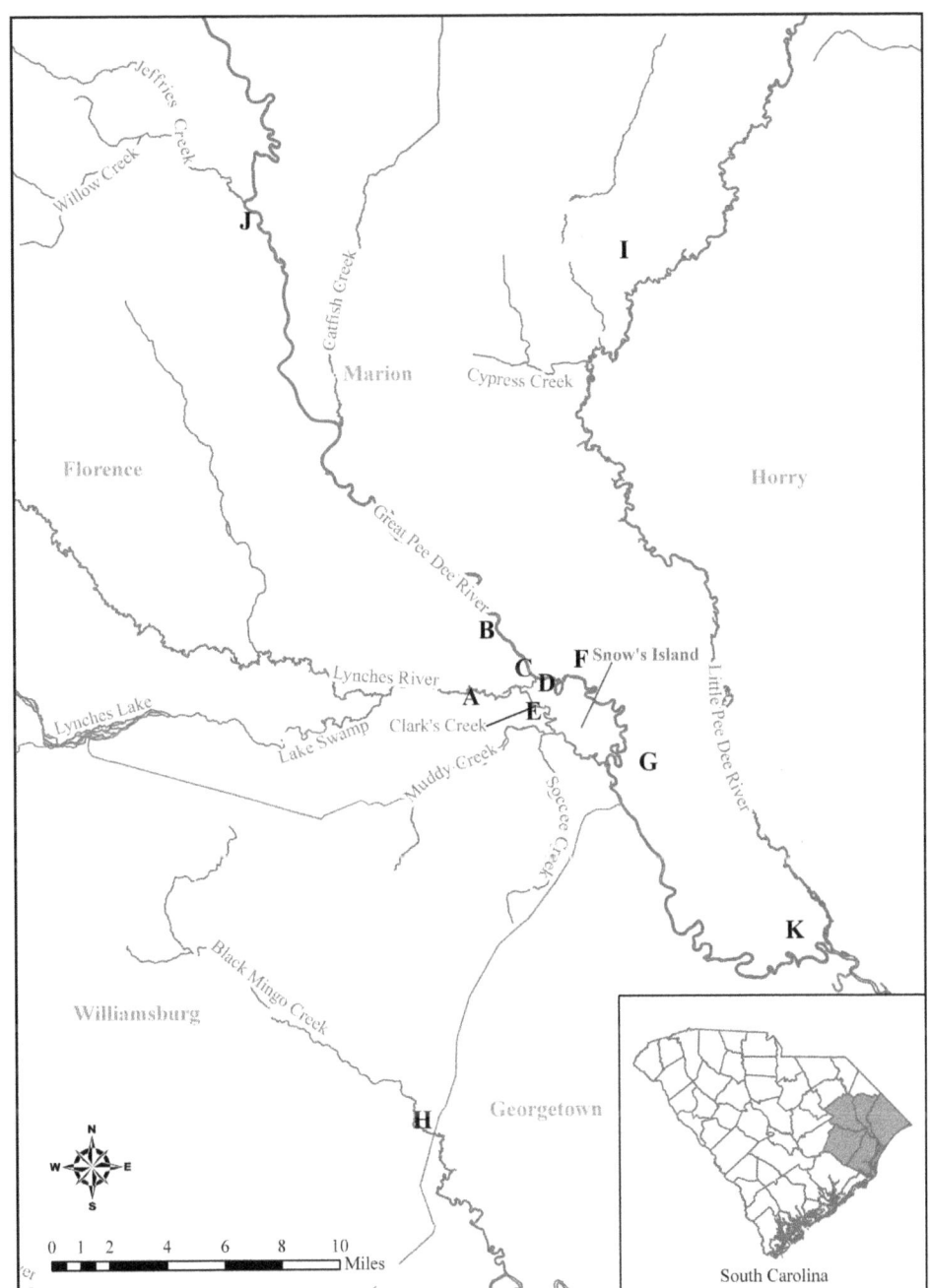

Figure 8.1. General location of Archaeological sites discussed in Chapter 8. A=38FL380, B=38FL409, 410, and 411, C=38FL282, D=38FL281, E=38FL280, F= 38MA207, 165, 81, G=38MA212, H=38WG170, 171, I=28MA206, J=38FL46, 50, K=38MA55. l=38MA205.

The primary metal detecting method used for the sites discussed in this chapter was a "search to find," or reconnaissance survey, by a team of two to three persons.[5] Historic document and map research narrowed the surveyor's search area to a reasonable area. The surveyors then walked the area along loose transects, sweeping the ground. If a metal signal was heard, the signal was excavated. When an artifact dating to the colonial period was found it was immediately retrieved, placed in a plastic bag, and the bag given a unique provenience (location) number. A pin flag was placed at the location and labeled with the same number. The location was recorded using a GPS instrument again using the same provenience number.[6]

The place was then more intensely covered by detectorists. Whenever possible the area around the artifact was blocked off in a square or rectangle defined by pin flags. Then, the detectorists walked adjacent transects (approximately 1.5 m wide), often overlapping, and reinforced by perpendicular transects, to thoroughly cover the zone where artifacts clustered. In thick woods, the block method is not possible; however, many sites in this chapter were in planted pine forests and could be covered systematically using the tree rows as guides. Eventually, a site map, consisting of artifact locations was generated using this method and the clusters were used to determine the placement of excavation units.

Excavations. Metal detecting finds sites but is not useful for excavating features or understanding site stratigraphy. Controlled, systematic hand excavations are the best means of revealing cultural features.[7] Excavation methods at 38FL282, 38MA207, and 38MA165 were each slightly different as the goals at the time were different. Site 38FL282 was excavated as a research project and several weeks were spent over two field seasons. Metal detecting, shovel testing, and block excavations were all used at 38FL282. Sites 38MA207 and 38MA165 were part of a project to find and identify sites associated with Francis Marion.[8] The goals at these two sites were simply to determine if the sites had archaeological integrity for future research.

Only one week was budgeted for hand excavations at both sites. These sites were in thickly planted pine forests. Trees were approximately 15 to 25 years old and spaced approximately every 0.5 to 1 m along rows. The rows were from 1.5 to 2 m (meters) apart. Therefore, at 38MA207, metal detected artifact locations defined the site area and a grid was imposed across the site using the total station, marked using pin flags. Trenches were then excavated along north/south and east/west grid lines to locate features. The trenches were 30 m. or one shovel, width wide and were excavated using shovel skimming and the floors were cleaned with shovels and trowels. The trench soils were not screened but they were inspected and where artifacts were seen in concentration, soils for that particular 1 or 2 m section of the trench were screened.

Once features were discovered, 2 x 2 m excavation units were placed within the suspected feature locale to better expose the feature. Additional block units were excavated adjacent to the original unit, either 2 x 2, 1 x 2 or 1 x 1 m as needed. Once these units were excavated, the floors were re-cleaned (troweled) to map and record the features.

All units were excavated in 10 cm (centimeters) levels and soils screened through ¼ inch mesh. Artifacts were provenienced (collected and cataloged as a group within a unit) within these 10 cm levels. The upper 20 cm of all the units were uniformly plow zone soils; artifacts were mixed within this upper level with no internal stratigraphy. The variation in plow zone depth was due to plow furrows and rows.

Artifacts from features (and levels) were bagged and their location information recorded separately. All artifact bags were labeled with provenience information. Feature and level forms were maintained. Feature details and stratigraphic profiles were drawn and photographed (digitally in the case of all sites except 38FL280, 38FL281, 38FL282).

At 38MA165, excavations consisted of three trenches excavated perpendicular to a berm or palisade wall to bisect it. These trenches were 1.5 m wide in order to expose a profile wall and for safety. The soils were not screened for artifacts as the goal was to reveal the cross section of the berm to determined if it was a cultural or natural feature. Shovel sorting of the soils revealed no artifacts in any case. Profiles were photographed and drawn for both walls. A Carbon[14] sample was taken from an organic layer.

Laboratory methods followed state guidelines.[9] All recovered cultural material was cleaned, stabilized when necessary, or treated in a manner appropriate for the kind of material collected. Artifact analysis was conducted to identify artifacts as to material type and function, with a description, and an artifact catalog was developed containing descriptive and provenience information for each artifact. At 38MA207, oyster shells recovered from features were sent to the Florida Museum of Natural History for seasonality analysis.[10]

38FL380 WITHERSPOON'S FERRY

Previous chapters described the importance of Witherspoon's Ferry to the Snow's Island community, not only as a strategic crossing point along Lynches Creek, but also as the site of Marion's first independent partisan command. It was at Witherspoon's Ferry that Marion met the Williamsburg militia and began his partisan campaign on 17 August 1780.

The general location of Witherspoon's Ferry is widely documented as being in the vicinity of where modern road SC51/175 crosses Lynches Creek (now River) at the northern edge of Johnsonville, South Carolina (Figures 3.4, 8.1). This location is depicted in *Mills' Atlas* as "Witherspoon's or Dubose's Ferry" (Figure 8.2).

The ferry was operated by Robert Witherspoon at the time of the American Revolution. The current highway bridge is located at the narrowest part of the river; a likely more precise location for the historic ferry crossing. If so, archaeological evidence of the ferry is probably gone since there has been extensive land modification as a result of bridge repair and a boat landing. The campground of Marion's militia would not have been there as it would have been in a swamp.

Across the river on the northern bank, the land is low and swampy for several hundred yards, and, for this reason, the modern highway on the north bank is a long causeway.

After the battle on Snow's Island, some histories state that the British camped on the north side. A careful reading of William Dobein James suggests that they were simply there scuttling the ferry boat. More likely they were camping on some higher ground to the north. Further, James states that Lynches Creek was "swoln, and at this place wide and deep" causing Marion, when he arrived, to travel upstream five miles above the ferry to find a place to cross the river (remember the ferry boat was scuttled, Marion needed a place to cross where he could swim the horses).[11]

About three-quarters of a mile downstream of the modern bridge, along the south bluff line is a projection of high land (Figure 8.3). Just across the river is a depression that leads to high ground. Could this be the actual location of Witherspoon's Ferry? There is a long narrow depression feature on the north bank that could be where the ferry reached dry land. There is good reason to believe this might be the ferry site location (see discussion below of the partisan landscape).

Unfortunately, although it runs into high ground, an industrial mine has turned that high ground into low ground. Today, this high ground immediately east of the modern bridge is occupied by Wellman Advanced Materials. The Wellman property has been landscaped and heavily modified by industrial buildings. In October 2000, archaeologist Michael Trinkley conducted a survey of the Wellman bluff tract east of the bridge and discovered a site recorded as 38FL380 (Figure 8.3).[12] This site, while heavily disturbed by both a 20th century homestead and Wellman Industries, contained colonial period artifacts including six white salt-glazed stoneware sherds, one undecorated Chinese porcelain sherd, five blue hand painted Chinese porcelain sherds, one

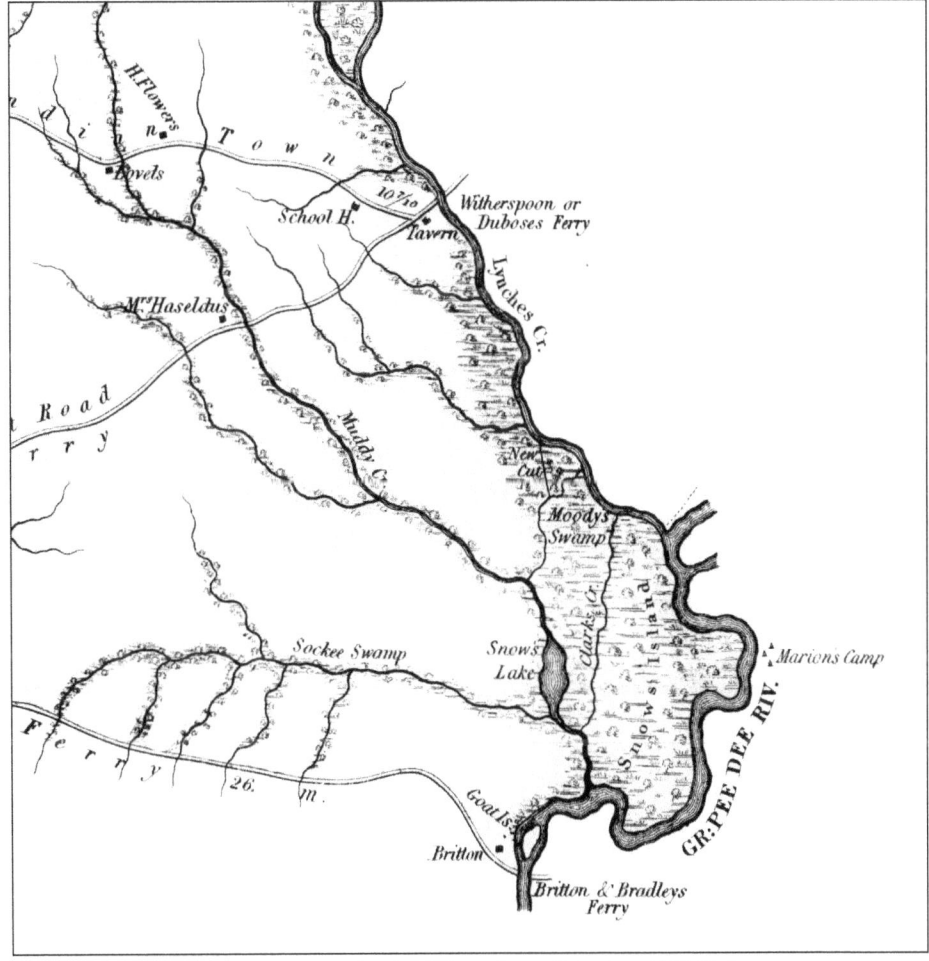

Figure 8.2. Detail of Williamsburg District, *Mills' Atlas*, depicting Witherspoon's Ferry and "Marion's Camp"

delft body sherd, one Westerwald sherd, a pipe bowl, and one "black" glass sherd.

While Trinkley calculated a mean ceramic date at 1744.5, the white salt-glazed and Westerwald stonewares are common Revolutionary period artifacts. No doubt this is a colonial site and I suspect that it was the campground of the Williamsburg militia or a colonial tavern or both. Unfortunately, it too has been destroyed by development.

38FL409, 38FL410, 38FL411 PORT'S FERRY

Marion crossed the Pee Dee at Port's Ferry several times during his partisan career (Figure 3.4). In fact, both sides of the river were utilized during the American Revolution. Port's Ferry was chartered in 1778 to Frances Port, Thomas's widow. As noted in Chapter 3, Benjamin Port owned property around Welsh Lake. According to local historian Tres Hyman, he probably ran another ferry there in conjunction with the original ferry during high water. It is also possible that Benjamin ran the ferry for Frances.

As described in Chapters 3 and 4, Port's Ferry provided access to Britton's Neck. Like Witherspoon's Ferry, there is a high side [west] and a low, swampy side [east]. The charter indicates four possible departure points on the east bank, according to land parcel researcher Deryl Young. These departure points were needed to adjust for the Pee Dee's seasonal water levels.

On the east side, Marion constructed a redoubt in September 1780. The redoubt was occupied by a detachment of his brigade under the command of Colonel Baxter later in the war. Marion may have camped on the west side, but others certainly camped there throughout the war as well. On 23 January, 1781, Colonel Henry Lee joined Marion at Snow's Island. At that time, he requested an additional 60 men to report to Benjamin Port's. After the failed attempt at Georgetown, Lee returned to Port's Ferry at the end of January. He was recalled by Greene but lingered into February (Chapter 6).[13] Frances Port's audited account includes records of several ferriages during the war including a large 1,600 man army passing through in January 1779.[14] Unfortunately, none of the ferriages include Marion's 1780 crossings.

Both sides of the ferry site were surveyed using metal detectors in 2006 and 2008 to locate evidence of the redoubt on the east side and camps on the west side. Three separate loci of colonial period artifacts were found on the west bank and designated 38FL409, 38FL410, and 38FL411 (Figure 8.4). Site 38FL409 was located at an old fish camp in a thick woods along the high west bank of the Pee Dee. Two side plates from British Brown Bess Sea

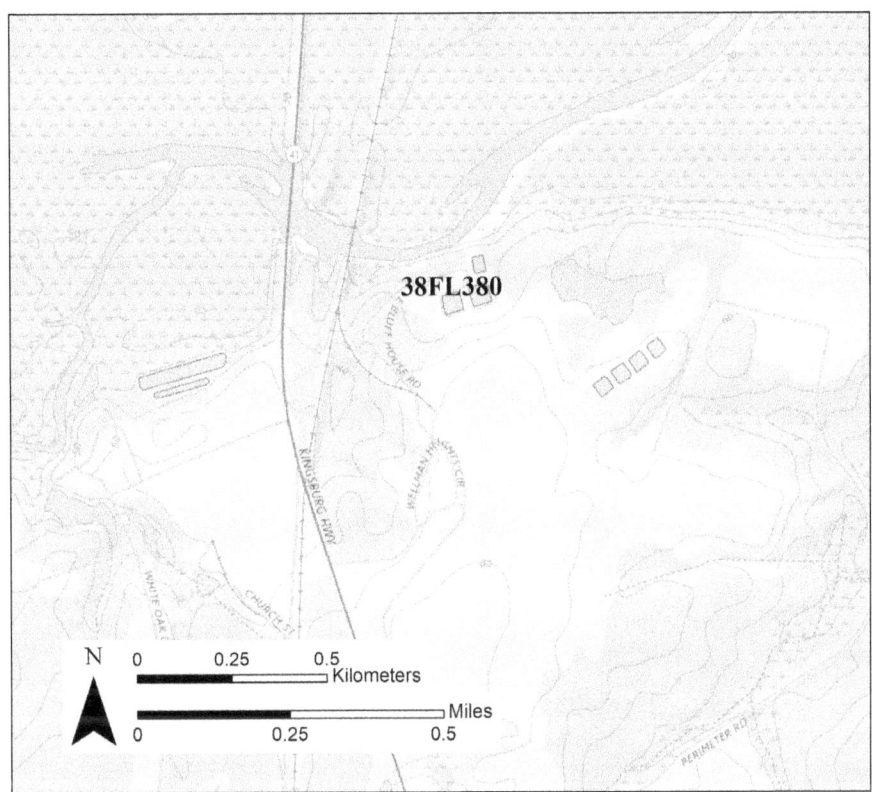

Figure 8.3. General location of archaeological site 38FL380 (USGS The National Map, modified by Brock Shattuck)

Service Muskets were recovered along with 18th century buttons, a colonial period horseshoe, buckles, lead seal, and several architectural items like door lock plates and hinges. All these artifacts were found in a very small area of about 20 m².

An informant suggested we survey a plowed field that local collectors called the "muster field" because they found musket balls and little else. Two buckshot and five lead shot identified as rifle balls were recovered by my team at this site (38FL410), which covered an area 250 by 250 m. Nothing else was recovered. Site 38FL411, another 18th century occupation, was found north of that location along the river. This site contained mostly buttons and a rifle ball.

All three sites provide evidence of colonial occupation. The Brown Bess Sea Service musket plates are probably an indication of a military occupation at 38FL409, but there was probably a domestic occupation there also. It is tempting to suggest that the pattern 1718-1757 Sea Service muskets were antiquated arms that might have been acquired by civilians turned partisans during the Revolution.[15] The lack of variety in the artifact assemblage of 38FL410 suggests a muster ground according to relic collectors, or a campground. The buttons and rifle ball at 38FL411 only indicate a colonial period site. It should be noted that historical records do not mention any British regulars or Loyalists camping at the ferry.

Across the Pee Dee, on its east side, the field team spent several days attempting to locate evidence of Marion's 1780 redoubt. According to Hugh Giles's audited account, it was located at Welsh (now Dog) Lake (Figures 3.7, 3.8). An Act of the State Legislature in 1826 described the transfer of Port's Ferry to Francis Davis: "Provided, he shall open and put in good order the roads leading to the new landings, to the satisfaction of the commissioners of the roads for Marion district; but the road leading from the ferry on the northeastern side of the river, shall be the same as in the lifetime of Mrs. Frances Port, passing out of the swamp at a place known by the name of the Old

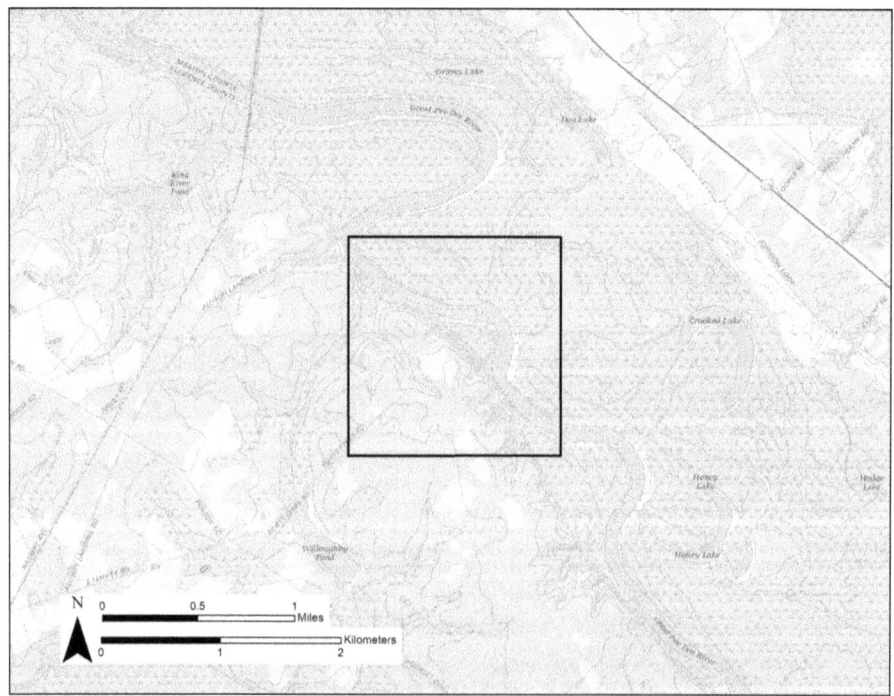

Figure 8.4. General location of Port's Ferry archaeological sites 38FL409, 38FL410, and 38FL411 (USGS The National Map, modified by Brock Shattuck)

Redoubt." Giles's account and the act narrowed the search area for the Port's Ferry redoubt to the south end of Dog Lake. That area was thoroughly searched and no evidence of the redoubt was found; however, the historic record seems clear that there was one in this vicinity. A small hill southeast of Dog Lake appeared to be a very likely location for this redoubt, but the site was covered with modern trash and there was no indication of redoubt walls. Archaeologist Carl Steen shovel tested the site during a separate archaeological project and found no evidence of colonial material.[16] I am personally convinced the redoubt was in this area and was subsequently destroyed.

38MA205 RICHARDSON'S

While searching for the 1780 redoubt, the team ran across what might be a small camp. Artifacts included a lead flint holder for a flintlock, a buckle fragment, a ring, a ring setting, melted lead, a dropped rifle ball, and two 18th century flat buttons (Figure 8.5). Although no shovel tests were excavated, no ceramics or other materials were found in the metal detecting holes to indicate it was a domestic site. This second site is not likely to be the Port's Ferry redoubt as it is approximately 1.5 mi. from Dog Lake.

The lack of ceramics supports the interpretation that this may have been an outlying piquet (guard) camp of Marion partisans or local militia. It is located along a bluff line that drops into the floodplain and perhaps along an old stage line road. It would be a good tactical location for such a guard post.

Meanwhile, between Dog Lake and 38MA205 is a high bluff that had a light artifact concentration of two rifle balls, a buckshot, and both colonial and 19th century ceramic and metal artifacts. The area (labeled Todd's on Figure 8.5) had been recently logged when my team visited the site and any surface features that might have remained were obliterated. Although this site is only a half mile from the south end of Dog Lake, its identity remains a mystery. It is possible this was in fact the site of the redoubt, however, in 1780, Marion and his militia camped around this redoubt for several weeks and there do not seem to be enough artifacts to support what would be expected for an extended stay. Another interpretation is that it is a colonial domestic occupation.

38MA212 HICKORY HILL

During the 2006 survey, the field team talked to many Florence and Marion citizens who were happy to help us locate sites. One provided a map that supposedly depicted a militia camp location along the Pee Dee River found by a relic collector.

In attempting to access the site (which was never found), the survey team discovered an 18th and 19th century occupation on a 25-ft.-high sand ridge on Britton's Neck known locally as Hickory Hill (Figure 8.6).

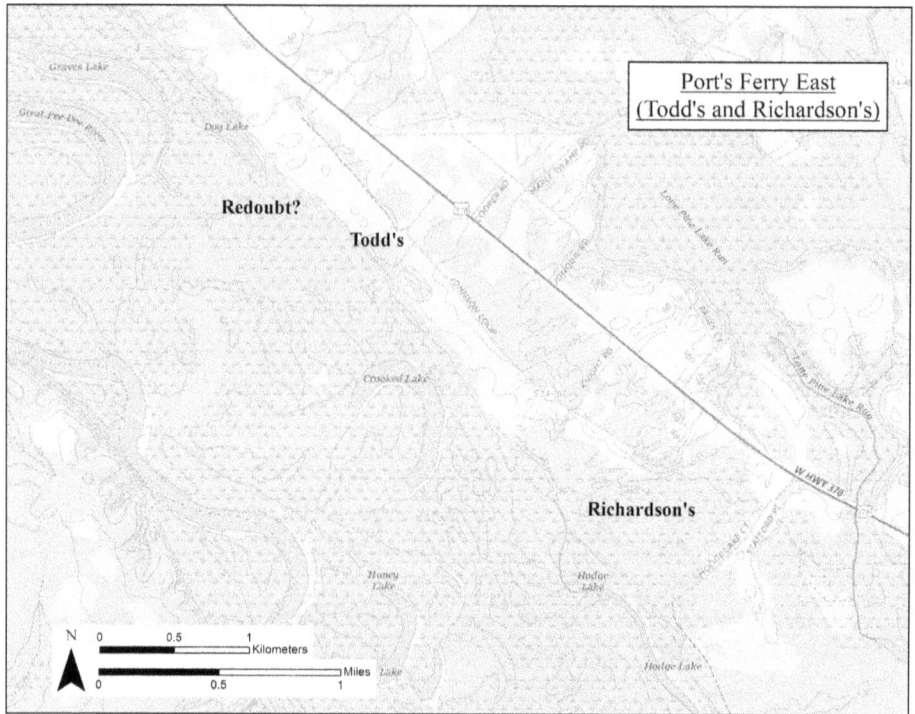

Figure 8.5. General location of archaeological site 38MA205 (Richardson's) and Todd's Site (USGS The National Map, modified by Brock Shattuck)

Just southeast of the site is the intersection of Woodberry Road with the road to Britton's Ferry. Woodberry Road runs from modern Highway 378 at the Old Neck Cemetery south to the Tanyard site (38MA55) (see below) at the confluence of the Little and Great Pee Dee Rivers. Today Britton's Ferry road (named Pet Larrimore Road on some maps) runs out of the swamp from Britton's Ferry north to modern Highway 378 and Potato Bed Ferry. During the colonial period it may have run up the Woodberry Road (see below).

From 1965 to 1980, genealogist Mrs. Phyllis B. Canady and Marion biographer Robert D. Bass carried on a great deal of correspondence about the region including the site at Hickory Hill. Their research concluded that Hickory Hill was either the location of Daniel or Francis Britton's house or the original location of the Old Neck Chapel. The Woodberrys also lived in the area in the 19th century.[17]

Colonial period artifacts were found scattered on the surface over the top of the ridge. A total of 44 metal items were collected using a metal detector and another 16 ceramic sherds were collected from the surface. The ceramics included 18th century delft, Staffordshire slipware, white salt-glazed stoneware, Buckley, creamware, clay pipe fragments, and 19th century blue shell-edged and transfer printed pearlware. Metal items included lead shot (rifle and buckshot), tombac buttons, buckles, one brass side-plate from a flintlock, wrought nails, an iron curry comb, and others.

The site is indeed a domestic site dating to the late colonial period. The assemblage collected there includes a rather high ratio of rifle balls and buckshot (18 separate items out of 44 metal items recovered, or 41%) suggesting the possibility that it was also occupied by a militia or partisan force.[18] Hickory Hill is the location of one of the Woodberry plantations on Britton's Neck, and it is quite logical that Marion or other militia forces camped there.

Four other locations nearby are important pieces of evidence regarding the partisan landscape and have been mentioned in previous chapters. The first is the location of the Widow Jenkins's house and boyhood home of Robert Bass (Figure 8.6). The survey team did not visit this site as the vegetation levels have always been prohibitive when opportunities became available. The team was not able to visit the Britton's Ferry site either, however, unlike the others, its location is firmly established. The third is the location of Rae's Causeway. Jenkins noted that Colonel Watson marched a mile up the Britton's Neck (Woodberry Road today) road and camped at "Rays." Bass believed that the camp was on the ridge at the causeway (Figure 8.6).[19] Finally, relic collectors tell of a camp on the neck near Potato Bed Ferry (Figure 8.6). They were convinced that it was not a house site because artifacts included 18th century buttons and "lots" of lead shot of miscellaneous calibers, and also believed the camp to be American, not British.

The site is located near a strategic point, Potato Bed Ferry. It is exciting to speculate that this site might have been Marion's camp of 15 October 1780 (see Chapter 6), as that is the only time that Marion is known to have camped on the Little Pee Dee. Today investigation of the site would likely reveal little as a large sand pit and cement factory are located there.

38MA55 THE TANYARD

The Tanyard is located at the very southern tip of Britton's Neck just upstream of the confluence of the Pee Dee and Little Pee Dee (Figure 8.7). Historian W.W. Sellers wrote that the site was the location of a tanyard run in the early 1700s by the Michalls family.

Although the site is approximately 11 miles south of Snow's Island and on the southern fringe of the Snow's Island region, it is quite possibly associated with Marion partisans. While there is no known historical documentation

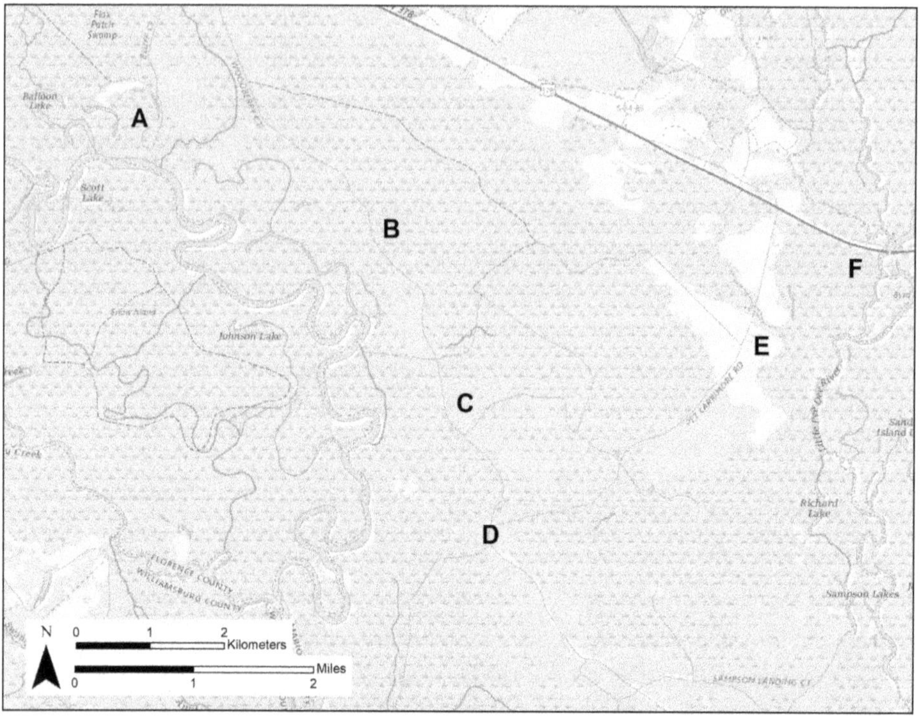

Figure 8.6. General location of sites and landscape features on Britton's Neck. A=38MA207, 38MA165, 38MA81 site complex, B=Rae's Causeway, C=Widow Jenkins Home, D=38MA212 Hickory Hill, E= Relic Collector Camp, F= Potato Bed Ferry (USGS The National Map, modified by Brock Shattuck)

connecting Marion to this site, local tradition has it that the site was a Marion camp and fortification.

Robert Bass initially did not think Marion or any of his detachments ever camped there, but changed his mind later, writing: "In 1915 a trench about knee deep ran to the westward and was said to be part of the defensive work thrown up by Marion to defend the landing from British vessels. A portion of this breastwork about six feet long can still be seen [1980] near the edge of the river." Numerous Marion County residents who I have interviewed remember this trench and I saw a remnant of it also in the 1990s. Based on conversations with South Carolina Department of Natural Resources personnel, the trenches were destroyed during logging operations.[20]

This site was first recorded as 38MA55 in 1975 by previous South Carolina Institute of Archaeology and Anthropology director, Dr. Robert Stephenson. A large collection of colonial materials, brick, and prehistoric artifacts were recorded, including a "musket ball."[21]

The Archaeology and Landscape of the Snow's Island Community | 185

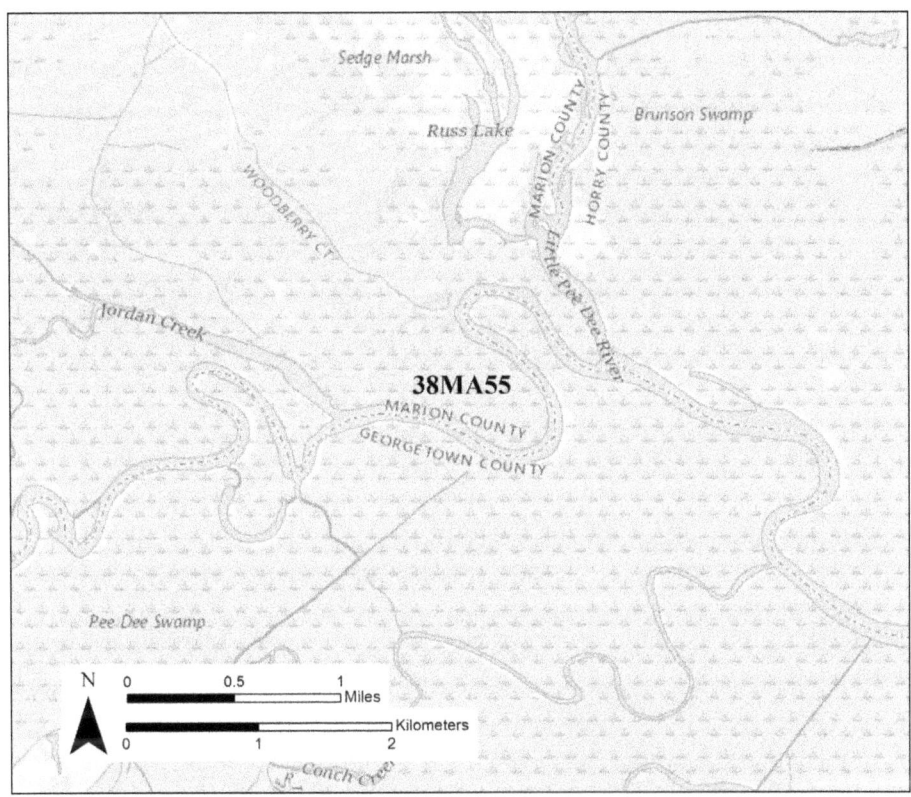

Figure 8.7. General location of archaeological site 38MA55, the Tanyard (USGS The National Map, modified by Brock Shattuck)

In 2006, I visited the site with the Francis Marion Trail Commission and a sample of artifacts was collected. The sample includes 25 historic ceramics dating to the 18th century including Chinese Export porcelain, Jackfield, Staffordshire slipware, and white salt-glazed stoneware sherds. A relic collector, who is now deceased, had in his collection a 2nd South Carolina Regiment button. The 2nd South Carolina was Marion's regiment during the early part of the war prior to the fall of Charleston. At one time, people who talked with this collector indicated that he said it came from the Tanyard. However, toward the end of his life he told others that he could not remember whether the button came from the Tanyard or from a site recorded by archaeologists as 38MA81 (see below).

38MA207 DUNHAM'S [DUNNAM'S] BLUFF

This site is an early rallying point for the militia and the campsite of one of Marion's detachment, perhaps that commanded by Colonel John Ervin. There also is a strong possibility that there was a domestic component, possibly the Dunham homestead. There is also intriguing evidence that it is the location of Marion's iconic "Snow's Island campsite." This evidence will be provided below for the reader to decide.

In any case, this is the first partisan campsite examined by a professional archaeologist and offers some insights as to the archaeological expression of a partisan camp. A detailed report of excavations was completed in 2009 for the South Carolina Francis Marion Trail Commission and the following summarizes the results.[22]

Earlier chapters have discussed the association of Dunham's Bluff with Francis Marion and the Snow's Island partisan community within the overall context of Marion's use of the Snow's Island region. This section summarizes that data for the reader and provides additional postwar documentation relating to the site's interpretation. The first necessary piece of information for understanding this context is that there are two archaeological sites interconnected in this discussion, the campsite at 38MA207 and the remains of a redoubt about 500 m away on the Pee Dee River bluff at Dunham's Bluff, 38MA165 (Figure 8.8).

The earliest record of a militia presence at Dunham's Bluff is the pension account of Joseph Davis. This account was written in 1851 (or 1857) by Davis's sons and daughters who were applying for their father's pension. Their account states that Joseph "volunteered at Ports Ferry on the great peedee and marched from thence in Company with Lieut. Benj. Munnerlyn, (afterwards promoted to a captain) Captain Shade Simons, Benjamin Davis, Moses King, Francis Goddard, Jonathan Collins, & others to the Rendezvous at Dunnam's Bluff, from thence to Charleston."[23]

From the context in the pension, Davis went from Dunham's Bluff to the first battle of Charleston in 1776; thus the site was an early militia camp, probably occupied numerous times throughout the war, and possibly a rendezvous for militia prior to the Revolution. This time frame, prior to Marion's association with the Snow's Island community, is further supported by John Rice's pension records. Rice's pension states that in the fall of 1779 he was under "Capt Munnerlyn–Col John Ervin. Under these officers he was stationed two months at a small redoubt on Great Pee Dee River in Marion Dist where he remained with some trifling exceptions the whole time."[24] While

The Archaeology and Landscape of the Snow's Island Community | 187

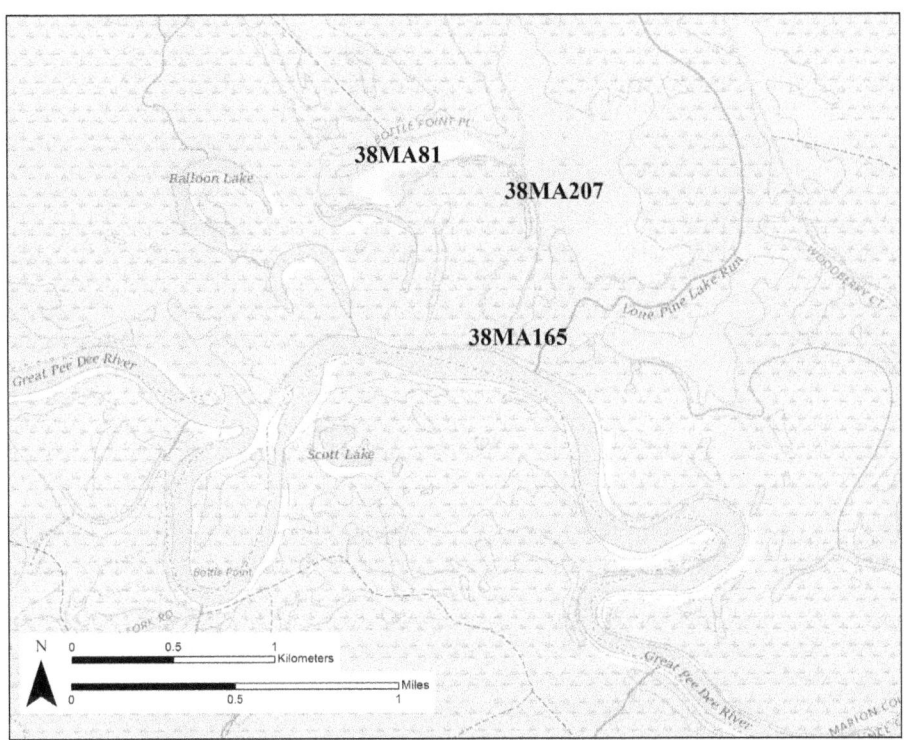

Figure 8.8. General location of archaeological sites 38MA207, 38MA165, and 38MA81 (USGS The National Map, modified by Brock Shattuck)

the date is probably wrong (Rice states he returned to militia service in 1780 and served under Marion at Beaufort and Wadboo, so its likely his chronology is confused), Rice had the officers correct and his pension provides yet another indication of a redoubt and camp on the Pee Dee, either Marion's redoubt at Port's Ferry or at Dunham's Bluff.

The existing historic records are confusing in regard to the redoubt and camp across from Snow's Island and the redoubt at Port's Ferry. Gregg's history of the Cheraws includes a picture of a redoubt that looks like the Dunham's Bluff redoubt, 38MA165. The caption of the picture states that it shows "The Site of Marion's Redoubt, Near Port's Ferry, at Dunham's Bluff."[25]

While nothing in Marion's correspondence mentions a camp at Dunham's Bluff, the key to understanding Dunham's connection to the Snow's Island story is the memoir of Reverend James Jenkins. Jenkins grew up in the Britton's Neck region and his brothers served with Marion. He was a young man at the beginning of the conflict but by war's end he was old enough to be called out for service in Colonel Baxter's Britton's Neck militia.

Importantly, Jenkins was very familiar with the region. In his memoir, he stated that his brothers took British Cornet Merritt to the redoubt "thrown up on the east side of the Great Pee Dee, by order of Colonel Irwin" before being transported to William Goddard's cabin. This testimony is presumably the evidence author Robert Bass used to conclude a redoubt was constructed at Dunham's Bluff. (Bass does not mention a camp at Dunham's Bluff, but it is logical to assume that if there was a redoubt, there would have been a camp since a redoubt is not something that soldiers live in.) Chapter 4 discusses the connection between the Ervins and Dunnams and it would make sense that Ervin turned to Robert Dunnam to build his fort on the Dunnam Plantation.[26]

Loftus Munnerlyn's pension account adds additional primary evidence for a camp at Dunham's Bluff, but in doing so adds to the confusion. As discussed in Chapter 6, his parents were taken to a camp "in the vicinity of the redoubt, which is situated on the right bank of the Pee Dee river opposite Snow's Island." Munnerlyn's account of his parents' move is made in the context of the battle of Blue Savannah, 5 September 1780. At that time, other primary sources solidly indicate that Marion was building a redoubt at Port's Ferry. Reverend Jenkins also mentions the Port's Ferry redoubt, where he was stationed later in the war, so it is unlikely that the Port's Ferry redoubt and the Dunham's Bluff redoubt discussed in the historic documentation are actually the same place. I believe that there were two redoubts in the Snow's Island region on Britton's Neck, one on the east side of Port's Ferry and one at Dunham's Bluff.[27]

Meanwhile, during the 19th century, the Dunham's Bluff redoubt and campsite became synonymous with Marion's Snow's Island camp. For instance, the *Mills' Atlas* map of Williamsburg District, published 44 years after occupation of the redoubt and camp, pinpoints the location of Marion's camp as being across the Pee Dee River from the actual island, or in other words, at Dunham's Bluff (Figure 8.2). I have researched Robert Mills's papers and have not discovered what information Mills had that would have prompted him to place the camp there. The location is not labeled as Marion's camp on the original survey maps Mills contracted to compile his atlas, therefore it was Mills who labeled the site, not the district surveyor.

Clearly, though, Mills had some information that led him to label this site as Marion's camp. I believe it was a plat of Snow's Island drawn by or for Peter DuBose as part of a petition for ferries in the area. The plat depicts the location of Dubose Ferry (which was previously Witherspoon's Ferry) and includes Snow's Island. Across the Pee Dee from Snow's Island, at the location of Dunham's Bluff, are two words: "Marion's Camp." Significantly, the petition is dated to 1813! This is the earliest date I have found in the records indicating that this camp is Marion's camp (Figure 8.9).²⁸

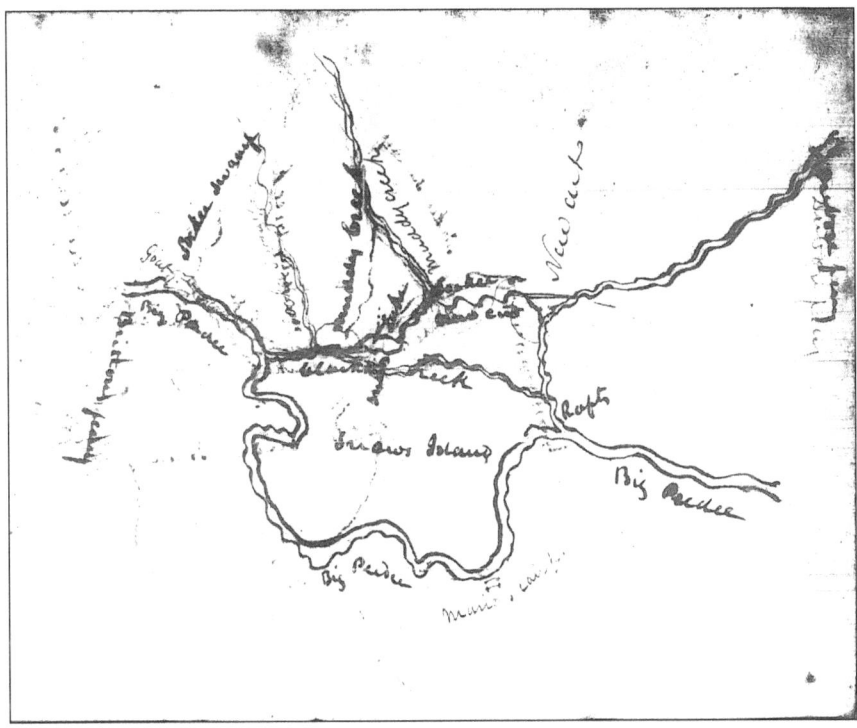

Figure 8.9. Plat Snow's Island Public Improvements Ferries-Petitions 1813 (SCDAH)

Mills also illustrated other Revolutionary War places in his atlas, including the Battles of Camden and Cowpens, and his locations are accurate within the scale of the atlas. Yet Mills also adds to the confusion between a camp on Snow's Island and the Dunham's Bluff camp in a book entitled *Statistics of South Carolina* that was published a year after the atlas. In this work, which describes each district in a narrative form, Mills writes that, in the Marion District:

> The principal lakes are Jordou's and Snow's lakes; the latter, ... The former designates a spot called Snow's Island, famous in the revolutionary war, as forming the secure retreat of Gen. Marion in the midst of the enemy, and from whence he could take them by surprise. This island lies immediately below the junction of Lynch's creek, with the Great Pedee, being bounded on two sides by these streams, and by Clark's creek on the west and south. Here, by having the command of the rivers, he could be abundantly supplied with provisions, and his post completely inaccessible except by water.²⁹

This description clearly places Marion's refuge on the physical location known as Snow's Island today. Yet, only a few pages later in his *Statistics* he writes under a section entitled, "Names of Places—Indian or Otherwise":

> Marion's camp, already noticed, opposite Snow Island, on the east side of the Great Pedee, is also noted.[30]

Clearly, the context here is that Marion's Snow's Island camp is *located* on the opposite side of the Pee Dee River from modern Snow's Island. This description fits archaeological site 38MA207.

There is more evidence that, during the 19th century, Marion's camp was considered to be on the east side of the Pee Dee. In 1858, a professor traveling through Marion County published his description of the county in *DeBow's Review*. He wrote that "about twenty three miles south of this place [Marion Court House] is another camp, called Marion's Redoubt on the Great Pee Dee river, opposite Snow's island."

One assumes that Steuckrath, a visitor to the region, must have been told where the redoubt was by proud local residents.[31] In fact, that is likely how he learned of the camp and redoubt at Dunham's Bluff. For instance, an 1828 letter to the editor in the *Charleston Courier* notes that July 4th was celebrated at the redoubt:

> When [Marion's men were] compelled by superior numbers to withdraw from the open country, they retreated to their native woods and fastnesses, until their forces were recruited. The remains of Marion's Fort, in Britton's Neck, are still perfectly visible. It stands opposite to Snow's Island, which was always his last, but perfectly secure, retreat. Some of the survivors of Marion's army, and many of the descendants of those, who have long since joined their leader in a better world, assembled at the old fort, to celebrate the birth-day of that Independence which they or their ancestors achieved.
>
> Toasts were proposed, including to "The spot on which we are assembled—The asylum of Marion and his little band," and to "Snow Island—The land opposite to us: the retreat of our fathers, who, when pursued and hunted, there found refuge and safety."[32]

Throughout the Antebellum, Marion citizens met at the redoubt. Another article in the Courier in 1832 reported that a public dinner was given to a Marion district state representative at the redoubt.[33]

The redoubt continued to be a place of patriotic celebration into the 20th century. In 1905, Reverend R.E. Stackhouse gave a speech before the Swamp Fox

Chapter of the Daughters of the American Revolution, in which he referenced the redoubt build by "Irwin [sic]" which he took "to be the redoubt still to be seen at Dunham's Bluff."[34] In 1908, Mrs. N.M. Johnson repeated this story. After noting the Port's Ferry redoubt was no longer extant, she stated that:

> There still exists at Dunham's Bluff a Revolutionary fortification, a part of which is in a good state of preservation. As Jenkins speaks of a redoubt thrown up on the east side of Pee Dee by Col. Irvin and occupied by him until driven out by the British, the Dunham Bluff redoubt is probably the one built by Irvin.[35]

To date, I have found no evidence of a Marion occupation on Snow's Island (see below) after many seasons of searching. The question remains: is 38MA207 the famous Snow's Island camp of Francis Marion, or a detachment camp? There is one other interesting and confusing piece of information. In Jenkins's memoir, he states that British Cornet Merritt was made prisoner and taken to William Goddard's cabin.

It has always been assumed that Goddard's cabin was on Snow's Island. But what if Goddard's cabin was on Goddard's Ridge, the high land along Lone Pine Lake Run instead? As noted in earlier chapters, Jenkins states that Francis lived there and moved his family down the neck during the early part of the war. If so, then 38MA207 almost has to be Marion's main depot and camp.

I am almost convinced that 38MA207 is the famous campsite (see below, Snow's Island), but there is still some lingering doubt. The history is clear that the British attacked Marion's Snow's Island camp in March of 1781. If the Dunham's Bluff site was Marion's main camp, the British would have had to cross the Pee Dee River. As this would have been a major undertaking, there should be some record in the historic documents of that event as such major landmarks are usually mentioned by military commanders, but I have found no such record. Furthermore, Marion's riflemen caught up with Doyle at Witherspoon's Ferry on Lynches Creek. If the British attacked a camp (or depot) on Snow's Island, then it would make sense for them to move west to Witherspoon's Ferry after the raid to block Marion as they made their way back to Camden. They likely crossed it when attacking the camp and retreated across it afterward.

If they attacked the camp on Dunham's Bluff, then they would have re-crossed the Pee Dee at Port's Ferry. They could, however, have run north up the east side of the Pee Dee and crossed at Burch's Ferry to get back to Camden.

As I said, I remain somewhat unsure that 38MA207 is Marion's main camp, but am convinced that it is at least a detachment camp, probably manned by Ervin and later by Colonel Baxter's militia. Within this camp, both partisan warriors and civilians would have been camped, the latter seeking the protection of Marion's warriors.

Metal Detecting. During the intensive effort to locate sites associated with Francis Marion for the Francis Marion Trail Commission, I decided to spend some of the time and effort budgeted for Snow's Island on a survey of the landscape across the island, based on the evidence provided in *Mills' Atlas*. Vegetation in the area made systematic survey impossible. The land was forested in 15- to 20-year-old planted pines and had recently been acquired by the South Carolina Department of Natural Resources.[36] The trees had been mechanically planted in raised soil beds.

By 2007, the soil banks had eroded, but some were still as much as 12 in. (30 cm) in height, spaced about 6 ft. (1.8 m) apart. To complicate matters, space between the tree rows was grown-up in thick understory. Metal detecting therefore consisted of the detectorists attempting to follow the furrows as best as possible and stopping to cover spaces between the trees on the beds. Repeated coverage of the rows was required during the months of January and February 2007. Eventually, an artifact concentration of 90 m north/south by 60 m east/west in size defined the borders of site 38MA207, along a gentle ridge (Figure 8.10).[37]

The results were exciting. A total of 216 metal objects were recovered from 38MA207 during the metal detecting. A total of 48, or 22%, of these were lead shot (another 11 lead shot were recovered by excavation, see below). Arms furniture included a fragment from a trigger guard, three flint holders, sprue from a buckshot gang mold, and two more sprue fragments. Metal clothing artifacts included 17 buttons (five sleeve buttons and a cuff link), one of which is a silver sleeve button with block "I" (Figure 8.11). Most interesting is a 2 lb. cast iron cannon ball (Figure 8.12).[38]

There was also an assortment of buckles, buttons, iron kettle fragments, a horse stirrup, and a complete candle holder. All the artifacts, including a large assortment of wrought nails (only a sample was collected), are consistent with an 18th century time frame.

Trench and Unit Excavations. With additional funding provided by the Francis Marion Trail Commission, a week of hand excavations was conducted to determine if the site contained intact features. Two types of excavation units were employed. First, the excavation team dug trenches across the site, focusing on a ridge line where artifacts were densely located. A total of 182 m of trenches, 30 cm wide, were excavated in a north/south and east/west

The Archaeology and Landscape of the Snow's Island Community | 193

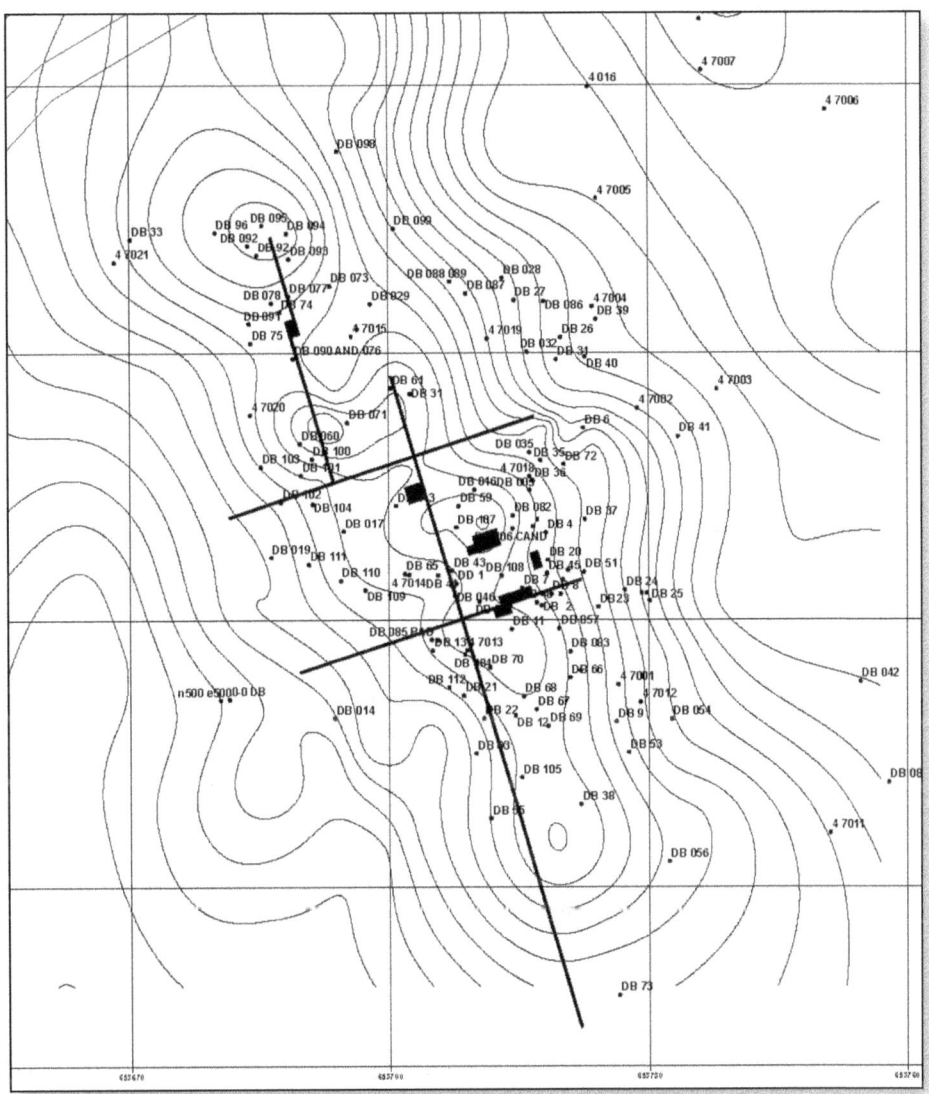

Figure 8.10. Site 38MA207 (Sean Taylor)

direction (Figure 8.10). All the trenches contained scattered artifacts, artifact concentrations, and features including postholes.

Not all features could be excavated in one week, but they were recorded. Two trenches (labeled A and C) encountered a hard-packed surface, indicating a what archaeologists call a living surface (a large, usually shallow, area of packed dirt that is the result of many people walking repeatedly over the same ground). Trench C also revealed a large posthole 20 cm wide (in profile). A 2x2-meter unit (Unit 4) was excavated at that location.

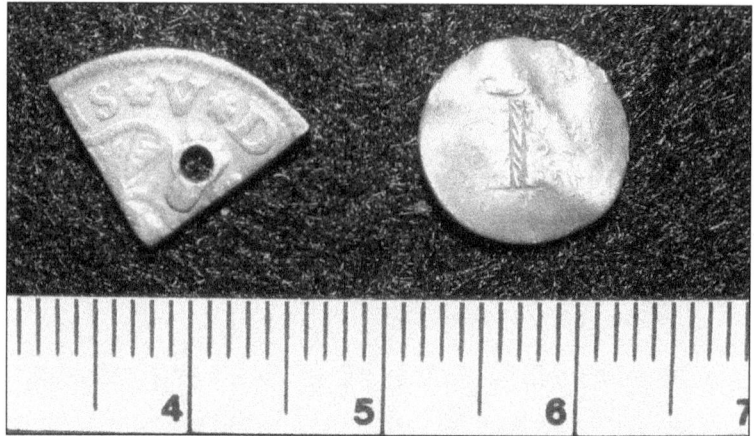

Figure 8.11. Block "I" silver sleeve button and "piece of eight" from 38MA207

Figure 8.12. A 2-lb. cannon ball with British "broad arrow" from 38MA207

Trench D revealed a feature consisting of dense artifacts, bone, shell, and large (football sized and larger) rocks. Unit 8 was excavated at this location.

Units 1, 2, and 3 were opened near where a brass candleholder was found during the metal detecting. A vaguely linear stain was revealed (Feature 1, Figure 8.13) at 45 cm below surface and it was decided to excavate a smaller unit to profile the feature in an attempt to determine both its possible

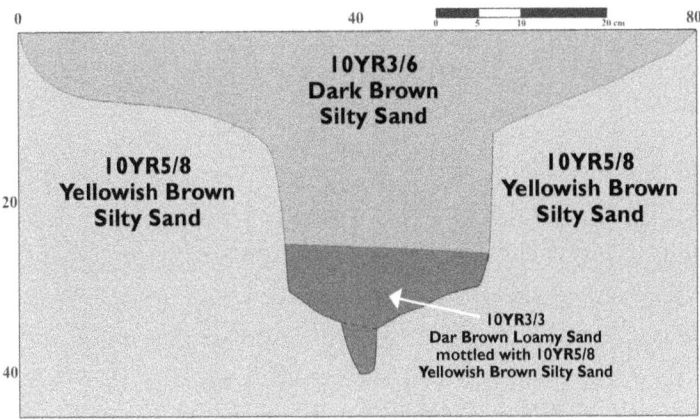

Figure 8.13. Feature 1 profile from 38MA207

function and shape. The cross section revealed a straight-sided trench feature that may have been a ditch for a domestic structure. It is also typical of a fort's palisade ditch.

Unit 4 revealed a hard-packed living surface about 35 cm below the topsoil. This level included uncounted small ceramic and glass artifacts (smaller than dime size) embedded in the hard surface. Obviously, repeated pedestrian traffic compacted the sands and ground the smaller ceramics into the hard surface, causing me to speculate that it could represent a tent floor, house front yard, or be evidence of an extended occupation campsite.

Units 5, 7, and 9 revealed another vaguely linear feature containing artifacts that is very similar to that found in Units 1, 2, and 3. Time constraints did not allow complete excavation, but a quickly excavated cross-section did not reveal a ditch like that seen in Units 1, 2, and 3. This may be a drip line for a structure.

Unit 8 revealed a shallow 5-cm sheet midden where two large non-local rocks were found at and just below the surface. The midden's size and depth were not determined as time did not permit full excavation. The sheet midden was contained within a 2 x 2 m unit, but the feature's bottom at the rocks was not discovered. A quick small excavation to locate its bottom extended 80 cm below the surface. This feature, or features was interpreted as a sheet midden and trash pit. The rocks may have been part of a fireplace or were used as foundations for a structure. Clearly the site has a number of intact features for future research.

Domestic Artifacts. The plow zone and features were full of 18th-century artifacts including ceramics, glass, and metal. A total of 153 American and European ceramics were recovered including blue on white Chinese porcelain lead glazed slipware, brown glazed stoneware, Westerwald stoneware, Astbury redware, white salt-glazed stoneware plate and teapot fragments, Whieldon ware, Jackfield, creamware, and single pearlware sherd.[39]

A mean ceramic date of 1747.8 was calculated for the artifacts. This seems early but is consistent with Revolutionary War period sites, and no sherds are dated later than the assumed date of Marion's camp or 1780-1783. Also, 45 colonoware sherds were recovered. These appear typical of Lowcountry types and are usually associated with slaves.

Glass artifacts are also less numerous than expected. Only 45 mostly dark green, "black" glass sherds (N=30) typical of the 18th and early 19th century were recovered. Only one bottle, with an applied string lip dating to the mid to late 18th century, was recovered along with a bottle base with a kick-up style suggesting an early 1780s timeframe.[40]

Lead Shot. The diameter of the lead shot that was recovered is very interesting as it is consistent with a pattern that is emerging as more and more Revolutionary War period sites are being excavated. Additional detail is furnished here as it is one of the more revealing aspects of the site and possibly most partisan camps and battlefields.

A total of 59 lead shot was recovered from both metal detecting and excavations. Eighteen examples (30%) of this shot are of the size associated with rifles or trade guns of the 18th century and early 19th century (Table 8.1). Two more could be either rifle or carbine shot and two more have size or markings attributable to a pistol. Only one lead shot is of the caliber (size) associated with a military weapon of the Revolution, that being a French Charleville musket ball. Most (N=36 or 61%) of the lead shot are buckshot (small shot less than .320" typically used to kill birds).

Some background information is necessary for the reader to understand the implications of these findings. For instance, regular British infantry were issued .75 caliber, brass-mounted "Long Land Pattern" and "Short Land Pattern" flintlock muskets, commonly known as "Brown Bess" muskets. Shot for these muskets consisted of a nearly perfectly rounded (having been tumbled) lead shot with a weight averaging 30.5 grams and a diameter of .680 to .695 in. American regular, or Continental, forces during the Revolution used British muskets and American-made copies early in the War, however, were armed with French Charleville muskets beginning around 1777—first as covert and later overt aid to the Americans through the American-French alliance.

The French Charleville was produced as several similar models, generally was iron mounted, and in .69 caliber. A lead ball fired from the Charleville has a diameter ranging from .620 to .660 in. and is typically .640 in. Charlevilles became the Continental infantry's standard weapon.

The British also armed an unknown number of their Loyalist militia units with captured French muskets after the fall of Charleston. For instance, Cornwallis reported capturing "80,000 musket cartridges" as the result of his victory at Camden. They would not go to waste.[41]

I have assumed that American militia and especially Marion's warriors would have been armed with old or captured British weapons and French muskets, especially in the fall of 1780 when they were partisans—including the period when camped at Dunham's Bluff. No lead shot normally associated with a British Brown Bess and only one possible French musket ball was found at Dunham's Bluff. Instead it appears, if this is a Marion camp and I am confident it is, that they were armed with rifles and/or trade guns.

Rifles of the period were more specialized with a wide variety of bore diameters, but all were of smaller diameter than the British or French muskets. (They were an American adaptation of German hunting rifles.) Every rifleman would have had to make shot for his own weapon using a bullet mold, and the lead shot diameter ranging widely from as small as large buckshot, .338 in., up to .600 in. Trade guns were smooth bored "rifles," of similar caliber and could also fire buckshot. They were originally made for the Native American trade and many colonists also owned them. Clearly the partisans at Dunham's were overwhelmingly armed with rifles or trade guns as 30% of the ammunition is rifle- or gun-sized lead shot.[42]

Furthermore, this type of ammunition assemblage (large ratio of rifle-sized balls versus military-sized lead shot) is seen at other Revolutionary War period and Francis Marion sites that I have surveyed or excavated. For instance, it was the same pattern seen at Port's Ferry (38FL409 through 411). At the site of the Black Mingo skirmish (see below), 19 or 36% of the 52 lead shot were rifle/carbine sized shot, and only one shot of a size associated with French Charleville muskets was recovered (the rest are buckshot see discussion, below). At the Parker's Ferry battlefield, another Marion battlefield, the balance is more even, with four rifle/carbine balls, and three musket balls (two Brown Bess, one Charleville). At Marion's Wadboo Plantation battlefield, 10 of 65 lead shot were rifle-sized balls. One was from a rifle/carbine, and another nine are confirmed carbine balls, only one shot was from a Brown Bess and four were fired from Charleville muskets (again the rest are buckshot, see below). At the nearby Waboo plantation campsite, 86 lead shot were recovered, 18 are rifle balls, 3 are rifle/carbine, 5 are Charleville sized, and 15 are carbine shot. No Brown Bess shot was found.

Marion was well known to have had excellent riflemen, and at the archaeological excavations at Fort Motte, a clear pattern around the fort indicates that Marion's men were firing rifles at the fort's walls and corner blockhouses. Again, it was assumed that most of his partisans were armed with muskets. It is beginning to appear that most were armed with rifles and trade guns.[43]

Most of the ammunition found at these sites was buckshot.[44] The historic records not only refer to Marion's partisans as armed with rifles (or guns as opposed to muskets), but also that they used buckshot extensively. For instance, in one of Marion's first commands to Peter Horry in August 1780, Horry is charged to find and procure "ball or swan shot" (the latter a form of buckshot). Marion's partisans fired "either a ball and buckshot, or heavy buckshot alone" at Parker's Ferry. Likewise, at Wadboo, Marion's men gave the British cavalry the "usual charge of heavy buckshot."[45]

At Dunham's Bluff, buckshot made up 36, or 61%, of the lead shot collected. Most are of the standard size (size .250 to .320 in.) (N=24). Six buckshot are smaller than the standard size and six are larger (only 16%). At the Parker's Ferry battlefield, 16 of 25 (64%) buckshot are greater than .320 in. At Fort Motte, another Marion battlefield, only six buckshot were recovered. However, this was at a siege site—the British were behind a fortified house, where buckshot would have been ineffective. Nevertheless, all buckshot recovered are .325 in. or greater, four are larger than .345 in. At Wadboo Plantation battlefield, 62% of the buckshot are over the standard size.

It is also worth noting that at two Upstate Revolutionary War battlefields where I have engaged in metal detection—Blackstocks and Williamson's Plantation—buckshot recovered were much less prevalent on the battlefield. Blackstocks combatants consisted of Sumter's militia (mostly riflemen) against Tarleton's dragoons and mounted 63rd Foot. In a collection of approximately 48 lead shot, only four buckshot were recovered at Blackstocks (even though Sumter was apparently wounded by buckshot in the battle). Two are larger than .320 in. (.333 in. and .342 in.). At Williamson's Plantation, an action between upstate American militia and a combination of British Legion, New York Volunteers, and Loyalist militia, no buckshot were recovered out of 25 shot, and all but two are rifle balls.[46]

If, as it begins to appear, that large buckshot can be associated with Marion partisans, the Dunham's collection does not appear to fit.[47] Even so, the Dunham's buckshot size may be an indication of an "early" Marion site, dating to the suspected historical date between August 1780 and April 1781, or even as early as 1776.

Table 8.1. Lead Shot from 38MA207

Ball Diameter	Fired	Unfired	Fired/Unfired?	Totals	Lead/Pewter
Rifle balls (5.3 g to 18.2 g)	13	2	3	18	
Rifle/Carbine	1		1	2	(1)
Gun/Pistol	2			2	
.69 Caliber Musket "Charleville"	1			1	
Standard Buckshot (.250" to .320")	8	8	8	24	(6)
Small Buckshot <.250"	3		1 + 2 wire shot=3	6	(1)
Large Buckshot/Small Rifle (.321" to .380")	2	4		6	(1)
Totals	30	14	15	59	(9)

Swan shot is normally considered to be small buckshot. Both Parker's Ferry and Wadboo were fought after the destruction of Marion's Snow's Island camp at the end of March 1781. The only occupants of Dunham's after that period would have been Baxter's militia.

Another interesting observation relates to the number of pewter or alloy shot found. At Dunham's Bluff, nine, or 15%, of the shot are composed of a combination of lead and pewter or other metal alloy, suggestive of the stretching of lead to make additional shot, which would be consistent with the lack of ammunition that posed a constant problem for Marion. Even at Wadboo Plantation near the end of the war, 10% of the battlefield shot recovered are pewter and at the campsite, 23%. This is in stark contrast to the Camden battlefield collection, a large battle with no partisans, where one pewter shot was found in the entire shot collection.[48]

Additional Metal Items. Metal items that might reflect warfare or military activity include the lead shot described above, three flint holders, sprue from a buckshot gang mold with five sprue remnants, two more sprue lead fragments, and a trigger guard fragment. There was also the silver sleeve button with block "I" (Figure 8.11). This artifact has been shown to several button and military sites archaeologists and the consensus is that it is a specially jeweled button for an officer, probably an officer in the 1st South Carolina Regiment.[49]

The gun furniture described above could also be associated with domestic hunting, however, the British 2-lb. cannon ball cannot. The cannon ball is cast iron, weights 1.87 lbs (a 2 pounder), and is marked with the British broad arrow (Figure 8.12), which has been used as the mark of the King's possessions since the 1300s and eventually became known as the mark of the British government.[50] The 2-lb. cannon ball is not a common size and weight for artillery of the period, but it is not unique either. Two-pounder cannon were referenced in technical reports on British smooth bore cannon and also mentioned as used by traders on the Mississippi in 1795. At the same time, light field cannon were usually 1.5, 3, 6, or 9 pounders during the American Revolution. For example, many lists of cannon size of the period do not include the 2 pounder.[51]

Given the above, a cannon ball of this size and at this site is intriguing. Marion had two-iron cannon at the Port's Ferry redoubt. These cannon were abandoned in the swamps when he retreated into North Carolina in late August 1780. Yet here at the Dunham's Bluff site a cannon ball was found, and of a size associated with small cannon not usually seen in the field during the Revolution. This small size suggests a pre-Revolutionary War light cannon, perhaps dating much earlier in the 18th century, which was appropriated by the local Williamsburg or Britton's Neck militia early in the war or prior to Marion's taking over command, and thus fitting the description by Simms. Finding the cannon ball here also reinvigorates the debate regarding the murky history of the Port's Ferry-Dunham's Bluff redoubt(s).[52]

Additional Artifacts. There are a large number of metal and other items associated with 18th century occupations elsewhere that are not necessarily revealing of partisan camps, including buttons, buckles, kettle fragments, leather bosses, and an excellent example of an iron stirrup, identical to those found at Revolutionary War military sites but not necessarily one of military issue. There were only 16 pipe stem fragments found.[53] A single glass bead was recovered and dates within a wide range from 1600 to 1836 and common to sites dating between 1700-1820.[54]

Faunal Analysis. Faunal analysis provided some interesting results. The pension and audited accounts indicate that Marion's partisans at Snow's Island and elsewhere were well supplied with beef, pork, lamb, corn, and rice. A total of 44 *identifiable* fragments of animal bone were recovered at this site (there were also over 300 small unidentifiable bone fragments). The majority of the bone came from the trash pit feature in Unit 8. Those identifiable to a particular species indicate only two individual specimens were represented—a single mature deer and a single mature hog. Only one bone has indications of butchering marks, a deer astragalus (ankle); another, a phalanx, was burned. One bone was classified as being from a Class VI-sized animal. A Class VI bone is of a size associated with a large mammal such as a cow or steer. This bone was found in Trench D, just south of Unit 8. Unit 1 also had a pig incisor and Unit 5/9 had a Class V mammal skull fragment. Class V mammals include deer and sheep. Unit 4 had yet another deer phalange.[55]

Also found in the same feature were mollusk shell fragments, including six oyster (*Crassostrea virginica*) and one hard clam (*Mercenaria mercenaria*). The shells were sent to the Florida Museum of Natural History for analysis, but they were poorly preserved. Still, analysis indicated some interesting observations. First, both oyster and hard clam are intertidal water species, thus the shells must have been carried from the coast to the site. Winyah Bay (Georgetown) is most likely their origin. Second, it is rare to see oysters at archaeological sites this far inland because it was traditionally believed that they would spoil rapidly. (In fact, oysters, if kept cool, will "live for weeks.")

According to hard clam expert Dr. William Arnold, clam will also survive about two weeks in cool weather. On the other hand, in warm weather, they will spoil rapidly. The presence of oyster and clam therefore tends to point to a time frame in the cooler months of the year. This supposition is supported by analysis from the Florida Museum, which indicates that these shells were likely obtained in cool weather.[56]

Why transport the shell nearly 40 miles inland when it appears from the historical record that the partisans were well supplied? Archaeologist Dr. Chester DePratter, who researches prehistoric shell middens, offered the suggestion that the shells were a convenient road food. Marion's partisans could have gathered a few oysters while maneuvering around Georgetown, and then eaten them on the return trip. The fact that only a few oyster and clams were found implies that was all that was left after they returned from the coast.[57]

Another important observation is that all the recovered oyster shells are left valve. These are the halves that are traditionally used to hold the oyster for eating.[58] So, where are the right halves? Perhaps in the rest of the feature, but more likely, the shells were deposited in the trash pit after eating, and not gathered and used for some other purpose such as making buttons.

Finally, the recovery of one pig, one deer, and the shell suggests that the trash pit items were the result of a single consumption event, such as a roast or feast for a large number of individuals, the remains of which were deposited in the pit and closed. If the trash pit remains represented several consumption episodes, a number of animals from the same species should have been represented in the same pit. Another interpretation may be that they are evidence of short-term camp behavior, rather than a long-term occupation, as in the case of a homestead.

Summary. Site 38MA207 represents the occupation of one of Francis Marion's detachments, perhaps on the site of the Dunnam homestead, and on a rendezvous site used by colonial militia. Also occupying the site were civilians, certainly the Munnerlyn family, and other civilians from the Snow's Island community. More than likely slaves were also there. The site is associated with the redoubt at Dunham's Bluff, 38MA165.

38MA165 DUNHAM'S BLUFF REDOUBT

The test excavations at 38MA207 presented the opportunity to investigate the earthen bank on the backside of Dunham's Bluff on the Pee Dee a few hundred yards south of the campsite and directly across from Snow's Island. Although antebellum newspapers indicated that Marion's redoubt was nearby (see history of Dunham's Bluff), this earthen bank, on the back side of a bluff and facing only a swamp, did not appear to be a likely tactical location for a redoubt. Besides those newspaper articles, however, there is even more evidence that this *was* the redoubt. For instance, Marion biographer Robert Bass wrote Mrs. Canady that he used to take school children to the redoubt at Dunham's Bluff. Furthermore, a 1926 booklet written by D.W. Stokes illustrated a colonial button supposedly found across from Snow's Island (Figure 8.14). These buttons, called rattlesnake buttons, with a snake and thirteen stars and stripes, are often found on Continental Army camps and around Charleston.[59]

Three trenches were excavated across the earthen bank.[60] Unfortunately, no artifacts were found in the profiles, which would have been a great help in dating the berm. A bullet mold for making rifle shot, however, was found during metal detecting. The trenches revealed an unexpectedly complex stratigraphy (Figure 8.15) which we asked a geologist with expertise in sedimentology to read for us.

Consequently, at the end of May 2007, two experts visited the site and offered their assistance.[61] Both agreed that the earthen berm was definitely man-made. Evidence from trench profiles indicated a dark organic stain approximately 1.2 m below the top of the berm. This stain ran at an approximate 10-degree angle downslope through the berm, then plunged into the swamp at a 45 degree angle. A carbon[14] sample was taken from this organic stain (buried A horizon) and provided a date of 1600-1610 +/- 40 years with a 95% probability. This

The Archaeology and Landscape of the Snow's Island Community | 203

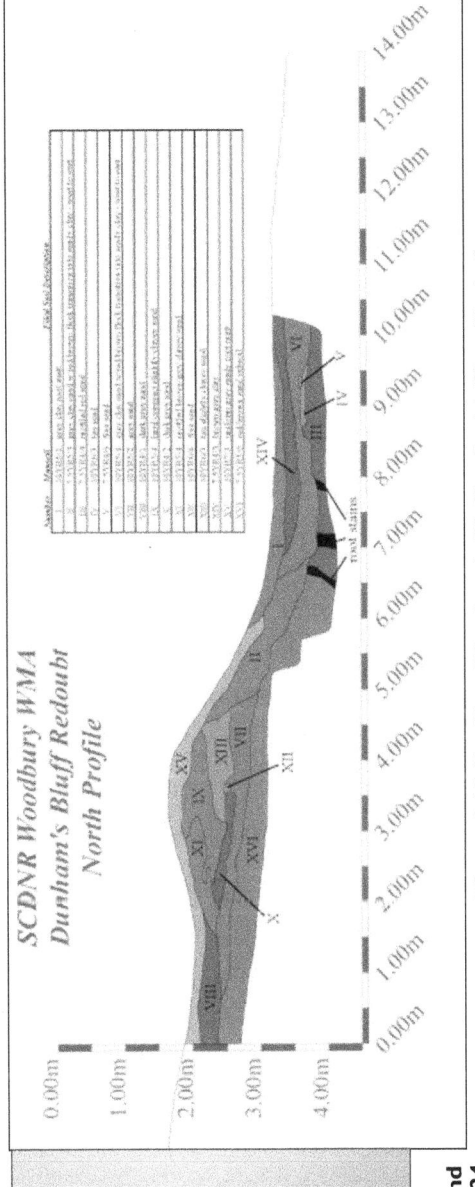

Figure 8.15. Profile of Dunham's Bluff redoubt (Sean Taylor)

**Figure 8.14
Rattlesnake button found
at Dunham's Bluff in 1924
(Stokes 1926)**

Button unearthed in January, 1924, just across the Pee Dee River from Snow's Island, by Mr. Arch McDuffie, of Britton's Neck. The button, being of silver and of special design and bearing a fox's h a v e been thought to have been worn by General Marion himself.

organic layer would have had to date earlier than Marion's redoubt (1780-81) when the A horizon (1780 surface) would have been sealed. "Hence, this is a 'good date' in that it is consistent with the interpretation that the earthen feature could well be attributable to Francis Marion." It is now clear that the feature is the remains of Marion's redoubt.[62]

38MA81 RICHBOURG'S

Approximately 700 yards west of the Dunham's Bluff site, 38MA207, the survey team discovered buckshot and a rifle ball in an open, plowed field (Figure 8.8). No ceramics were seen. Normally, a random rifle ball and buckshot would not be good evidence of an occupation as it is common knowledge among active relic collectors that one can find a random ball or two in any field; however, I had interviewed two relic collectors about 38MA207 and learned more about 38MA81.

At first, both acknowledged having a collection of lead shot from the location of 38MA207 but once I showed them a map of the site, neither had been to that actual location and, instead, insisted that their collections came from 38MA81. I have not seen either collection, but both assured me that they had found a colonial site at Richbourg's (named for the property owner). Site 38MA81 is probably either a piquet post for 38MA207 or, a detached camp of its own.

38FL280 AND 38FL281 SNOW'S ISLAND

Although a good argument can be made that 38MA207 is Marion's legendary Snow's Island camp, an equally good argument can be made that Marion's main depot was on Snow's Island. Robert Bass states that Marion's Snow's Island camp was at William Goddard's Plantation. Goddard owned and farmed the northern part of Snow's Island (see Chapter 4). Bass claimed further that Goddard's Plantation was "on the high ground toward the middle of the island, safe above the flood waters of the Pee Dee." Marion's men built lean-tos and used Goddard's barn for prisoners, calling it the "bull pen."[63] Bass grew up in the area, and although he was not precise in his references, my respect for his local knowledge has grown as the Dunham's Bluff camp and redoubt, which he wrote about, were confirmed archaeologically. Primary source material is, as usual, vague regarding the exact location of Marion's camp, but during Marion's winter 1781 occupation of the island, he wrote of being at "the mouth of Lynches Creek." Marion then wrote Greene a series of letters in January 1781, addressed from locations including "Snow's Island," "Lynches

Creek," and "Goddard's Plantation" (see Chapter 6). The letters addressed specifically as Snow's Island were written on 14 January and 18 January. Various Marion biographers have assumed, logically, that these postmarks are actually the same physical location; that being a camp somewhere on the north end of Snow's Island where Lynches Creek enters the Great Pee Dee. There is also the possibility that he was moving around.

Now we know his men occupied the camp at Dunham's Bluff and most likely had several detached camps in the Snow's Island region. Furthermore, there is the possibility that all these addresses were merely generalized locations, as the entire region, including the camp at Dunham's Bluff, was known as "Snow's Island." Archaeologist Lawrence Babits calls this conceptualization of the name a "mailbox," meaning that to an 18th-century partisan, Snow's Island was not an exact place. Instead, it was a place along the Pee Dee everyone knew as generally along the river near the mouth of Lynches Creek. Once you got to the Snow's Island region, you had to look further for the exact location where Marion was camping at that time.

In the case of Colonel Henry Lee, for instance, Marion's scouts found him first and guided him to the camp (see Chapter 6). The point is that neither Greene nor Lee knew exactly where Marion's camp on Snow's Island was. Scouts or messengers went to the "mailbox" and either found Marion or were found by Marion's scouts.

Hypothetically, Hugh Miscally, the Loyalist who guided British Colonel Doyle to the island, only knew where Snow's Island was, and guided them to that location where they were challenged by Marion's guards. Once on the island and in a running battle, the scouts retreated toward the actual camp. By defending the camp, they led the British to its exact location.[64]

In any case, my first attempt to find the camp on Snow's Island in 1993 was at the instigation of a relic collector who had found 18th-century bottle glass in the water near the mouth of Lynches Creek. Since this site fit the location of Goddard's Plantation, I conducted a survey. Three colonial sites were discovered, 38FL280, 38FL281, and 38FL282 (Figure 8.16). None were "smoking guns" for Marion's famed camp. Instead, they just added to the mystery.

The first, 38FL280, is located just across Clark's Creek from Snow's Island and was revealed as a result of a bulldozer cut. Relic collectors already had found iron kettle fragments, a pistol barrel, two brass buttons, buck shot, and a file. The survey team found a gun flint, five "black" glass bottle sherds (two bases are probably 18th century), seven pipestems, three bowl fragments, a delft sherd, three Staffordshire sherds, three Jackfield sherds,

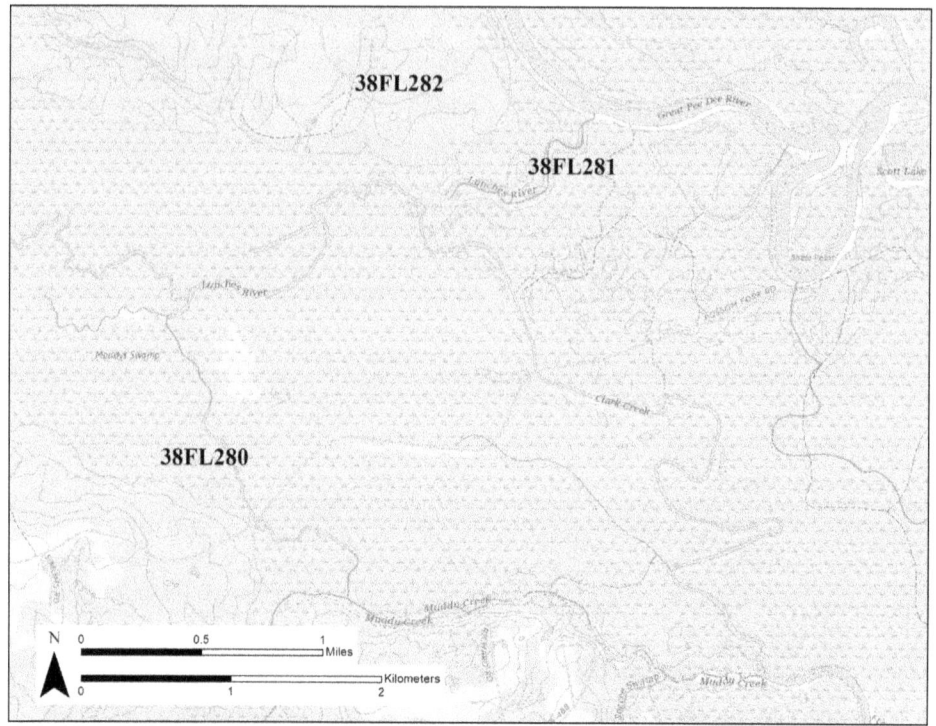

Figure 8.16. General locations of sites 38FL280, 38FL281, and 38FL382 (USGS The National Map, modified by Brock Shattuck)

one flat brass button with iron shank, two thimbles, two pewter buttons, one lead seal, one strap buckle, daub, brick in very poor condition, and colonoware sherds.

A damaged feature was excavated, its function unknown as the site had been essentially destroyed by the bulldozer work. Impressions at the time were that the site predated the American Revolution. Given what has been learned to date from other colonial sites, these impressions may not be accurate, but no other interpretation is possible except that the site is an 18th century domestic site, possibly dating to Marion's occupation.

Site 38FL281 consists of a large 2,000 x 500 m stretch of land on Snow's Island from the mouth of Lynches Creek upstream along the south bank where relic collectors found "black" glass bottles. The relic collectors also found a pewter spoon, button, lead "patch" kettle fragments, and a Spanish four *real* coin dating to 1783 (post Revolution). At the time of survey, this part of Snow's Island was planted in young pine trees like Dunham's Bluff. Bedding had not been done, so the land was not textured with long rows of plowed banks.

On the other hand, space between the trees was thickly covered in underbrush making metal detecting impossible except along the road that parallels the bank. The landowners, Sonoco Products Company, assisted the team by bulldozing lanes between the trees, skimming away the underbrush, and leaving clear open lanes approximately 10-15 meters wide from the mouth upstream. This made metal detecting conditions ideal.

Amazingly, though, hardly anything was found. One rifle ball and one colonial period sleeve button are the only items of interest besides numerous 19th century nails and logging equipment. The location fit all historical descriptions, but nothing was found indicating a partisan camp or even evidence of a domestic site.

I returned for a one-day visit around 2009 when I received word that the property owners had timbered the area. Once there, I and two colleagues walked several hundred acres of cleared land, finding no surface indications of a camp. Surely, if this had been the location of Marion's camp, some 18th century ceramics would have been found on the surface.

38FL282 GODDARD'S PLANTATION

Since nothing was found at what was considered the most likely location based on the historic record, the survey team concluded that Marion's correspondence listing such locations as "mouth of Lynches Creek," "Goddard's Plantation" and "Lynches Creek" could refer to either side of Lynches Creek. Across from Snow's Island, the land rises as much as 39 ft. above sea level and 15 ft. above the highest elevation on Snow's Island at the mouth of Lynches Creek. On the bluff line just above the mouth of Lynches Creek, the survey team located a large late 18th-century domestic occupation, which I believe is Goddard's Plantation. *Mills' Atlas* depicts "Goddard's" 19th-century house at this location (Figure 8.17). The atlas was published 40 years after Marion's occupation of the region, however, and the Goddard's on Mills's map could easily have been built on top of the colonial occupation, which actually appears to be the case, based on the material culture recovered. In 1993, 1994, and 2000, a team under my direction conducted metal detecting and shovel testing and excavated formal hand units at the site. The following presents a summary of those excavations.

Metal Detecting. The site was in a planted pine plantation; however, the trees were probably 5 to 10 years older than those at Dunham's Bluff and had been through at least one thinning (another thinning occurred after 1993). There was much less underbrush to deal with. A total of 358 metal items

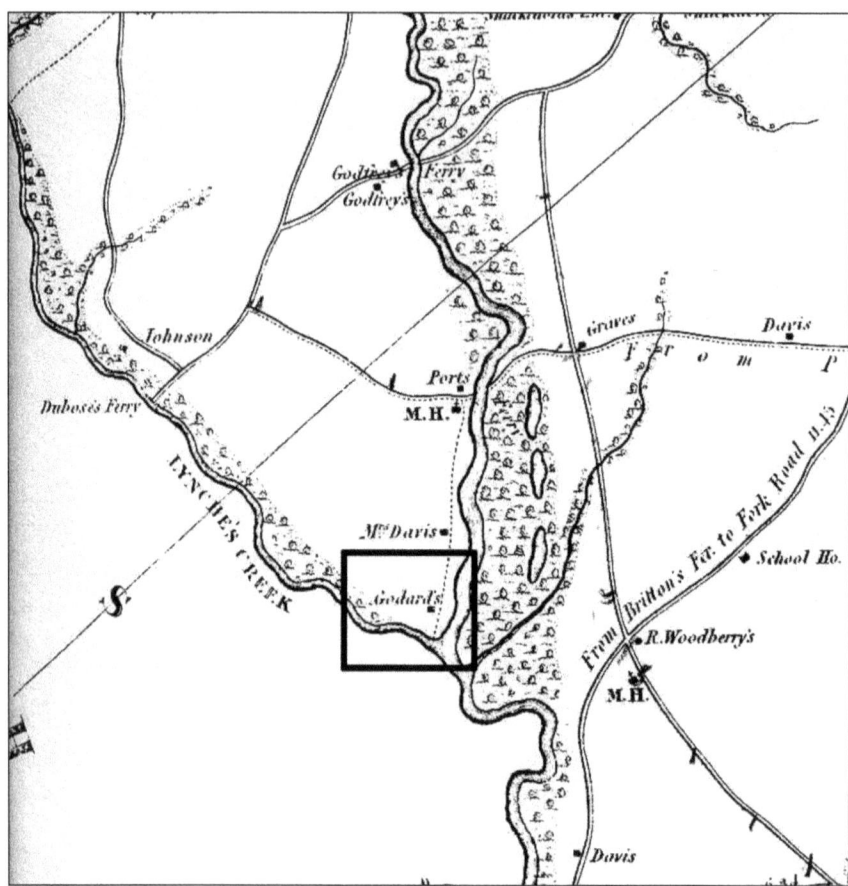

Figure 8.17. Goddard's Plantation on *Mills' Atlas* (1825)

were recovered. The vast majority (N=184) are broken iron kettle fragments, another 55 are unidentified iron objects, many of which are probably kettle and nail fragments. Most are smaller than three inches in diameter and were scattered across the site. Nails were not collected. Other metal items include 27 flat buttons of the colonial period, 2 cuff links, 12 pieces of lead sprue, 3 other lead chunks, 3 pewter pieces, 2 thimbles, 4 shoe buckles, 2 strap guides, 3 pieces of chain, 2 file fragments, 8 plow fragments, 2 unidentifiable coins (probably King George pennies), 2 knife fragments, 2 furniture pulls, 1 folding ruler fragment, 13 unidentified copper fragments, 1 axe blade, 2 hooks, 1 key fragment, and 3 spikes. There are also 24 lead shot mostly from rifles and trade guns (Table 8.2). None of the shot is of standard military caliber.

Excavations. Excavations revealed a late colonial to early 19th-century occupation including at least two large post-in-ground or earthfast buildings

(Figures 8.18, 8.19). Artifacts from the site consist of large amounts of creamware, colonoware, dark green "black" glass, lead glazed slip-decorated earthenware, pipestems, salt-glazed stoneware, Westerwald stoneware, and combed slipware, typical of late 18th century sites.

The first building was a very large, rectangular structure 6.75 x 4.5 m. in size or approximately 22 x 14 ft. (Figure 8.18). The structure was oriented north/south along its long side and the west side consisted of nine postholes, representing an earthfast building. In 1993, the west side and south end of the structure were excavated, and the north end was shovel skimmed to see if a hearth could be located. No hearth was found. In 1994, a small team of excavators returned to reveal the east wall, but a logging skidder from tree thinning had so damaged the structure that in the limited time funded for excavations, it was never clear that the team was excavating the east wall of a single structure or the wall of another adjacent structure. In any case, plow zone artifacts were numerous, but two features, one from each season, provide data of interest.

Feature 11, from the 1993 excavation, was identified as a posthole with post mold approximately 20 x 40 cm. In the bottom of the feature was a concentration of 18 sherds from a single badly burned salt-glazed stoneware plate. The heat from a fire was so hot that the glaze had puddled on some sherds. Half the sherds are larger than a quarter. In the upper soils of the feature there were also recovered a combed slipware sherd, and an unburned green glass sherd, a burned glass sherd, and many brick fragments.

Feature 17, from the 1994 excavation, was identified as another posthole feature, also containing many sherds. The feature included 22 colonoware sherds, many showing signs of burning. There are also 49 historic European ceramic sherds. These sherds are both creamware and salt-glazed stoneware types but the exact identification for individual sherds could not be done because of the fire damage. Nevertheless, enough were cross mended to form parts of a single salt-glaze stoneware mug and at least one creamware plate. There are also 7 combed slipware sherds (also burned), and 12 lead glazed earthenware sherds that were mended to form parts of a jug. More evidence from the fire include 4 melted clear glass blobs, 6 green glass blobs, 3 blue glass blobs, and 10 green glass sherds. Three other clear glass sherds are curled from being near a fire. Two nails and a brick fragment complete the artifacts from this single post hole.

As noted, Structure 1 could be a single structure or two adjacent buildings. It appears that the artifacts from this structure, or structures, are probably from an earlier occupation than that represented by the postholes. In other words, the

210 | *Francis Marion and the Snow's Island Community*

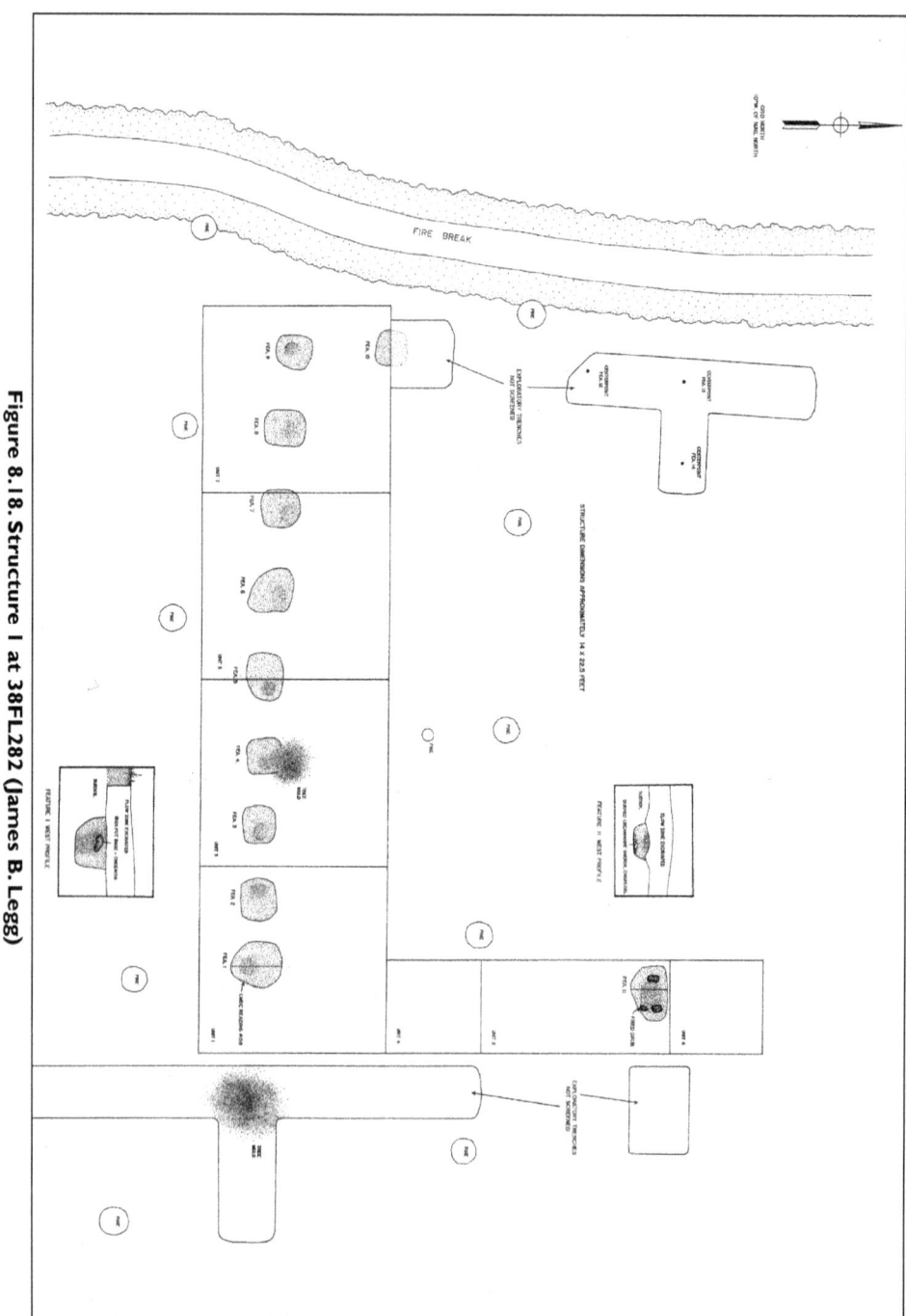

Figure 8.18. Structure 1 at 38FL282 (James B. Legg)

Table 8.2. Lead shot from 38FL282

Ball Diameter	Fired	Unfired	Fired/Unfired ?	Totals	Lead/Pewter
Rifle balls (5.3 g to 18.2 g)	7	3	3	13	(2)
Rifle/Carbine		1	1	2	
Standard Buckshot (.250" to .320")	2	1		3	
Small Buckshot <.250"	3			3	
Large Buckshot/Small Rifle (.321" to .380")	2		1	3	
Totals	14	5	5	24	(2)

artifacts inclusion in the postholes is the result of digging the posthole and, in backfilling, the builders threw in artifacts from a previous structure. There was no evidence in the post molds that would indicate the actual posts burned, yet the artifacts had clearly been subjected to an intense fire. This suggests that the structure, or structures, represented by Features 11 and 16, were replacements for an earlier structure, possibly not an earthfast structure, and that the previous structure occupied the same space as Structure 1. The absence of a hearth suggests that Structure 1 was possibly agricultural in function rather than domestic.

Structure 2, excavated during the 2000 season, was fully exposed and was approximately square, 4.5 m. on a side (14 ft.), and consisted of eight postholes and was another earthfast structure. A hearth was found in the center of the south wall (Figure 8.18). In contrast to Structure 1, the artifacts from this structure are not burned and were universally small fragments. Features contained very few artifacts as did the upper plow zone. Feature 4, the structures northeast corner, contained only one creamware sherd, a colonoware sherd, and an unidentified metal fragment. In the five 2 x 2 m. units, six 1 x 2 m. units, and five 1 x 1 m. units, only 19 creamware, 42 colonoware, an alkaline glazed sherd, and one combed slipware sherd were recovered.[65] Only seven green glass sherds and three dark green "black" glass sherds were found. Prehistoric artifacts (ceramics and lithics) outnumber the historic artifacts in the plow zone. A flat button was also recovered as were a few nail fragments. Again, none of the ceramics or glass show signs of burning.

212 | *Francis Marion and the Snow's Island Community*

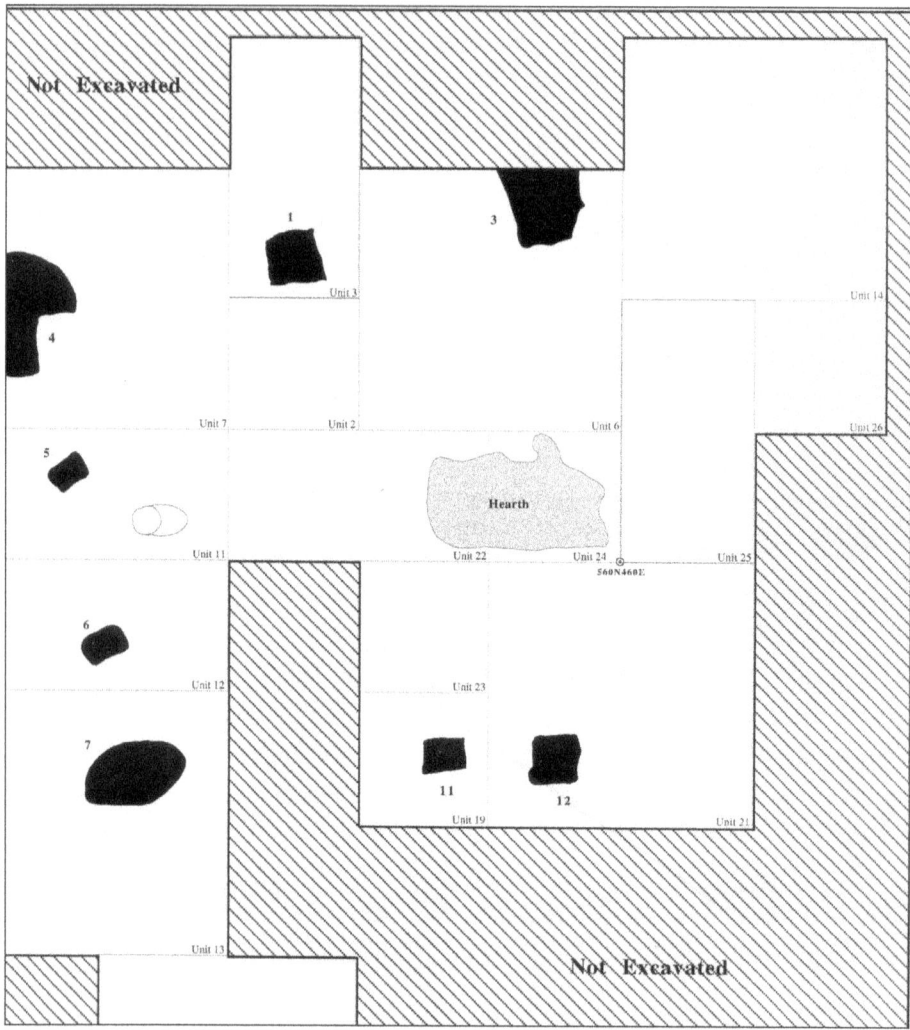

Figure 8.19. Structure 2 at 38FL282 (Mona M. Grunden)

Archaeologists have excavated many earthfast structures in South Carolina. Some have asserted that this technique was most popular at slave or low status households in the Lowcountry between 1740s and 1790s. All these sites were dated based on the associated artifacts. It must be mentioned that such structures are also found at 17th century sites in Virginia; however, it is becoming clear that they died out in the Lowcountry of South Carolina in the early antebellum period.[66]

Interpretation. Based upon documentary evidence, artifacts and structural features, this site appears to be William and Frances Goddard's late 18th century colonial plantation and the early 19th-century plantation depicted in *Mills' Atlas* as "Goddard's." Goddard's Plantation, according to Bass, was on Snow's Island. In fact, Goddards owned land on both the north and south banks of Lynches Creek at Snow's Island.[67]

As much as I would like this to be a Marion campsite, there is virtually no archaeological evidence of a military presence, although the artifacts date to the correct time period. There does not appear to be enough lead shot to argue that it was occupied by militia. All that can be said is that the site was probably occupied during the Revolution and that, as it is near Snow's Island, Marion could have visited it or had a piquet post there. Perhaps the colonial occupation is part of Goddard's main plantation house while the field hands were housed on the island where there is historical evidence that he owned land and had agricultural fields. Marion's men probably occupied Goddard's slave quarters on the island, as he had done elsewhere like Wadboo Plantation. After the war, it would appear that at least some slaves occupied the upper (northern) part of the plantation, as Structure 2 was likely a slave quarter. Meanwhile, the exact identity of Structure 1 (or structures) is as a plantation outbuilding because it seems too large for a slave quarter and there is no evidence of a hearth.[68]

The evidence of burning at Structure 1 is very intriguing and leads to additional supposition. It is reasonable to speculate that the artifacts from the area of Structure 1 represent Goddard's Revolutionary period occupation, burned by Wemyss during his 1780 raid or Doyle's raid on Snow's Island. After the war, Goddard rebuilt his plantation on the same location as represented by Structures 1 and 2. Thus, this site is closely associated with the Snow's Island community even if there is little evidence that it is directly associated with Marion.

38WG170 BLACK MINGO, 38WG171 BLACK MINGO NORTH

Fifteen miles south of Snow's Island, Marion defeated a detachment of Loyalists camped around Dollard's Tavern at the end of September 1780 (Figures 3.5, 3.6, 3.9, 4.1). This battle was briefly described in Chapter 6. Liscomb placed Dollard's Tavern just south of Sheppard's Ferry and east of Willtown, a well-known colonial village. Taverns were often located near ferries to serve waiting ferry customers. In a field just south of the modern Highway 41/51 bridge across Black Mingo Creek and the suspected site of the old ferry, local relic collectors and Revolutionary War enthusiasts reported ceramics and glass (Figure 8.20). The survey team visited this field and its surrounding woods several times over the course of 2006 and 2007, and eventually recovered artifacts indicating that this was the location of Dollard's Tavern and at least a portion of the battlefield. Many artifacts came from near a large pile of colonial brick. A collection of over 120 metal items was assembled as a result of this metal detecting visit, including flat buttons, melted lead, and colonial period buckles. There is little evidence of a later 19th century occupation. The collection includes 32 buckshot, 19 rifle/carbine-sized lead balls, and 1 musket ball probably fired from a French Charleville musket. Other items of interest are a gun trigger guard, a bayonet/sword scabbard clip, the ramrod pipe from a British Brown Bess musket, the tang of a gun butt plate, a pistol or trade gun side plate, lead sprue from a buckshot mold, and a King George penny dating from the 1750s.

The Black Mingo region was used often by Marion's men as a campground and as a reserve depot for supplies from Georgetown once it was in American

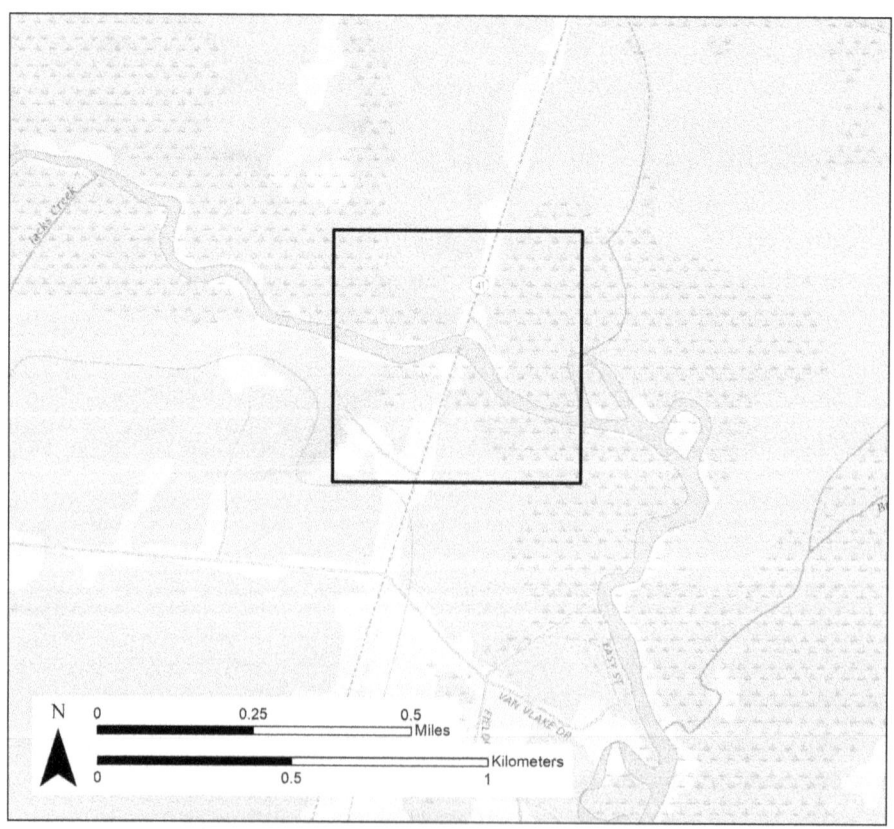

Figure 8.20
General location of sites 38WG170 and 38WG171
(USGS The National Map, modified by Brock Shattuck)

hands. Marion camped there on 17 November 1780. He also sent Captain Postell to the area in January 1781. In March 1782, Marion, acting on Governor Mathews's orders, planned to use Black Mingo as a safe haven for the residents and merchants in Georgetown including moving their property there. Further, on 13 March 1782, Marion suggested that Horry post a guard and camp at Black Mingo for those stores, including constructing a redoubt with a block house in the center: "Your situation should be such as to command the river within musket shot."[69]

One relic collector who had seen newspaper articles on the Dunham's Bluff excavations contacted me and offered to show me his collection from the Black Mingo area. He said he found a considerable number of musket balls across the river. I visited the collector and was shown an amazing assortment of flat buttons, rifle and musket balls, fragments of musket side plates, a cartridge box finial, and a sword scabbard tip. The collector also had a coffee can nearly full of buckshot, which he had collected from the site, but did not believe they were connected to the occupation. He thought they were modern buckshot and had collected them simply to clear the area so that he could find more interesting artifacts. An examination of a sample of the buckshot demonstrated that the vast majority were not modern.

I then surveyed the location he showed me (Figure 8.20). The team recovered 25 metal items, including 9 buckshot, 8 rifle/carbine lead balls, 1 flat button, 1 lead seal, and 1 colonial period buckle. This site, 38GW171, has to be one of Marion's or Horry's campsites (or perhaps a Loyalist camp), a rare one in that there is no evidence of ceramics—as is the usual case. In other words, this was a campsite that does not appear to be located around a domestic structure like a plantation house or ferry.

38MA206 BLUE SAVANNAH

Survey goals for the Francis Marion Trail Commission in 2006 and 2007 included a search for the Blue Savannah battlefield. This battle, as described in earlier chapters, was along the Little Pee Dee in Loyalist territory and, according to Loftis Munnerlyn, was instigated by Loftis and his brothers insisting on rescuing their father, who was a prisoner of the Loyalist militia there. The battle occurred 4 September 1780, only a few weeks after Marion took charge of the Snow's Island community militia.

The battle was two skirmishes, perhaps as much as two to three miles apart. From Port's Ferry, Marion set out to the east to find the Loyalists and disperse them (and perhaps rescue Munnerlyn's father and mother). Marion's vanguard was under Major John James, who found Loyalist commander Major Micajah Ganey and a mounted detachment. James immediately attacked and routed Ganey. From the prisoners, Marion learned that the Loyalist infantry were camped three miles farther ahead. Arriving near the infantry camp, Marion found some 200 men, formed up in line under the command of Captain Jesse Barefield. Marion retreated, but near "Blue Savannah," he set up an ambush. Barefield pursued, fell into the ambush, fired a volley, and then retreated into a nearby swamp.

Genealogist Jo Church Dickerson has devoted many hours attempting to find the skirmish sites and generously provided her knowledge of the area where she believed the battle occurred.[70] Among her findings is an 1865 plat of Thomas M. Munnerlyn, son of Loftus, which depicts the "blue savannah" (Figure 8.21). The location corresponds to *Mills' Atlas*, which depicts Loftus Munnerlyn's house along the old Little Pee Dee River Road (Figure 3.7). This might be the 1780 Munnerlyn house, but it does not have to be. The location is near a savannah-like landscape feature (a Carolina bay); Highway 41 cuts through the savannah today. This evidence provided a searchable area for metal detecting.

In 2006 and 2007, the survey team conducted two metal detecting reconnaissance surveys in the region. Survey conditions were mixed and included, pastures, plowed fields, planted pines, and woods with heavy undergrowth. Two artifact concentrations were discovered. Five buckshot (one pewter) and a rifle ball were recovered at the first site. Within 100 m. of the first, a light scatter of 18th century artifacts was found on the surface. On this second site, nine artifacts were collected, including a wrought nail (there were several other examples on the surface), three kettle fragments, "black" glass, a slipware sherd, two buckshot, and a rifle ball. This latter site appears to be a colonial domestic site, or less likely, a camp. One isolated rifle ball was found at least 100 yards from the other two concentrations.

Normally, the low number of shot recovered would not be good evidence of a battle site. The combined archaeological and historical data is tantalizing and lends support that one of the skirmish sites has been located. Both skirmishes were brief affairs in which one or two volleys were exchanged; probably neither side were armed with muskets, hence the absence of musket balls. In summary, the team found suggestive evidence in a location that fits the historic description but nothing that would confirm that we had found the battlefields.

The Archaeology and Landscape of the Snow's Island Community | 217

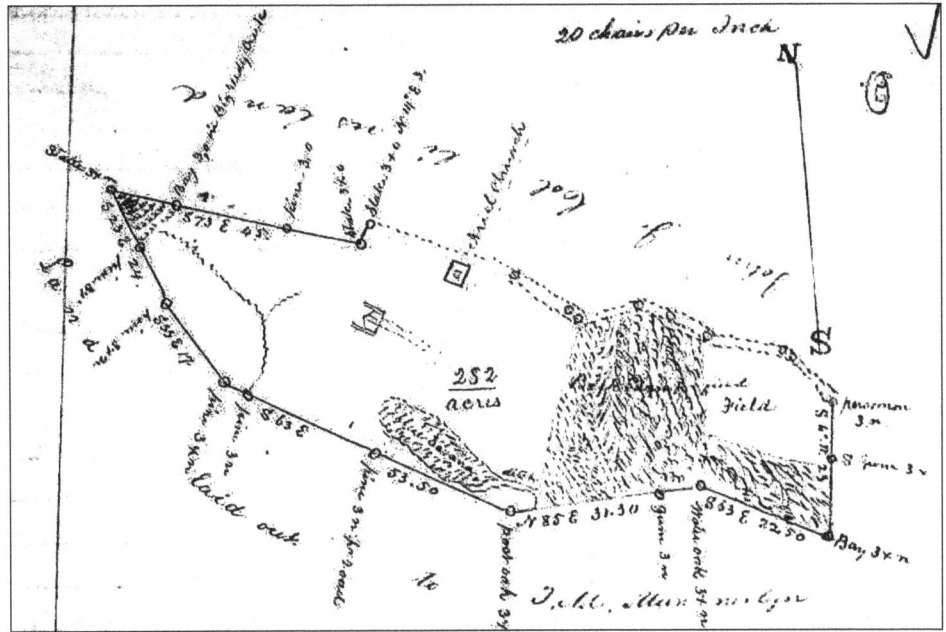

Figure 8.21. Thomas M. Munnerlyn 1865 plat depicting blue savannah and homestead (Marion Deed Book II:92, courtesy Jo Church Dickerson)

BURCH'S [BURCHES] MILL, 38FL46 AND 38FL50

Joseph Burch's plantation, ferry, and mill were scenes of important events in the Marion story. Many of these were discussed in earlier chapters. Besides Marion, it is quite likely that other militia units camped at the plantation many times. Although I did not included Burch's contributions to the cause in earlier chapters, as he was at the northern edge of the Snow's Island community, Burch was a strong supporter of the Revolution, and he received a total of 70 Pounds, 17 Shillings, and one half penny Sterling as compensation for provisions and forage provided to the militia from 1780 through 1783.

Both American and British troops made use of Joseph Burch's mill and plantation on various occasions during the American Revolution. The earliest known visit by Francis Marion was on 20 and 21 February, 1781 and he camped at the plantation. Colonel Doyle camped at Burch's on 28 March 1781 after destroying Marion's camp at Snow's Island. Burch met Marion's men and told them Doyle had been at the camp. Marion's orderly book indicates he camped at the "Burke's Mill" on 1 April 1781 and this is probably Burch's Mill. Toward the end of the war, Marion was ordered to pursue North Carolina/Little Pee Dee Loyalists. On his way to meet the Loyalists he wrote Loyalist Major

Micajah Ganey to negotiate a truce before more blood was spilled. The letter does not specify the mill, ferry, or plantation, just "Birche's." This is repeated in a letter on June 3, and again it was "Mr. Birches'." On 8 June 1782, Marion and Ganey signed a treaty at Burch's. Marion also writes two letters after the signing, on 9 and 15 June. Both are noted as "Burch's." Marion's orderly book addresses orders from "Burches Mill," on June 3 and "Camp at Burches Mill 7 June 1782." Marion also wrote General Nathanael Greene on 9 June, "Burches on PD," and "Burches" on 16 June.[71]

Like other sites in the area, there are no colonial records indicating that Joseph Burch owned a mill or ferry prior to the American Revolution. Plat and deed research indicates that he owned large tracks of land "north of Jeffries Creek in the neck, and south of Jeffries creek on Willow Creek." He established a ferry across the Pee Dee in 1790 after the war and owned two boats, one of which Colonel Henry Lee borrowed during the war and never returned (Figure 3.4).[72] Nevertheless, I believe that Burch operated the ferry prior to and during the war.

Historian G. Wayne King places Burch's Plantation "between Hopewell Church and Willow Creek Bridge." Archivist Terry Lipscomb further pinpointed the location of Burch's in Florence County east of SR 57, about a mile south of the confluence of Jeffries Creek and the Pee Dee River. At this location there is a small creek running east to the Pee Dee called Mill Branch, a modern mill pond, and nearby, archaeological sites 38FL46 and 38FL50. These sites consist of scattered colonial period ceramics.[73]

Mr. Deryl Young was contracted by the Francis Marion Trail Commission to conduct map and plat research in the area of the mill pond to see if historic documentation could be found indicating Burch's presence. This research furthered the mystery of Burch's Plantation and Mill. The area of the mill pond was owned by the Hewson family at the time of the Revolution. Edward Hewson was granted land to build a mill there in the 1750s. An adjacent plat even calls the creek flowing into the pond Hewson's Mill Creek. This creek was also mentioned as being the general location of the first Aimwell Church established by the Witherspoons.[74]

Burch did own property nearby, however. His will indicates that he was living on the property just north of Hewson's. There are two colonial period sites recorded in that location, 38FL46 and 38FL50 (Figure 8.22). Burch's Ferry, 38FL46, appears to have been officially established in 1790. There is an undated petition (circa 1801-1802) by residents of the Warhee region complaining that Burch's Ferry rates were too high. Apparently they needed

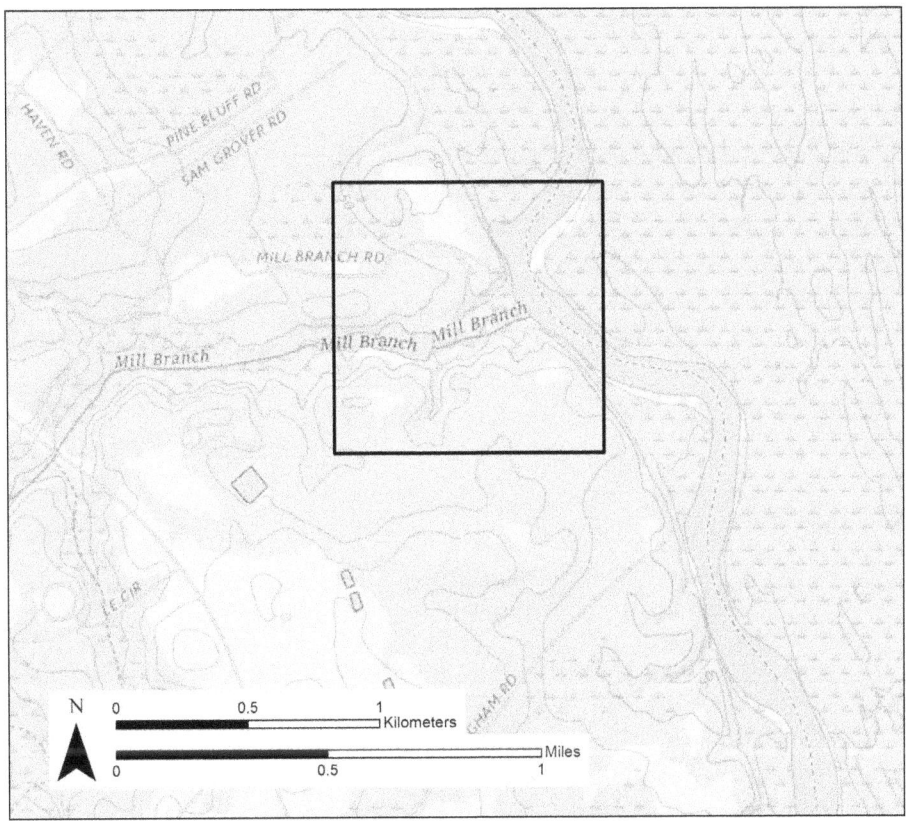

Figure 8.22. General locations of sites 38FL46, 38FL50, and suspected location of Burch's Mill (USGS The National Map, modified by Brock Shattuck)

to use this ferry to get to Burch's Mill to grind their corn. Young believes that at the time of the Revolution, Burch was leasing the mill from Hewson and perhaps later purchased it. Another possibility is that Hewson was the owner but Burch was the miller and active partner.[75]

During the Francis Marion Trail survey in 2007, the survey team was able to survey a 378-acre plot of land that included both sides of Mill Branch. The mill pond area had recently been subjected to landscape clearing and large areas around the mill pond were clear of debris and vegetation. Unfortunately, the survey team found no evidence of colonial artifacts or mill foundations. Although the mill pond shoreline was cleared, land at the immediate eastern end, the most likely mill location, was in woods. Nothing was seen there, but the landscape looked as if had been severely impacted by heavy equipment sometime in the past. Meanwhile, at the ferry site 38FL46 and adjacent 38FL50, a plowed field, 18th-century ceramic artifacts were observed.

After my project, Mr. Neil Myers, who has an interest in families in the area of Jeffries Creek did more extensive research into the Burch's mill mystery. He contacted the landowner at the mill pond and was given permission to dig around. He turned up laid stone in a trench between the mill dam and the Pee Dee.[76] Myers strongly believed he had found Burch's Mill and, in 2020, I conducted a two-day investigation at that location, finding only a few wrought nails, soft brick, and three 18th-century sherds. The archaeological evidence indicates an 18th-century site, and the most logical purpose of the laid stone is as a mill race. Mr. Myers site, most likely is Burch's Mill.[77]

The landscape around the mill site, consisting of high banks adjacent to the site on the south and Mill Branch on the east, totally precludes any possibility that Marion signed the treaty with Ganey at the mill site. Marion must have signed the treaty at Burch's Plantation, and both troops, Marion's and Ganey's, camped at the plantation.

THE PARTISAN COMMUNITY LANDSCAPE

This section discusses the colonial landscape around Snow's Island and its transformation into a partisan landscape as a result of the war. For this discussion, I am making some assumptions about site functions based on interpretations presented in the previous section. For example, I do not know with absolute certainty that colonial artifacts discovered at site 38FL380 represent the camp location of the Williamsburg militia. All that is certain is that it is an archaeological site dating to the colonial period. In this case, it is not necessary to be certain, because the historical record firmly establishes that: 1) Witherspoon's Ferry was in the immediate vicinity, and 2) Marion took command of the Williamsburg militia camped at Witherspoon's Ferry. It is reasonable to assume that militiamen either camped there or nearby.

Chapter 3 presented the history of settlement of the Snow's Island region. The evidence presented indicates that the region consisted of a dispersed, rural, agricultural community settled by Protestants and their slaves beginning around 1740. The initial colonists were land speculators who purchased large tracts to sell to settlers. They were followed by a combination of Scots-Irish and Irish immigrants who settled first in Williamsburg Township and by Welsh settlers from Pennsylvania. Many Welsh quickly moved north upstream to better agricultural lands.

Settlement in the Snow's Island region was thwarted by the swamp-filled landscape of the Pee Dee Drainage and Carolina bays. Those people that stayed turned to cattle and hog raising to make a living. The swamps turned out to be great foraging areas for livestock and allowed settlers to purchase tracts of land that included both swamps and highlands. Homesteads were built in the highlands near the swamps and the cattle and hogs were turned loose in the swamps.

When indigo became a profitable cash crop, Snow's Island settlers found it could be grown in the region, although herding continued as the primary commodity up to the American Revolution. Indigo increased the need for a labor source and brought an increased number of slaves to the region.

As colonists continued to flow into South Carolina through the first half of the 18th century, a pattern developed in the northeastern part of the colony. Settlement and development first concentrated along the Waccamaw, Santee, Black, and lower Pee Dee Rivers. Large tracts of land that became rice plantations were purchased, especially along the Waccamaw. Settlement steadily increased along the Santee and Black Rivers in Williamsburg Township. Likewise, along the upper Pee Dee from around Jeffries Creek north to the area called the Welsh Tract (for its numerous Pennsylvania Welsh), a backcountry community developed. Between the Williamsburg and Welsh settlement was the Snow's Island community—with a less dense but well-distributed settlement focused along the Pee Dee and its branches, like Lynches Creek.

In other research, I have labeled a sparsely settled region surrounded by more densely concentrated settlements as an "Interior Frontier." Frontiers are generally considered regions beyond developed settlements where the process of initial settlement is just beginning. Frederick Turner saw a frontier as a "migrating region, a state of society rather than a place." For Turner, the frontier was "a stage of settlement that 'passed through' an area, to be replaced by a second, more stable stage." Today a more nuanced understanding includes the concept that frontiers are a peripheral place in which actors (usually colonists and indigenous peoples) vie in a contest of cultures between the core and the frontier periphery.

It is not my intent to discuss the imagined nature of the frontier, but rather to point out that settlement does not progress as a wave of people pushing into this periphery. The boundary between the core and the periphery is not like a bubble expanding westward. Instead, settlement and interaction on the colonial frontier in South Carolina, and the American frontier after the American Revolution, was dendritic and rapid, flowing up- and down-stream along major rivers, mountain passes, and buffalo trails. This rapid movement created interaction zones and contested spaces along migration routes while it also created pockets (both geographical and cultural) where the mindset and state of frontier society long persisted. These interior frontiers were formed because the initial settlers were always agriculturalists. Thus, they were interested in the best, most fertile lands. The Georgetown region was fertile for rice and indigo. The uplands of Cheraw were also fertile for growing crops. These regions were settled first. In between, the Snow's Island region, was less attractive to agriculturalists. That is why it was bypassed and why I believe it became an interior frontier, a region of light but well-distributed settlement, isolated by the nature of the landscape and surrounded by more concentrated settlement and development. In this case, it was a swampland, not suitable for large scale agriculture, and thought to be unhealthy. As historian Susan Linder stated when I asked her why she thought there was so little information about the region— "It has always been an isolated region."[78]

Another example of Snow Island's isolation is the apparent lack of mills. Mills were essential to colonial and pioneer families and usually one of the first industries in any pioneer setting. Lawrence Babits has demonstrated the importance of mills to Revolutionary War armies. Babits used orderly books to plot the route of General Greene's army in North Carolina. He knew the army usually camped at or near mill sites, as they were essential for grinding corn. He hypothesized that the army should camp within six miles (10 km) of a mill each day, although there was some evidence that armies used mills as far as 14 miles away from camp. The six-mile distance is based on central place theory, and research into medieval markets and Romano-British settlements. Six miles is an average distance that can be made on foot from home to market and back in a single day. Babits mapped 72 American campsites of Greene's army from 6 June 1780 to 15 April 1781. Babits concluded that "The Chi-square statistic suggests that while the army did not always camp at mills, there was a high degree of association between the duration of military camps and mills." Or, "If the army camped for more than one night, then the camp was invariably at a mill and... if the army camped for only one night, then the majority of cases the camp was located at a mill. So, since Marion had a camp at Snow's Island and Dunham's Bluff during the period from mid-November 1780 to end of March 1781, and possibly longer, where was the mill they used?[79]

There is no historical or archaeological evidence of a colonial mill within six miles of Snow's Island. However, like the question of Marion's camp on Snow's Island—absence of evidence is not evidence of absence. *Mills' Atlas* depicts a mill on Cypress Creek at Dog's Bluff on the Little Pee Dee approximately eight to nine miles from Dunham's Bluff (Figure 3.7). I have no information about whether this mill was in operation some 40 years before the printing of the map. In Chapters 6 and 7, I have demonstrated that this creek was a focal point of Loyalists in the Snow's Island region.

Meanwhile there were mills at the fringes of the community. Most famous was Burch's Mill, where Marion camped and signed the treaty with Major Ganey. As noted, this mill is probably located on Mill Branch. This mill, however, was nearly 18 river miles upstream from Dunham's Bluff. Another mill below Britton's Neck, called Smith's Mill, was just two river miles south of the mouth of Clark's Creek on the Pee Dee as depicted on a 1889 Corps of Engineer Map.[80] It is not known if this mill was operating during the Revolution. Marion camped at a "Smith's Mill" on 27 June 1782. The historic record indicates that he was in the Santee region at this time, so perhaps there was a mill just south of Britton's Ferry during the Revolution.

The bottom line is that while mills were essential to colonial agriculturalists, I have found no historic record of a mill within the core region of Snow's Island during the American Revolution. While there most certainly should be one, the absence of evidence points to another reason why I consider the region an isolated interior frontier. No one wrote much about its history although there were a reasonable number of people living there.

If the region is painted as an interior frontier, Snow's Island and the region around it became an ideal hiding place for Marion's partisans. As discussed in Chapter 1, partisans need a base camp, secure from their enemies. These base camps are always in remote areas or areas far from "civilization" and where access is difficult. Typically, guerrilla base areas are in mountainous regions, not only far from areas of population and development but also where the partisans can control access points like passes. As mentioned in the first chapter, guerrilla warfare strategist Mao Tse-tung also recognized swamps and marshes as landscape suitable for guerrilla operations. The landscape that made the Snow's Island region an isolated or interior frontier was its swamps, swales, oxbows, and Carolina bays. "Geography is the guerrilla's ally, as much as it is the invader's enemy. Guerrillas know the land by heart; it is their home. They hide in the native mountains, swamps, jungles, farmlands, or urban sprawl, places where an outsider would seldom dare go."[81]

The Snow's Island region was remote in terms of distance from the main concentrations of colonial settlement (Charleston, Camden, Cheraw, and Georgetown), which the British captured and controlled during Marion's partisan career. It was also remote as a result of its complex river system including the Great Pee Dee, Little Pee Dee, Black Mingo Creek, Lynches and Clark's Creek, Muddy Creek, and Lynches Lake. These rivers did not restrict human access to the region so much as channel access via the ferry system. In turn, the location of ferries informed the transportation network into and around the region.

Indeed, the ferries were the keys to access and transgress through the Snow's Island region. Witherspoon's, Port's, Britton's, Burch's, and Potato Bed Ferries were critical (Figure 3.4). With the war, ferries became strategic and tactical points as the colonial landscape was transformed into a partisan landscape. At the beginning of the war, they were used as rallying and rendezvous points. Already well-known points on the colonial landscape, many, like Port's Ferry, probably had been rallying or muster grounds for militias prior to the war. When Marion arrived at Witherspoon's in August 1780, the Williamsburg militia was already camped there. North of Witherspoon's Ferry, Giles's Britton's Neck militia was camped at Giles Bluff, a high bank overlooking the Pee Dee (Figure 3.7). They were probably stationed there because Giles's militia had been isolated and immobilized by General Horatio Gates's defeat at Camden and Giles was supplying his militia from his own plantation's resources.

When Marion arrived, he must have recognized the importance of the ferry crossings as control points for access into and through the Snow's Island region. Partisan warfare is a strategically defensive posture, but, on the tactical level, partisans need to act offensively through raids and ambush. Mobility is critical. Marion's partisans not only needed to control access into the Snow's Island region, but also be able to slip out and back. In both instances, ferries were essential.

Although limited, the historical and archaeological evidence reveals that these sites were guarded by Marion; the archaeological evidence shows the nearby campsites. It is reasonable to assume the Williamsburg militia camp was occupied by a Marion detachment guarding Witherspoon's Ferry whenever Marion was in the area in any reasonable strength level (Figure 8.3). On the west bank of Port's Ferry, there is archaeological evidence of a muster ground or a campsite or two (Figure 8.4). On the east bank, although I have not found any evidence, historical sources strongly indicate that there was a redoubt on the high ground just as one comes out of the swamp of Dog (Welsh) Lake (Figure 3.8). At Britton's Ferry, the landscape and tactical equivalent of the Port's Ferry redoubt exists at the Hickory Hill site. Hickory Hill is located on the first terrace above the swamp at Britton's Ferry (Figure 8.6). It is also on higher ground than the surrounding terrace. It guards access to and egress from Britton's Ferry at a crossroad. The high number of lead shot recovered suggests a militia presence. Up the road at Potato Bed Ferry, relic collectors have found a campsite nearby, close enough to the ferry to guard it. It is also near a road junction, guarding the road down the neck to Potato Bed Ferry (Figure 8.6).

One rare historical insight regarding the importance of ferries to the tactical landscape at Snow's Island is a letter from British Colonel Balfour to Georgetown Commandant Colonel Saunders. After British Colonel Doyle destroyed Marion's camp on Snow's Island, Balfour wrote Saunders that "C. Doyle is in possession of the ferries on Lynchs Creek and I would hope the Loyal militia of the other side will assist in driving them [Marion's men] off – your post [Georgetown] is now in that situation, that no effort from it can be of assistance."[82] In other words, controlling the ferries was as important as taking the camp. Another was Colonel Robert Gray's observation during the war that a post at Port's Ferry would control Witherspoon's Ferry and the larger region.

If I am correct that Marion placed detachments and guards to control the access points (in this case ferries) to the Snow's Island region and his camp, then is the Dunham's Bluff redoubt protecting an access point to Snow's Island? Was there a road or trail from Dunham's across to Snow's Island? Was this the main access point to the Snow's Island camp from Britton's Neck? Based on the above evidence this seems to be the case. The Reverend James Jenkins seems to suggest this as British Cornet Merritt was taken to the redoubt and made prisoner, being confined at William Goddard's house (see above discussion of Dunham's Bluff).[83] If so, then why was it placed at the rear of the bluff? Placed as it was, it could not protect the landing from the Pee Dee. Another explanation for the redoubt at Dunham's Bluff is necessary and will be presented below. First, though, additional observations are offered regarding ferries and their importance to the region.

At the tactical or micro landscape level, there is clearly a pattern in the topography of colonial ferry crossings. For some reason, every ferry site mentioned in this region consists of a high bluff on one bank and low swampy land on the opposite bank. Port's Ferry is so low that it required two ferries— one to get across the Pee Dee and the other to get across Dog (Welsh) Lake when the water was high. Witherspoon's, Port's, Britton's, and Burch's all have high banks right up against the river and a low swamp across from the bluff line. Port's and Britton's west banks are as much as 40 ft. higher than the land opposite. Unlike the other sites, the riverbanks at Potato Bed Ferry are wide, low, and swampy on both sides, with causeways rising above the swamp to the high ground, which is only perhaps 15 ft. above the river.

Second, it is interesting to note how both the Americans and British, regulars and militias, held ferries somewhat sacrosanct. Marion's first order from Gates transferred to Horry was to go to the Santee and burn all plantation boats and ferry boats in the hopes of trapping the British on the north bank of the Santee and cutting their supply line between Charleston and Camden. After the British destroyed the Snow's Island base camp, they were caught in the act of destroying the ferry boat at Witherspoon's when Marion's riflemen arrived on the south bank and challenged them. Yet, during most of the war, it appears that ferry boats were not regularly destroyed except as a desperate act. Sometimes even then, the ferry boats were not destroyed. For instance, when Marion retreated into North Carolina, there is no indication that he destroyed the ferry boats to protect his rear as he rode north. Even when Marion set off at the end of August to burn boats along the Santee, he must not have burned those along the Pee Dee and at Witherspoon's Ferry, as he quickly crossed these ferries on his return after the skirmish at Great Savannah. While Marion was famous for simply swimming his horses when in a hurry, it is doubtful swimming was the preferred method of crossing major rivers.[84] On many occasions he crossed at ferries and bridges. For instance, his attack at Black Mingo was all but thwarted when he crossed the bridge above the ferry and the noise of his horses warned the British camped at Dollard's Tavern. There is no record of Marion or the British destroying the ferry boat at Sheppard's Ferry where Dollard's Tavern was located. No doubt he swam his horses when needed, but as a regular practice, it would have tended to scatter his forces at each crossing (for example, Horry nearly drowned attempting to swim across Lynches Creek when the ferry boat had been scuttled by the British at Witherspoon's Ferry). As far as the ferries around Snow's Island were concerned, he possibly hid the boats he needed to be used as necessary.

The Snow's Island ferries generally remained in operation during the war, probably even during his January 1781 stay on Snow's Island when he collected boats and supplies to secure the area. In a rare example of documentary evidence supporting this contention, Frances Port's audited account records six instances of ferriage in 1779 for troops, wagons, cattle, and horses. There are also three in 1781, and at least six more for 1782 (writing difficult to read). On one receipt it includes ferriage for 322 men, 122 horses, and swimming 123 head of cattle. Interestingly, none of these receipts are dated to the fall 1780 when Marion was actively using this ferry on various occasions as a full partisan warrior.[85]

Ferries are good indicators of the road and transportation system. There are no detailed contemporary maps documenting routes used by the colonial community and Marion's partisans within the Snow's Island region. James claims that Marion made his own trails, which became well-used routes after the war: "Many of the general's trails remained for a long time after, and some are now roads." But there was a colonial road network (albeit poorly maintained) before Marion got there. These roads have significance to understanding the partisan landscape as did the ferries.[86]

The major routes on historic maps include the road leading north out of Williamsburg from Black Mingo (Sheppard's) Ferry and crossing Lynches at Witherspoon's Ferry, and another branching off from that road to Britton's Ferry. These roads are depicted on Faden's, Mouzon's and Cook's maps of the period (Figures 3.5, 3.6, 3.9). The road crossing at Witherspoon's ran up the Pee Dee, paralleling that stream on the west bank, and it is reasonable to assume that the "old river road" SSR 57 roughly follows that route (Figure 3.4). This was probably the general route Wemyss took when he burnt the Whigs out in the fall of 1780.

Today the road from Black Mingo to Britton's Ferry is probably County Line Road SSR5 (Figure 3.9). On the Britton's Neck side, it is rarely used today, but a dirt road (named Pet Larrimore Road) connects to it at the Woodberry Road intersection. From there, the colonial road ran north along the bluff line on the west bank of the Little Pee Dee and continued to the state line on the Mouzon and Faden maps. Running south of Black Mingo, the road split, with branches to Georgetown and Kingstree.

Obviously, there were other roads and trails during the colonial period and hints to this system can be seen on *Mills' Atlas* (Figure 3.7). Although nearly 40 years after the Revolution, the atlas provides rare details about the colonial road system that I believe are relevant to the earlier time period. For instance, it is clear that Marion traveled to places like Indiantown from the Snow's Island region during the Revolution—and Mills's map of Williamsburg District in 1825 does show such a road. Also, *Mills' Atlas* depicts points identified in Watson's campaign against Marion in 1781 along the Santee River Road. It is reasonable to assume that many other roads on *Mills' Atlas* existed during the colonial period. Since there are no roads on Britton's Neck depicted on the Mouzon, Faden, and Cook maps except the road out of Britton's Ferry, *Mills' Atlas* assists in learning more about the road system on Britton's Neck around the time of the American Revolution. At that time, the road from Britton's Ferry passed by Hickory Hill and appears to turn north up what is now Woodberry Road before going up the west side of the Little Pee Dee. This road today would be roughly State Roads 908 and 41. The road from Britton's

Ferry also goes northeast to Potato Bed Ferry, but travelers from Britton's Ferry on their way up the Little Pee Dee probably would have taken the Woodberry route (Figures 3.7 and 8.6). Meanwhile, the trail to Norman's Landing (Figure 3.7) may have been to Woodbury's [Woodberry's] Landing at the time of the Revolution.

Mills' Atlas depicts a road north of Lynches Creek running to Port's Ferry that crosses at Port's and runs straight east to join the road along the Little Pee Dee. This is probably Paul Richardson's Road or SSR 207 today. The atlas also depicts a road on the Pee Dee's east bank that runs south to Potato Bed Ferry and may be modern Highway 378 today; however, a more likely suspect is another road that follows the Pee Dee ridgeline. Only fragments remain today but it can be seen on more detailed maps like topographical maps (Figure 3.8). On this map, there is a dirt road that follows the ridgeline very closely. It is not certain that this road, or all of it, dates to the colonial period, however, assuming that it does, it provides additional insights regarding the partisan landscape. First, the Port's Ferry redoubt at Welsh Lake (shown as Dog Lake) was placed at a tactically sound location guarding both the road coming out of Welsh Lake and the road paralleling the ridgeline (Figures 3.8, 8.5, 8.6, and 8.8). Continuing down the road in a southernly direction is site 38MA205 (Richardson's), a small collection of colonial artifacts (Figure 8.5). If this site is actually a piquet camp, then it too is tactically well placed along the ridge road at a junction with another road from Port's Ferry. The latter road continues down toward Britton's Neck and, near Big Ben Port Lake, relic collectors and I have located another apparent collection of lead shot at 38MA81, which I believe is an outlying camp of Marion's Dunham's Bluff camp (Figure 8.8). From 38MA81, the road continues straight into 38MA207, "Marion's Camp" according to many 19th century maps and random literature. From here, travelers can turn south to Dunham's Bluff and cross over to Snow's Island or continue to the Woodberry Road. Marion's enemies attempting to get to Snow's Island would have had to contend with the Dunham's Bluff redoubt at this point. The presence of the redoubt here then is an argument that there was a camp on Snow's Island, as the redoubt was meant to guard this access point.

Moving farther south through the Dunham's Bluff camp onto a small ridge and then crossing Lone Pine Lake Run, one could cross onto Rae's Hill or to the Woodberry Road. Once on the Woodberry Road, one could travel down Britton's Neck to Britton's Ferry, but again would run into Hickory Hill and the possible camp there. On Woodberry Road, one could follow another ridgeline to Potato Bed Ferry. If so, the traveler would come straight to the campsite found by relic collectors and now destroyed (Figure 8.6).

Returning to Dunham's Bluff and the redoubt, its placement behind the high ground on the bluff at first seems to be a tactical blunder (Figure 8.8). It could not have stopped anyone coming up the Pee Dee as it was placed behind the bluff and did not even have a field of fire to the Pee Dee. From a partisan perspective, however, it is brilliantly placed. First, in looking at the road system described above, the redoubt controls access to Snow's Island from the river road on Britton's Neck. Second, as a partisan, one wants to be hiding first and foremost. A large enemy force coming upstream along the Pee Dee would pass Dunham's Bluff without seeing the redoubt. If the enemy did land on the bluff to attack the camp, then Marion's partisans could fire from the redoubt to stop the attack. Third, I believe that Lone Pine Lake Run was navigable at the time of the Revolution. In fact, this seems to be the most likely route into the camp from the river. If so, any enemy coming upstream to attack the camp that tried to attack from Lone Pine Lake Run would also have to contend with the redoubt. Finally, as placed, it is close enough to the road, the bluff, and the stream to protect all avenues of approach using rifle fire. The redoubt is positioned less than 200 yards from the road, the bluff line, and the stream. Artillery would be useful but not necessary with the redoubt placed as it is.

On the Britton's Neck side, defensive positions were constructed. But there is no evidence in the historic record—or archaeologically—of defensive positions on the west side of Snow's Island (save perhaps for site 38FL280). During field and archive research on Snow's Island camps, I assumed a literal translation of the letters written by Marion during his January presence on Snow's Island. As discussed in Chapter 6, these letters were addressed as "Snow's Island," "Lynches Creek," "Mouth of Lynches Creek," and "Goddard's Plantation." This led to fieldwork concentrated along the south bank of Lynches Creek with negative results. Bass, on the other hand, wrote that the site of Goddard's cabin was on the northern side, but was "toward the middle of the island," whatever that means.[87] Assuming that it means a central location on the island, then it would make some tactical sense. That is, hiding the camp in the deep swamp would require firsthand knowledge of its location to find and attack the camp, while a campground near the mouth of Lynches Creek might be seen from the bluff line across the creek at Goddard's Plantation. If there was a camp on Snow's Island, then Marion was relying on the swamp only as a means of defense. All in all, the camp at Dunham's Bluff was better protected than one on Snow's Island.

Far down the Woodberry Road, at the confluence of the Little and Great Pee Dee, was the Tanyard site (Figure 8.7). This is the final known earthen fortification—perhaps another redoubt—in the region. Bass believed the trench line was constructed under orders from Marion. There is no historic record of this fortification, but if it was a Marion earthwork, then its obvious purpose was to oppose enemies coming up the Pee Dee. At the tactical level, this earthen feature is positioned to stop traffic coming up the Pee Dee, not the Little Pee Dee, unless artillery was available. It is not located at the mouth of the Little Pee Dee but rather upstream from its mouth on a large bend that would provide defenders ample opportunity to fire upon boats coming up the Great Pee Dee. The placement was obviously only to deter river traffic, as it was so far down the neck that anyone attempting to attack Snow's Island would simply bypass it by crossing onto Britton's Neck at Britton's Ferry or Potato Bed Ferry.

In a nutshell, *the Snow's Island region was the Snow's Island camp.*[88] The archaeological evidence supports Marion's correspondence that his partisans were widely dispersed in small camps across the Snow's Island community. From Port's Ferry to Hickory Hill, from Witherspoon's Ferry to Dunham's Bluff, the archaeological expression of Marion's Snow's Island base camp, the partisan landscape, and the landscape of resistance, is the broad region of Snow's Island and its immediate vicinity, with multiple points or components consisting of camps and defensive fortifications to protect access routes into the region. The partisans made use of the Whig community's homes and resources, such as the house sites at Dunham's Bluff, Hickory Hill, and perhaps the Tanyard. There are most likely other examples, but this is the only known archaeological evidence available to date. Overall, except for the defensive fortifications, the archaeological expression of a partisan presence is largely as ephemeral in the archaeological record as the partisans were to the British.

Endnotes for Chapter 8

1 Isbell 2000; Hegmon 2002.

2 When an archaeological site is investigated by an archaeologist, it is given a unique number and often a name. In South Carolina, site numbers consist of three parts. The first number is 38 for South Carolina (of 50 states). The second part of the number are two letters representing the county in which the site is found. Marion County is MA. The last number is the next number in sequence of recorded sites. So archaeological site 38MA207, the Dunham's Bluff site, is the 207nd site to be officially recorded in Marion County, South Carolina.

3 Smith 2008a; Smith 2009.

4 Archaeologists are focused on preserving the exact location of every artifact they find. Thus, few professional archaeologists would touch a metal detector because they were associated with relic collecting for profit and digging the metal artifact destroyed any information about the artifact's depth. Archaeologist Doug Scott finally demonstrated their utility on battlefields in the 1980s and now they are the go to instrument for battlefield archaeologists. See Scott et al. 1989; Smith 1994; Conner and Scott 1998; Espenshade et al. 2002; Legg et al. 2005.

5 Legg et al. 2005:80. Metal detectors have different capabilities and it is usually a best practice to use several different models for different soil and landscape conditions. The primary detector used by operators at the sites discussed in this study was a Tesoro Cibola ®. This machine is lightweight with excellent discrimination and depth. Also used was a Fisher 1270 ®. It also has excellent discrimination and depth. Normally they had 8 in. coils. A 3 in. coil was also used at the Dunham's Bluff site (38MA207). Smaller coils are useful for distinguishing different types of metal within a dense cluster of metal artifacts. Archaeological sites 38FL280, 38FL281, and 38FL282 were investigated in 1993 and these detectors were not available at that time. For those sites, detectorists used a "Double Eagle" with a 15 in. coil and a White's Sierra Madre ® with a 9 in. coil. The Double Eagle was a hand-crafted detector popular with relic hunters in North Carolina at that time and worked well in sandy soils. It had practically no ground balance or discrimination. Likewise, the White's machine did not have a discriminator.

6 Trimble ® model Global Positioning System (GPS) data loggers were used in this study. Usually a Geoexplorer, or Geoexplorer 3; however we also used a TDC-1 model and a Geo XH. Pathfinder Office ® software was used for post-processing GPS data. The Geographic Information System (GIS) mapping software used for analysis was ArchGIS ® version 9. At 38MA207, metal detector artifact locations were recorded using a Sokkia ® SCT6 total station (electronic transit) for those artifacts discovered during the week that hand excavations were conducted.

7 In archaeological terms, a feature is the remains of some non-portable aspect of a site, which has a vertical aspect as well as horizontal aspect, usually located in the ground. Pits, trenches, post holes, wells, building foundations are all examples of features. One way to think of features is that you can't take it back to the laboratory. You must excavate it, to see its components. They are very important components of a site, because the artifacts found within the feature are known to have been used and discarded when the feature was abandoned or purposely filled in.

8 Smith 2008a.

9 Council of South Carolina Professional Archaeologists 2005.

10 All artifact bags were labeled on the exterior using permanent ink. Labels consisted (as appropriate) of the site number, catalog number, project name, provenience information, investigator's affiliation, recovery date, and bag number. All boxes in which artifacts were packaged were acid-free and medium sized (ca. 1 ft^3). A box inventory was inserted in each box and affixed to the outside for easier relocation of artifacts within the site collection. All associated record data (field notes, analysis sheets, artifact catalogs, etc.) were also boxed with the collection. Collections of artifacts from most sites are housed at SCIAA. Those artifacts from sites that were investigated for the Francis Marion Trail Commission were given to Francis Marion University at the request of the commission, except those on federal lands.

11 James 1821:105.

12 Trinkley 2000:37.

13 Jenkins 1842:29; Lee to Greene, 23 January 1781, GP, Vol. VII:177; Lee to Greene, 27 January 1781, GP, Vol. VII:206.
14 Port A.A. 6031.
15 Bailey 1997:59.
16 Giles A.A. 2817; South Carolina Statutes at Large, 1826, Act 2399:527; Carl Steen 2010, pers. comm.
17 Bass Tour notes, 1980, Bass-Canady Correspondence.
18 Arguing that a high ratio of lead shot to other metal items represents a possible militia presence is subjective and not meant to be a statistically valid statement. The detectors used provide the ability to distinguish lead, brass, and iron before excavation of the object and not all iron reading were recovered.
19 Jenkins 1842:27.
20 Sellers 1902:105; Bass Tour notes 1980, Bass-Canady Correspondence.
21 Stephenson 1975.
22 Smith 2009.
23 Joseph Davis Pension S10534.
24 John Rice Pension R8747.
25 Gregg 1925:595. Gregg cannot be held accountable for this confusion as the picture is in an addendum included by the Pee Dee Historical Society. The addendum also states that after the Battle of Blue Savannah, Marion "Return[ed] to Port's Ferry, he threw up a redoubt on the east side of the river, at what is now called Dunham's Bluff. He mounted a cannon and left an officer and men in charge. There is no record how long they remained" (Dargan 1905:596).
26 Jenkins 1842:18.
27 L. Munnerlyn Pension S18136; Jenkins 1842:29.
28 Plat-Snow's Island, Public Improvements Ferries-Petitions 1813, Peter DuBose, Sumter District. SCDAH. There are two types of ink on the plat. One set is bold and the other is lightly written. The "Marion's camp" is light. Its possible someone labeled the map with the camp after it was originally done, however, to my untrained eye, the handwriting looks the same.
29 Mills 1826:624.
30 Mills 1826:627.
31 Steuckrath 1858:122.
32 "To the Editor," *Charleston Courier*, 12 July 1828.
33 *Charleston Courier*, 29 October 1832.
34 Stackhouse 1905:17-18.
35 Johnson 1908:990.
36 In fact, during the 1993 survey of Snow's Island, I sent a survey team through this same location but the trees were so small and thick that they could not penetrate the woods.
37 Taylor 2008:3.
38 Credit for discovering the site goes to my colleague Mr. Spencer Barker. Spencer was part of the team and convinced us to return to the area after we had made a pass through and found little. Upon returning to the site, Spencer found the cannon ball.
39 Smith 2009:28.
40 Noel Hume 1991:68.
41 Peterson 1968: 27-29, 36-38; Darling 1970; Neumann 2001; Moore 1967:63,93-99; Neumann 2002; Tarleton 1787:139. Of course, it is not this simple. There were other caliber weapons. For instance, British cavalry and dragoons were armed with a .65 caliber carbine, which fired lead shot averaging a diameter of .600 in. (Peterson 1968:44-45; Moller 1993:256-265). Horse pistols were either .65 or .69 caliber, averaging a diameter of .540 in. and .640 in. (Peterson 1968:46-48). American regular dragoons were armed with a French carbine of .67 caliber, firing a ball with a diameter of .629 in. (Neumann and Kravic 1975:65). Only four (6%) shot with these characteristics were found at Dunham's Bluff.
42 Legg 2007:3.

43 Smith 2008a:41-44, 80; Smith 2008b:15-16; Smith et al. 2007a. This pattern is also reflective of relic collector activity to some unknown degree. That is, there are few, if any sites in South Carolina that have not been subjected to relic collecting since the 1970s. Musket balls are larger than rifle balls and thus easier to detect. Sites collected by relic collectors in the 1970s and 1980s would have lost much of their complement of musket balls at that time, while the rifle balls (and especially buckshot) would have been more likely to have been overlooked to be collected later by detectorists using more sophisticated machines. Still, the apparent pattern of extensive use of rifles by Marion's partisans is real.

44 Continental soldiers fired not only a large lead ball but loaded their muskets with a standard cartridge that contained powder for both the shot and priming pan, a lead ball, and three buckshot with a diameter of about .300 in.

45 Peterson 1968:60-61; Legg et al. 2005:101-103; Marion to Horry, 17 August 1780, James 1821:Appendix 11; James 1821:128, 179.

46 Smith et al. 2007a; Smith 2006b; Smith et al. 2007b; Boatner 1966:78-79.

47 This is not to say that the dominance of buckshot at a Revolutionary War battle site means it must be a Marion battlefield or camp. At the Camden battlefield (Smith et al. 2009) the combatants included American Continentals (Charleville muskets and cartridges), North Carolina and Virginia militia (muskets, probably Charlevilles), Loyalists (probably Charleville muskets and cartridges), British regulars (Brown Bess muskets), and British regular cavalry (carbines and swords). There were no known rifle units at Camden. A total of 817 buckshot were recovered by archaeologists at this site, while only 58 Brown Bess and 80 Charleville sized lead shot were recovered (Smith et al. 2009:64-65). There are only 56 lead shot of miscellaneous sizes including carbines, rifles, trade guns, fowlers, and case (artillery) shot in the collection. Only four were confirmed as fired rifle balls.

48 Smith et al. 2009.

49 Lawrence Babits, pers. comm. 2007.

50 Walton 1894:736. Colonel Clifford Walton, in his history of the British army from 1660 to 1700, noted that the ordinance regulations for 1683 stated that henceforth small arms would be marked with the King's mark. In 1699, this extended to all British ordinance including cannon balls.

51 McConnell 1988:288; Russell 1980:253.

52 Simms 1844:124; James 1821:56.

53 Archaeologists have come up with a a method of relative dating pipestems by measuring bore size. Archaeologists Lewis Binford and Ivor Noel Hume believe the method is not accurate for sites post dating 1760. For what it is worth, though, the pipestem bores were measured and a date of 1754 was calculated.

54 Neumann and Kravic 1975:157; Binford 1978; Noel Hume 1991:299-301; Brain 1979:plate 1 and 101.

55 Wallman 2009:Appendix A, 1-2.

56 Wellman 1917; William Arnold 2009, elec. comm. Irv Quitmyer 2009, pers. comm.

57 Chester DePratter 2009, pers. comm.

58 Irv Quitmyer 2009, pers. comm.

59 Bass-Canady Correspondence; Heider 1980; Stokes 1926; Troiani 2001:146.

60 Sean Taylor, archaeologist with the South Carolina Department of Natural Resources, is thanked for leading this investigation.

61 Geoarchaeologist Dr. Mark Brooks, South Carolina Institute of Archaeology and Anthropology, and Dr. Paul G. Nystrom, geologist from the South Carolina Department of Natural Resources, provided their expertise.

62 Smith 2009:37; Brooks 2009:B1-2.

63 Bass 1959:104.

64 Marion to Greene, 28 December 1780, GP, Vol. VII:13; Marion to Greene, 14 January and 18 January 1781, GP, Vol. VII:121,143; Babits 2009, pers. comm.

65 The colonoware sherds are less than a quarter in size. At that level it is difficult to distinguish

66 Drucker and Anthony 1979; Wheaton et al. 1983:338; Groover 1992; Wheaton 2002:36-37; Adams 2002:69; Epps 2006; Noel Hume and Noel Hume 2001.
67 Bass 1959:104, 157.
68 Smith 2008b.
69 Lipscomb 1975:38; Marion to General William Harrington, 17 November 1780, in Bass 1959:91; Marion to Greene, 8 March 1782, GP, Vol. X:462; Marion to Horry, 13 March 1782, Gibbes 1853:272.
70 Dickerson 2006.
71 O'Kelly 2006:513-514, 525; Rudisill 1993:205; Rankin 1973:179; Marion to Greene 16 June GP, Vol. XI:341; Smith et al. 2008, Gibbes, Vol. 3: 183-191.
72 Young 2007:2.
73 King 1981:27; Lipscomb 1981:36.
74 Young 2007.
75 Young 2007.
76 Neil Myers, 2010 elec. comm.
77 Myers 2006; Smith et al. 2020. Prior to my investigation, Jon Leader, the State Archaeologist ran a gradiometer over the site and found a strong metallic anomaly. We placed an excavation unit over the anomaly, and it turned out to be a cluster of soft red 18th century bricks. We found no artifacts reflecting a mill. This work was sponsored by the Florence County Museum.
78 Smith 2008c; Mitchell 1998:2-3; Mitchell 1998:3; Lightfoot and Martinez 1995; Linder 2010, pers. comm. Here I am emphasizing actual settlers. I know the first in any region were hunters, foresters (loggers), and speculators. Hunters and loggers usually moved on, and speculators were just that. The settlement of the upland South was completed by agriculturalists. After publication of my dissertation, I found that I was not the first to come up with this idea. In the 1960s, John Prescott, labeled these regions, passed over during the initial settlement of a region because of less desirable lands, as "secondary" frontiers (Prescott 1965).
79 Babits 1982:64, 88.
80 Linder 1984:113.
81 Tierney 2006:17.
82 Balfour to Saunders, 2 April 1781, Saunders Papers.
83 Jenkins 1842:19.
84 James 1821:70.
85 Frances Port A.A. 6031.
86 James 1821:70.
87 Bass 1959:104.
88 I give credit to Dr. Edward Carr, a member of my dissertation committee who made this comment. Ed summarized my dissertation in one sentence. Edward Carr 2006, pers. comm.

CHAPTER 9

FRANCIS MARION, SNOW'S ISLAND, AND AMERICAN MEMORY

There were other partisan leaders during the revolution in the South. Thomas Sumter, Isaac Shelby, William Bratton, for example, also kept the cause alive through the summer and fall of 1780 when Charleston fell and General Gates's army was destroyed. Today, however, we do not hear much about these American heroes. They do not have innumerable biographies or days named after them. Disney did not devote a TV series to them. So, if children still learn anything about the American Revolution in South Carolina, why is it Francis Marion they remember?

This chapter attempts to explain how South Carolina and America came to remember and construct a national memory of Francis Marion as the legendary "Swamp Fox."[1] It focuses largely on the period from immediately after the war up to the middle of the 19th century. As part of this examination, I will also discuss how Snow's Island fits into this national narrative, as the island became the "Sherwood Forest" of America's Robin Hood.[2]

From the vast body of literature devoted to Francis Marion today, those unfamiliar with Marion would hardly conclude that his life is wrapped in mystery and legend. A "selected" bibliography published in 1999 listed 21 biographies.[3] The bibliography also included 14 books of fiction with Marion as the inspiration. The bibliography did not include any articles, chapters, poetry, dictionary entries, or other literature discussing Francis Marion. Nor did it include numerous discussions of Marion by military historians, in which Marion is held as a classic guerrilla (see Chapter 1). For proof of Marion's enduring legacy even today, the reader is invited to do an internet search. From this vast body of literature, one would have to conclude that the world knows quite a bit about Francis Marion.

HORRY, WEEMS, JAMES, AND SIMMS

The short answer to this question is that Marion got good press early. All of this Marionology—the books, articles, movies (*The Patriot*), and television (Walt Disney Productions 1960s TV series)—relies to some degree or another on the first full biography published in 1809 by the Reverend Mason Locke Weems, a book still in print.[4] The Horry-Weems biography, in conjunction with the 1821 biography by William Dobein James and the 1844 biography by William Gilmore Simms, comprise a literary trilogy that constructed an American memory of Francis Marion.

The story of how the Horry-Weems biography came to be is important to our understanding of the biography's enduring influence and the role of early 19th-century publishers in constructing national memory. Previous chapters have hinted at the long friendship, sometimes tested, between Peter Horry and Francis Marion. Horry served as a colonel under Marion throughout the war and, around 1803, completed a manuscript of his service. Horry asked the Georgetown Library Society to publish the work, but they thought it would be too expensive to publish. That decision turned out to be a real shame for historians since Horry's manuscript has been lost. On the other hand, it was the springboard for Marion's national recognition. Seeking another publisher, Horry met the Reverend Mason Locke Weems.[5]

Peter Horry
courtesy of the
Caroliniana Library

Weems was an established Virginia bookseller, author, and publisher of religious and moral tracts. Through his publications, he actively sought to evangelize "republican and Christian principles, two concepts he equated." His publications championed national unity. According to biographer Jill Acree, Weems wanted Americans to see themselves as "one distinctive people."[6] "Weems's life and texts help explain how the Enlightenment currents of the eighteenth-century Atlantic world fed into the evangelical, republican nationalism of the nineteenth-century United States."[7] Weems was also an entrepreneur and, as early as 1797, he suggested to his publishing partner Mathew Carey that they publish a series of books on Revolutionary War heroes, specifically mentioning George Washington, Anthony Wayne, Nathanael Greene, and Israel Putnam. Marion was not among those named. Weems immediately saw an opportunity when Washington died in 1799, and decided to publish his own biography of Washington, which would "teach virtue to youth" and enhance his and Carey's wealth.

His timing was perfect. The Washington biography was an immediate success and with successive editions he added more anecdotes to the work; the famous cherry tree anecdote appearing in the 1806 fifth edition. During a southern tour to sell his books, he met Peter Horry.[8] Imagine Horry's delight in having a nationally recognized publisher interested in his memoir of Francis Marion after being rejected by the Georgetown Library Society. Naturally, Horry handed Weems his manuscript for editing and publishing, while asking Weems not to alter its sense. Horry's delight was shattered when he saw the final product. Weems had not just edited it, but also rewritten the manuscript into another of Weems "republican biograph[ies]" modeled on the successful Washington biography. An enraged Horry wrote Weems that it was now a "military romance." Weems, he said, had "carved & mutilated it with so many erroneous statements…" Crushed, Horry lamented that it was "most Certainly tis not my history, but your romance."[9]

Weems, who believed in his cause, was equally shocked. From his perspective, Horry's demand for accuracy was secondary to the important lesson of teaching virtue, religious toleration, and republicanism through the Washington and Marion biographies. Furthermore, across the young nation, anti-British sentiment was growing that would eventually result in the War of 1812. Weems explicitly fed this mood by turning the British into irreligious "fiends devoid of human compassion" in the Marion biography.[10]

Marion was made a champion of American values. Weems had Marion delivering long orations in which, for example, he declares to a British officer that "I am in love; and my sweetheart is LIBERTY." To which Horry wrote in the margins of his own copy, "General Marion never made a Speech any where." Weems's Marion even delivers a long speech before his death on another of Weems's favorite themes—the importance of public education. To add to Horry's humiliation, Weems kept Horry's name as the author and did not add his own until the fourth edition in 1816.[11]

Anyone who has read the biography will agree with Peter Horry that the biography was indeed a romance; but Horry was dead wrong about one thing. The exasperated Horry wrote Weems in response to Weems's explanation of the bio-novel:

> A History of Realities turned into a Romance? The idea alone Militates against the work. The one as a history would be always read

with Pleasure, as real performances—The other as ficticious Inventions of the Brain."[12]

In fact, Horry's Weems-tainted biography of Francis Marion was a huge success, widely accepted by hero-seeking Americans. By 2011, some 50 editions had been published. The Marion biography has been lauded as Weems's best work and one 20th century critic, Lawrence Wroth, declared it the "American *Mort d'Arthur.*"[13]

The influence of Weems in building the imagined American narrative cannot be understated. Weems was right that Americans were seeking a national identity and national heroes. Washington's and Marion's reputations grew. Historian François Furstenberg has said of Weems that he was "Not a great man, perhaps, but a maker of great men." He noted that "Weems helped make Washington into the nation's common father."

In the post-Revolutionary War period, Furstenberg notes, Americans "were bombarded" with biographies, pamphlets, almanacs, broadsides and prints by publishers like Weems, Carey, Caleb Bingham, and Noah Webster. "Eventually, these texts would persuade a fractious, rebellious, polyglot people to unite in adulation of the nation's founding fathers and to celebrate its most important documents as nothing less than sacred scripture."[14] In discussing the Washington Weems created, Furstenberg's observations can also be applied to the Marion Weems created:

> Indeed, one might even say that it was through Weems that Washington was transformed into an icon suitable for American audiences. Through his efforts, Washington went from being an eighteenth-century member of the planter elite to being a backwoods, up-by-his-bootstraps, evangelical figure who could appeal to a mass audience.[15]

With the publication of the Horry-Weems biography, Marion was "nationalized."[16] As frontier Americans sought inspiration and justification for their migration west after the revolution, the Weems biographies were carried with them along with the family bible. An example of how ubiquitous the Marion and Washington biographies were in 19th-century pioneer communities was recently demonstrated to me while researching antebellum settlement in south central Indiana. Among the few books children had in school in 1840s Indiana, "the 'Life of Marion' was not uncommon." Weems wrote the Marion biography for children, and generations would learn of the Swamp Fox. Their parents named 29 towns, 17 counties, and uncounted children for Francis Marion.[17]

Certainly, the Marion imagined by Weems lives on even today and while there is value in his creation, it does make it difficult for historians to objectively evaluate Marion's life and career. Early 20th-century South Carolina historian A.S. Salley lamented:

> ...the falsehoods that Weems concocted—sometimes in malice—have been accepted as truth and retold throughout the United States and used in encyclopaedias [sic] and textbooks, government reports and political speeches.[18]

All post-Weems biographers have had to deal with the Weems biography without the benefit of Horry's original eyewitness account[19]—all except William Dobein James, who was another of Marion's partisans to write a biography of him. At one time, I saw James's biography as a better, more accurate Marion, but today I take a more cautious approach. James's account has an air of authenticity not found in Weems's account and, although historian George F. Scheer wrote "that no more accurate or valuable book on Marion exists," I have come to believe that it also adds to the Marion legend in its own subtle manner.[20] James's Marion has issues. First, for the period when Marion was a partisan (August 1780 to April 1781), James was ill and left in North Carolina. When he returned, he was confined to bed with smallpox. Thus, for the period of Marion's famous partisan and Swamp Fox exploits, James was not an eyewitness but instead relied on others, including Snow's Island community members Gavin and Robert Witherspoon. Second, James's chronology is often not in sync with Marion's correspondence. Third, James built on Weems's account, and in the Snow's Island example, adds to Weems's mythology as will be demonstrated later in this chapter.

Indeed, while Weems imagined Marion through Horry, James enhanced the legendary Marion under the guise of an eyewitness account. In James's introduction to his Marion biography, he notes that he had read Weems and had used the five volumes of Marion correspondence collected by Horry, "but it appears he [Weems] made no use of them in his life of Marion." For these reasons, I now see James's biography as a more subtle form of constructed memory.[21]

The third volume of the Marion trilogy was the biography written by "the most prolific, the most versatile, and the most successful Southern antebellum man of letters," William Gilmore Simms. Simms wrote some 100 volumes in his life including two Marion biographies, one as a book and the other as a series in *Russell's Magazine*—and also as a poem. In addition, he made

Marion the main historical character in at least two novels, *Mellichampe*, and *Katharine Walton*. Simms disparaged both Weems and James. He wrote of Weems that he "had rather loose notions of the privileges of the biographer" and that while "we are more secure" of James's facts, his work is "quite devoid of merit as a literary performance." Yet, Simms's biography of Marion is also full of flowery speeches and facts difficult to sort in juxtaposition to Marion's correspondence. The key to understanding Simms's Marion is to see Simms as he saw himself—as a deconstructionist of mythology but with a literary heart.[22]

Indeed, in retrospect, Simms had similar, nearly identical, goals to Weems regarding nation building. Historian Charles Watson states: "Starting in the 1820s, he joined wholeheartedly the efforts in progress to shape the culture, the politics, and the thought of the fledgling nation. His overriding objective was the development of a great nation, which need defer to none."[23] Like Weems, he saw this need not only as a historian but also as a writer of fiction. "Simms perceived that his chief duty as a man of letters lay in the articulation of a distinctively American history and literature, distinguished from that of Europe."[24] Simms saw the American Revolution as a "confrontation between the Old World, with its traditional values, its established mores, and its rigid conventions, to which the Tories and Loyalists are committed, and the New World, with its fresh values, its emerging mores, and its unstructured freedom, to which the Patriots are committed."[25] Through some eight Revolutionary War novels, Simms championed the virtues of "honor, duty, integrity, compassion, fairness, [and] patriotism."[26] In an essay on the "True uses of History," he wrote that the job of the romancer was to develop "national characteristics."[27]

For Simms, art was superior to historicity. As Lisa Kay Miller explains, "Like [James Fenimore] Cooper, Simms believes that the creator of the American epic must be truthful, but of course not bound to mere fact. Instead, he is bound to truth in essence—the truth of human nature." So, while Simms appears not as radical to facts as Weems, he still saw that a biography could be romantic, while needing to be "true to the letter of history as research could make it." Indeed, historian Sean Busick recently defended Simms's work as the "highest standards of scholarship when it was written." Simms's Marion thus could be described as the work of a literary Goldilocks, not too hot (romantic Weems), and not too cold (factual James), but just right (true myth Simms).[28]

Simms's biography of Marion, while closer to reality, still followed the national memory first imagined by Weems and James. For instance, Simms, like Weems, pointed to the similarities between George Washington and Marion, such as their common birth dates, their youthful desire for the sea, their early desire for self-improvement, their common agricultural background, and their similar even temperaments.[29]

Weems and Simms were literary giants constructing national memory using Francis Marion as a model of American virtue. Simms, however, lived in an era of a growing national rift that would result in the Civil War. As the nation drew towards open conflict, Simms became a defender of the South and a secessionist who increasingly saw the North as the 19th-century equivalent of Great Britain.[30] Simms saw his turn toward sectionalism as rooted in nationalism. Another Simms scholar, David Moltke-Hansen, asserts that Simms was not a nationalist, then a sectionalist, but both simultaneously, and indeed, Simms wrote that to be national one must be sectional and that to depict a section (i.e., the South) faithfully is to illustrate the nation.[31] During the contentious era leading to Civil War, then, Marion's memory would be associated with a growing Southern identity of independence and revolution. Marion's name would be invoked in the defense of the South.[32]

> In the troubled decades preceding the Civil War, tales of Revolutionary bravery and patriotism had offered encouragement to a nation suffering the strain of growing and insistent internal differences; the increasingly isolated South had, perhaps, more than her neighbors, sought that reassurance and had found much comfort and guidance in the worship of her old heroes, including Francis Marion.[33]

The examples of Marion invocation are numerous. For instance, a radical named Nathaniel Beverley Tucker urged South Carolina to provide leadership in the move toward Secession, writing that "Is she not the land of MARION? Let his spirit animate her."[34] During the Civil War, guerrilla fighters like General John Morgan would be likened to Francis Marion, enhancing the reputation of both.[35] While Washington became the nation's "common father," Marion became the South's common father. "Marion biographers repeatedly used the legendary Marion to prove the South's martial past."[36]

Weems, James, and Simms all contributed in varying degrees to constructing a Francis Marion around the needs of a young nation pushing westward.[37] As the nation split under the pressure of slavery and states' rights, Marion's memory was evoked in the South as a revolutionary spirit. The forms in which the imagined nation of antebellum America embraced its hero, Francis Marion, can be best illustrated in two examples, the memory of Francis Marion as the Swamp Fox, and the local and national memory of the Snow's Island.

MARION, THE SWAMP FOX

Francis Marion will always be the Swamp Fox.[38] The construction of Marion as the Swamp Fox follows the conventions of the three critical 19th century biographers discussed above with the enthusiastic assistance of other antebellum historians. The first published use of this *nom de guerre* appears in Horry and Weems, and Weems uses it symbolically as might be expected. Weems makes use of the fox metaphor thrice before he associates Marion as the Swamp Fox. In Chapter 6 of Weems's biography, Peter Horry attacks a party of vagrants and thieves, charging them like a "troop of red foxes dashing into a poultry yard."[39] In Chapter 9, British soldiers celebrating their capture of Charleston "flourish their swords, and 'whoop' and 'hoic' it away like young fox hunters, just striking on a fresh trail." Later they are described as "young foxes." Finally, in Chapter 16, Horry sets an ambush along a road near Georgetown. Down the road comes a "courting party" consisting of two young ladies in a chair accompanied by British officers:

> On getting into the gloomy woods, the girls were taken with a quaking fit for their sweethearts, lest that vile "swamp fox," as they called Marion, should come across them.[40]

There is an interesting variation in the 1809 first edition. The phrase first appears as "*vile swamp fox.*" Later editions changed the punctuation to "vile 'swamp fox,'" perhaps to emphasize the Swamp Fox, and as will be discussed, the fact that "Swamp Fox" changed from a pejorative to a sobriquet as Marion's legend grew.

No additional mention of Marion as the Swamp Fox appears in Horry and Weems. The pejorative is used almost as an afterthought, or throwaway, not worth further exposition. It is William Dobein James, the unpretentious eyewitness who calls his work a "domestic history," who picks up the fox theme in his biography and runs with it. James puts the *nom de guerre* in British Colonel Tarleton's mouth.[41]

> On the morning after the retreat, Tarleton found Marion's trail across the Woodyard, but went round it, and pursued, as he says, "for seven hours, through swamps and defiles." In fact, he pursued about twenty-five miles, when arriving at Ox swamp, which was wide and miry and

without a road to pass it, he desisted, saying to his men, "Come my boys! let us go back, and we will soon find the game cock [Sumter], but as for this d——d *old fox*, [italics in original] the devil himself could not catch him." After this, the two generals were thus characterized.[42]

Tarleton's memoir does not describe Marion as a fox.[43] Although James institutes Marion as the "old fox" and Sumter as the "game cock," he too makes no more of it afterwards, never actually calling Marion the "Swamp Fox."

It is not until around the late 1830s and early 1840s that Marion is tagged with the full title Swamp Fox in national memory through American literature. Alexander Garden includes the Tarleton story in his 1822 *Anecdotes of the Revolutionary War in America,* but calls Marion the "Fox," not the "Swamp Fox."[44] Likewise, William Cullen Bryant's circa 1831 poem *Song of Marion Men,* does not use the Swamp Fox title. However, there *is* an allusion to Snow's Island in the lines:

> Our fortress is the good greenwood,
> Our tent the cypress-tree;
> We know the forest around us,
> As seamen know the sea.
> We know its wall of thorny vines,
> Its glades of reedy grass,
> Its safe and silent islands
> Within the dark morass.[45]

H.N. Moore's biography, published the same year as Simms's, does *not* put the Swamp Fox *nom de guerre* in Tarleton's mouth, and a quick review of the Moore biography indicates Moore did not use it at all. But Simms uses it in his 1840 history of South Carolina, published five years before his Marion biography.[46]

The key difference is that while Weems called Marion a "vile swamp fox" and James called Marion an "old fox," it is Simms who uses it positively instead of negatively. It is Simms who uses it as a sobriquet.[47] Simms, with his desire to be accurate yet literary, combines the Weems's and James's accounts:

> He turned the head of his column at the very moment when his object was attainable. Popular tradition represents him as expressing himself discouraged at the sight of Ox swamp, and exclaiming, "Come, my boys! let us go back. We will soon find the Game Cock (meaning Sumter), but as for this d———d Swamp Fox, the devil himself could not catch him." From this speech of Tarleton, we are given to understand that

the two popular names were derived, by which Sumter and Marion were ever after known by their followers.[48]

Karl Heider saw the significance of Marion's link to the Swamp Fox *nom de guerre* as an example of "Good Form in an American Totemic Set," meaning one of three totemic names of South Carolina Revolutionary War partisan generals, Francis Marion (Swamp Fox), Thomas Sumter (Gamecock), and Andrew Pickens (Wizard Owl). Heider found no indication that the Swamp Fox was used "in a friendly sense" prior to Simms. "After Simms, 'Swamp Fox' was no longer a vile pejorative but a heroic title."[49] After Simms, the use of the Swamp Fox sobriquet was not only standard but enhanced further. For instance, just after Simms, historian J.T. Headley's 1847 biographies of Washington's generals included the Tarleton story as "this d____d swamp fox." And the name continued to grow along with the appearance of other anecdotes to strengthen the bond between Marion and the moniker. Heider, for example, notes an 1893 article in which Marion's men are reported to have used fox tails in their caps as a badge of identity. As noted in Chapter 8, Heider mentions the button found across from Snow's Island and illustrated in a 1926 book on Marion as an example. The button's animal was identified as a fox in the book, and the book's author suggested that it was worn by Francis Marion (Figure 8.14). (The button is actually a rattlesnake button.) Heider rejects the idea that its owner was Francis Marion. I agree the button could never be proven to be Marion's; however, it is now evident that the button probably did come from Marion's men. Heider makes the reasonable, but now known to be erroneous statement that, "It is unimaginable that he [Marion] would have been wearing, much less losing, silver buttons at Snow's Island." As we now know, the silver "I" button found at Dunham's Bluff indicates that someone in Marion's partisan band was indeed wearing silver buttons (Chapter 8).[50]

Thus, Weems was the first literary agent to associate the Swamp Fox *nom de guerre* with Francis Marion. At that time, it was a phrase of derision. As America remembered the Revolution and created its heroes, it became a sobriquet, made popular by Simms and part of a totemic set for South Carolina heroes. As remembrances of Marion were reconstructed during the years preceding the Civil War, Marion became a symbol and hero of the South:

> Thus elevated by Weems from neighborhood hero almost to the level of Founding Father, the Marion persona was subsequently pressed into service by other writers, often as a medium through which to advance political ends, or as a motif by which to suggest excitement in historical fiction.[51]

SNOW'S ISLAND IN AMERICAN MEMORY

As America imagined Francis Marion as the Swamp Fox, his lair likewise became a mythological and romantic landscape. Again, the significance of Snow's Island grew in the telling by the three biographers, Horry-Weems, James, and Simms. Weems, labeled by modern historians as the most romantic and prone to fictive themes, in fact makes less of Snow's Island than the other two. It is not until Chapter 22 that Snow's Island is even mentioned by Weems as Marion's "old place of retreat."[52] Then in Chapter 24, he describes the island camp:

> For this purpose he always kept a snug hiding-place in reserve for us: which was Snow's Island, a most romantic spot, and admirably fitted for our use. Nature had guarded it, nearly all around, with deep waters and inaccessible marshes; and the neighboring gentlemen were all rich, and hearty whigs, who acted by us the double part of generous stewards and faithful spies, so that, while there, we lived at once in safety and plenty.[53]

This is the extent of Weems's exposition on Snow's Island. If one removes the phrase "a most romantic spot," this paragraph accurately summarizes the Snow's Island landscape and the Snow's Island Whig community, largely without embellishment. He even notes that while there, they lived "in safety and plenty," suggesting they were not starving on sweet potatoes as James and Simms will later claim. Indeed, the pension applications, audited accounts, and the archaeological remains at Dunham's Bluff all suggest they were not starving. James, on the other hand, begins the construction of Snow's Island memory as a landscape reminiscent of the ancients, by comparing Marion to King Alfred the Great (849-899 A.D.) and Snow's Island to the marshes of Athelney. (These marshes were the king's hideout when he was forced to retreat to them in his battles against the Danes.)

> This island became henceforth the most constant place of his [Marion's] encampment; a secure retreat, a depot for his arms and ammunition; and, under similar pressures, a second Athelney, from which he might sally out upon the modern, but no less ferocious plunderers than their ancestors, the Danes. Snow's Island, not quite so marshy as was the retreat of the great Alfred.[54]

James goes on to describe the geography of the river system, the abundant livestock, the men forced to sleep in the open air, and feeding "chiefly upon sweet potatoes."[55] This dietary reference plays another part in the Snow's Island legend (see below).

Although James's use of the Swamp Fox is largely pejorative, his use of the swamp by Marion begins the transition of the memory of Snow's Island from a disgraceful, unhealthy, dark landscape to a romantic landscape. He indicates that "At the time [American Revolution] the marshes of Black creek, and the bogs of Black river, were impassible (except to Marion) on any direct route to Camden…" Thus, instead of a place where Tories hid out, James is the first to use the swamp as a place for cunning, fox-like men such as Francis Marion.[56]

Simms elaborates further on the swamp theme, expanding its mythological qualities. As far as I know, he is the first to associate Marion with Robin Hood and thus Snow's Island with the mythological landscape of Sherwood Forest:

> Marion's career as a partisan, in the thickets and swamps of Carolina, is abundantly distinguished by the picturesque; but it was while he held his camp at Snow's Island, that it received its highest colors of romance. In this snug and impenetrable fortress, he reminds us very much of the ancient feudal baron of France and Germany, who, perched on castled eminence, looked down with the complacency of an eagle from his eyrie, and marked all below him for his own. …The love of liberty, the defence of country, the protection of the feeble, the maintenance of humanity and all its dearest interests, against its tyrant—these were the noble incentives which strengthened him in his stronghold, made it terrible in the eyes of his enemy, and sacred in those of his countrymen. Here he lay, grimly watching for the proper time and opportunity when to sally forth and strike. His position, … was wonderfully like that of the knightly robber of the Middle Ages. True, his camp was without its castle—but it had its fosse and keep—its draw-bridge and portcullis. There were no towers frowning in stone and iron—but there were tall pillars of pine and cypress, from the waving tops of which the warders looked out, and gave warning of the foe or the victim. No cannon thundered from his walls; no knights, shining in armor, sallied forth to the tourney. He was fond of none of the mere pomps of war. He held no revels—'drank no wine through the helmet barred,' and, quite unlike the baronial ruffian of the Middle Ages, was strangely indifferent to the feasts of gluttony and swilled insolence. … Art had done little to increase the comforts or the securities of his fortress. It was one, complete to his hands, from those of nature—such a one as must have delighted the generous English outlaw of Sherwood forest—isolated by deep ravines and rivers, a dense forest of mighty trees, and interminable undergrowth. The vine and briar guarded his passes. The laurel and the shrub, the vine and sweet scented jessamine, roofed his dwelling, and clambered up between his closed eyelids and the stars. Obstructions, scarcely penetrable by any foe, crowded the pathways to his tent;—and no footstep, not practised in the secret, and 'to the

manner born,' might pass unchallenged to his midnight rest. The swamp was his moat; his bulwarks were the deep ravines, which, watched by sleepless rifles, were quite as impregnable as the castles on the Rhine."[57]

The symbolism of the swamp is critical to understanding Simms's use of Snow's Island in the construction of Francis Marion as the Swamp Fox. As alluded above, at the time of the Revolution, swamps were considered dark places, and impossible only to traverse except by the most cunning. As we have seen, they were places where only a "vile swamp fox" would go. Marion himself saw swamps as vile, dark, secretive places. In Chapter 6, I quoted Marion's letter to General Horatio Gates describing the skirmish at Blue Savannah, where he chased the Loyalists into the swamps "impossible to all but Tories."[58]

Not only in his Marion biography but also in his novels, Simms elaborated on the swamp theme, painting the swamp as both a desolate place of gloom and disease, and also lovely and inviting. Furthermore, the swamp was "historically…a symbol of the American resistance in South Carolina, for it was the partisans primary shelter" and "[as] a generous source of food, the swamp protects the partisans also from hunger." According to Carol Niemi, who analyzed Simms's novels in regard to nature, the British were depicted as uncomfortable in or around swamps, while swamps were a comfortable home for Marion and his partisans. Thus, Simms transforms the dark period of the Revolution (when the British were in control of South Carolina and Marion and his partisans were forced to hide in swamps) into a landscape of resistance inhabited by a community of resistance, a safe haven where only the most expert woodsmen survived.[59]

As the symbolism of Snow's Island and the swamp are linked to Marion, it becomes the setting for one of the most famous and oft-repeated Marion anecdotes—the story of a British officer who visited Francis Marion's camp under a flag of truce to negotiate a prisoner exchange. As told by Weems, the location of this negotiation is *not* clearly linked to Snow's Island. Instead, it is told immediately after another anecdote in which a mutiny occurs while Marion is camped near Georgetown at Mr. Cross's home. Thus, it is logical that the negotiation occurred at Cross's home. The story is summarized herein.

The unnamed British officer was at Marion's camp under a flag of truce. After the meeting, the officer was ready to leave when Marion invited him to dinner. The officer looked around the camp and saw nothing but sweet potatoes, which Marion's servant was roasting for their dinner.[60] In a flowery exchange between the two, the officer learns that this is the best food they have

Furthermore, he learns from Marion that Marion's men are serving without pay. It is also here that Weems has Marion tell the officer that he is in love with liberty. The British officer is so taken aback by the sacrifices of Marion and his men, camping in swamps, living on sweet potatoes, and serving without pay, that upon his return to Georgetown, the officer resigns his commission, or as Weems quotes the officer to his commander: "Why, sir, I have seen an American general and his officers, without pay, and almost without clothes, living on roots and drinking water; and all for LIBERTY! What chance have we against such men!'"[61]

This story had wings, as it encapsulates the Marion mystique most popularly. James does not include this anecdote in his biography, yet he has his own sweet potato motif, reminiscent of Weems. James records that while camped at White Marsh, North Carolina, Marion invited him to dinner. "The dinner was set before the company by the general's servant, Oscar, partly on a pine log, and partly on the ground; it was lean beef, without salt, and sweet potatoes." James is honored to share his hominy with Marion.[62]

As might be expected, Simms moves the anecdote to a more romantic landscape. Simms places the exchange on Snow's Island where he can better compare Marion to Robin Hood. Simms's version covers four pages in which he adds a contrasting image of "portly" British officers as opposed to Marion's "slight" frame. While Weems places the sweet potato story immediately after the mutiny, Simms reverses the order, relating first the sweet potato story on Snow's Island, followed immediately by the story of the mutiny, which occurs at "Mr. Crofts."[63]

In defense of Simms it would have shown remarkable restraint not to relate the sweet potato story in his Marion biography. The anecdote was already a 19th century hit. After Weems related it, Alexander Garden included it in his 1822 *Anecdotes of the Revolutionary War in America,* though again, not specifically placing it on Snow's Island. The story dominated the entry on Marion in a 1831 book of "Military Biography" of Revolutionary War officers, the author fully quoting Horry and Weems for four pages of the seven-page entry (an entry that does not refer to Marion as the Swamp Fox).[64] The entry also cites the story in reference to an earlier publication called the *American Biographical Dictionary.* Post-1809 editions of Horry and Weems included an illustration of the scene, which according to Nell Weaver Davies, began with the 1812 edition, although the South Caroliniana Library's own 1814 edition is not illustrated. Furthermore, the anecdote received wider national attention when in 1836 artist John Blake White painted the scene of Marion offering the potatoes to the British officer, further enhancing Marion's national memory, cementing his Swamp Fox image, and, most importantly, providing the visual link to the swamp landscape.[65] Indeed, the painting was a 19th century mnemonic of Marion and the Snow's Island landscape. The scene has been copied and modified numerous times. White himself created three versions and a version was used on Confederate currency during the Civil War (*see* cover painting and page v).[66]

The story's wide appeal is evident and perhaps was commonly told before Simms's biography. Pee Dee locals, perhaps old Snow's Island community members, used the story as a tourist attraction. In 1843, an anonymous author published a travel story in *The Knickerbocker*, a literary journal, entitled "Sketches of South Carolina." In that journal, the author visited the "Georgetown District" where he met an "old soldier, whom I met by accident at the ferry-house on the banks of the Pedee," and who "conducted me to the spot where General Marion invited the British officer to dinner—a scene immortalized by the pencil of White." Historian Joseph Johnson included the story in his *Reminiscences* in 1851, and Benson Lossing follows Simms and places the incident on Snow's Island. By the Civil War, no one could write about Marion without using the Swamp Fox sobriquet and the sweet potato anecdote.[67]

FRANCIS MARION, MEMORY, AND LIVING LEGEND

Scholars Paul Shackel, Benedict Anderson, and Edward Linenthal argue that the construction of memory follows the predetermined agenda of the dominant ideology.[68] Memory is constructed expressly to impose a set of meanings over and above other possible meanings, often for political and almost always for ideological reasons. One cannot argue with this in regard to the memory of Francis Marion and Snow's Island, as both Weems and Simms explicitly state their agenda is to construct a national image, instruct moral values, and change how Americans remember their past.

That said, I believe it also undervalues the foundations of memory. I suggest a more complex interplay is necessary to fully understand the creation of memory and mythology. I suggest that mythology cannot succeed unless it is linked, however loosely, to verifiable facts and events. These facts, though often stretched and enhanced, are the glue that holds a memory together.[69]

The academics discussed above would take issue with this. As Linenthal writes, "Ultimately, the vibrant activity at our nation's memory terrains reveals more about our own labors of shaping cultural identity than about getting the past 'just right.'"[70] Perhaps they are right, but in my experience, it is the argument over getting the past "just right" that is at the heart of competing interests, regardless of uses.[71] In the case of Weems's interpretation of Francis Marion, for example, we are today amused by Weems for his inventions and the flowery speeches placed in the mouth of Francis Marion, however, without our knowledge and/or a feeling of certainty that they *were* inventions, Linenthal has no argument. For mythology to be mythology in our Western zeitgeist, it has to contrast with fact. Post Revolutionary War Americans sought American heroes, not Greek gods.

Furthermore, community members must play an active role in constructing this memory. Archaeologist Paul Shackel describes it this way: "The individual memory is closely linked to a community's collective memory, and there is sometimes a struggle to create or subvert a past by various competing interest groups."[72] Community members are agents for the production of memory, and while certain people carry authority in the community, those who have no authority do not follow blindly. Thus, having demonstrated the constructed memory of Francis Marion and the landscape of memory of Snow's Island, I now turn back to the earliest memories of Marion and Snow's Island to see how reality, in the form of community memory, combines with the imagination of shapers (like Weems) to create a national memory or narrative.

To understand my point, it is first important to note that the war did not end with a flourish. Although the British evacuated Charleston in December 1782, the colonies were in limbo regarding additional conflict until Congress agreed to articles of peace in April 1783, which did not result in a treaty until September 1783. As noted in Chapter 7, the militia was in arms through much of 1783. For the next several years, the colonies struggled with forming a nation and did not ratify a constitution until 1788. The point is that, for several years after Marion dismissed his men at Wadboo Plantation in December 1782, most Snow's Island community members, along with many South Carolinians, were in a period of social and political flux. Heroes and hero worship would come later, after Weems, James, and Simms constructed a national memory.

However, the "mystic chords" of memory of Francis Marion were being played in the minds of the Snow's Island community long before Weems set them to music. Before there was Weems, there was the Snow's Island community and it remembered Marion not through memory, but as a colleague—or as Karl Heider pointed out, for them Marion was a living legend.[73]

Indeed, Marion's reputation was growing toward national recognition immediately upon the conclusion of the war.[74] The Continental Congress promoted him on 30 September 1783 to a full colonel in the Continental line (along with 26 others), a largely symbolic gesture, but recognition just the same.

That same year, officers of the Continental Army formed a brotherhood called the Society of the Cincinnati to promote liberty and friendships among fellow officers. Marion was a founding member of the South Carolina society. The new governor, with the approval of the State Legislature, recognized Marion's contribution, and as his estate had been destroyed in the war, they named him Commandant of Fort Johnson in 1785. This carried a salary, allowing him a respectful manner to recover property lost during the war. Furthermore, he was voted back to the state Senate, and was part of the 1790 South Carolina Convention which wrote a new state constitution. He remained in the state militia up to a year before his death in 1795. Again, the point is that Marion was not forgotten even as the state and country attempted to figure out who they were and what they would be. Marion was a local hero and nationally recognized prior to Reverend Weems.[75]

And, the Snow's Island community recognized their commander long before Horry and Weems. In 1794, Marion was honored with an address from the citizens of Georgetown "to Convey [their] Grateful sentiments for your former numerous Services." Their address closed with:

> Continue Citizen General in peace to till those Acres which you once wrested from the hands of an Enemy Continue to Enjoy Dignity accompanied with Ease & quiet & to lengthen out your days, blessed with Consciousness of a Conduct Unaccused of Rapine or Oppression & of Actions ever directed by the Purest patriotism.[76]

The address was signed by 148 citizens of Georgetown, including Snow's Island community members John Dunnam, Shadrach Simons, Hugh Giles, Gavin Witherspoon, [unreadable] Witherspoon, Andrew Johnston, and J. Baxter. It also included many former Marion partisans not living in the Snow's Island region but who were part of the wider community of resistance including—first on the list—Peter Horry. Also signing were P. Trapier, John Postell, William James, John Roberts, Maurice Simons, Anthony Potts, Hugh Horry, Erasmus Rothmahler (owned land south of the Brittons on Britton's Neck), and John McCrotty.

To further support Marion's "real-time" celebrity status, he was recognized for his contribution to the cause in the very earliest histories of the war. In the first history of the American Revolution in South Carolina, published only two years (1785) after the signing of the Treaty of Paris, David Ramsay included Marion as playing a respectable, if not central, role. He is mentioned in six different places in the book. As might be expected, he is not called the Swamp Fox, nor does Snow's Island figure in this history. However, Ramsay, only two years after signing of the Treaty of Paris, already records characteristics of Marion's tactics and personal character that will be repeated, enhanced, and otherwise used to construct the Marion memory.

> This valuable officer, to whom Charleston is much indebted, had retired from Charleston during the siege, having most fortunately for his country fractured his leg, which rendered him incapable of commanding his regiment.
>
> Unfurnished with the means of defense, he was obliged to take possession of the saws of the sawmills, and to covert them into horsemen's swords. So much was he distressed for ammunition, that he has engaged when he had not three rounds to each man of his party.
>
> For several months he and his party were obliged to sleep in the open air, and to shelter themselves in the thick recesses of deep swamps. From these retreats he sallied out whenever an opportunity of harassing the enemy or of serving his country presented itself. This worthy citizen, on every occasion, paid the greatest regard to private property, and restrained his men from every species of plunder.
>
> General Marion, though surrounded by enemies, had defended himself with a few faithful militia in the swamps and morasses of the settlements near Charleston..." Having mounted his followers, their motions were rapid, and their attacks unexpected.[77]

Furthermore, Ramsay's inclusion of Marion was repeated in the earliest postwar histories of the United States, like William Gordon's 1788 history. Only five years after the war, Gordon wrote of Marion:

> For months he and his party slept in the open air, and sheltered themselves in the thick recesses of deep swamps; from whence he sallied out, whenever an opportunity of harassing the enemy, or of serving his country presented itself. He paid the greatest regard to private property, and restrained his men from every species of plunder.[78]

In these early years, Marion's exploits at Great Savannah, Forts Watson and Motte, and Eutaw Springs are usually mentioned along with his swamp retreats.

By the time of Horry and Weems's publication, Marion's role was already growing in American memory. David Ramsay's *History of South Carolina*, first published in 1809, increases Marion's role in the war, largely due to William Dobein James. As James mentions in his biography, his first attempt to write about Marion was for Ramsay's history. "I hastily sketched out from memory a short history of Marion's brigade, for him; which he inserted in fifteen pages of his first volume." James's account in Ramsay has an interesting place in the memory of Francis Marion. It was written sometime after 1798, when Ramsay wrote a circular letter to prominent citizens to gather information for his 1808 history. James states that he used Horry's five volumes of letters for his full biography, but it appears he did not have them for the 15-page excerpt in Ramsay. In any case, James's short excerpt in Ramsay's 1809 history probably should be considered the very first biography of Marion. The structure of this biography follows James's later biography and a thorough analysis of it (beyond that necessary herein) might offer many insights between James's and Weems's biographies. For my purposes, James's narrative mentions Snow's Island in a straightforward manner, with no flourishes. "Here, by having command of the rivers, he could be abundantly supplied with provisions, and his post was inaccessible except by water." No mention of the sweet potato story in this account, nor is Marion called the Swamp Fox.[79]

Further indication that Marion was recognized as a hero prior to Weems is that as veterans of the war began writing their memoirs, Marion was not forgotten. William Moultrie wrote in 1802 that Marion:

> Took the saws from the mills, and set the smiths to work, to turn them into horsemen's swords; he frequently engaged when he had only three or four rounds to a man; his little party would sometimes be reduced to five and twenty men...who always lay in the woods, in most unfrequented places, with nothing but their blankets to cover themselves.[80]

Colonel Henry Lee, writing in 1811, continues the theme:

> Fertile in stratagem, he struck unperceived; and retiring to those hidden retreats selected by himself in the morasses of the Pedee and Black River, he placed his corps not only out of the reach of his foe, but often out of the discovery of his friends.[81]

Thus, the *themes* of the Swamp Fox and Snow's Island existed prior to Weems. Or, critically, Weems and later Simms constructed memory not out of whole cloth but built on widely accepted, acknowledged, appreciated, and verified events in the living past as witnessed by contemporaries. These agents provided the foundation of memory for Weems, James, and Simms.

Furthermore, Marion, at least at the state level, was already being compared to legendary heroes and guerrillas of the past. For instance, on 28 June 1804, the Palmetto Society of South Carolina held their meeting on Sullivan's Island and at dinner that evening saluted General Moultrie, the President, George Washington, the Navy, the Governor, the United States, the U.S. militia,

Nathanael Greene, the "Fair" of South Carolina, Christopher Gadsten, our "Ministers abroad," and "The memory of general Francis Marion—the Fabius of South Carolina."[82] Fabius was a Roman dictator and military officer who defended Rome from Hannibal by harassment and attrition rather than open battle, much as Marion had done to the British.

Much can be learned about a person by his or her enemies. In Chapters 6 and 7, I have provided evidence enough of British attitudes toward Marion as a menace to their goal of subduing the colony. During the war, he went from being labeled derisively as "Mr. Marion," to "Colonel Marion" as the British gave him reluctant respect. They also knew better than to place Loyalist militia against him unless they were protected by regular soldiers. None of this led to them calling him a Swamp Fox (unless one believes that Tarleton uttered his famous "d___ed old fox" epithet), but it does indicate that Marion was a formidable and respected foe.

Was he a swamp fox? Amazingly, there is even some contemporary evidence that the British or Loyalists had indeed labeled Francis Marion the Swamp Fox during the American Revolution. As Karl Heider insightfully notes, the Swamp Fox sobriquet might have come from "living legend."[83] By this, I understand him to mean that the term Swamp Fox might have been created not only as a 19th-century need for "good form" but that those living during the Revolutionary War actually did call Marion a Swamp Fox.

The evidence is circumstantial, but it is worthy of consideration. In 1782, Charleston was controlled by the British. Likewise, the Charleston *Royal Gazette* newspaper was controlled by Loyalist printers. In the 13 March edition, under the headline "Intelligence Extraordinary from Philadelphia," the byline reads "The following Books are in the press, and will speedily be published." There follows a list of titles of these books. Among the titles listed are, "A topographical description of the northern parts of South Carolina, betwixt Peedee and Santee, illustrated with a map, wherein are accurately delineated all the thickets and swamps in that country, from an actual survey by Brigadier General Marion," and "Select maneuvers for cavalry; to which are added practical observations on the most soldier-like manner of swimming rivers in a route, by the same." These titles are a joke at Marion's expense. Philadelphia at the time was under the control of the Americans and a center for the publication of Whig propaganda. Among additional book titles in this article are, for instance, "Description of the strong brick castle at the Eutaws, by General Greene," making sport of Greene's army at the Battle of Eutaw Springs. During that battle, Greene was on the verge of winning until British soldiers barricaded themselves in a brick house and fired from the windows, stopping the American advance.[84]

The jokes may seem weak today, but they clearly illustrate the fact that the British and Loyalists at the time of the Revolution were spoofing the Americans, including Francis Marion's intimate knowledge of "thickets and swamps." Further, he is derided for not crossing rivers like a gentleman—"soldier-like"—but was forced by the British to swim his horses in an undignified manner. Again, the swamps were undesirable places (unhealthy!) and this is contemporary evidence of the British derogatorily associating Marion with swamps. This spoof does not quite call him a Swamp Fox, but to put it in William Gilmore Simms terms, the sense is there, and this is proof that the idea existed during the war.

It is also interesting to note that in all the pension applications by Marion's veterans, not one that I have seen designated Marion as the Swamp Fox. He is always referred to as General or Colonel Marion. A keyword search for "swamp fox" in the searchable pension applications at *www.fold3.com* did not reveal an example. A search of 8,431 transcribed pension applications did not reveal one, either. The only use of the term "fox" I found was in the pension application of John Hill, who called Lord Cornwallis the "old fox." I believe this is evidence that, until Simms changed the term from a pejorative to a sobriquet, calling Marion the Swamp Fox would have been an insult. At least Marion's veterans and the Snow's Island community were not using the phrase Swamp Fox nor seeing themselves as swamp foxes.[85]

The absence of the descriptor in the pension applications is more curious if one considers that there is evidence that at least some Snow's Island community veterans had an acquaintance with the histories written in the late 18th and early 19th centuries—including the Horry and Weems biography. It is notable that certain Marion skirmishes show up in the pension applications more often than others. The actions at Great Savannah, Blue Savannah, Tearcoat Swamp, Fort Watson, Fort Motte, Eutaw Springs, and, to a lesser degree, Quinby Bridge and Parker's Ferry, are the most often noted. I have not counted the number of pensioners mentioning Fort Motte, but one is given the impression that if all of the pensioners who mentioned Fort Motte were actually there, Marion might have just rolled over the fort Alamo-style.

These are the actions mentioned in the earliest histories of Ramsay, James, and Horry and Weems, and it would be natural for old war veterans, who might not remember where they were at a specific time, to turn to these histories to make their cases for pensions. This is not to imply that they were lying outright, but rather it is reasonable to assume that, often marching in the dead of night to places previously unknown, they had little idea where they were at the time of any particular action. Reading, or having someone read to them these histories, assisted them in recall of the past—"I think I was there… it sounds familiar." Thus, it is reasonable to assume that Ramsay, James, and Horry and Weems helped reconstruct memories of the war in the veterans' minds. In other words, myth and fact intertwine to construct an authoritative memory. This again adds to the curiosity of why no pensioner or pensioner's family titled Marion the Swamp Fox in these records and leads once again to the conclusion that during the Revolution, a "swamp fox" was a term of derision and that it was only by the time of Simms that it had become a popular sobriquet, after most pensioners were in their graves. William Boddie further asserts in his 1938 biography that aside from Peter Horry, Mrs. Marion and many of Marion's veterans (Snow's Island community members) were infuriated with what Weems had done to Horry's biography. Mrs. Marion, according to Boddie, wanted to horsewhip Weems and that "so displeased… were Marion's veterans in Williamsburg that all of them brought their copies to the Court House on a certain salesday and made a bonfire of them." Boddie claims to have found one of these "half-burned" copies in an old box.[86]

There is direct evidence that the early biographies were used by the pensioners. One of the most interesting examples appears to be an eyewitness account of the legendary sweet potato story. Samuel Weaver, serving in the North Carolina militia, was detached briefly to Marion's command. The time frame is vague but appears to be between the fall of Charleston (May 1780) and the battle of Guilford Court House (March 1781) and the location was "on Pedee river or some of its waters." While serving under Marion, Weaver wrote:

> …a Brittish Officer as he was told, come into Camp, but from what he does not know, which [strike which] he was Cooking [strike Cooking] roasting & baking sweet potatoes on the Coles—General Marion [strike ?] steped up with the Brish Officer and remarked he believed he would take up [strike up] Breakfast, he felt proud of the request, Puled out his potatoes, wiped the ashes off with a dirty handerchief, placed them on a pine log (which was all the provision they had) and General Marion and the British Officer partook of them. He has been told by some, that this has been recorded in the life of the General as dinner, but this was a breakfast.[87]

Although this appears to be an eyewitness account of the incident, and at least one historian implies that it is confirmation of the event,[88] I have to say that I cannot agree. First, the phrase "as he was told" indicates to me that he was told of the event rather than witnessing it. In fact, the "W" used on the pension indicates it was his widow's application, not his. Second, Weaver includes details that are right out of Weems—including "roasting" the potatoes, placing the food on a "piece of bark," and the potatoes as being "the best we have."[89] Interestingly, Weaver's complaint was that it was actually *breakfast* rather than dinner. This application is dated 1839, prior to Simms's biography, so Weaver has to be referencing Horry and Weems or, less likely, James's biography. Weaver had previously made an application in 1836 and does not mention this story in that application. It is added to the more elaborate statement made three years later. More important than whether or not Weaver was an eyewitness to the story is the evidence that Weaver was familiar with a Marion biography and was likely using it to assist his reconstruction of events. (Weaver also mentions that he met George Washington.) We know that Weaver could not write and therefore probably could not read. Admittedly, this is an example where what might have been fabricated in the name of nationalism is entwined into the historicity of Francis Marion and makes scholars fools.

Still, Weaver was not the only one to claim to be an eyewitness to the sweet potato story. Alexander Garden relates the story and claims that J.H. Stevens, a soldier in Maham's unit, was an eyewitness.[90] Incidentally, Garden does not specifically place the incident on Snow's Island.

Another example where anecdote becomes history is the claim of Thomas Jackson. Jackson's story found its way into a history of the Baptists of Louisiana by William Paxton. In this late 19th-century history, Jackson was named as a prominent member and founder of a Baptist church in East Feliciana Parish. During the Revolution, Jackson was "a faithful soldier, and accompanied the old 'Swamp Fox' throughout the entire campaign." Paxton's history relates the sweet potato story and concludes that "Thomas Jackson was the man who roasted that lot of potatoes." Jackson's pension application makes no mention of the sweet potato story, although in the file, a letter written in 1934 requesting information about Jackson states that "I know that he served for a time under Gen. Francis Marion and family tradition says he served the dinner of roasted potatoes to the British General." Thus, by the late 19th century, the story was entrenched in Marion lore and families included it in their memories of ancestral war service. These were not the veterans and living members of the Snow's Island community.[91]

Finally, in keeping with the concept that memory and historicity must combine for constructed memory to have authority, one can turn back to Weems. Even in Weems there are events that can be verified by primary documents, indicating that not all Weems is pure fiction. No one would question that Weems was following the general flow of Revolutionary War events and that the foundation of his romance was Horry's eyewitness manuscript. If we can trust Horry, and there is no reason to doubt him, Weems must have left nuggets of authentic events that he did not totally mangle, which only adds to scholar's frustration.

Two examples serve to illustrate that there is something for Marion scholars interested in historicity to mine even from Horry and Weems. First is the incident at the Sampit Bridge during Colonel Watson's retreat to Georgetown. In Chapter 6, I have related that Watson's force arrived at the Sampit Bridge to find Marion's riflemen had already reached the bridge and stood on the opposite bank to stop his crossing. Watson sent his men forward, and Marion's riflemen fell back instead of fighting, allowing Watson to get his force across the river. In Weems's account, Horry condemns the commander of the rifleman, who he sarcastically calls "my brave Scott" and then labels him an "Infamous poltroon" for retreating. Scott's men are recorded as "calling him a coward to his face." Being called a coward in a popular book read by a young nation is not what someone would want to own up to. Yet, there was a John Scott in Marion's brigade and in his pension account, he says that he was with 32 riflemen at Sampit Bridge and that, being outflanked, he retreated. Scott may have never known he was singled out as a poltroon in Horry and Weems's book, but, one must assume that Scott was there and Weems, through Horry, reported the event accurately.[92]

Another example of accurate recording or historicity within Horry and Weems includes the observation that Weems gets Hugh Miscally's name correct. Weems spelled his name Mizcally, while Levi Smith (also named in Horry and Weems) spelled it Maskelly. There are other examples, but the point is that, while there is no doubt that much of Weems's version of Horry and Weems is fictitious, there are nuggets of reality within that might be the key to all biographies of Francis Marion.[93]

Jill Acree asserts that Weems's book "rescued Marion from near obscurity." Likewise, Blocker D. Meitzen concluded that Marion "slipped quietly from the popular national consciousness" after the Civil War.[94] If one is familiar at all with the books of Francis Marion and the continuing fascination with him, these assertions are at odds with the facts. Marion and his mythology are alive and well today in such examples as an Francis Marion annual symposium in Manning, South Carolina; the state's South Carolina Francis Marion Trail Commission; and any number of biographies and articles as seen by an internet search and my references. Admittedly these modern memories have been shaped by the Marion trilogy—Horry and Weems, James, and Simms.

To some immeasurable extent, South Carolina's and America's memory of Francis Marion was established by Weems, expanded by James, and enhanced especially by William Gilmore Simms. These authors, primarily Weems and Simms, were expressly and openly attempting to construct a national memory built upon religious freedom and national values of freedom and independence—using the exploits of Washington, Marion, and others to exemplify model American citizens. Weems and Simms, and to a lesser extent James, were the apostles of American memory.[95]

Furthermore, Marion was re-imagined by the South in the years prior to and during the Civil War to be an agent of resistance standing against northern aggression. The South saw itself as an underdog and turned to a memory of Francis Marion as a successful underdog who overthrew oppression. Within that memory, Snow's Island became a constructed landscape of memory symbolizing the safe haven of underdog partisans who emerged to smite the British Empire.

Yet, this memory was not created *ex nihilo*. Community memory is certainly influenced by shapers like Weems and Simms, but they rely on agents for the seeds of that myth, and these agents must be active in the acceptance or rejection of that myth. In memory, fact and fiction intertwine and support each other. This is best seen in the postwar pension applications of Marion's partisans, in which places and events are mentioned in support of the applicant's veteran status.

At the beginning of this chapter, I stated that the short answer to why we remember Marion, as opposed to other partisans, is that Marion had good press. The long answer is that the seeds of Marion's memory were planted shortly after the war—while he was alive—by Marion's men. Weems, through Horry, cultivated that memory and made it bloom. In the end, perhaps Simms had it right. It is the duty of the shaper to fit the memory to certain facts in a literary style. It was most important to get the sense of history correct. As Peter Horry noted, it was important that the myth fit the facts.

Importantly, images of community only have authority in that they pay homage in some manner to a past image. This is called tradition. It is the democracy of the dead. Tradition refuses to submit to the small and arrogant oligarchy of those who merely happen to be walking about.[96]

Endnotes for Chapter 9

1. Modified versions of this chapter (Smith 2013) have appeared in an edited volume on William Gilmore Simms entitled, *William Gilmore Simms's Civil War,* edited by David Moltke-Hansen, and an introduction by me to another republication of Simm's *Life of Marion* in 2016 (Smith in Simms 2016).
2. Anderson 1991. Smith 2000:xi . The memory of Francis Marion today is especially reinforced yearly in such examples as the Francis Marion Trail Commission and an annual symposium on Francis Marion in Manning, South Carolina, as well as the continued biographies written about Francis Marion; John Otter's being the latest. For purposes of brevity, I will look at the creation of this national memory rather than its maintenance in the 20th and 21st centuries. Still, there will be opportunities to mention current memories of Francis Marion.
3. Moore 1999. There have been four since then, including William Willis Boddie's 1938 biography first published in 2000 (Boddie 2000).
4. Horry and Weems 1891.
5. Smith 2000:xxiv; Wates 1980:353.
6. Acree 2007:2, 45.
7. Furstenberg 2006a:106-107.
8. Acree 2007:86, 112.
9. Acree 2007:138. Horry to Weems, 4 February [circa 1811], Peter Force Papers, LOC.
10. Acree 2007:157, 243, 246.
11. Horry and Weems 1891:155; Horry, Notes in Horry and Weems, Guignard Papers, SCL-USC; Acree 2007:153.
12. Horry to Weems, 4 February [circa 1811], Peter Force Papers, LOC.
13. Acree 2007:163, 211. The number of editions is widely varied in the various critiques of the biography. I am using Acree's number, but in any case, the editions keep coming out.
14. Furstenberg 2006b:1-3.
15. Furstenberg 2006a:143.
16. Marr 2007.
17. Smith and Cohran 2010; Banta 1888:377; Pogue 2003:1.
18. Anderson 1991; Salley 1948.
19. Smith 2000:xxiv. Horry's original manuscript has been lost. That tale is another long story, and quite confusing, but the short version is that it probably was destroyed either in the burning of Columbia during the Civil War, or survived the war and was with a large number of randomly organized state documents at the State House. While late 19th century renovations were being completed, these papers were stored unceremoniously on the third floor and some were burnt by workers to keep warm. Those that survived were finally given to the state historical commission to serve as the foundation for the state archives, but much had been lost through neglect, including, most likely, Horry's original manuscript (Wates 1980:360). However, in writing his manuscript, Horry made use of five volumes of Marion's correspondence (and other Revolutionary War figures), most of which has been published by Robert Gibbes as the *Documentary History of the American Revolution* and the Papers of Nathanael Greene. Two other Marion biographers, William Dobein James and William Gilmore Simms made use of these volumes for their treatments of Francis Marion. Horry also wrote an autobiography, parts of which are also missing but contain a few reminiscences of the Revolutionary War (Shillingsburg 1967:5-7).
20. Scheer 1948:248.
21. James 1821:vi.

22 Holman 1966:vii; Miller 1987:43; Simms 1844; Simms 1858; Simms 1858-59; Smith 2000:xxv; Simms 1844:Preface.
23 Watson 1993:1.
24 Miller 1987:44.
25 Brown 1978:72.
26 Brown 1978:146.
27 Watson 1993:2.
28 Miller 1987:49; Busick 2005:7, 50.
29 Busick 2005:46.
30 Watson 1993:74.
31 Moltke-Hansen 2009:16.
32 Meitzen 1987:113; Blocker Dodson Meitzen wrote an excellent thesis on the symbolism of Francis Marion and this work has greatly assisted in my own thinking about Marion's symbolism.
33 Meitzen 1987:113.
34 Watson 1993:110.
35 Meitzen 1987:116.
36 Pogue 2003:35.
37 Prior to the Civil War, there were other biographies that also added to Marion's legacy, but these seem only to repeat the narrative provided by the three. Among other biographies at this time were those of Horatio N. Moore (1845), Benson J. Lossing (1858), and Cecil B. Hartley (1866).
38 A hat tip to University of South Carolina anthropologist Karl Heider, who in 1980 published a delightful article on the sobriquets of Francis Marion as the Swamp Fox, Thomas Sumter as the Gamecock, and Andrew Pickens as the Wizard Owl.
39 Horry and Weems 1891:51. As mentioned previously, the chapters are different in the first edition due to a typographical error repeating Chapter IV in the first edition and the addition of illustrations in later editions. I am citing the 1891 edition.
40 Horry and Weems 1891:73-74, 134.
41 James 1821:vii.
42 James 1821:62-63.
43 Tarleton 1787.
44 Garden 1822:267.
45 Bryant 1912.
46 Heider 1980:18.
47 Heider 1980.
48 Italics in original, Simms 1844:152.
49 Heider 1980:1, 12. There is one possibility of a positive use around the same time as Simms. Tarleton Brown, a veteran wrote in an 1843 memoir that "It was from craftiness and ingenuity of Marion, the celerity with which he moved from post to post, that his enemies gave to him the significant appellation of the 'Swamp Fox'" (Brown 1999:19). The memoir was published in the Charleston Rambler, and Brown, old at the time, died in 1845. Most likely his memoir was taken down by his granddaughter's husband, Charles Colcock Hay (Brown 1991:i). So Colcock, having read Simms, may be the one who added the "literary flourish" of the Swamp Fox. In demonstrating the evolution of the Swamp Fox sobriquet, Heider notes that Simms' 1840 edition of his *History of South Carolina* labels Marion the Swamp Fox only once while subsequent editions add another instance.
50 Headley 1847:421; Heider 1980:13; Stokes 1926.
51 Meitzen 1987:152.

52 Horry and Weems 1891:176.
53 Horry and Weems 1891:189.
54 James 1821:67.
55 James 1821:73.
56 James 1821:118-119.
57 Simms 1844:166-167.
58 Horry and Weems 1891:134; Marion to Gates, 15 September 1780, SRNC, Vol. 14:617.
59 Niemi 1982:25-28, 67.
60 Horry and Weems 1891:147. Horry and Weems named this servant Tom, but later historians will identify the servant as Oscar, AKA "Buddy," Marion's lifetime servant (Johnson 1851:280).
61 Horry and Weems 1891:156.
62 James 1821:57.
63 Simms 1844:76, 179-180.
64 Stavely 1831:207-213.
65 Nell Weaver Davies dates the painting between 1810 and 1815 (Davies 1999:16). I can not find any source backing up this early date. Most internet sources either do not date it or indicate a circa 1836-1837 date. White lived from 1781 to 1859.
66 Horry and Weems 1891:153; Davies 1999:16, 20; Scheer 1963:260.
67 Clark 1973:210; Johnson 1851:280; Lossing 1858:159.
68 Paul Shackel 2001; Benedict Anderson 1991; and Edward Linenthal 2001.
69 This leaves open a long discussion of what are "facts." Rather than detour into an existential debate on reality, I define facts as "what really happened" and for archaeologist and historians, "data told twice." That is, at least two independent sources corroborating phenomena or events. Such evidence is made stronger by competing interests corroborating these phenomena or events.
70 Linenthal 2001:xii.
71 One only must attend a single Francis Marion symposium to see this. Marion enthusiasts compete vigorously over the most minute facts and events in Marion's life, vying to get the facts correct.
72 Shackel 2001:2.
73 Heider 1980:5.
74 He was also recognized during the war. Greene introduced himself to Marion with the words, "I have not the honor of your Acquaintance but am no stranger to your Character and merit" (Greene to Marion, 4 December 1780, GP, Vol. VI:519).
75 Rankin 1973:292-293.
76 15 November 1794, Horry Collection, Peter Force Papers.
77 Ramsay 1785:176-178, 209.
78 Gordon 1788:454-457.
79 James 1821:vi; James in Ramsay 1809:233-234.
80 Moultrie 1802:233.
81 Lee 1812:174.
82 *The Carolina Gazette*, 6 July 1804:3.
83 Heider 1980:5.
84 *Royal Gazette* 13 March 1782:3.
85 http://southerncampaign.org/pen/; John Hill pension application S2615.
86 Boddie 2000:284.
87 Weaver Pension W8993.
88 Davies 1999.

89 Horry and Weems 1891:154.
90 Garden 1822:21.
91 Paxton 1888:593; Jackson Pension S31166.
92 Horry and Weems 1891:480; Scott Pension S32508. Rifles may be more accurate than muskets, but they take a long time to reload and did not take a bayonet. Facing regulars with muskets with bayonets attached and at close quarters is suicide for riflemen and I give Scott some slack for his decision.
93 Horry and Weems 1891:222; Smith et al. 2007a:28.
94 Meitzen 1987:152.
95 Anderson 1991.
96 Chesterton 1908.

CHAPTER 10
FRANCIS MARION AT SNOW'S ISLAND

In the previous chapters, I demonstrated that during the latter part of the 18th century, a sparsely settled region around Snow's Island, South Carolina, included several closely related families that joined the Whig resistance against the British during the American Revolutionary War.

Through the early part of the war, members of this community of resistance supported the rebel cause with soldiers, livestock, forage, and crops. With the British capture of Charleston in 1780 and their subsequent conquering of the backcountry, this community of resistance was transformed into a partisan community, a community of warriors and citizens surrounded by Loyalist and British strongholds like Camden and Georgetown. Under the leadership of Francis Marion, this community was organized, and its landscape fortified into a place of refuge until it was invaded in the spring of 1781. Marion's camp or camps were destroyed, however, the community quickly reformed. Although under continued threat from nearby Loyalists, the community continued to support the cause until the end of the war.

This chapter returns to the question asked in Chapter 2, summarizes the answers discovered in previous chapters, and offers further thoughts.

In Chapter 2, I proposed the following questions:

1. How was the colonial population around Snow's Island transformed into a community of resistance as a result of revolution? How was it maintained by Francis Marion as a distinct partisan community?
2. What is the archaeological manifestation of the partisan community?
3. How was the partisan community and Snow's Island redefined in 19th century memory?
4. What can the Snow's Island partisan community tell us about communities of resistance in general?

To address these questions, I proceed from the particular to the general, from the historical to the anthropological, first reviewing the history of the Snow's Island region's settlement and the development of the Whig community. I then review Marion's use of the partisan community during the American Revolution. From this discussion the character of partisan communities is revealed.

The final section of this chapter offers anthropological observations on communities of resistance and communities in general, including observations on how communities are maintained through memory—essentially, a review of Chapter 9. Some of the discussion in this chapter is redundant, but as the chapter is meant to stand alone, the redundancy is intentional.

A HISTORICAL REVIEW OF THE SNOW'S ISLAND COMMUNITY

With a nod in recognition of the earliest explorers and traders, European settlement in the Snow's Island region began around the 1740s, shortly after the Scots-Irish and Irish settlement of nearby Williamsburg Township west of Snow's Island. The Williamsburg settlers first came to the Santee and Black Rivers, but certainly by the 1760s were well established along Lynches Creek, Lynches Lake, Muddy Creek, Soccee Creek, and Snow's Island. The first settlers around Britton's Neck and immediately north were largely Welsh from the northern colonies. The Snow's Island region was agriculturally poor, swampy, and unhealthy; many Welsh moved up the Pee Dee River to the Cheraw and Society Hill regions.

Speculators purchased large tracts of land in the Snow's Island region, including the island itself. Eventually lower- and middle-class settlers arrived and found the swamps abundantly supplied with forage for cattle and hogs. Furthermore, there was a demand for these meats in Georgetown, Charleston, and even in the far northern colonies, and some of these colonial cowboys became quite wealthy. Indigo soon proved to be another profitable commodity for the region. Indigo processing was labor intensive and, as a result, the slave population grew along with the new settlers. By the 1760s, the Snow's Island community settlement was sparse compared to the Upcountry and its residents widely distributed.

Meanwhile, the population north of Snow's Island had reached the point where having the seat of colonial government in Charleston ceased to be practical. Most critical to the frontier backcountry community was the need for a police force. As unchecked violence and crime increased, the call for stronger government representation in the backcountry also increased.

Typically, centralized government does not give up power voluntarily, and the first South Carolina resistance movement emerged in the form of the vigilante Regulators, seeking to force the government in Charleston to act upon their needs for local law enforcement. Forced to respond by the Regulator and Anti-Regulator movement, the colonial government established backcountry representation.

An important precedent had been set, seeds of resistance had been sown, and lessons learned. Taking matters into one's own hands worked. Rebellion got results. Although there may not have been great participation in the Regulator movement in the Snow's Island region, it is likely the community took note of the results.

In the grand scope of colonial history, the Regulator movement might be viewed as part of the larger Whig resistance movement in the late 18th century, in which Americans began to see themselves as having an identity apart from Great Britain. Chapter 5 demonstrated that as early as 1775, the Snow's Island community was involved as resistors against the British colonial government. The community sent its leading citizens to the South Carolina resistance movement represented as the Continental Association and the Provincial Congresses. The Snow's Island community joined the Whig resistance early.

Since winners write the history, it is not clear how unanimous the resistance was within the Snow's Island community, however a letter written by Thomas Port to the First Council of Safety, requesting militia appointments, indicates wide—even unanimous—support. The letter is a single reference and perhaps Port overstated the case to assure his militia commission. It does seem, however, that most families in the core Snow's Island community supported the resistance. Miscally is the only known exception.

The overall South Carolina population quickly split into regions of Loyalist and Whig strongholds or the "pieces of patchwork" Loyalist officer Robert Gray described later. Through the first five years of war, much of the military action was down country around Charleston and farther south. The Snow's Island community responded by joining militia companies, sending these companies beyond the region as requested, and by providing meat and grain to the American cause. After the fall of Charleston, under the initial leadership of prominent local Whigs, the South Carolina resistance movement resorted to partisan warfare. Within the Snow's Island community region, the Whig community of resistance became more active and its membership more clearly defined, while just upstream along the Little Pee Dee, a Loyalist community also became more clearly defined.

Within the core Snow's Island region, families such as James, Port, Witherspoon, Potts, and Giles organized the partisan community. With the arrival of General Horatio Gates and his Continental Army in August 1780, Whigs in the region grew confident; Hugh Giles, an unsung hero of the war, gathered cattle and supplies in and around Snow's Island, and with many families supporting the resistance within an isolated swamp environ, Snow's Island became a logical base for partisan activities, while former militia men gathered at Witherspoon's Ferry and Giles Bluff to prepare for warfare in their own neighborhood.

Francis Marion arrived in August 1780. The two militia forces were awaiting leadership from constituted authority and it is possible that Snow's Island was already being used as a supply depot. Under Marion's direction, the two forces—the Williamsburg militia and the Britton's Neck militia—consolidated and reorganized.

The Snow's Island community region was fortified, although the description may be too strong a notion. Perhaps it would be better to say that the partisans took advantage of the landscape to secure the region as best as possible. Camps, piquet posts, supply depots, and at least one small redoubt were built at strategic access points like roads, bridges, and ferries. These were more for warning of approaching enemies than strong defensive positions.

If Snow's Island proper was not in use as a supply depot and camp before Francis Marion's arrival, at least by late November, the island had become the geographical focal point of partisan activity and the partisan community of resistance in the greater region. Or perhaps, if there was no camp physically located on Snow's Island, then Dunham's Bluff across from Snow's Island was that focal point. In either case, by November 1780, Marion had made several forays against the British along the Santee. He was then forced to retreat to North Carolina, returned to surprise the British at Black Mingo, again retreated to North Carolina, and again returned to reestablish his control over the Snow's Island community. From at least November 1780 until March 1781, Snow's Island served as the base of Marion's partisan operations while the Whig community served as a sympathetic civilian population providing logistical support.

Local civilians and Marion entered a symbiotic relationship. Marion and his warriors provided some security, while the civilian community provided food and forage. Resources from the surrounding communities were gathered at depots on and around Snow's Island. Alone in the Pee Dee drainage from August to December 1780, Marion and the Snow's Island community survived as a result of an aggressive tactical offense and strategic defense (fight and flight) assisted by fortunate distractions in the larger Whig resistance across South Carolina.

With General Nathanael Greene's introductory letter in early December 1780, the strategic situation changed in South Carolina. Prior to that point, Marion and his partisans were on their own, fighting to survive and keep the Whig resistance alive. With the arrival of Greene, Marion and his partisans could now establish a link to the greater strategic revolutionary cause and work in cooperation with regular forces. Unfortunately, Greene arrived during the winter, thwarting close coordination due to the rising Pee Dee River.

Ironically, the American victory at Cowpens by General Morgan reversed Marion's strategic situation again, forcing Greene out of South Carolina and placing Marion's partisans back into a strategic defensive partisan posture. This time the British were able to take advantage of the situation. Using two separate forces, they managed to keep Marion busy with one force, while the other invaded the Snow's Island region and destroyed the camp, ostensibly on Snow's Island.

Although Marion stopped Colonel Watson's first attack from the Santee River, the invasion of Colonel Doyle from Camden followed by Watson's second invasion from Georgetown demonstrates the porous, fragile, and weak nature of the Snow's Island partisan community as a conventional fighting force, but also its resilience as a partisan community. Marion stopped Watson along the Santee and Black Rivers, however, while Marion was fighting Watson, Doyle marched to Snow's Island and after only a brief fight, destroyed the depot. When Marion turned to catch Doyle, Watson marched from Georgetown north through Britton's Neck without the slightest resistance.

The Snow's Island civilian community dispersed into the swamps as Marion had done when threatened in September 1780. Marion alone was too weak to turn back the challenge of Watson, but with Nathanael Greene's return to South Carolina, the partisans and civilians returned to the community region, reestablished their homes, their networks, and their logistical support of Marion's Brigade. Once again, the adage that it "takes infantry to hold ground" proved true.

For the British to have subdued the Snow's Island partisan community, they would have had to establish a permanent presence. Why the British did not establish a series of posts up the Pee Dee River from Georgetown to Cheraw in August 1780 is an interesting question, but part of the answer likely lies in the remoteness of the Snow's Island region as an isolated frontier (see below), combined with its recognition as a partisan stronghold. Colonel Balfour admitted as much in a letter written to Lord Rawdon "Pedee firmly held by enemy; need for post between Camden & Georgetown."[1]

After the Snow's Island camp was destroyed, Marion never used the region as a base camp again. Still the Snow's Island partisan community and the region remained critical to the larger Whig resistance in three important ways. First, Snow's Island partisan warriors remained in Marion's ranks and fought more and more like regular soldiers as the war progressed. Although they continued to come and go as their militia time expired, they were at least willing to venture beyond their own neighborhood to fight along the Santee, in the Lowcountry south of Charleston, and around Charleston. Second, the Snow's Island community region continued as an important region for resource exploitation. It had been, and continued to be, a classic catchment zone for Marion and the larger Continental Army under Nathanael Greene. Even after six years of warfare, the region in 1782 still had many head of cattle and hogs and many bushels of corn for both Marion and Greene. Livestock was rounded up and driven to those parts of South Carolina where the war continued. Likewise, vegetables and salt from the coast was gathered and shipped. Third, small detachments of militia/partisans remained in the area to fend off Loyalists from the nearby neighborhoods of the Little Pee Dee.

Although not the focus of the main effort against the British, the Snow's Island region remained important enough to Marion and Greene that Marion eventually had to return to settle affairs with neighboring Loyalists. Thus, throughout the war, the Snow's Island community was an integral part of Marion's war effort, first as a recruitment area, second as a base camp, third as a logistical military "rear." This continued even beyond Marion's eventual retirement from action in December 1782.

THE LANDSCAPE OF PARTISAN COMMUNITIES AND PARTISANS

The Snow's Island pre-war community was a dispersed settlement within a marginal region. Elsewhere, I have called such a region an "interior frontier."[2] An interior frontier is a pocket of isolated settlement surrounded by more accessible regions of concentrated settlement. In the vernacular, an interior frontier is a region "off the beaten path." Evidence indicates that the Snow's Island-Britton's Neck region was settled later and remained a rural, isolated region in comparison with the upper Pee Dee, Georgetown, and Williamsburg settlements during the colonial period.[3]

Marion, of course, was ordered to the Snow's Island community by either Governor Rutledge, General Horatio Gates, or both. Still, Marion needed not to have chosen the region as his base of operation. While we cannot know the mind of Francis Marion, it appears that the locality was chosen as a refuge for two reasons. First, it was an isolated, swampy, landscape conducive to hiding and defense. Second, the settlers there consisted primarily of a tight community of Whig families or a community of resistance. Certainly, the British were too weak to cover all of South Carolina. That the British did not drive Marion from the region until the late spring of 1781 supports the notion of a frontier landscape consisting of both geographical isolation and strong community support.

In the face of concentrated force, however, the Snow's Island community was both porous and resilient. As previously mentioned, partisans cannot stand in full battle against regular forces. When the British concentrated a force, such as Wemyss's, Doyle's, or Watson's invasions, the community offered little resistance. In all cases the people quickly reformed.

I do not want to imply that because the area was geographically isolated it was totally cut off from Georgetown, Williamsburg, or Cheraw as a result of the Pee Dee drainage system. Indeed, it seems that neither Marion nor the British had trouble crossing Lynches Creek, the Pee Dee River, or the numerous other rivers and creeks close by when necessary. There is also evidence that, prior to the Revolution, people crossed these streams to go to church and on other missions, indicating that the river crossing was not overly cumbersome. Only once were Marion's plans delayed by the Pee Dee and that was in the winter of 1780, when the river rose so much that he planned to leave Snow's Island for higher ground. In fact, it was so high that he could not get supplies to Greene's camp upstream. That Marion crossed seemingly at will is amazing to me. Even when the river level is low, the river appears dangerous to my 20th century eyes.

Interior frontiers, as I have defined them, are not only geographically isolated but are often also culturally isolated. Certainly, at the time of the American Revolution, the Snow's Island cultural development was less complex than that at Georgetown and possibly the Cheraw regions. Georgetown and Williamsburg became regional centers of wealthy high-status peoples, church formation (at the time the focal point for societal development), and cultural development. For example, in the 1740s, the local Georgetown elite formed the Winyah Indigo Society, "Georgetown's answer to the Charleston Library Society. With the formation of the [Society] there henceforth existed in Georgetown a library, a school, and something of an intellectual center."[4] Georgetown was also the source of medical doctors and a social movement establishing early schools.

Some large landowners in Georgetown owned plantations in the Snow's Island region and probably ran them as absentee planters. Likewise, Williamsburg society was focused around Kingstree, with the elite plantation society settling along the Santee and Black Rivers. They arrived as strong Presbyterians and Church of England members and formed their churches early.[5] Above Snow's Island, the people in the Cheraw region developed a backcountry society. While farther from Georgetown and Charleston than the Snow's Island region, the people in the Cheraw region seem to have formed a more complex colonial community earlier than those in the Snow's Island region. Again, the initial development came from the Welsh and the Welsh Neck Baptist Church. As Susan Linder states:

> The Welsh Neck ministers were in many ways typical of the back country planter class that developed before the Revolution. Frontier planters provided a variety of essential services to their less prosperous neighbors and thus rose to wealth and power within the framework of an economy based on the family or household as the fundamental unit of social order.[6]

The Cheraw District was active in the Regulator movement. During the Revolution, the St. David's Society developed a seminary of learning in the Cheraw District.[7]

I do not want to make too much of this apparent cultural isolation. However, the lack of information about Snow's Island's regional development, in comparison to the areas surrounding this landscape, hints that the typical colonial societal organizations were slower to develop in the Snow's Island community than in the surrounding regions.

That the Snow's Island region developed a colonial society slower than the surrounding regions does not imply that social integration between families was less developed or complex. Indeed, I would argue that with a less populous community, and government infrastructure weakened by its distance from the region, people and families around Snow's Island tended more often to turn to their neighbors for support and social infrastructure. Kinship ties became a major aspect of community cohesion. Logically, the reason the community became a stronghold of Whig resistance was the result of close kinship ties between many core families living in and around the area.

As I indicated in Chapter 1, historians, due to a lack of primary sources and perhaps interest, have underplayed Marion's talent for organization and logistical skills, paying more attention to his tactical brilliance. In the case of Francis Marion and the partisan community, however, the two were not necessarily distinct. To be tactically brilliant required logistical skills and Marion demonstrated the latter, gathering cattle, forage, slaves, and boats from beyond the Snow's Island region and consolidating these resources within the Snow's Island community. Within the region, he widely dispersed these resources over several camps and depots. In this manner, he solved several tactical problems. For instance, no one place, no single large depot, became too important to his or the community's survival. Dispersal was also needed to guard the many approaches or access points into the region. Dispersal solved the problem of keeping his horses and cattle fed. Finally, as Nathanael Greene mentioned in his introductory 1780 letter (see Chapter 4), dispersal kept Marion from being surprised by the enemy.

From an archaeological perspective, the partisan community included of several dispersed locales consisting of farmsteads (plantations), depots, campsites, piquet posts, and even some indications of parade or muster grounds. It can be argued that there was no single Snow's Island camp in the legendary notion of a Sherwood Forest. It is argued herein that by drawing a circle around Snow's Island from Port's Ferry west to Witherspoon's Ferry southeast down to Britton's Ferry, across Britton's Neck to Potato Bed Ferry that all this region was "Marion's Camp" (Figure 3.4). Essentially, the geographical core family region of the larger Snow's Island region *was* in fact Marion's Snow's Island camp and depot.

Furthermore, from this area, Marion drew food, forage, sundries, and other resources like boats, lead shot, and salt. The Snow's Island region, then, was a classic catchment area.[8] However, this catchment area was much larger than Flannery envisioned in his studies. Marion's partisans ranged up to twenty miles beyond Snow's Island to gather resources. Proximity did play a factor, but because of horsepower, the area of proximity was larger. Furthermore, the Snow's Island catchment area was not defined geographically as bounded by river basins or mountains or swamps as often is the characteristic of archaeologically defined catchment regions. More definitive of the catchment area was the partisan community, a social-political construct. Beyond the friendly confines of the Snow's Island community, Loyalist communities existed, which made foraging more dangerous, but not necessarily out of bounds entirely.

A paradoxical aspect of the Snow's Island community is its central place in Marion's campaigns. In conventional warfare, we traditionally think of a regular army's frontline being away from central supply depots, with a logistical chain linking the army to a frontline facing the enemy. This was the case for the British. Backcountry strongholds like Camden, South Carolina, were linked to their Charleston supply base along an extended supply line protected by a series of small forts like Fort Watson and Fort Motte.

As noted in Chapter 2, Lawrence Babits' study of the conventional army of Nathanael Greene revealed that as the army marched it camped at the homes, ferries, plantations, or mills of local prominent citizens. These places became central places for resource exploitation. The troops foraged around these campsites like army ants gathering supplies and bringing back to the camps.

On the other hand, during Marion's partisan campaign in the fall of 1780, Marion and his partisans seemed to rely very much on the Snow's Island community as a fixed region for exploitation. Campsites in the community became the partisan's depot, training center, and resting place, to which Marion repeatedly returned when threatened. Even after the partisan phase of his career ended, the community remained as supply source for food and forage. Marion relied on mobility to survive, but he appeared to be very much tied to the Snow's Island region in the fall of 1780 while surrounded by the British in Charleston, Camden, Georgetown, and to the northeast—a strong Loyalist community.

THE ARCHAEOLOGICAL MANIFESTATION OF PARTISAN COMMUNITIES

Partisans are ephemeral on the landscape and thus the archaeological expression of partisans and partisan communities are likewise ephemeral. Except for a redoubt like 38MA165, my research to date has found no "smoking gun" in the archaeological record that points to partisans absent supportive evidence from the historical record. I expected to find military buttons and military accoutrements at sites in the region. These were found at sites like Port's Ferry (38FL409, 38FL410, 38FL411) and a single cannon ball and two buttons from Dunham's Bluff (38MA207), but this is hardly a large data base. Nothing in the artifact assemblage from Goddard's Plantation (38FL282) indicates a military presence—a site that the archaeological evidence dates to the latter part of the 18th century. The only evidence of military activity at this site is damage from a very hot fire at Structure 1, suggestive of British Major Wemyss' 1780 raid.

Part of the artifact problem is, of course, due to continued erosion of artifactual evidence by relic collectors. The campsite near Potato Bed Ferry was reported to have had numerous buttons, and there was at least one 2nd

South Carolina Regiment button found either at the Tanyard or another site in the Britton's Neck region. Nevertheless, military accoutrements in the form of military arms, furniture, and buttons were/are rarely found at these sites. Clearly though, Marion's partisans used fewer military arms than expected. Whether this is a pattern that can be extended to all partisans or Marion's alone is at this point unknown; however, I suspect this pattern will be seen at other sites where militia made up most of the military force present.

For instance, this artifact pattern was evident at a recent metal detecting survey at Williamson's Plantation battlefield in York County, South Carolina.[9] It is becoming more evident that to find partisan camps, or evidence of a partisan presence, the archaeologist must rely on the historic record for supportive evidence. This is certainly the case at the Snow's Island/Dunham's Bluff complex.

Furthermore, the nature of partisan warfare, specifically the need for a sympathetic civilian population, means that there will be few "pure" partisan occupations to be found in the archaeological record. I did not find any, although the site reported by the relic collector near Potato Bed Ferry might be an example. Regardless, partisans camped near strategic points (in this case, ferries), or mills (Burch's Mill, for instance) or plantations (Goddard's Plantation and Dunham's).

The data suggest, then, that the archaeological expression of partisan activity will usually be masked by the evidence of domestic occupation. This remains a problem in the interpretation of the Dunham's Bluff site. Small fortifications like the Dunham's Bluff redoubt are rare. In fact, they should be unexpected. As one of the classic attributes of partisan warfare is rapid maneuver (for which Francis Marion is especially noted), the presence of one known (Dunham's Bluff) and one well-documented (Port's Ferry) redoubt in the Britton's Neck area only reemphasizes Marion's commitment to the Snow's Island community as a base of operation. There is also the fortification at the Tanyard, which for all appearances may also have been a redoubt but certainly was an earthen fortification of one sort or another. In all, these earthworks are more typical of regular army defensive tactics and one could speculate that the presence of these fortifications represents Marion's previous classic 18th century training, and his continued desire and commitment to regular 18th century warfare. As I argued in Chapter 4, Marion was a reluctant partisan. His goal was to lead a regular, standing army that could stand against the British as they eventually did at Eutaw Springs. That he did so well as a partisan speaks volumes of his military skills.

Another observation about these redoubts is that they are architectural fixtures on the landscape. In the cases of Dunham's Bluff and the Tanyard, they are visible reminders of resistance. In the case of the Snow's Island partisan community, they are the *only* visible reminders of the resistance, as were architectural structures the main archaeological evidence for Preucel in his study of the people of Kotyiti, New Mexico (discussed in Chapter 1).[10]

PARTISAN COMMUNITIES REMEMBERED

After the war, the Snow's Island community returned to its agrarian ways. The evidence indicates that community connections forged prior to and during the war remained strong afterward, and even included former Loyalists. Over time, members of the partisan community south of Lynches Creek and west of the Pee Dee River probably had less connection with those on Britton's Neck as the Snow's Island region was organized into different districts—Williamsburg and Marion. Still, the partisan community remained in community and national memory.

As America established itself as a new and distinct nation, it turned toward its war heroes (and villains) in building a national identity. Distinctive past events were mixed with a sense of the past to forge a new memory—a nationalized memory of the war, of the partisan community, and of Francis Marion. Memory served to smooth dramatic historical events, sanding the rough edges of the complexity of what had actually transpired.

In this case, the Whig community elite were those who wrote the postwar history. Such historians as Weems, James, and Simms, each in their own way, provided a narrative that, if not always completely accurate, as Simms noted, caught the sense of the time. Since each generation rewrites its history, we look back at the Weems and Simms versions of the Revolution with a certain disdain for their hero worship, simplicity, and sentimentality. Still, it has to be recognized that, however he did it, Marion took a community of cattle and hog farmers, organized them into a partisan band, and held the Snow's Island region against a superior force until help arrived in the form of Nathanael Greene. Then, these same partisans became reliable militia and stood in the ranks in formal battle array against the British at Eutaw Springs.

Modern scholars would argue that the postwar partisan community was an imagined community. Yet two things are obvious to me. First, that the partisan community was not imagined *ex nihilo*. Their memories were founded on past events and records of past events. Even Weems, who appears to have played fast and loose with many facts, was tied to *these* facts.

Furthermore, our lack of respect for Weems today, our amusement at his sentimentality, our disdain for his biography, are all based ultimately on his lack of allegiance to the overall body of the historic record. Memory may not always get it right, but we strive to get it right and we spend much energy arguing the "rightness" of our history.

Archaeologists and anthropologists have long recognized the symbolic importance of landscape. Snow's Island was an integral part of the antebellum partisan memory of the war and Francis Marion. Today, Snow's Island serves as a perfect example of a "Traditional Cultural Place" in the National Park Service sense. Although it is on the National Register and now recognized as a National Landmark, we have no archaeological evidence of Snow's Island or Marion's presence, but the living memory of Francis Marion alone establishes it as a place of importance in the American narrative.

FRANCIS MARION, THE PARTISAN COMMUNITY, AND COMMUNITIES OF RESISTANCE

To conclude this book, I offer some general thoughts from an anthropological perspective. In Chapter 4, I discussed that the pre-war Snow's Island community consisted of several families connected through a combination of geographical proximity and social arrangements like kinship, marriage, religion, and ethnicity. It is reasonable to suppose that business relations, such as group cooperation in getting cattle to market would also be a tie that helped glue the pre-war community together. These families consisted of people of a range of economic means. Geographical proximity was an important attribute of the community but perhaps the least important. Kinship and marriage seem to be the strongest social relationships of the remaining community attributes, followed by church membership. These ties were reinforced through business or legal arrangements such as landholdings, wills, and judgments.

People and families within the Snow's Island region joined the Whig resistance early and strongly supported the cause throughout the war. When war threatened, the prominent families in the Snow's Island community, especially the core region, rallied together and organized the community. It is reasonable to assume that the community went through a period of, for lack of a better term, rarefaction, during the first years of the conflict. That is, those who did not join the Whig resistance left or were removed. The only evidence of loyalism within the Snow's Island core community was the Miscallys.

I speculate that Hugh Miscally at first joined the Whig resistance and then changed his mind. Assuming this is correct, his initial support gave him the opportunity to visit Marion's camp and later lead the British to its location on Snow's Island. If so, Miscally was not alone.

The historic documents indicate that there were others who changed their allegiance throughout the war. Although the people of Britton's Neck near Snow's Island were Whigs, just outside of the core region was a pocket of Loyalists along Cypress Creek. Cypress Creek marked the northeastern boundary of the Snow's Island region and families north of the Creek (not counting some Jenkins and Munnerlyns) were mostly Loyalists. The Cypress Creek Loyalists seemed to be a tight-knit community of their own. The historic record does not tell us much about the interaction between these people and the Snow's Island community prior to the war. Despite their loyalism, they quickly resettled and apparently were not ostracized for very long after the war. As speculated in Chapter 7, this is probably the result of their joining the Whig cause close to the end of the war.

Thus, the evidence presented in Chapters 5, 6 and 7 demonstrates that Francis Marion inherited the Snow's Island partisan community, initially organized by prominent local citizens, who turned to him for leadership and, most importantly, authority. How did Francis Marion maintain the community? I believe that the Snow's Island partisan community—and partisan communities and communities of resistance in general—are held together through a dynamic tension between the elites and followers. In my dissertation, I labeled the prominent families "drivers," while those of lesser prominence in the community were "adherents." *Drivers* in the community established community institutions. Community leaders, such as church elders, entrepreneurs, and government officials, established the social community in peacetime, and at the time of war or resistance, became lead actors in the community of resistance. By maintaining the community of resistance generally and the local partisan community specifically, these drivers maintained their position in the community. Likewise, then, in pockets of loyalism, leaders would choose to maintain their community as Loyalists. It was to their benefit and survival to remain with the King.

At the beginning of the war, prominent citizens were elected to serve the community in Charleston during the associations in 1775 and 1776, and later established the Snow's Island community of resistance in the late 1770s. From Prince Frederick Parish, leaders like John James, Hugh Giles,

John Witherspoon, Thomas Potts, Francis Britton, and William Snow were all members of the association.[11]

There were others. Recall that it was Thomas Port who called together the community to reform the militia. Shade Simons, John Ervin, John Dozier, and others were elected militia officers, indicating their acceptance as leaders in the community. These men were from established families in and around Snow's Island and would have been the initial instigators of Whig opposition. They first gained leadership positions as a result of wealth, but not wealth alone. They provided pre-war leadership in societal organizations, like religious and civic functions, and previous militia leadership. Mere landownership or the holding of a single government office did not necessarily mean one would become an officer during the war. Only those who were already identified as leaders in pre-war society could have transformed their leadership in a wartime society.

These leaders not only risked their lives but also their fortunes. As can be seen in Chapters 5, 6 and 7, these individuals contributed a great number of cattle, corn, and other food substances to the cause. Since many were officers in Marion's partisan corps, it is reasonable to assume that their contributions were voluntary.

I have also demonstrated that Marion's partisans included many others, less wealthy or prominent, who were loyal to the community but came and went as their militia terms expired or joined Marion for their own safety. These I call the *adherents*.

In Chapters 6 and 7, I listed several people (Jesse White, John Might, George McCall, William Vaughan) who were with Marion because their own homes were in Loyalist pockets and Marion provided them security. Their allegiance was more fragile than those living in and around Snow's Island and I suspect they were less committed to the partisan community. They came and went as victories and defeats were experienced. Marion's appeal to authority sometimes had to be enforced by threat to be effective in maintaining these partisans in the community.

Meanwhile, there were other types of adherents in the community. They were tied to the community as a result of living largely on Britton's Neck. They also had property to risk but were not among pre-war community leadership for whatever reason, and, I speculate, they were also among those who joined Marion or left him as circumstances dictated. Hugh Miscally may be such an example. Then, there are members whose membership was coerced. In the Snow's Island community, these were the largely invisible slaves (historically speaking).

Another form of community member was the *ideological partisan*. They were committed to the cause and remained with Marion throughout. The Munnerlyns are an example. They joined early, remained with Marion with only short visits home, and were able to negotiate action on Marion's part in getting him to assist in the rescue of their father.

A characteristic of American society is the ability to rise and fall within social classes. Benjamin Munneryln, probably not among the wealthy, became an officer and demonstrates that participation in the resistance transformed some peacetime non-elites into elites. Nathan Savage may also be an example. Serving as a private during the war, afterward he became a leading citizen in the community. It is possible that the reputation gained as a result of his service during the war prompted his postwar leadership.

On the other hand, there were other partisans like David and Henry Britton, the Dunhams, and Joseph Graves, who were from prominent community families but served as privates.

In Chapters 3 and 4, I demonstrated that those community drivers and adherents in the Snow's Island community were held together in a dynamic tension by several forces, or motivators, imposed from within and beyond the community. For the Snow's Island partisan community and communities of resistance, the first motivator was a common decision to resist constituted authority. Resistance to oppression is political action. Communities of resistance are made of individual members each making a political decision informed by a variety of social factors such as kinship or religion, and more visceral reactions such as fear, revenge, or the seeking of justice. Once that decision was made, the partisan community was bound together by the possible consequences of that decision. Threat of death and the destruction of personal property was a strong motivator. However, the community still sought out authority as a force for holding members together within the community. The leaders were seeking legal authority when they made their request to the Whig governor and General Horatio Gates for a Continental officer. This action brought Francis Marion to Witherspoon's Ferry.

Marion represented legal authority and an authorized link to the larger Whig resistance. In turn, Marion used his authority and the established leadership within the community to further militarize the community for resistance. In essence, he used the pre-war community structure to maintain the wartime partisan community by accepting that structure and promoting, from within the community, pre-war leaders into positions of authority. They, in turn, recognized his authority and allied themselves to him and the larger Whig resistance.

Another way to look at this appeal to authority is within the realm of societal traditions—again using the pre-war community to control partisan community infrastructure. The community had already elected the leaders. Importantly then, despite being revolutionaries, the Whig revolution in America was a political, not social, revolution because it preserved the pre-war community structures. Within the Snow's Island community, the social infrastructure remained. Traditional roles were maintained. The Snow's Island community was simply transformed into a militarized society that I have called the partisan community.

It is worth remembering that one of the larger mistakes the British made after the fall of Charleston was their promotion of prominent Loyalists into positions of authority *formerly held by the pre-war community leaders who during the war had become members of the resistance.* This not only increased the wrath of the Whig leaders but their followers as well.

Another method Marion used to maintain the partisan community was to establish a network of logistical support. Marion supported the community not only by providing security but also in rationing valuable consumables, like salt. Salt was a colonial necessity not only for food preservation but also for digestion. Salt was used as a means of population control. This is not to say that without salt, Marion would not have been able to maintain the community, but it was a means by which favor could be gained, a means of, pardon the pun, adding spice to the relationship.

Another method of maintaining the community was the provision of security. The presence of Marion's warriors dispersed across the Snow's Island community region decreased dissent within the community and provided protection from incursions by Loyalists. Partisans were not strong enough to stand against regular soldiery, but were usually able to check weak Loyalist forces. That is the nature of partisan warfare.

Communities are not bound by power forced downward, but by negotiation between established leadership and followers, drivers and adherents. In fragile partisan communities, this becomes even more critical to community cohesion. Leaders cannot act without appeal to the agency of their followers. Marion's authority alone did not rally the troops to action. His calls for consolidation were not always answered or answered quickly. Even threats did not always bring community action. Repeatedly, Marion's desires and goals were thwarted by the actions of soldiers who returned home after a victory or defeat, ignoring his orders or calls for consolidation—or as a result of their fear of the greater strategic situation.

In at least one instance, they forced Marion into action. The Munnerlyn brothers' desire to rescue their father and mother forced Marion's hand, spurring him to attack Loyalist militia along the Little Pee Dee, which resulted in the battle of Blue Savannah. It was as if Marion jumped out in front of the charging troops and yelled, "Follow me!"

Time and again, Marion not only had to contend with the British but with his own warriors and civilians in the partisan community. Marion was forced to retreat early in battles like Parker's Ferry as a result of panic among the troops. Or disperse after victory like at Black Mingo. Marion's desire to attack the Loyalists in North Carolina was thwarted because to do so would have left the Snow's Island community open to attack, which he knew would cause his men to desert. Thus, the Snow's Island community informed his strategic and tactical situation. He could not afford to lose the community, which was not only his refuge, but also his source of manpower, food, and forage.

Finally, we do not know exactly the impact of the "invisible community" of slaves on Marion's actions. We do know that Marion deliberately rounded up slaves from the surrounding region, keeping this "resource" from the British and Loyalists, and that, besides civilians taking refuge in his camps, there were also an unknown number of slaves. Both slaves and civilians had to be fed and protected. In the case of slaves, they also had to be watched so as to keep them from escaping. All these factors, too, shaped the nature of Marion's interaction with the Snow's Island partisan community.

Community, as viewed through an anthropological perspective, is always a result of circumstance. Community is always situational. The situation may be local, requiring cooperation between human groups in face-to-face association, like families attempting to survive, react to threat, or resist a common enemy, as in the case of the Whig community in South Carolina as a whole or as partisans, as in the Snow's Island community.

As situations change, community identification, membership, and boundaries change. Communities are indeed human associations based on contingency. Community members will seek the preservation of the community largely for individual purposes like security, but by acting in self-interest, members strengthen and enhance community infrastructure and tighten community bonds.

Within communities, no matter how they are politically and/or socially created, the members organize themselves hierarchically. There always exists a pecking order. This pecking order is divided largely into two general groups, leaders and followers, drivers and adherents. Leaders create action, order, and community cohesion. Followers act on community goals either voluntarily or under coercion. There is always a dynamic tension between these two groups that helps maintain community identity through negotiation.

And, regardless of how a community organizes itself, there is always an ultimate leader. In the case of the Snow's Island partisan community, Francis Marion was the ultimate leader. Initially, his position was purely the result of the community's voluntarily accepting allegiance to the greater Whig resistance. As their successes mounted, security was provided, resources were shared, Marion's authority increased. Despite their revolutionary ideology, the partisan community—this community of resistance against British authority—still needed an authority figure, and an established pecking order in which to function.

As anthropologist Laura Nader reminds us, we need to study all members, from ordinary individuals to the elites to fully understand society and community.[12] Or as the quote at the beginning of this book noted:

> History is said to be the biography of society. Society is composed of individuals—and the biography of an individual who has exerted a wide influence in the community of which he was a member is actually the history of that community.[13]

In this vein, the history of the Snow's Island partisan community *is* the biography of Francis Marion.

Endnotes for Chapter 10

1 Balfour to Rawdon, 26 October 1780, CP, P.R.O. 30/11/3.
2 Smith 2008c.
3 Linder and Thacker 2001.
4 Rogers 1970:87, 94-95.
5 Boddie 1923.
6 Linder 2000:66.
7 Linder 2000:74.
8 Flannery 1976.
9 Scoggins et al. 2010.
10 Preucel 2000.
11 Rogers 1970:115.
12 Nader 1972.
13 *Southern Quarterly Review* July 10, 1846. The author is anonymous. I believe it was William Gilmore Simms.

BIBLIOGRAPHY

The following sources were used in this book. Historical archaeologists have a difficult dilemma regarding the citation of source material. Historians have a style which better supports the citation of primary documents, while archaeologists use a citation style that works well for their discipline. Historical archaeologists work in both disciplines but when it comes to citation of their source materials, there is no perfect fit, especially for primary sources. I have used the style guide for the *Society for Historical Archaeology* as my guide, with some modifications for clarity.

PRIMARY SOURCES (MANUSCRIPTS, DIARIES, COLLECTIONS, PAPERS)

Accounts Audited (AA) of Claims Growing out of the Revolution in South Carolina, 1775-1856, South Carolina Department of Archives and History, Reels RW2685-RW2849.

Bass, Robert and Phyllis B. Canady
1965-1980 Clippings, Articles, Correspondence with Phyllis B. Canady. Marion County Archives and History Center, Marion, SC.

Canady, Phyllis B., compiler
2001 Britton Family First Three Generations In South Carolina. Three Rivers Historical Society, Williamsburg County Library, Hemmingway, SC.

Charleston Will Book and Indexes. South Caroliniana Library, University of South Carolina, Columbia.

Clinton, Sir Henry. Clinton Papers, William Clements Library, University of Michigan, Ann Arbor, MI.

Cornwallis, Lord Charles. (CP) Papers, Public Record Office (now National Archives of Great Britain). P.R.O. Volumes 30/11/ 1-7, 63-71, 77-89. London, England. Transcription by Mr. Ross St. George, Wilmington, NC.

Deeds, Plats, Wills. South Carolina Department of Archives and History, Columbia, SC. Items cited by Series, Reel or Volume number, and item or page number. For example S109803:16,34, indicates Series 109803, Reel 16, page 34. Also found on the SCDAH on-line Records Index http://www.archivesindex.sc.gov/.

De Kalb, Johann. Papers, Manuscript Division, South Caroliniana Library, University of South Carolina, Columbia, SC.

Dozier, A.W.
1868 Letter to R. Steven D. Smith, Collection, South Carolina Institute of Archaeology and Anthropology, University of South Carolina, Columbia, SC.

Force, Peter. American Archives Collection, Library of Congress.

Gates, Horatio. The Horatio Gates Papers, Microfilm, Thomas Cooper Library, University of South Carolina, Columbia, SC.

Gates, Horatio. Gates Papers, Houghton Library, Harvard University, Cambridge, MA.

Greene, Nathanael. The Papers of General Nathanael Greene. (GP) See Published Primary Sources. Series of published Greene correspondence abstracted.

The Papers of General Nathanael Greene. William Clements Library, University of Michigan, Ann Arbor, MI. Complete letters. (GP-WCL)

Greene, Nathanael. Greene Papers, Library of Congress (LOC).

Guignard Family Papers. South Caroliniana Library, University of South Carolina, Columbia, SC.

Horry, Peter. Transcripts of Francis Marion Letters, 1779-1782, 5 volumes, most published by Robert Gibbes (see Published Primary Sources). Peter Force Papers, Microfilm Series P900013, RW3365 South Carolina Department of Archives and History, Columbia, and Library of Congress, Washington, DC.

Johnstone, Gilbert. Papers. South Caroliniana Library, University of South Carolina, Columbia.

Lipscomb, Terry W.
1974ca A Guide to Manuscript Sources Relating to Snow's Island. Manuscript South Carolina Department of Archives and History, Columbia, SC.

Maybin, Nellie Chappell and Mrs. Clinton W. Foxworth
1957 Genealogical Records 1957, Richard Winn Chapter, Jenkinsville, SC, South Carolina Society D.A.R. Daughters of the American Revolution Library, Washington, DC.

Marion, Francis. Papers, South Caroliniana Library, University of South Carolina, Columbia, SC.

Marion, Francis. Papers, Huntington Library, San Marino, CA.

Marion, Francis. Orderly Book, 1775-1782. Huntington Library, San Marino, California. (See also Published Primary Sources)

Moultrie, William. Papers, South Caroliniana Library, University of South Carolina, Columbia, SC.

Nase, Henry. Diary of Henry Nase, King's American Regiment, 26 December, 1775 to 29 January 1784. Transcribed by Todd Braisted in 1991. Nase Family Papers, New Brunswick, Museum, Archives Division.

Papers of the Continental Congress (PCC). Microfilm, Thomas Cooper Library, University of South Carolina, Columbia, SC and South Carolina Department of Archives and History, Columbia, SC.

Revolutionary War Pensions and Bounty Land Warrant Application Files. National Archives Microcopy M804, South Carolina Department of Archives and History, SC, and www.footnote.com.

Saunders, John. 1754-1834. Saunders Papers, Loyalist Collection, Harriet C. Irving Library, University of New Brunswick, Fredericton, NB, Canada. Transcription courtesy Jim Piecuch.

Sparks, Jared. Collection of American Manuscripts (MS22), Houghton Library, Harvard, MA.

Stub Entries to Indents Issued in Payment of Claims Against South Carolina Growing Out of the Revolution. (See also Published Primary Sources).

PUBLISHED PRIMARY SOURCES

Ashford, Elizabeth Jeannette
1982 The Bellune Family. Elizabeth Jeanette Ashford, Pawleys Island, SC. Williamsburg County Library, Hemingway, SC.

Civil and Military Engineer of the State of South Carolina
1818 Report of the Civil and Military Engineer of the State of South Carolina for the Year 1818. In *Internal Improvements in South Carolina 1817-1828*, David Kohn and Bess Glenn, editors, pp. A-1-22. Privately printed, Washington, DC.

State Records of North Carolina
1907 *The State Records of North Carolina*, Volume 14, edited by Walter Clark, Nash Brothers, Goldsboro, NC.

Conrad, Dennis M. editor
1995 *The Papers of Nathanael Greene, Volume VIII, 30 March-10 July 1781.* The University of North Carolina Press, Chapel Hill, NC.

Frierson, John
1999 The South Carolina Campaign of 16 February to 28 Dec. 1781, as Noted in General Francis Marion's Order Book. John Frierson, Lexington, SC. Footnote.com (now Fold3.com) 2010, Scanned Original Pension Applications From National Archives, Records of the Veterans Administration, Record Group 15.

Gibbes, Robert
1853 *Documentary History of the American Revolution. Volume 1, 1781 and 1782.* Banner Steam-Power Press, Columbia, SC.
1855 *Documentary History of the American Revolution. Volume 3, 1776-1782.* D. Appleton & Co., NY.

Gray, Colonel Robert
1910 Colonel Robert Gray's Observations on the War in Carolina. *South Carolina Historical and Genealogical Magazine* XI(3):1-139-159.

Hartman, Bushy
2005 *South Carolina Early Wills Collection, Williamsburg County Series, Will Book A of Williamsburg County, 1806-1826.* Deadly Serious Genealogy, Moncks Corner, SC.

Hendrick, Ge Lee Corley and Morn McKoy Lindsay
1975 *The Jury Lists of South Carolina 1778-1779.* Privately printed, Greenville, SC.

Jervey, Elizabeth H.
1943 Abstracts From Records of Court of Ordinary, 1764-1771. *South Carolina Historical and Genealogical Magazine* XLIV(3):173-183.

Lipscomb, Terry W., and R. Nicolas Olsberg, editors
1977 *The Colonial Records of South Carolina: The Journal of the Commons House of Assembly, November 14, 1751-October 7, 1752.* University of South Carolina Press, Columbia, SC.

Montgomery, Elizabeth Witherspoon
1835 *An Early Manuscript Copy of The Witherspoon Family Chronicle & Later Notes on Related Families.* The State Printing Company for the Williamsburg County Historical Society, Columbia, SC.

National Archives and Records Administration
1974 Descriptive Pamphlet for *Revolutionary War Pension and Bounty-Land Warrant Application Files,* M804, Washington, DC.

O'Kelley, Patrick
2006 *"Unwaried Patience & Fortitude": Francis Marion's Orderly Book.* Infinity Publishing, West Conshohocken, PA.

Rudisill, Horace Fraser
1993 *The Diaries of Even Pugh (1762-1801).* St. David's Society, Florence, SC.

Salley, A.S. Jr., editor
1900 Letter of Thomas Post [Potts] to the Council of Safety in Charles Town. Papers of the First Council of Safety of the Revolutionary Party in South Carolina, June-November 1775. *South Carolina Historical and Genealogical Magazine* I(2):128-129.
1910 *Stub Entries to Indents Issued in Payment of Claims Against South Carolina Growing out of the Revolution, Books L-N.* The Historical Commission of South Carolina, Columbia, SC.
1915 *Stub Entries to Indents Issued in Payment of Claims Against South Carolina Growing out of the Revolution, Books O-Q.* The Historical Commission of South Carolina, Columbia, SC.
1917 *Stub Entries to Indents Issued in Payment of Claims Against South Carolina Growing out of the Revolution, Books R-T.* The Historical Commission of South Carolina, Columbia, SC.
1918 *Stub Entries to Indents Issued in Payment of Claims Against South Carolina Growing out of the Revolution, Books U-W.* The Historical Commission of South Carolina, Columbia, SC.
1925 *Stub Entries to Indents Issued in Payment of Claims Against South Carolina Growing out of the Revolution, Book X-Part 1.* The Historical Commission of South Carolina, Columbia, SC.
1925 *Stub Entries to Indents Issued in Payment of Claims Against South Carolina Growing out of the Revolution, Book X-Part 2.* The Historical Commission of South Carolina, Columbia, SC.
1927 *Stub Entries to Indents Issued in Payment of Claims Against South Carolina Growing out of the Revolution, Books Y-Z.* The Historical Commission of South Carolina, Columbia, SC.
1934 *Stub Entries to Indents Issued in Payment of Claims Against South Carolina Growing out of the Revolution, Book B.* The Historical Commission of South Carolina, Columbia, SC.
1935 *Accounts Audited of Revolutionary Claims Against South Carolina, Volume 1.*

Salley, A.S. Jr., The Historical Commission of South Carolina, Columbia, SC.
1937 Journal of General Peter Horry. *South Carolina Historical and Genealogical Magazine,* Volume XXXVIX(3):125-128.
1938 *Accounts Audited of Revolutionary Claims Against South Carolina, Volume 2.* The Historical Commission of South Carolina, Columbia, SC.
1939 *Stub Entries to Indents Issued in Payment of Claims Against South Carolina Growing out of the Revolution, Book I.* The Historical Commission of South Carolina, Columbia, SC.
1943 *Accounts Audited of Revolutionary Claims Against South Carolina, Volume 3.* The Historical Commission of South Carolina, Columbia, SC.

Salley, A.S. Jr., contributor
1959 Horry's Notes to Weems's *Life of Marion. South Carolina Historical Magazine* LX(3):119-122.

Showman, Richard K., General Editor, Dennis M. Conrad, Editor, Roger N. Parks, Senior Associate Editor, Elizabeth C. Stevens, Associate Editor
1991 *The Papers of General Nathanael Greene, Volume VI, 1 June 1780-25 December 1780.* The University of North Carolina Press, Chapel Hill, NC.

Showman, Richard K., General Editor, Dennis M. Conrad, Editor, Roger N. Parks, Senior Associate Editor, Elizabeth C. Stevens, Associate Editor
1994 *The Papers of General Nathanael Greene, Volume VII, 25 December 1780-29 March 1781.* The University of North Carolina Press, Chapel Hill, NC.

Southern Campaigns of the American Revolution
2010 Transcribed Pension Applications, http://southerncampaign.org/pen/.

Superintendent of Public Works
1825 Report of the Superintendent of Public Works of South Carolina for the Year 1825. In *Internal Improvements in South Carolina 1817-1828*, David Kohn and Bess Glenn, editors, pp. 367-386. Privately printed, Washington, DC.

Warren, Mary Bonderant
1977 *South Carolina Jury Lists 1718 through 1783.* Heritage Papers, Danielsville, GA.

Wates, Wylma Anne, editor
1955 *Stub Entries to Indents Issued in Payment of Claims Against South Carolina Growing out of the Revolution, Books G-H.* South Carolina Archives Department, Columbia, SC.
1956 *Stub Entries to Indents Issued in Payment of Claims Against South Carolina Growing out of the Revolution, Book K.* South Carolina Archives Department, Columbia, SC.
1957 *Stub Entries to Indents Issued in Payment of Claims Against South Carolina Growing out of the Revolution, Books C-F.* South Carolina Archives Department, Columbia, SC.

Utley, Lucille
1981 Marion County Extracts From Equity Rolls. Three Rivers Historical Society, on file, Williamsburg County Library Hemmingway, SC.

Utley, Lucille and Teri Dalrymple
2002 Marion County Court Records, Court of Common Pleas, 1788 to June 1861. Three Rivers Historical Society, Williamsburg County Library, Hemmingway, SC.

Utley, Lucille and Alita White Sutcliffe
1997 Marion County South Carolina Abstracts of Deeds, Volume 2, Books F-I & K, 1811-1823. Forebears Press, Charlotte, North Carolina. Williamsburg County Library, Hemmingway, SC.

Utley, Lucille, Margie Collins, Glenda Watts, and John M. Gregg
2005 Selected Marion County Judgment Rolls [1802-1870]. Three Rivers Historical Society, Williamsburg County Library, Hemmingway, SC.

Utley, Lucille and Danny Smith
1985a Marion County Probate Records Volume II. Three Rivers Historical Society, Williamsburg County Library, Hemmingway, SC.
1985b Marion County Probate Records Volume III. Three Rivers Historical Society, Williamsburg County Library, Hemmingway, SC.

Utley, Lucille, Danny Smith, Ferrell and Nancy Prosser
1985 Marion County Probate Records Volume I. Three Rivers Historical Society, Williamsburg County Library, Hemmingway, SC.

Utley, Lucille, Angela Turner, and Billie Eaddy Cribb
2003 Abstracts of Marion County [SC] Deed Books L-M-N, 1824-1831. Three Rivers Historical Society, Williamsburg County Library, Hemmingway, SC.

PRIMARY SOURCES CONSULTED

Cornwallis, Lord Charles. (CP-SCDAH) Papers, Microfilm, Series B800121, Reels RW3145A-RW3150, South Carolina Department of Archives and History, Columbia, SC.

Eaddy, Elaine Y.
[1981] Williamsburg County Probate Records 1806- ca. 1900 and Notes From Other Miscellaneous Sources. Three Rivers Historical Society. Williamsburg County Library Hemmingway, SC.

Three Rivers Historical Society
Federal Census of the United States, State of South Carolina, District of Williamsburgh 1790, 1800, 1810, 1820, 1830, 1840, Bound by the Society.

Winslow, Edward. Winslow Papers, Two volumes, edited by W.O. Raymond, Microform, Volume 2. Harriet Library, University of New Brunswick, Fredericton, NB, Canada. Transcription courtesy Jim Piecuch.

SECONDARY SOURCES

Acree, Jill
2007 *The Sorrows of Parson Weems: His Life and Legacy*. Doctoral dissertation, Department of History, Claremont Graduate University, Claremont, CA. Microfilms International, Ann Arbor, MI.

Adams, Natalie P.
2002 A Pattern of Living: A View of the African American Slave Experience in the Pine Forests of the Lower Cape Fear. In *Another's Country: Archaeological and Historical Perspectives on Cultural Interactions in the Southern Colonies*, J.W. Joseph and Martha Zierden, editors, pp. 65-78. University of Alabama Press, Tuscaloosa, AL.

Adams, William H.
1977 *Silcott, Washington: Ethnoarchaeology of a Rural American Community*. Reports of Investigations, No. 54, Washington State University, Pullman, WA.

Anderson, Benedict
1991 *Imagined Communities: Reflections on the Origins and Spread of Nationalism*. Verso, London, UK.

Anschuetz, Kurt F., Richard H. Wilshusen, and Cherie L. Scheick
2001 An Archaeology of Landscapes: Perspectives and Directions. *Journal of Archaeological Research* 9(2):157-211.

Arensberg, Conrad M., and Solon T. Kimball
1995 *Culture and Community*. Harcourt, Brace and World, New York, NY.

Arkush, Elizabeth N., and Mark W. Allen, editors
2006 *The Archaeology of Warfare*. University Press of Florida, Gainesville, FL.

Ascher, Robert
1968 Times Arrow and the Archaeology of a Contemporary Community. In *Settlement Archaeology*, K.C. Chang, editor, pp. 43-52. National Press Books, Pal Alto, CA.

Asprey, Robert B.
1975 *War in the Shadows: The Guerrilla in History*. Two Volumes, Doubleday & Company, Garden City, NY.

Babits, Lawrence E.
1982 *Military Documents and Archaeological Sites: Methodological Contributions to Historical Archaeology.* Doctoral dissertation, Brown University, Providence, RI. Microfilms International, Ann Arbor, MI.
1998 *A Devil of a Whipping: The Battle of Cowpens.* University of North Carolina Press, Chapel Hill, NC.
2004 Asymmetrical Warfare During the American Revolution's Southern Campaign. Paper presented at the Annual Meeting of the Society for Military History, Charleston, SC.
2006 Eutaw Springs, South Carolina. In *Encyclopedia of the American Revolution, Volume 1, Second Edition*, Harold E. Selesky, editor in chief. pp. 343-347. Library of Military History, Thomson Gale, New York, NY. Original entry 1966, by Mark M. Boatner, first edition, pp. 350-357. David McKay, New York, NY.

Babits, Lawrence E., and Joshua B. Howard
2009 *Long, Obstinate, and Bloody: The Battle of Guilford Courthouse.* University of North Carolina Press, Chapel Hill, NC.

Bailey, De Witt
1997 *Pattern Dates for British Ordnance Small Arms 1718-1783.* Thomas Publications, Gettysburg, PA.

Bailey, N. Louise
1984 *Biographical Directory of the South Carolina House of Representatives, Volume IV, 1791-1815.* University of South Carolina Press, Columbia, SC.

Bailey, N. Louise, and Elizabeth Ivey Cooper
1981 *Biographical Directory of the South Carolina House of Representatives, Volume III, 1775-1790.* University of South Carolina Press, Columbia, SC.

Banta, D.D.
1888 *History of Johnson County, Indiana.* Brant & Fuller, Chicago, IL.

Barmeyer, Niels
2003 The Guerrilla Movement as a Project: An Assessment of Community Involvement in the EZLN. *Latin American Perspectives*, Issue 128, 30(1):122-133.

Barnett, Roger W.
2003 *Asymmetrical Warfare: Today's Challenge to U.S. Military Power.* Brassey's, Washington, DC.

Bass, Robert D.
1959 Swamp Fox: The Life and Campaigns of General Francis Marion. Alvin Redman, London, UK.
1977 Some Names in Britton's Neck. *Names in South Carolina* (XXIV):19-21.

Barry, John M.
1980 *Natural Vegetation of South Carolina.* University of South Carolina Press, Columbia, SC.

Bellesiles, Michael
2006 Savannah, Georgia. In *Encyclopedia of the American Revolution, Volume 2, Second Edition*, Harold E. Selesky, editor in chief, pp. 1036-1040. Library of Military History, Thomson Gale, New York, NY. Original entry 1966, by Mark M. Boatner, first edition, pp. 982-988. David McKay, New York, NY.

Ben-Ari, Eyal
1998 *Mastering Soldiers: Conflict, Emotions and the Enemy in an Israeli Military Unit.* Berghahn, Oxford, UK.

Binford, Lewis
1978 A New Method of Calculating Dates from Kaolin Pipe Stems Samples. In *Historical Archaeology: A Guide to Substantive and Theoretical Contributions*, Robert Schuyler, editor, pp. 66-67. Baywood Press, Farmingdale, NY.

Blankenstein, Henry and Dianne
2010 "Dozier." Blankenstein [genealogy website]. http://pages.prodigy.net/blankenstein/Dozer.htm

Boatner, Mark M.
1966 *Encyclopedia of the American Revolution*. David McKay, New York, NY.

Boddie, William Willis
1923 *History of Williamsburg*. The State Company, Columbia, SC.
2000 *Traditions of the Swamp Fox: William W. Boddie's Francis Marion*. The Reprint Company, Spartanburg, SC.

Borick, Carl P.
2006 Siege of Charleston. In *Encyclopedia of the American Revolution, Volume 1, Second Edition*, Harold E. Selesky, editor in chief, pp. 192-195. Library of Military History, Thomson Gale, New York, NY.

Brain, Jeffery P.
1979 *Tunica Treasure*. Papers of the Peabody Museum of Archaeology and Ethnology, Volume 71, Harvard University, MA.

Brooks, Mark
2009 Appendix B: Natural Vs. Anthropogenic Depositional Processes: Summary of a Day in the Field at Dunham's Bluff. In *Archaeological Evaluation of the Dunham's Bluff Sites, 38MA207 and 38MA165*, Steven D. Smith, pp. B1-B3. South Carolina Institute of Archaeology and Anthropology, Columbia, SC.

Brown, Jerome King
1978 *William Gilmore Simms and the American Historical Romance*. Doctoral dissertation, Department of English, University of Kansas, Lawrence, University Microfilms International, Ann Arbor, MI.

Brown, Richard Maxwell
1963 *The South Carolina Regulators*. The Belknap Press of the Harvard University Press, Cambridge, MA.

Brown, Tarleton
1999 *Memoirs of Tarleton Brown: A Captain in the Revolutionary Army, Written by Himself, With a New Introduction by Terry W. Lipscomb*. Brown County Museum and Historical Board, Barnwell, SC.

Bryant, William Cullen
1912 Song of Marion. In *Historic Poems & Ballads*, Rupert S. Holland, editor. George W. Jacobs, Philadelphia, PA.

Buchanan, John
2019 *The Road to Charleston: Nathanael Greene and the American Revolution*. University of Virginia Press, Charlottesville.

Busick, Sean R.
2005 *A Sober Desire For History: William Gilmore Simms as Historian*. University of South Carolina Press, Columbia, SC.

Butler, Lindley
1994 David Fanning's Militia: A Roving Partisan Community. In *Loyalist and Community in North America*, Robert M. Calhoon, Timothy M. Barnes, and George A. Rawlyk, editors, pp. 147-157. Greenwood Press, Westport, CT.

Calhoon, Robert M.
1965 *The Loyalists in Revolutionary America 1760-1781*. Harcourt Brace Jovanovich, New York, NY.

Calhoon, Robert M., Timothy M. Barnes, and George A. Rawlyk
1994 *Loyalist and Community in North America*, Greenwood Press, Westport, CT.

Carman, John, and Patricia Carman
2007 Mustering Landscapes: What Historic Battlefields Share in Common. In *Fields of Conflict: Battlefield Archaeology From the Roman Empire to the Korean War*, Douglas Scott, Lawrence Babits, and Charles Haecker, editors, pp. 39-49. Praeger Security International, Westport, CT.

Casey, Edward S.
2008 Place in Landscape Archaeology: A Western Philosophical Prelude. In *Handbook of Landscape Archaeology*, Bruno David and Julian Thomas, editors, pp. 44-59. Left Coast Press, Walnut Creek, CA.

Chacon, Richard J., and Rubén G. Mendoza, editors
2007 *North American Indigenous Warfare and Ritual Violence*. University of Arizona Press, Tucson, AZ.

Chang, K.C.
1968 Toward a Science of Prehistoric Society. In *Settlement Archaeology*, K.C. Chang, editor, pp. 1-9. National Press Books, Pal Alto, CA.

Chesterton, Gilbert S.
1980 *Orthodoxy*. J. Lane, New York, NY. Original 1909.

Clark, Murtie June
1981 *Loyalists in the Southern Campaign of the Revolutionary War*. Volume 1, Genealogical Publishing Company, Baltimore, MD.

Clark, Thomas D. (editor)
1973 A Yankee View, 1843. *South Carolina The Grand Tour 1780-1865*, pp. 201-214. University of South Carolina, Columbia, SC.

Coker, Kathy Roe
1987 *The Punishment of Revolutionary War Loyalists in South Carolina*. Doctoral dissertation, Department of History, University of South Carolina, University Microfilms International, Ann Arbor, MI.

Conner, Melissa, and Douglas D. Scott
1998 Metal Detector Use in Archaeology: An Introduction. *Historical Archaeology* 32(4):76-85.

Cook, Harvey Toliver
1926 *Rambles in the Pee Dee Basin, South Carolina*. The State Company, Columbia, SC.

Cooper, James F.
2007 *An Historical Sketch of Indiantown Presbyterian Church*. Indiantown Bi-Centennial Committee, Bound by Rivers Historical Society, Williamsburg County Library, Hemingway, SC.

Council of South Carolina Professional Archaeologists
2005 *South Carolina Standards and Guidelines for Archaeological Investigations.* Council of South Carolina Professional Archaeologists, South Carolina Department of Archives and History, Historic Preservation Office, and the South Carolina Institute of Archaeology and Anthropology, Columbia, SC.

Dargan, John J.
1905 History of the Old Cheraws Addenda and The Contributions of the Pedee Counties, Pee Dee Historical Society. In *History of the Old Cheraws*, Rev. Alexander Gregg, editor, pp. 551-635. The State Company, Columbia, SC, 1925, original 1867, Richardson and Company, New York, NY.

Darling, Anthony D.
1970 *Red Coat and Brown Bess.* Museum Restoration Service, Bloomfield, ON, Canada.

Davies, Nell Weaver
1999 New Facts About an Old Story. *Carologue* 15(4):16-21.

Dawson, Doyne
1999 The Origins of War: Biological and Anthropological Theories. *History and Theory* Vol. 35(1):1-28.

Dederer, John
1983 *Making Bricks Without Straw: Nathanael Greene's Southern Campaigns and Mao Tse-tung's Mobile War.* Sunflower University Press, Manhattan, KS.

Dickerson, Jo Church
2005 Address to the Pee Dee Chapter, South Carolina Genealogical Society, 13 November. Steven D. Smith Collection. South Carolina Institute of Archaeology and Anthropology, Columbia, SC.
2006 Blue Savannah. Packet of research compiled by Jo Church Dickerson for Steven D. Smith and the Francis Marion Trail Commission. South Carolina Institute of Archaeology and Anthropology, SC.

Dornfest, Walter T.
1997 John Watson Tadwell Watson and the Provincial Light Infantry, 1780-1781. *Journal of the Society for Army Historical Research* 77:220-229.

Drucker, Leslie M., and Ronald W. Anthony
1979 *The Spiers Landing Site: Archaeological Investigations in Berkeley County, South Carolina.* Carolina Archaeological Services, Columbia, SC.

Dunham, James T.
2010a Descendants of John Dunnam http://freepages.genealogy.rootsweb.ancestry.com/~pastor/johndunnam.htm
2010b The Robert Commander Dunnam, Sr. and Jr. Families of Baldwin & Wilcox Counties, Alabama. http://freepages.genealogy.rootsweb.ancestry.com/~pastor/rcdwil.htm

Edgar, Walter B.
1998 *South Carolina, A History.* University of South Carolina Press, Columbia, SC.
2008 *Partisans and Redcoats: The Southern Conflict that Turned the Tide of the American Revolution.* William Morrow, New York, NY.

Edgar, Walter B., and N. Louise Bailey
1977 *Biographical Directory of the South Carolina House of Representatives, Volume II: The Commons House of Assembly 1692-1775.* University of South Carolina Press, Columbia, SC.

Eller, Jack D.
1999 *From Culture to Ethnicity to Conflict: An Anthropological Perspective on International Ethnic Conflict.* University of Michigan Press, Ann Arbor, MI.

Ember, Melvin
1982 Statistical Evidence for an Ecological Explanation of Warfare. *American Anthropologist* Vol. 84(3):645-649.

Epps, Katrina Small
2006 *Intra-Regional Interactions in the Lowcountry of South Carolina.* Stanley South, editor. Volumes in Historical Archaeology, XLV, South Carolina Institute of Archaeology and Anthropology, University of South Carolina, Columbia, SC.

Epstein, Beryl William and Samuel Epstein
1956 *Francis Marion, Swamp Fox of the Revolution.* J. Messner, New York, NY.

Ervin, Sam J., Jr.
1978 Entries in Colonel John Ervin's Bible. *South Carolina Historical Magazine* 79(3):219-227.

Espenshade, Christopher T., Robert L. Jolley, and James B. Legg
2002 The Value and Treatment of Civil War Military Sites. *North American Archaeologist* 23(1):39-67.

Ewald, Johann
1991 *Treatise on Partisan Warfare.* Introduction, annotation, and translation of 1785 edition by Robert A. Selig and David Curtis Skaggs. Contributions in Military Studies, No. 116. Greenwood Press, New York, NY.

Ferguson, Clyde R.
1979 Functions of the Partisan-Militia in the South During the American Revolution: An Interpretation. In *The Revolutionary War in the South: Power, Conflict, and Leadership*, W. Robert Higgins editor, pp. 239-258, Duke University Press, Durham, NC.

Ferguson, E. James
1961 *The Power of the Purse.* University of North Carolina Press, Chapel Hill, NC.

Ferguson, Leland G.
1975 *Archeology at Scott's Lake, Exploratory Research 1972, 1773.* Research Manuscript Series 68, South Carolina Institute of Archaeology and Anthropology, University of South Carolina, Columbia, SC.

Ferguson, R. Brian
2006 Archaeology, Cultural Anthropology, and the Origins and Intensifications of War. In *The Archaeology of Warfare*, Elizabeth N. Arkush and Mark W. Allen, editors, pp. 469-523. University Press of Florida, Gainesville, FL.

Ferguson, R. Brian, and Neil L. Whitehead, editors
1992 *War in the Tribal Zone: Expanding States and Indigenous Warfare.* School of American Research Press, Santa Fe, NM.

Fitz-Simons, Daniel E.
1995 Francis Marion the 'Swamp Fox': An Anatomy of a Low-Intensity Conflict. *Small Wars and Insurgencies* 6(1):1-16.

Flannery, V. Kent (editor)
1976 *The Early Mesoamerican Village.* Academic Press, New York, NY.

Frost, John
1847 *Life of General Francis Marion; Embracing Anecdotes Illustrative of his Character.* Lindsay and Blakiston, Philadelphia, PA.

Furstenberg, François
2006a *In the Name of the Father: Washington's Legacy, Slavery, and the Making of a Nation.* The Penguin Press, New York, NY.
2006b Spinning the Revolution. *The New York Times.* July 4.

Garden, Alexander
1822 *Anecdotes of the Revolutionary War in America.* A.E. Miller, Charleston, SC. Reprinted by the Reprint Company, 1972, Spartanburg, SC.

Gerson, Noel B.
1966 *The Swamp Fox, Francis Marion.* Doubleday, Garden City, NY.

Geier, Clarence R., David G. Orr, Matthew B. Reeves
2006 *Huts and History: The Historical Archaeology of Military Encampment During the American Civil War.* University of Florida Press, Gainesville, FL.

Gimelson, Bruce
2007 Autographs, Paintings, Americana. http://www.brucegimelson.com.

González, Roberto J.
2007 Towards Mercenary Anthropology: The New Counterinsurgency Manual FM 3-24 and the Military-Anthropology Complex. *Anthropology Today* 23(3):14-19.

Gordon, William
1788 *The History of the Rise, Progress, and Establishment of the Independence of the United States, Volume III.* Reprint 1969 by Books for Libraries Press, Freeport, NY.

Graves Family Association
2010 Descendants of Joseph Greaves and Mary Bennett of England & South Carolina. http://www.gravesfa.org/gen156.htm.

Greer, Shelley, Rodney Harrison, and Susan McIntyre-Tamwoy
2002 Community Based Archaeology in Australia. *World Archaeology* 34(2):265-387.

Gregg, Reverend Alexander
1925 *History of the Old Cheraws.* The State Company, Columbia, SC. Original 1867, Richardson and Company, New York, NY.

Griffith, Samuel B.
1978 *Mao-Tse-tung on Guerrilla Warfare.* Double Day, Garden City, NY.

Groover, Mark D.
1992 *Of Mindset and Material Culture: An Archaeological View of Continuity and Change in the 18th Century South Carolina Backcountry.* In Volumes in Historical Archaeology XX, Stanley South, editor. South Carolina Institute of Archaeology and Anthropology, University of South Carolina, Columbia, SC.

Gupta, Akhil, and James Ferguson
1997 Culture, Power, Place: Ethnography at the End of an Era. In *Culture, Power, Place: Explorations in Critical Anthropology*, Akhil Gupta and James Ferguson editors, pp. 1-32. Duke University Press, London, UK.

Haecker, Charles M., and Jeffrey G. Mauck
1997 *On the Prairie of Palo Alto: Historical Archaeology of the U.S.-Mexican War Battlefield.* Texas A & M Press, College Station, TX.

Headley, Joel T.
1847 *Washington and His Generals.* A.L. Burt Company, NY.

Hegmon, Michelle
2002 Concepts of Community in Archaeological Research. In *Seeking the Center Place: Archaeology and Ancient Communities in the Mesa Verde Region*, Mark D. Varien and Richard H. Wilshusen, editors, pp. 263-279. The University of Utah Press, Salt Lake City, NV.

Heider, Karl G.
1980 The Gamecock, The Swamp Fox, and the Wizard Owl: The Development of Good Form in an American Totemic Set. *Journal of American Folklore* 93:367(1-22).

Holbrook, Stewart Hall
1959 *The Swamp Fox of the Revolution.* Random House, New York, NY.

Hole, Frank and Robert F. Heizer
1973 *An Introduction to Prehistoric Archaeology.* Third edition, Holt. Rinehart and Winston, Inc, New York, NY.

Hollman, C. Hugh
1967 William Faulkner: The Anguished Dream of Time. *Three Modes of Modern Southern Fiction.* University of Georgia Press, Athens, GA.

Holtorf, Cornelius
2005 *From Stonehenge to Las Vegas: Archeology as Popular Culture.* AltaMira Press, Walnut Creek, CA.

Horry, Peter and Mason L. Weems
1891 *The Life of Marion, A Celebrated Partisan Officer in the Revolutionary War, Against the British and Tories in South Carolina and Georgia.* Philadelphia, PA. First Edition 1809.

Howe, George
1870 *History of the Presbyterian Church in South Carolina.* Volume 1, Part 2, Duffie & Chapman, Columbia, SC.

Hoyt, Epaphras
1811 *Practical Instructions For Military Officers: Comprehending A Concise System of Military Geometry, Field Fortification and Tactics of Riflemen and Light Infantry. Also The Scheme for Forming a Corps of a Partisan, and Carrying on the Petite Guerre, by Roger Stevenson, Esq. Revised, Corrected, and Enlarged.* John Denio, Greenville, MA.

Isbell, William H.
2000 What We Should be Studying: The "Imagined Community" and the "Natural Community." In *The Archaeology of Communities: A New World Perspective*, Marcello A. Canuto and Jason Yaeger, pp. 243-266. Routledge, London, UK.

James, William Dobein
1821 *A Sketch of the Life of Brig. General Francis Marion, and A History of His Brigade.* Reprinted 1948 by Continental Book Company, Marietta, GA.

Jenkins, James
1842 *Experience, Labours and Sufferings of Reverend James Jenkins of the South Carolina Conference.* Privately Printed, n.p.

Joes, Anthony James
1996 *Guerrilla Warfare: A Historical, Bibliographical, and Bibliographical Sourcebook.* Greenwood Press, Westport, CN.
2000 *America and Guerrilla Warfare.* University of Kentucky Press, Lexington, KY.

Johnson, Mrs. N.M.
1908 Bits of History. Daughters of the American Revolution, *American Monthly Magazine* XXXIII, July No.1:989-991.

Johnson, Joseph
1851 *Traditions and Reminiscences Chiefly of the American Revolution in the South*. Charleston, SC.

Keithly, David
2001 Poor, Nasty and Brutish: Guerrilla Operations in America's First Civil War. *Civil Wars* 4(3):35-69.

King, G. Wayne
1981 *Rise Up So Early A History of Florence County*. The Reprint Company, Spartanburg, SC.

King, Leslie J.
1984 *Central Place Theory*. SAGE Publications, Beverly Hills, CA.

Kohn, David, and Bess Glenn, (editors)
1938 *Internal Improvements in South Carolina 1817-1828*. Privately Printed, Washington, DC.

Kovacik, Charles F., and John J. Winberry
1987 *South Carolina: A Geography*. Westview Press, Boulder, CO.

Kruijt, Dirk
2008 *Guerrillas: War and Peace in Central America*. Zed Books, London, UK.

Lambert, Robert S.
1987 *South Carolina Loyalists in the American Revolution*. University of South Carolina Press, SC.

Landers, Erma Poston, and James Allen Poston
[1965] *A Poston Family of South Carolina*. Bound by the Three Rivers Historical Society, Williamsburg County Library, Hemingway, SC. No date.

Laqueur, Walter
1976 *Guerrilla: A Historical and Critical Study*. Little, Brown, and Company, Boston, MA.

Leatherman, Thomas
2005 Poverty and Violence, Hunger and Health: A Political Ecology of Armed Conflict. In *Globalization, Health and the Environment: An Integrated Perspective*, Greg Guest, editor, pp. 55-80. Altamira Press, Walnut Creek, CA.

Lee, Henry
1998 *The Revolutionary War Memoirs of General Henry Lee*. Edited by Robert E. Lee, with an introduction by Charles Royster, Da Capo Press, NY. Original, 1812. Original title, *Memoirs of the War in the Southern Department of the United States*.

Legg, James B.
2007 Appendix I: Analysis of Small Arms Ammunition From Fort Motte. In *"Obstinate and Strong": The History and Archaeology of the Siege of Fort Motte*. By Steven D. Smith, James B. Legg, Tamara S. Wilson, and Jonathan Leader, pp. 11-18. South Carolina Institute of Archaeology and Anthropology, University of South Carolina, Columbia, SC.

Legg, James B., Steven D. Smith, and Tamara S. Wilson
2005 *Understanding Camden: The Revolutionary War Battle of Camden As Revealed Through Historical, Archaeological and Private Collections Analysis*. South Carolina Institute of Archaeology and Anthropology, Columbia, SC.

Lewis, J.D.
2007 The Royal Colony of South Carolina. http://www.carolana.com/SC/Royal Colony/sc royal colony townships established.htmlaccessed 25 February 2010.

Libbie, C.F. & Co.
1895 *Catalogue of the Collection of Autographs and Coins of the Late Charles H. Bell, Esq.* C.F. Libbie & Co., Boston, Mass. No. 364. Marion, Col. Francis Autographed Receipt. Steven D. Smith Collection, South Carolina Institute of Archaeology and Anthropology, Columbia, SC.

Lightfoot, Kent G., and Antoinette Martinez
1995 Frontiers and Boundaries in Archaeological Perspective. *Annual Review of Anthropology* Vol. 24:417-192.

Linder, Suzanne Cameron
2000 *A River in Time: The Yadkin-Pee Dee River System*. With Emily Linder Johnson, Palmetto Conservation Foundation, Columbia, SC.

Linder, Suzanne Cameron and Marta Leslie Thacker
2001 *Historical Atlas of Rice Plantations of Georgetown County and the Santee River*. South Carolina Department of Archives and History, Columbia, SC.

Linenthal, Edward T.
2001 Foreword. In *Myth, Memory, and the American Landscape*, Paul A. Shackel, editor, pp. xi-xii. University of Florida Press, Gainesville, FL.

Lipe, William
1970 Anasazi Communities in the Red Rock Plateau, Southwestern Utah. In *Reconstructing Prehistoric Pueblo Societies*, William A. Longacre, editor, pp. 84-139. University of New Mexico Press, Albuquerque, NM.
1992 *The San Canyon Archaeological Project: A Progress Report*. Crow Canyon Archaeological Center Occasional Paper No. 2. Crow Canyon Archaeological Center, Cortez, CO.

Lipscomb, Terry
1973-1983 South Carolina Revolutionary War Battles, Parts 1 Through 10. *Names in South Carolina*, Volumes XX through XXXI, University of South Carolina, Columbia, SC.

Lossing, Benjamin
1858 Francis Marion. *Harpers New Monthly Magazine*. No. XCVIII, July XVII:145-170.

Lumpkin, Henry
1981 *From Savannah to Yorktown: The American Revolution in the South*. University of South Carolina Press, Columbia, SC.

Mao Tse-tung
1978 *Mao Tse-tung on Guerrilla Warfare*. Edited by Samuel B. Griffith. Anchor Press, Garden City, NY.

Marcus, Joyce
2000 Toward an Archaeology of Communities. In *The Archaeology of Communities: A New World Perspective*, Marcello A. Canuto and Jason Yaeger, editors, pp. 231-242. Routledge, London, UK.

Marr, Timothy
2007 Abstract. Dredging the Swamp Fox: Francis Marion in the Circuits of Cultural Memory. Paper presented at the Annual Meeting of the American Studies Association, Philadelphia, PA.

McConnell, David
1988 *British Smooth-Bore Artillery: A Technical Study*. National Parks and Historic Sites, Environment Canada-Parks, Ottawa, ON, Canada.

McFate, Montgomery
2005 Anthropology and Counterinsurgency: The Strange Story of Their Curious Relationship. *Military Review* March-April 24-28.

Meitzen, Blocker Dodson
1987 Francis Marion: His Life as Symbol. Master's thesis, Department of History, Auburn University, Auburn, AL.

Meriwether, Robert L.
1974 *The Expansion of South Carolina 1729-1765*. Porcupine Press, Philadelphia.

Michie, James
1980 Expectations of Archeological Site Locations Within Floodplain and Peripheral Upland Areas. Prepared for S.C. Water Resources Commission, South Carolina Institute of Archaeology and Anthropology, Columbia, SC.

Miller, Lisa Kay
1987 *The Artist as Historian: The Southern Frontier and the Writing of History in the Fiction of William Gilmore Simms, William Faulkner, and Eudora Welty*. Doctoral dissertation, University of Missouri, Columbia, University Microfilms International, Ann Arbor, MI.

Mills, Robert
1825 *Mills' Atlas of the State of South Carolina*. Reprint 1980, Southern Historical Press, Greenville, SC.
1826 *Statistics of South Carolina: Including a View of its Natural, Civil, and Military History, General and Particular*. Hurlbut and Lloyd, Charleston, SC.

Mitchell, Robert D.
1998 The Southern Backcountry: A Geographical House Divided. In *The Southern Colonial Backcountry*, David Colin Crass, Steven D. Smith, Martha A. Zierden and Richard D. Brooks, editors, pp. 1-35. University of Tennessee Press, Knoxville, TN.

Moller, George
1993 *American Military Shoulder Arms, Volume 1: Colonial and Revolutionary War Arms*. University of Colorado Press, Denver, CO.

Moltke-Hansen, David
2009 Southern Literary Horizons in Young America: Imaginative Development of a Regional Geography. *Studies in Literary Imagination* 42(1):1-31.
2013 editor, *William Gilmore Simms's Unfinished Civil War: Consequences for a Southern Man of Letters*, University of South Carolina Press, Columbia.

Moore, Alexander
1999 The Swamp Fox in History and Literature. *Carologue* Winter 15(4):14-15.

Moore, Horatio Nelson
1845 *The Life and Times of Francis Marion, with an Appendix. Containing Biographical Notices of Greene, Morgan, Pickens, Sumpter, Washington, Lee, Davie, and Other Distinguishing Officers of the Southern Campaign During the American Revolution*. J.B. Perry, Philadelphia, PA.

Moore, Warren
1967 *Weapons of the American Revolution: and Accoutrements*. Funk and Wagnalls, New York, NY.

Moss, Bobby Gilmore
1983 *Roster of South Carolina Patriots in the American Revolution.* Genealogical Publishing Company, Baltimore, MD.

Moss, Bobby Gilmore, and Michael C. Scoggins
2004a *African American Patriots in the Southern Campaign of the American Revolution.* Scotia-Hibernia Press, Blacksburg, SC.
2004b *African American Loyalists in the Southern Campaign of the American Revolution.* Scotia-Hibernia Press, Blacksburg, SC.

Moultrie, William
1802 *Memoirs of the American Revolution so far as it Related to the States of North and South Carolina.* David Longworth, New York, NY.

Munnerlyn, James
2010 Website PhPGEDView. http://www.munnerlyn.info/phpgedview/indilist.php?alpha=M,

Murdock, George P.
1949 *Social Structure.* The Macmillan Company, NY.

Murdock, G.P, C.S. Ford, A.E. Hudson, R. Kennedy, L.W. Simmons, and J.W.M. Whiting
1945 Outline of Cultural Materials. *Yale Anthropological Series* II.

Myers, Neil O.
2007 *Myers and Neighbors of Jeffries Creek.* Privately printed, Aiken, SC.

Nader, Laura
1972 Up the Anthropologist—Perspectives Gained from Studying Up. In *Reinventing Anthropology*, Dell Hymes, editor, pp. 284-311. Random House, New York, NY.

Neumann, George C.
2001 The Redcoats' Brown Bess. *American Rifleman* April:48-53, 87.
2002 The 'Revolutionary' Charleville. *American Rifleman* May:52-57, 99, 101-102.

Neumann, George C., and Frank J. Kravic
1975 *Collector's Illustrated Encyclopedia of the American Revolution.* Scurlock Publishing Company, Texarkana, TX.

Niemi, Carol Superfine Blair
1982 *Toward a Perfect Security: Images of Natural Process in The Revolutionary War Novels of William Gilmore Simms.* Doctoral dissertation, University of Georgia, Athens, University Microfilms International, Ann Arbor, MI.

Noel Hume, Ivor
1991 *A Guide to Artifacts of Colonial America.* Vintage Books, New York, NY.

Noel Hume, Ivor and Audrey Noel Hume
2001 *The Archaeology of Martin's Hundred: Part I: Interpretive Studies.* University of Pennsylvania Museum of Archaeology and Anthropology Philadelphia, PA.

Oller, John
2016 *The Swamp Fox: How Francis Marion Saved the American Revolution.* Da Capo Press, NY.

Otterbein, Keith F.
1999 A History of Research on Warfare in Anthropology. *American Anthropologist* 101(4):794-805.
2004 *How War Began.* Texas A& M Press, College Station, TX.
2009 *The Anthropology of War.* Waveland Press, Long Grove, IL.

Pancake, John S.
1985 *This Destructive War: The British Campaign in the Carolinas, 1780-1782.* University of Alabama Press, University, AL.

Parker, John C.
2013 *Parker's Guide to the Revolutionary War in South Carolina.* Infinity Publishing, West Conshohocken, PA.

Paxton, William E.
1888 *A History of the Baptists of Louisiana, from the Earliest Times to the Present.* C.R. Barnes Publishing Company, St. Louis, MO.

Peterson, Christian E., and Robert D. Drennan
2005 Communities, Settlements, Sites, and Surveys: Regional Scale Analysis of Prehistoric Human Interaction. *American Antiquity* 70(1):5-30.

Peterson, Harold
1968 *The Book of the Continental Soldier.* Stackpole Books, Harrisburg, PA.

Petty, Julian J.
1943 *The Growth and Distribution of Population in South Carolina.* Bulletin No. 11, South Carolina State Planning Board, State Council For Defense, Columbia, SC.

Piecuch, Jim
2008 *Three Peoples One King: Loyalists, Indians, and Slaves in the Revolutionary South, 1775-1782.* The University of South Carolina Press, Columbia, SC.

Pitts, James J., Travis A. Dudley, Benjamin N Stuckey Jr., E E. Herren, and C. J. Mitchell
1974a *Soil Survey of Marion County, South Carolina.* United States Department of Agriculture, Soil Conservation Service, Columbia, SC.

Pitts, James J., F.L. Green, and T. R Gerald
1974b *Soil Survey of Florence and Sumter Counties, South Carolina.* United States Department of Agriculture, Soil Conservation Service, Columbia, SC.

Pogue, Lauren
2002 Francis Marion, the Swamp Fox: The Man and the Myth. Honor's Thesis, Department of History, University of North Carolina, Chapel Hill, NC.

Powell, William S.
1975 Gilbert Johnstone. Written for *Dictionary of North Carolina Biography.* University of North Carolina, Chapel Hill.

Preucel, Robert W.
2000 Making Pueblo Communities: Architectural Discourse at Kotyiti, New Mexico. In *The Archaeology of Communities: A New World Perspective*, Marcello A. Canuto and Jason Yaeger, pp. 58-77. Routledge, London, UK.

Pringle, Elizabeth W.A.
1916 *The Register Book for the Parish Prince Frederick Winyaw.* The National Society of the Colonial Dames of America, Williams & Wilkins Company, Baltimore, MD. Reprint by the Three Rivers Historical Society, Hemmingway, SC.

Prescott, John Robert Victor
1965 *The Geography of Frontiers and Borders.* Hutchinson University Library, University of Michigan, Ann Arbor.

Ramsay, David
1785 *History of the Revolution in South Carolina, from a British Province to an Independent State, Volume 2.* Isaac Collins, Trenton, NJ.
1809 *History of South Carolina, From its First Settlement in 1670 to the Year 1808.* David Longworth, Charleston, SC.

Rankin, Hugh F.
1973 *Francis Marion: The Swamp Fox.* Thomas Y. Crowell Company, New York, NY.

Rhame, Col. J.A.
1915 *The Battle of Willow Grove and Other Revolutionary Matters.* Jane Campbell Chapter, Daughters of the American Revolution. https://www.lynchburgpresbyterianchurchandcemetery.org/the-battle-of-willow-grove#!, accessed 18 March 2020.

Rogers, George C. Jr.
1970 *The History of Georgetown County, South Carolina.* University of South Carolina Press, Columbia, SC.

Rouse, Irving
1968 Prehistory, Typology, and the Study of Society. In *Settlement Archaeology,* K.C. Chang, editor, pp. 10-30. National Press Books, Pal Alto, CA.

Russell, Carl P.
1980 *Firearms on the Early Frontier.* Reprint, Google Books. Original 1957 University of California Press, Berkeley, CA.

Sabine, Lorenzo
1979 *Biographical Sketches of Loyalists in the American Revolution With an Historical Essay.* Genealogical Publications, Baltimore, MD. Original 1864.

Salley, A.S.
1948 Introduction to New Edition. In *A Sketch of the Life of Brig. General Francis Marion, and A History of His Brigade.* William James, editor. Reprint 1948, Continental Book Company, Marietta, GA.

Salo, Edward George
2009 *Crossing the Rivers of the State: The Role of The Ferry in The Development of South Carolina, Circa 1680-1920s.* Doctoral dissertation, Department of History, Middle Tennessee State University, Murfreesboro, TN. Microfilms International, Ann Arbor, MI

Sassaman, Kenneth E.
2001 Hunter-Gatherers and Traditions of Resistance. In *The Archaeology of Traditions: Agency and History Before and After Columbus,* Timothy R. Pauketat, editor, pp. 218-236. The University Press of Florida, Gainesville, FL.

Sauer, Carl
1963 The Morphology of Landscape. *In* John Leighly, editor, *Land and Life: A Selection From the Writings of Carl Ortwin Sauer,* pp. 315-350. University of California Press, Berkeley, CA. Original 1925.

Scheer, George F.
1963 Francis Marion: The Elusive Swam Fox. In, *The American Heritage New Illustrated History of the United States, Volume 3: The American Revolution, by* Robert G. Athearn, pp. 261-268. Dell Publishing Company, New York, NY.

Schram, Stuart R., Translator
1966 *Mao Tse-tung Basic Tactics.* Frederick A. Praeger, New York, NY.

Scoggins, Michael C., Steven D. Smith, and Tamara S. Wilson
2010 *Defining the Williamson's Plantation: Huck's Defeat Battlefield.* Report presented to the American Battlefield Protection Program, National Park Service, by the York County Cultural and Heritage Museums, Rock Hill, SC.

Scott, Douglas D., Richard Fox, Jr., Melissa A. Conner, and Dick Harmon
1989 *Archaeological Perspectives on the Battle of the Little Bighorn.* University of Oklahoma Press, Norman, OK.

Sellers, W.W.
1902 *A History of Marion County, South Carolina.* The R.L. Bryan Company, Columbia, SC.

Shackel, Paul
1994 Town Planning and Everyday Material Culture: An Archaeology of Social Relations in Colonial Maryland's Capital Cities. In *Historical Archaeology of the Chesapeake*, Paul Shackel and B.J. Little, editors, pp 85-96. Smithsonian Press, Washington, DC.
2001 *Myth, Memory, and the American Landscape.* University of Florida Press, Gainesville, FL.

Shaw, R. Paul, and Yuwa Wong
1989 *Genetic Seeds of Warfare: Evolution, Nationalism, and Patriotism.* Unwin Hyman, Boston, MA.

Shillingsburg, Peter LeRoy
1967 The Use of Sources in Simms's Biography of Francis Marion. Master's thesis, Department of English, University of South Carolina, Columbia, SC.

Showman, Richard K., and Dennis M. Conrad
1991 Introduction. In, *The Papers of General Nathanael Greene, Volume VI, 1 June 1780-December 1780*, Showman, Richard K., Dennis M. Conrad, Roger N. Parks, and Elizabeth C. Stevens, editors, pp. xi-xix. University of North Carolina Press, Chapel Hill, NC.

Simcoe, Colonel John G.
1844 *Simcoe's Military Journal: A History of Operations of a Partisan Corps Called the Queens Rangers.* Bartlett & Welford, New York, NY.

Simms, William Gilmore
1844 *The Life of Francis Marion.* Henry G. Langley, New York, NY.
1858 Marion-The Carolina Partisan. *Russell's Magazine* I(IV):1-16, 113-128.
1858-59 Marion [poem]. *Russell's Magazine* III(IV)212-218. IV(IV):312-321, V(IV) 406-415, VI(IV):505-509).
2016 *The Life of Francis Marion.* University of South Carolina Press, Columbia.

Simons, Anna
1999 War: Back to the Future. *Annual Review of Anthropology* 28:73-108.

Smith, Steven D.
1994 Archaeological Perspectives on the Civil War: The Challenge to Achieve Relevance. In *Look to the Earth: Historical Archaeology and the American Civil War*, Clarence R. Geier, Jr., and Susan E, Winters, editors, pp.3-20. University of Tennessee Press, Knoxville, TN.
2000 Introduction. In *Traditions of the Swamp Fox: William Boddie's Francis Marion*, by William Boddie, pp. xi-xliv. The Reprint Company, Spartanburg, SC.
2006a Francis Marion, Revised. In, *Encyclopedia of the American Revolution, Volume 2, Second Edition*, Harold E. Selesky, editor in chief, pp. 677-680. Library of Military History, Thomson Gale New York, NY. Original entry 1966, by Mark M. Boatner, first edition, pp. 675-679. David McKay, New York, NY.

Smith, Steven D. (continued)
2006b Letter Report of Findings At The Blackstocks Battlefield. Report to the Palmetto Conservation Foundation, from the South Carolina Institute of Archaeology and Anthropology, University of South Carolina, Columbia, SC.
2008a The Search For Francis Marion: Archaeological Survey of 15 Camps and Battlefields Associated with Francis Marion. With Contributions by Tamara S. Wilson and James B. Legg, South Carolina Institute of Archaeology and Anthropology, Columbia, SC.
2008b Archaeological Evaluation of Wadboo Plantation, 38BK464. With Contributions by Tamara S. Wilson and James B. Legg, South Carolina Institute of Archaeology and Anthropology, University of South Carolina, Columbia, SC.
2008c Interior Frontiers: Historic Settlement in Western Louisiana and Middle Missouri. Paper presented at a conference entitled, "The Social Archaeology of Southeastern Colonial Frontiers," University of South Carolina, Columbia, April 11, 12th.
2009 Archaeological Evaluation of the Dunham's Bluff Sites, 38MA207 and 38MA165. With Contributions by Tamara S. Wilson, Sean Taylor, Mark Brooks, and Diane Wallman, South Carolina Institute of Archaeology and Anthropology, Columbia, SC.
2013 Imagining the Swamp Fox: William Gilmore Simms and the National Memory of Francis Marion. In, David Molke-Hansen editor, *William Gilmore Simms's Unfinished Civil War: Consequences for a Southern Man of Letters*, pp. 32-47. University of South Carolina Press, Columbia.
2016 Critical Introduction to the Life of Marion. In, William Gilmore Simms, *The Life of Marion*, Simms Initiative, University of South Carolina Press, Columbia, SC.

Smith, Steven D., David F. Barton, and Timothy B. Riordan
1982 *Ethnoarchaeology of the Bay Springs Farmsteads: A Study of Rural American Settlement*. National Technical Information Service, Washington, DC.

Smith, Steven D., Christopher Ohm Clement, and Stephen R. Wise
2003 GPS, GIS and the Civil War Battlefield Landscape: A South Carolina Low Country Example. In, Paul Shackel, editor, Remembering Landscapes of Conflict, *Historical Archaeology* 37(3):14-30.

Smith, Steven D., and Chris J. Cochran
2010 The History of American Settlement at Camp Atterbury. Report to the US Army Corps of Engineers, Engineer Research and Development Center, Champaign, IL. From the South Carolina Institute of Archaeology and Anthropology, Columbia, SC.

Smith, Steven D., James B. Legg, Tamara S. Wilson, and Jonathan Leader
2007a "Obstinate and Strong": The History and Archaeology of the Siege of Fort Motte. South Carolina Institute of Archaeology and Anthropology, Columbia, SC.

Smith, Steven D., James B. Legg and Tamara S. Wilson
2007b The Search for Williamson's Plantation: Huck's Defeat Battlefield. Report to the York County Culture and Heritage Museums from the South Carolina Institute of Archaeology and Anthropology, University of South Carolina, Columbia, SC.

Smith, Steven D., James B. Legg and Tamara S. Wilson (continued)
2009 The Archaeology of the Camden Battlefield: History, Private Collections, and Field Investigations. Report to the Palmetto Conservation Foundation and the National Park Service, Save America's Treasures, from the South Carolina Institute of Archaeology and Anthropology, University of South Carolina, Columbia, SC.

Smith, Steven D., Brian Mabelitini, James B. Legg, and Ellan Hambright
2019 "Two Revolutionary War Expedient Fire Arrows From Archaeological Contexts in South Carolina." *Military Collector & Historian*, 71(3):243-246.

South Carolina Statutes at Large
1826 2399, Port's Ferry Transfer to Francis Davis.

Southern Quarterly Review
1846 Review: *The Study of History: Introductory Lectures on Modern History* by Thomas Arnold, M.D., edited by Henry Reed, M.A., Appleton & Co., New York. In *Southern Quarterly Review*, July 10.

Stackhouse, Rev. R.E.
1905 Marion County in the Revolution: An Address Delivered before the Swamp Fox Chapter, D.A.R. *The State*, November 19th, Columbia, SC.

Stanley, Victory Bland Jr.
1938 *Marion Churches and Churchmen 1735-1935: A Narrative of the Church of England and Its Successor, the Episcopal Church.* Southern Printing and Publishing Company, Charleston, SC.

Starn, Orin
1991 Missing the Revolution: Anthropologists and the War in Peru. *Cultural Anthropology* Volume 6(1):63-91.

Stauffer, Michael E.
1994 *The Formation of Counties in South Carolina.* South Carolina Department of Archives and History, Columbia, SC.

Stavely, William
1831 *American Military Biography, Containing the lives and characters of the Officers of the Revolution.* William Stavely Publisher, Philadelphia, PA.

Stephenson, Robert
1975 Archaeological Site Form, 38MA55. South Carolina State Site Files, South Carolina Institute of Archaeology and Anthropology, Columbia, SC.

Steuckrath, George
1858 Extract of Letter. *Debow's Review* XXV, 1(1):122.

St. Georges, Laurent M.
1988 Population Control and Guerrilla Warfare As Decisive Factors in the American Revolution. Master's thesis, Department of History, University of South Carolina, Columbia, SC.

Stokes, D.W.
1926 *The Life of Francis Marion: Being a Brief Account of the Deeds of the "Swamp Fox" and a List of Marion's Men.* Pamphlet for Francis Marion Hotel, Charleston, SC, South Caroliniana Library, Columbia, SC.

Stone
2010 The Stone Family Website http://jaimeadams.com/stone.html#austin.

Stovall, Rayburn Clifton
1971 Francis Marion: 1780-1782. School of Social Science, Master's thesis, Morehead State University, Morehead, KY.

Strang, Veronica
1999 Competing Perceptions of Landscape in Kowanyama, North Queensland. In *The Archaeology and Anthropology of Landscape,* P. Veko, and R. Leyton editors, pp. 206-218. Routledge, London, UK.

Suttles, Gerald D.
1972 *The Social Construction of Communities.* University of Chicago Press, Chicago, IL.

Tarleton, Banastre
1787 *A History of the Campaigns of 1780 and 1781, in the Southern Provinces of North America.* T. Cadell, London, UK.

Taylor, Sean
2008 An Investigation of the Effects of Timber Harvesting on Artifact Locations. Report. South Carolina Department of Natural Resources, Columbia, SC.

Thayer, Bradley A.
2004 *Darwin and International Relations: On the Evolutionary Origins of War and Ethnic Conflict.* University of Kentucky Press, Lexington, KY.

Tierney, John J., Jr.
2006 *Chasing Ghosts: Unconventional Warfare in American History.* Potomac Books, Washington, DC.

Trinkley, Michael
2000 *Archaeological Survey of the Wellman Bluff Tract.* Chicora Research Contribution 307, Chicora Foundation, Columbia, SC.

Troiani, Don
2001 *Military Buttons of the American Revolution.* Thomas Publications, Gettysburg, PA.

Tuomey, Michael
1848 *Report on the Geology of South Carolina.* A.S. Johnson, Columbia, SC.

Turney-High, Harry Holbert
1971 *Primitive Warfare: Its Practice and Concepts.* Second edition. University of South Carolina Press, Columbia, SC.

United States, Census Bureau
2000 Census Bureau. http://censtats.census.gov/, accessed 14 August 2010.

Varien, Mark D.
1999 *Sedentism and Mobility in a Social Context: Mesa Verde and Beyond.* University of Arizona Press, Tucson, AZ.

Varien, Mark D., and James M. Potter, (editors)
2008 *The Social Construction of Communities: Agency, Structure, and Identity in the Prehistoric Southwest.* AltaMira Press, Lanham, MD.

Waghelstein, John D.
1995 Regulars, Irregulars, and Militia: The American Revolution. *Small Wars and Insurgencies* 6(2):133-158.

Wallace, David Duncan
1951 *South Carolina: A Short History 1520-1948.* University of South Carolina Press, Columbia, SC.

Wallace, Rev. James A.
1856 *History of Williamsburg Church.* Bell & James Printers, Salisbury, NC.

Wallman, Diane
2009 Appendix A, Faunal Report. In *Archaeological Evaluation of the Dunham's Bluff Sites, 38MA207 and 38MA165.* Steven D. Smith, pp. A1-A5. South Carolina Institute of Archaeology and Anthropology, Columbia, SC.

Walton, Colonel Clifford
1894 *History of the British Standing Army, 1660-1700*. Harrison and Sons, London, UK.

Wates, Wylma Anne
1980 Meanderings of a Manuscript: General Peter Horry's Collection of Francis Marion Letters. *South Carolina Historical Magazine* 81(4):352-361.

Watson, Charles S.
1993 *From Nationalism to Secessionism: The Changing Fiction of William Gilmore Simms*. Greenwood Press, Westport, CN.

Ward, Bobby J., Roland Morton, Leander Brown, Ben Stuckey, J.J. Pitts
1989 *Soil Survey of Williamsburg County, South Carolina*. United States Department of Agriculture, Soil Conservation Service, Columbia, SC.

Weigley, Russell F.
1970 *The Partisan War: The South Carolina Campaign of 1780-1782*. Tricentennial Booklet Number 2, University of South Carolina Press, Columbia, SC.

Weir, Robert M.
1970 *"A Most Important Epocha" The Coming of Revolution in South Carolina*. Tricentennial Booklet Number 5, University of South Carolina Press, Columbia, SC.

Weller, Jac
1977 Irregular But Effective: Partisan Weapons and Tactics in the American Revolution Southern Theater. In *Military Analysis of The Revolutionary War: An Anthology by the Editors of Military Affairs*, pp. 131-144. KTO Press, Millwood, NY.

Wellman, Mabel T.
1917 *Food Study*. Little, Brown, and Company. <http://chestofbooks.com/food/science/Food-Study/Oysters.html.> Accessed 12 February 2009.

Wheaton, Thomas R.
2002 Colonial African American Plantation Villages. In, J.W. Joseph and Martha Zierden, editors, *Another's Country: Archaeological and Historical Perspectives on Cultural Interactions in the Southern Colonies*, pp. 30-44. University of Alabama Press, Tuscaloosa, AL.

Wheaton, Thomas R., Amy Friedlander, and Patrick H. Garrow
1983 *Yaughan and Curriboo Plantations: Studies in Afro-American Archaeology*. prepared for the National Park Service, and Charleston District Corps of Engineers Soil Systems, Marietta, GA.

Wickham-Crowley, Timothy P.
1992 *Guerrillas and Revolution in Latin America: A Comparative Study of Insurgents and Regimes Since 1956*. Princeton University Press, Princeton, NJ.

Williams, Heather
2003 *Parachutes, Patriots, and Partisans: The Special Operations Executive and Yugoslavia*. University of Wisconsin Press, Madison, WI.

Williams, Otho
1822 A Narrative of the Campaign of 1780. In *Sketches of the Life and Correspondence of Nathanael Greene, Major General of the Armies of the United States in the War of Independence*, Volume 1, William Johnson, pp. 485-503. A.E. Miller, Charleston, SC.

Wilson, Daniel H.
2001 *General Francis Marion: The Swamp Fox and Marine Corps Warfighting Doctrine*. Master's thesis, Marine Corps Command and Staff College, Quantico, VA.

Wright, John W.
1931, 1932, 1933 Some Notes on the Continental Army. *William and Mary Quarterly Historical Magazine* 2(11)2:81-105, 2(11)3:185-209, 2(12)2:79-103, 2(13):85-97.

Wright, Robert K. Jr.
2000 *The Continental Army*. Army Lineage Series, Center of Military History, United States Army, Washington, DC.

Yaeger, Jason and Marcello A. Canuto
2000 Introducing an Archaeology of Communities. In *The Archaeology of Communities: A New World Perspective*. Marcello A. Canuto and Jason Yaeger, editors, pp. 1-15. Routledge, London, UK.

Young, Deryl
2007 Letter Report on Burch's Mill to Robert C. Barrett, Francis Marion Trail Commission. Steven D. Smith Collection, South Carolina Institute of Archaeology and Anthropology, Columbia, SC.

MAP FIGURES

USGS The National Map: National Boundaries Dataset, 3DEP Elevation Program, Geographic Names Information System, National Hydrography Dataset, National Land Cover Database, National Structures Dataset, and National Transportation Dataset; USGS Global Ecosystems; U.S. Census Bureau TIGER/Line data; USFS Road Data; Natural Earth Data; U.S. Department of State Humanitarian Information Unit; and NOAA National Centers for Environmental Information, U.S. Coastal Relief Model. Data refreshed February, 2020.

NEWSPAPERS

Charleston Courier, Genealogy Bank, Genealogybank.com.

The Carolina Gazette. Microfilm, South Caroliniana Library, University of South Carolina, Columbia, SC.

The South Carolina and American Gazette. Microfilm, South Caroliniana Library, University of South Carolina, Columbia, SC.

Royal Gazette, Charleston. Microfilm, South Caroliniana Library, University of South Carolina, Columbia, SC.

Royal Georgia Gazette. Microfilm, Thomas Cooper Library, University of South Carolina, Columbia, SC.

INDEX

A

Acree, Jill, 236, 258
Adams, David, ix
Adams, William H., 18
African Americans, 163-164
Aiken, Scott, xxi
Aimwell Presbyterian Church, 65-66, 79-80, 91, 218
Alison, Frances Rebecca, 90
Alison, Francis, 90
Alison, Hugh James, 75, 90
Alison, James, 75, 90
Alison, John Balloon, 75, 90
Allison, John, ix
Allston, Peter, 50
Alston, Joseph, 48
Ami's Mill, 108, 110
Anderson, Benedict, 30, 249, 262
Arensberg, Conrad, 16
Arnold, William, 201, 233
Athelney, 245
Avant, John, 49
Awendaw Creek, 53

B

Babits, Lawrence, ix, 29, 205, 222, 233, 274
Bailey, N. Louise, 63, 74, 80, 88-92, 169
Bakers Swamp, 62
Balfour, Nisbet, 112-113, 115, 128, 132, 138, 141, 143, 225, 270
Ball Slough, 68
Ball, Sarah, 68
Barefield, Elisha, 164
Barefield, Jesse, 161-162, 216
Barker, Spencer, ix, 232
Barmeyer, Niels, 20
Barrett, Bob, ix
Barrow, James, 87, 96
Barrow, John, 96
Bass, Nancy, 83

Bass, Robert, 41, 61-62, 68-69, 73, 91, 112, 120, 133, 144, 182-184, 188, 202, 204
Batchelor, Ann, 73
Baxley, Charles, ix
Baxter, John, 84, 155, 157, 168, 178, 187, 192
Bay Springs (Miss.),18
Beale, Othniel, 48-50
Bellune [Balloon, Bullen] Family, 44, 61
   Mary, 86
   William, 61, 70, 75-76, 89-90, 96, 98
Benbow's Ferry, 113, 118
Bennett, Rebecca, 70
Bethea, P. Y., xiii, 85
Big Swamp, 73
Billum, Francis, 61
Binford, Lewis, 233
Bingham, Caleb, 238
Black Creek, 53, 246
Black Mingo, viii, 8, 35-36, 39, 61, 67, 77, 109, 115, 120, 156, 197, 213-215, 224, 226-227, 268, 282
Black Mingo Creek, 35-36, 39, 61, 77, 109, 156, 213, 224
Black Mingo, Skirmish at, 109, 197, 213-214, 226, 268
Blue Savannah, viii, xiv, 73, 101, 107, 137, 161, 188, 215-217, 232, 247, 255, 282
Blue Savannah, Battle of, 73, 188, 232, 282
Blueford Plantation, v
Boddie, William, xxi, 71, 77-78, 109, 256, 260
Booth, John, 87, 98-99, 101, 107, 110, 147, 167
Bottle Point, 35
Bratton, William, 235
Bridges Campaign, 128-131, 143
Brittains Ferry, 134
Britton Family, 58-61
   Abraham, 63
   Daniel, 60, 86, 90, 94, 96, 182
   Elizabeth, 69, 72, 81, 86
   Francis, 58, 60, 69, 86, 90, 93-94, 182, 278

Frankey, 63
Hanna, 58, 76
Henry, 60, 86, 94, 280
James, 72, 83, 96, 144
Joseph, 58, 60, 69, 89, 96, 164
Mary Goddard, 60-61
Moses, 60, 78
Philip (Phillip), 69, 76
Sarah, 60
Stephen, 61, 89, 96
Thomas, 60, 93, 278
Timothy, 58, 69, 89
William, 49, 61, 78, 89-90, 93, 96, 278
Britton's Neck, xiii-xiv, 5, 24, 33, 35, 41-42, 45, 48, 51, 53, 55, 58-66, 68-70, 72-73, 76, 80-81, 86, 88, 93-94, 96-98, 104-105, 107-110, 112, 115, 120, 128, 133-134, 137, 144, 152, 157, 161, 163, 169, 178, 181, 183-184, 187-188, 190, 200, 223-225, 227-230, 251, 266, 268-269, 273, 275-276, 278-279
Brooks, Mark, ix, 233
Brown, Joanna, ix
Brown, Joseph, 64
Brown, Tarleton, 261
Browngard, Jasper, 163
Bryant, William Cullen, 243
Buchanan, Jack, ix
Buckholtes [Buckholts, Buckholtz] Family, 81-82
  Abraham, 81-82
  Jacob, 81-82
  Peter, 82, 98, 138-139, 159, 160, 164, 167, 169
Burch, Joseph, 168, 217-218
Burch's Ferry, 41, 44-45, 191, 217-219
Burch's Mill, viii, xiv, 80, 135, 144, 157, 169, 217, 219-220, 223, 275
Burke, Thomas, 155, 168
Burn(e), Andrew, 65, 98
Burne, Susan, 64
Burris, Samuel, 83
Busick, Sean, 240
Butler, Lindley, 19

C

Camden, Battle of, xvi, 104-105, 189
Campbell, William, 94
Canady, Phyllis B., xiii, 59, 76, 88, 182
Canuto, Marcello, 16
Capers, Jim, 164
Carey, Mathew, 236

Carr, Edward, ix, 234
Carter, Fred, ix
Case, John, 162
Casey, Joanna L., ix
Cashaway Baptist Church, 89
Cassells, C., 115
Cassels, James, 115
Caswell, Major General, 136
Catfish Creek, 33, 44, 47, 50, 53, 62, 71, 81-82, 84, 86, 88, 134, 161-162
Cedar Swamp, 65-66
Chandler, Bill, ix
Chang, K. C., 17
Cheraw District, 53, 63, 101, 145, 149, 272
Cheraw Hill, 88, 95-96, 101, 266
Cherokees, 6-7, 95
Clark, William, 48
Clement, Chris, ix
Clinton, Henry, xvi, 1, 98-99
Coates, John, 150
Cobb, Charlie, ix
Collins, Jonathan, 62, 73, 84, 87, 95, 98-99, 137, 168, 186
Collins, Margaret, 64
Collins, Rachel, 73-74
Conn, Mary, 80
Conn, Thomas, 80
Continental Congress, xv, 93, 117, 138, 250
Conyers, James, 135, 148
Cook, Harvey, 47
Cooper, Elizabeth Ivey, 63, 74, 80, 88-92, 169
Cooper, Wm James, 142
Copp, Robin, ix
Cornwallis, Lord Charles, xxii, 1, 12, 99, 104, 108, 115, 117, 124, 126, 132, 146, 152, 255
Cowpens, Battle of, 189
Cowpens, Battle of, 124, 126, 189, 269
Craven County Petition, 62, 67, 69-70, 73, 76-77, 80-81, 83-84, 101, 164
Cullen, Brett, ix
Cypress Creek, 61, 134, 161-163, 169, 222, 278
Cypress Creek Bay, 61
Cypress Swamp, 169

D

Darlington District, 82
Davies, Nell Weaver, 248, 262
Davis Family, 62-63
  Ann, 63-64, 67

Benjamin, 60, 62-64, 70, 74-75, 89-90, 95-96, 101, 164-165, 167, 186
Daniel, 61
David, 63, 159, 165, 168-169
Elizabeth T., 91
Francis, 62-63, 89, 95, 97, 99, 101, 137, 160, 165, 180, 186
Henry, 62-63, 67, 74
James, 89, 134
John Calhoun, 90
Joseph, 62-63, 70, 75, 89, 91, 95-96, 101, 165, 186, 232
Lieutenant Henry, 63
Margaret, 90
Mary, 62, 64, 68
Mary Ann, 64
May Benjamin, 167
Miles, 63
Nancy, 75, 90
Thomas, 63, 75, 90
William, 62-64, 70, 74-75, 89-90, 96, 164
Dawsey, Fowler, 87, 96
Dawson, Audrey, ix
de Kalb, Johann, 104, 136
DePratter, Chester, 201, 233
Dickerson, Jo Church, ix, xiv, 66-67, 89, 216-217
Doyle, Welbore Ellis, 131-132, 142, 159, 205, 217, 225, 269
Dozer [Dozier] Family, 63-64
    Dozer (Dozier), Leonard, 63, 68
    Dozer, Ann, 76
    Dozer, A. W., 40, 53
    Dozier, John, 62-63, 67-68, 89, 94, 96, 120, 144, 279
Drayton, Ed, ix
Drowning Creek, 108, 149, 156, 161-162
Dubose Ferry, 176, 188
Dubose, Captain Daniel, 97
DuBose, Peter, 188, 232
Duncan, Graham, ix
Dunham's (Dunnam's) Bluff, viii, xiii-xiv, 40, 44, 45, 61, 64, 67, 69, 74-75, 95, 118, 120, 124, 133-134, 137, 140, 158, 186-191, 197-200, 202-207, 215, 222-223, 225, 228-232, 244-245, 268, 274-276
Dunham [Dunnam] Family, 64-65
    Robert, 64
    Ann, 62
    Ebenezer, 64, 74, 89, 96, 165, 167
    James T., 64
    John, 64-65, 90, 96, 251

Dunnam Plantation, 188
Dupree, Josias Garnier, 49

E

Enfield Plantation, 144
Ervin Family, 65-66
    John, 60, 65, 72, 74, 79, 83, 98, 101, 120, 132, 140, 144, 159, 168-169, 186, 279
    Hugh, 65-66, 79, 110, 125, 141, 155, 168
    James, 74
    Margret, 65
    Mary, 72
    Robert, 72, 77, 79, 188
    Samuel, 65, 79
Euhaney Ferry, 123
Eutaw Springs, 6, 27, 151-152, 252, 254-255, 276
Eutaw Springs, Battle of, 151, 254
Evans, Elizabeth, 70

F

Fairlawn Plantation, 153
Fanning, David, 19, 156
Fenimore, James, 240
Ferguson, Clyde, 7
Ferguson, E. James, 26
Ferguson, Leland, 167
Ferguson, R. Brain, 30
First Council of Safety, 94, 267
First Provincial Congress, 6, 74
Fladger Family, 66-67
    Hugh, 67, 74, 96
    Charles, 66, 89, 96, 137
    Elizabeth, 66, 89
    Henry, 67, 74
    Hugh Giles, 67, 96
Flannery, V. Kent, 17
Fletcher, Elizabeth, 66-67
Fletcher, John, 87, 167
Florence County Historical Society, i, ix, xix
Folsome, Ebenezer, 136
Fore, Sam, ix
Forsyth, Robert, 158
Fort Dorchester, 6
Fort Granby, 127, 148
Fort Johnson, 13, 251
Fort Motte, 7-8, 12, 142, 146-148, 167, 198, 252, 255, 274
Fort Motte, Siege of, 7, 148
Fort Watson, 8, 12, 124, 127-128, 146-148, 167, 252, 255, 274

Foxworth, Maxcy, ix
Francis Marion Memorial Day, xxii
Francis Marion Trail Commission, ix, xix, xxii, 172, 185-186, 192, 215, 218, 231, 259-260
Frierson, John, ix, 108
Fullwood, William, 140
Fulmer, Henry, ix
Furstenberg, François, 238

G

Gadsten, Christopher, 254
Galivants Ferry, 35
Ganey, Ananias, 162
Ganey, Micajah, 105, 134, 149, 152, 155, 161-162, 216, 218, 223
Ganey, Stephen, 164
Garden, Alexander, 243, 248, 257
Gasque, John, 87, 164
Gasque, Loveless, 79
Gasque, Robert, 79, 87, 162, 164
Gasque, Thomas, 164
Gates, Horatio, xii, xv, 99, 101, 104, 115, 136-137, 139, 224, 235, 247, 268, 271, 280
General Assembly, 62-63, 66, 68, 72, 74, 77-78, 80, 84, 94-95
George, Laurent St., 12
George, Ross St., ix
Georgetown District, 33, 53, 62, 249
Gervais, John, 140
Gibbes, Robert, 260
Giles Bluff, 44-45, 68, 107, 116, 137, 224, 268
Giles Family, 67-68
  Abraham, 63, 66-68, 89, 165
  Abram, 67, 96, 112, 125, 138, 141
  Elizabeth, 63, 66
  Hugh, 50, 64, 66-68, 70, 79, 83, 90, 93-94, 96-99, 101, 104, 107, 112, 116, 118, 136-137, 139, 180, 251, 268, 278
  John, 63, 67, 83, 93, 278
  Robert, 63, 66-67, 89
Gilpha, James C., 61
Glover, Joseph, 127, 144
Goddard Family, 68-70
  Ann, 60, 77
  Billy, 165, 169
  F., 92
  Frances, 69, 212
  Francis, 48, 58, 60, 62, 69-70, 72, 77, 86, 90, 95-96, 101, 168, 186
  Jane, 58
  Mary, 58, 60-61, 69
  Thomas, 60
  William, 48-49, 50, 61, 68-69, 72, 78-79, 86, 88, 90, 133, 188, 191, 204, 212, 225
Godfrey, Benjamin, 90
Godfrey, Rebecca, 90
Godfrey, Richard, 75, 77, 79, 89
Gonzalez, Roberto J., 30
Goose Creek, 144, 149
Gordon, James, 48-49, 262
Gordon, William, 252
Grant, James, 6
Graves [Greaves] Family, 70-71
  Benjamin, 96
  James, 71, 96
  Joseph, 94, 96, 98, 280
  Rachel, 90
  Robert, 71
  Bennett, 70, 75
  Elizabeth, 61
  Francis, 70, 77, 79, 165
  John, 61, 70, 98-99
  Joseph, 70, 83, 89, 96, 125, 164-165, 167
  Thomas, 75, 164
  William H., 70, 75
Gray, Robert, xxv, 100-101, 105, 110, 126, 138, 149, 154, 157, 161, 225, 267
Great Savannah, 105, 226, 252, 255
Green, William, 49, 75, 90
Greene, Nathanael, xii, xxii, 8, 12, 24, 26, 51, 103, 117-118, 123-125, 132-133, 135, 140-141, 145, 152, 154, 157, 159, 167-168, 218, 222, 236, 254, 269-270, 273-274, 276
Gregg, Alexander, 88-89
Grice, James, 164
Grice, Thomas, 87, 107, 120, 139, 157, 159, 164, 169
Grifis, William, 140
Grunden, Mona M., xiv, 212
Guatemalan National Revolutionary Unity, 20
guerrilla warfare, xviii-xxiv, 1, 8, 12-13, 16, 30, 223
Guilford Court House, 132, 151, 256

H

Hallman, Blake, x
Harden, Colonel William, 151
Harley, Thomas, 76
Harrington, Henry William, 137-139, 234
Harrison, John, 108, 111, 129
Hartley, Cecil B., 261
Hartley, William, 87

Hay, Charles Colcock, 261
Headley, J. T., 244
Heider, Karl, 244, 250, 254, 261
Hewson, Edward, 218
Hickory Grove, 134
Hickory Hill, viii, xiv, 42-43, 45, 60, 181-184, 224, 227-228, 230
Hicks, George, 52, 63
High Hills, 113, 118, 128, 147, 150
Hill, John, 255, 262
Hinson, Frances, 74
Hobkirk, Battle of, 147
Holiday, Giles, 67
Hood, Robin, 23, 235, 246, 248
Hopewell Meeting House, 91
Hopewell Presbyterian Church, 91, 218
Horry, Daniel, 99, 140
Horry, Hugh, 99, 112, 116, 129, 167, 251
Horry, Peter, xii, xvii, xxi, 5, 12, 22-23, 39, 97, 104-105, 116, 121-123, 127, 129, 132, 134, 136, 144, 147, 149, 152, 154, 156, 163, 168, 198, 236-237, 242, 251, 256, 259, 262
Hudgins, Gretchen, ix
Huger, Francis, 136
Huger, Isaac, 141
Humphries, Elizabeth Witherspoon, 75, 90
Humphries, Thomas, 75, 90-91
Huntington, Samuel, 117
Hux, Joseph, 163-164
Hyman, Tres, ix, 91, 178
Hyrne, Ann, 58

I

Indiantown Presbyterian Church, 60, 66, 71-72, 79, 83
Irvin, Moses, 163, 169
Irwin, Thomas, 140

J

Jacks Creek, 140
Jackson, John, 148
Jackson, Thomas, 257
James Family, 71-72
    David, 71, 162
    Elizabeth, 66
    Gavin, 66, 71, 96, 138
    Jane, 79
    John, xvi, 71-72, 74-75, 78-79, 90, 93-94, 104, 107-108, 126, 129, 134, 140-141, 147, 152, 156, 216, 251, 278

    Mary, 70, 72, 80
    Nathaniel, 71
    Robert, 71-72, 239
    William, v, 5, 12, 22, 39, 71-73, 75, 77, 89, 96, 121, 132, 136, 138, 143, 147, 164-165, 176, 236, 239, 242, 251-252, 260
Jefferson, Thomas, 117
Jeffries Creek, 33, 44, 47, 63, 77, 81-83, 88, 91, 96, 127, 132, 152, 157, 218, 220-221
Jenkins Family, 72-73
    James, 69, 72, 90, 97, 120, 132, 134, 143-144, 151, 157, 169, 187-188, 225, 234
    John, 72, 97, 133, 169
    Joseph, 73, 116, 139, 164
    Samuel, 69, 72-73, 164, 167-168
    Widow, xiv, 43, 45, 86, 133-134, 183-184
Johnson, Andrew Farwell, 61, 88
Johnson, James, 87, 169
Johnson, Joseph, 249
Johnson, N. M., 191
Johnson, Robert, 44
Johnston, Andrew, 48, 50, 251
Johnston, Archibald, 48, 50
Johnston, William, 80
Johnston(e), Gilbert, 136
Jolley, Hester, 58

K

Keen, Ann Lewis, 66
Keen, James, 89
Keen, Sarah, 74
Keene, Elizabeth, 66
Kelly, Kenneth G., ix
Kendle, William, 140
Kennedy, James, 163
Kimball, Solon, 16
King, G. Wayne, 218
King, Moses, 62, 186
Knox, Henry, 117
Kolb, Abel, 123
Kolbs, Tilmon, 67
Kozak, Ginnie, ix
Kruijt, Dirk, 20

L

Lacandona, Selva, 20
Laurens, John, 95
Leader, Jon, ix, 234
Leatherman, Tom, ix

Lee, Henry, xii, xxiv, 5, 12, 103, 124-125, 135, 141, 146, 178, 205, 218, 253
Legg, James B., ix, xiv, 210
Lesser, Charles, ix
Lewis, Elizabeth, 66
Lexington, Battle of, 94
Lincoln, General Benjamin, 99
Linder, Susan, 222, 272
Linenthal, Edward, 249, 262
Lipe, William, 17
Lipscomb, Terry, ix, 54, 69, 218
Little Pee Dee River Road, 216
Long Bluff, 40, 108, 152
Lossing, Benson, 249, 261
Lower Bridge, 129
Lumber River, 36, 51, 108, 110, 156
Lynches (Lynchs, Linches) River (Creek), xvi, xviii, xxii, 5, 12, 33, 35-37, 39-41, 44, 47-48, 51, 53-55, 58, 60, 65-66, 69-72, 74, 77-80, 82-83, 91, 94, 98, 104, 107-109, 112, 115-116, 122, 126-127, 132, 144, 152, 157, 167-168, 176, 191, 204-207, 213, 221, 224, 226-229, 266, 271, 276

M

McCall, George, 82, 91, 97, 99, 107, 110, 137, 140, 167-168, 279
McCoy, Redden (Reddin), 84, 92, 110, 137, 139, 159, 167-169
McCrotty, John, 251
McCrotty, William, 129
McLeroth, Robert, 115, 117-118
McMasters, Kris, ix
Maham, Hezekiah, 146, 153-154
Marcus, Joyce, 29
Marion County Court House, 61, 68, 190
Marion District, xiii, 33, 45, 65, 74, 80, 86, 90, 101, 145, 180, 186, 189-190
Marion, Esther, 5

MARION, FRANCIS
against Cherokees, 6-8
attacks against Georgetown, 103, 111-115, 124-125, 138n34 and 35, 141n74, 148, 167n1, 178
birth, 5
Bridges Campaign against Watson, 128-131
early life at sea, 6
leaves Charleston, 7, 98

on Britton's Neck, 5, 105, 107, 109-110, 178, 183, 186-204, 225, 229-230, 275
organizes brigade, 119-120, 140n66, 142n89
takes command of militia, xvi-xvii, 11n10, 93, 104-105, 136n2, 176, 268
and Nathanael Greene, xxii, 7, 24, 51, 103, 117-118, 122-124, 127, 140n66, 145, 146, 148-151, 204-205, 218, 269-270, 273, 276
and Horatio Gates, xv-xvi, 100, 104, 110, 115-116, 118, 136n2, 5 and 10, 139n47, 226, 271, 280
and Henry Lee, 5, 11n10, 103, 124-125, 135, 141n80 and 81, 143n103, 146-148, 150, 178, 205, 253
and Major Micajah Ganey, 105-106, 134-135, 149, 152, 155-157, 161-163, 168n26 and 43, 216, 220, 223
as Continental officer, xv, 6-7, 95, 136n5, 250-251
as Swamp Fox, xxii, 2, 235, 238, 242-249, 253-256, 261n39 and 49
at Ami's Mill, 108, 110
at Benbow's Ferry, 113, 118
at Black Mingo, 8, 109, 115, 197, 213-215, 226, 268, 282
at Blue Savannah, 105-107, 137n12, 161, 188, 215-217, 232n25, 247, 255, 282
at Burch's Mill and Ferry, 127, 133, 135, 144n112 and 113, 157, 169n43, 217-221, 222-224, 225, 275
at Dunham's [Dunnam's] Bluff, 118, 120, 124, 186-204, 229-230, 244-245, 268, 275
at Fort Johnson, xi, 12n, 251
at Great Savannah, 105, 226, 252
at Lower Bridge, 129
at Ox Swamp, 131, 242
at Parkers Ferry, 151, 197-199, 255, 282
at Port's Ferry, 40, 105, 107, 109, 112, 116, 136n10, 137n12, 178-181, 186-188, 191, 200, 215, 232n25
at Richardson's Plantation, 113
at Sampit Bridge, 131, 144n112, 258
at Shubrick's Plantation, 150-151
at siege of Fort Motte, 7, 8, 11n10, 77, 142n100, 146, 148, 167n12, 198, 251, 255
at siege of Fort Watson, 146-147, 167n12, 255
at Siege of Savannah, xi, 6, 98
at Snow's Island, vi, xviii, xxiii, 5, 10, 11, 15, 81, 103, 112, 116, 118-125, 139n55, 140n66, 141n81, 165, 186-207, 225, 229-230, 245-249, 270, 273-274
at Tidyman's Plantation, 156
at White Marsh, 108, 140n68, 248

Marion, Gabriel, 5, 138
Marion, Oscar, ii, 262
Mars Bluff, 157
Mathews, John, 155, 157, 215
McCall, Charles, 82
Martin, James, 87
Meitzen, Blocker Dodson, 258, 261
Meriwether, Robert, 47
Merritt, Thomas, 132, 188, 191, 225
Michie, James, archaeologist, 38
Michie, James, all others, xiii, 36, 50, 69, 161
Middle Swamp, 44, 82-83
Might, John, 140, 279
Mill Creek, 108, 218, 222
Miller, Lisa Kay, 240
Miscally, Hugh, 82, 131, 143, 148, 159, 205, 258, 278-279
Mixan (Mixon), Michael, 60
Moltke-Hansen, David, ix, 241, 260
Moore, Horatio N., 243, 261
Morgan, Daniel, xii, 26, 124, 126, 141, 241, 269
Morgan, John, 241
Morris, Nell, ix
Motte, Rebecca, 77
Moultrie, William, 6, 253
Mount Hope Swamp, 129
Muddy Creek, 39, 71, 78, 82, 159, 224, 266
Munnerlyn Family, 73-74
  Benjamin, 62, 73, 84, 95, 98, 101, 105, 110, 136-137, 139, 164, 186, 280
  Francis, 62, 74, 137
  James, 73, 164
  Jason, 89
  John, 74, 89, 98, 140, 162, 167, 186
  Joseph, 89
  L., 90, 101, 137, 140, 168, 232
  Loftis (Loftus), 73, 97-99, 120, 137, 162, 165, 169, 215-216
  Sarah, 74, 76
  Thomas, xiv, 73, 216-217
Murdock, George, 16
Murphy, Maurice, 110, 139, 152, 168
Murphy, Morris, 52
Myers, George, 82-83
Myers, John, 82-83
Myers, Neil, ix, 220, 234

N

Nader, Laura, 283
Nase, Henry, 143
Nash, Abner, 117
Native American(s), 44, 95, 197
Neilan, David, ix
Nelson, John, 112, 140, 143
Nettles Family, 83
  George, 138
  Joseph, 83, 138
  Robert, 83
Niemi, Carol, 247
Noel Hume, Ivor, 232-234
Nystrom, Paul G., 233

O

Old Neck Cemetery, 182
Old Neck Chapel, 62, 182
Old River, 35, 43-44, 227
Oller, John, ix, xxii, 143
Orangeburg District, 126
Otter, John, 260
Owens, David, 162
Ox Swamp, 71, 80, 131, 242-243

P

Palmer, David, 162
Parker, John C., 143
Paxton, William, 257
Pee Dee River, xviii, 28, 35-36, 41, 53, 58, 61, 76, 82, 84, 120, 140-141, 182, 186, 188, 190, 205, 224, 230
Perkins, George, 164
Perkins, Jacob, 164
Perkins, Lewis, 87, 99, 136, 139, 169
Perkins, Thomas, 75
Petit (Petite) Guerre, xxiv
Philips, Ann, 162
Philips, William, 162
Pickens, Andrew, 244, 261
Pickering, Timothy, 26
Piecuch, James, ix, 169
Pond Bluff Plantation, 6, 159
Port Family, 74-76
  Benjamin, 62, 73, 76, 88, 90, 96, 99, 101, 116, 125, 139, 141, 165, 178
  Frances, 41, 61, 74-75, 88, 90, 141, 144, 178, 180, 226, 234
  Francis, 90, 125

John Peter, 64, 75
Little Ben, 43
Peter, 64, 75, 87, 96
Rachel, 64
Thomas, xiii, 41, 48, 64, 74-76, 80, 90-91, 94, 96, 178, 267, 279
Port's (Ports) Ferry, viii, xiv, 40-41, 44-45, 47, 53, 61-63, 67-70, 72-77, 83, 88, 91, 95, 105, 107, 109, 111-112, 116, 123, 125, 136-138, 140, 157, 178, 180-181, 183, 186-188, 191, 197, 200, 215, 224-225, 228, 230, 232, 273-275
Postell, James, 126, 140-141, 251, 164
Postell, John, 75, 120, 122-123, 133, 140-142, 215, 251
Poston Family, 83
   John, 83, 96, 164
   Joseph, 83, 96, 164
Potato Bed Ferry, xiv, 41-42, 45, 66, 81, 108-109, 144, 146, 182-184, 224, 225, 228-230, 273, 275
Pott, Thomas, 108
Potter, James, 29
Potts Family, 83-84
   Anthony, 251
   John, 93, 141, 278
   Thomas, 83-84, 93-94, 96, 116, 142, 278
   William, 84, 108, 139
Powell, George Gabriel, 62-63, 70, 162
Power, Tracy, ix
Powers, Tom, ix
Prescott, John, 234
Preucel, Robert, 21
Prévost, Augustine, 98
Prince Frederick Parish, 53-54, 60, 66, 68-70, 73-74, 77-78, 80, 82-83, 86, 88, 93, 139, 278
Prince George Parish, 62, 73, 88
Provincial Congresses, 6, 74, 78, 93-94, 267
Pugh, Evan, 64, 67-68, 89, 139, 144
Putnam, Israel, 236

Q

Queensborough Parish/District, 46
Quitmyer, Irv, 233

R

Rae [Rea] Family, 76
   Hanna Britton, 76
   John, 67, 69, 76, 91, 96, 134, 157, 168-169
   William, 76, 96

Ramsay, David, 108, 251-252
Rankin, Hugh, 133
Rawdon, Francis (Lord), 113, 117, 126, 128, 132-133, 138, 150, 270
Rawlins, Richard, 140
Ray, Edmund, 76, 96
Ray, William, 76, 96
Reedy Creek, 73, 163
Reedy River, 94
Regiment of Foot, 129
Reid, James, 136
Rhame, J. A., 143
Rice, John, 87, 140, 157, 169, 186, 232
Richardson, Paul, 228
Richardson's Plantation, 113
Richbourg, Henry, 129
Roberts, John, 140, 251
Roberts, Robert, 140
Rooney, Kevin, ix
Rothmahler, Erasmus, 251
Ruewer, David, ix
Rutledge, John, 7, 99, 127, 136, 140, 151, 154, 168, 271

S

Salley, A.S., 31, 239
Sampit Bridge, 131, 144, 258
Sampit River, 49, 131, 144
Sandinista National Liberation Front, 20
Santee River, xv, 6, 39, 47, 98, 104-105, 113, 117, 124, 127-129, 131, 146, 156, 221, 227, 266, 269, 272
Sassaman, Kenneth E., 21
Sauer, Carl, 29
Saunders, John, 133, 142-143, 225
Savage Family, 77
   Nathan, 77, 79, 96-97, 108, 116, 147, 280
   Peniah, 79
Savannah River, 97
Saxe Gotha, 93
Scape Whore (Scape Ore), 127
Scheer, George F., 239
Scoggins, Mike, ix
Scott, Doug, 231
Scott, John, 140, 258
Screven, Benjamin, 48, 84
Screven, Elisha, 48-49
Screven, Samuel, 48, 54

Second General Assembly, 68, 78
Second Provincial Congress, 74
Sellers, W. W., 51, 62, 183
Shackel, Paul, 249-250, 262
Shackelford, Stephen, 65
Shaw, William, 84, 96, 110, 137, 139, 164
Shelby, Isaac, 235
Sheldon Church, 98
Sherwood Forest, xviii, 11, 23, 235, 246, 273
Shubrick's Plantation, 150
Silcott (Wash.), 18
Simcoe, John, 132
Simms, William Gilmore, xxi, 22, 133, 150, 236, 239, 255, 259-260, 284
Simons, Anna, 30
Simons, Maurice, 251
Simons, Shadrach (Shade), 84, 86, 95, 186, 251, 279
Singletary, Elizabeth, 78
Singleton Swamp, 78
Skeen, Alexander, 50
Smith, Jessy, 87, 96
Smith, Levi, 258
Smoot, Elias, 99
Snipes, William Clay, 126
Snow Family, 77-78
   Ann(e), 69, 90
   George, 69, 77-78, 91, 168
   Hanna, 159, 169
   James, 48-49, 69, 78, 90, 119, 139-140, 143, 155, 164, 168
   Mary Port, 75, 78, 90
   Nathaniel, 69, 77-78
   Natt, 90
   Samuel, 75, 91
   William, xiii, 61, 78, 84, 90, 93, 119, 121, 139, 165, 169, 278
   Camp on Snow's Island, v, xiii, 27-28, 68, 84, 103, 116, 118-119, 121, 131, 133, 139, 141, 143-144, 159, 164, 167, 172, 187-191, 199, 204-205, 217, 222, 225, 228-230, 246, 269-270, 273
Soccee Creek, 39, 266
Soccee Swamp, 39, 84
Society Hill, 50, 89, 266
South Carolina Regiment of Infantry, 6
Sparrow Swamp, 82
Spring Hill, 6, 98
Spring Swamp, 60
St. David's Parish, 52-54, 70, 74, 77

St. David's Regiment (Militia), 62-63, 70, 94-95, 162
St. David's Society, 272
Stanley, Victor, 67
Starn, Orin, 20
Steen, Carl, 181, 232
Stephenson, Robert, 184
Stevens, J. H., 257
Stewart, Alexander, 151
Stokes, D. W., 202
Stone Family, 78-79
   Stone, Austin, 77-79, 91, 167
Stovall, Rayburn, 12, 167
Strang, Veronica, 19
Sullivan, Battle of, 101
Summers, Carole, ix
Sumner, Jethro, 136
Sumter District, 84, 232
Sumter, Thomas, xvii, 12-13, 26, 30, 127, 151, 167, 235, 244, 261
Sun Tzu, 13
Swager, Christine R., ix
Swamp Fox, viii, xxii, 2, 23, 25, 190, 235, 238-239, 242-245, 247-249, 252-257, 261
Swamp Fox Murals Trail Society, xxii
Sweet, Anthony, 165, 169
Swinton Family, 86
   Hugh, 138
   William, 86

T

Tarleton, Banastre, 99, 113, 124, 138, 242
Taylor, Mike, x
Taylor, Sean, ix, xiv, 193, 203, 233
Tearcoat Swamp, 112, 255
The Oakland Club, v, xii
Thicketty Creek, 93
Thompson, Hugh, 69, 168
Thompson, Samuel, 82
Tidyman's Plantation, 156
Tierney, John, 5
Tindal, John, 164
Tindall, James, 163
Tisdale, Tom, ix
Trinkley, Michael, 177
Tse-tung, Mao, 8, 13, 223
Tucker, Nathaniel Beverley, 241
Turnbull, George, 138
Turner, Frederick, 221

Turney, Harry Holbert, 13, 30
Tyler, John, 87, 98
Tyler, Samuel, 87
Tynes, Samuel, 112

U

Utley, Lucille, 88

V

Varien, Mark, 29
Vaughan, William, 140, 279

W

Waccamaw River, 36, 123, 136
Wadboo Plantation, xiii, 24, 138, 153, 158, 197-199, 213, 250
Wade, Thomas, 158-159, 167
Wall, Michael, 164
Wall, Wright, 162, 164
Wallace, James, 71
Walton, Clifford, 233
Walton, Katharine, 240
Wannamker, Doraine, ix
Wannamaker, Luther, ix
Washington, George, xxi, xxiv, 12, 117, 236, 241, 254, 257
Washington, William, 99
Wateree River, 7, 52, 147
Wates, Wylma, 31
Watkins, Dick, ix
Watson, Charles, 240
Watson, John Tadwell, 128, 134, 140, 143, 146-147, 183, 258, 269
Wayne, Anthony, 236
Weaver, Samuel, 256
Webster, Noah, 238
Weems, Mason Locke, xii, xxi, 5, 12, 22-23, 39, 235-239, 243, 245, 248, 251-252, 259, 262
Wemyss, James, 107-108, 274
White, Jesse, 140, 279
White, John Blake, ii, v, xviii, 248
White Marsh, 108, 140, 248
Wiboo Swamp, 129
Wickham-Crowley, Timothy, 20
Wiggens, Elias, 162
Wiggins, Jesse, 87, 137, 168
Wiggins, Thomas, 84
Will, John Dozier, 89
Williams, Alaina, ix

Williams, Henry L., 76
Williams, Mesech (Meschack, Mesesh), 162-163
Williams, Otho Holland, xv, 104, 136, 163
Williamsburg District, xiv, 33, 39, 44, 46, 84, 119, 167, 177, 188, 227
Willow Creek, 44, 218
Willow Grove, 143
Willow Grove, Battle of, 143
Witherspoon Family, 79-81
 David, 71, 79-81, 91, 95, 101, 132, 143
 Gavin, 64-66, 72, 79-80, 96, 98, 105, 125, 138, 167, 239, 251
 Jane, 65, 79
 John, 94
 John, 64-65, 71, 76, 79, 93-94, 96, 138, 278
 Robert, 66, 72, 79-80, 176, 239
 William, 71, 164
Witherspoon's Ferry, viii, xiv, xvi, xix, 12, 35, 41, 66, 79-80, 83, 93, 104-105, 107, 109, 111-112, 116, 133, 136, 138, 151-152, 156, 176-178, 188, 191, 220, 224-227, 230, 268, 273, 280
Wizard Owl, 244, 261
Woodberry Family, 81
 George W., 76
 Richard, 41, 61, 81, 91, 109, 162, 164
Woodberry Road, 42-43, 62, 76, 182-183, 227-228, 23
Woodbury, John, 64
Woodbury, Jonah, 64
Wragg, Samuel, 64
Wroth, Lawrence, 238

Y

Yadkin River, 36
Yaeger, Jason, 16
Yauhannah Ferry, 144
Young, Deryl (Daryl), ix, xiii, 53, 59, 90-91, 178, 218

Z

Zeigler, Benjamin T., iii, ix, xix

About the Author
Steven D. Smith, Ph.D.

STEVEN D. SMITH, PH.D. is a Research Professor at the South Carolina Institute of Archaeology and Anthropology, University of South Carolina. He received his Master's Degree from the University of Kentucky in 1983 and his Ph.D. in Anthropology from the University of South Carolina. He has over 30 years' experience in historical archaeology with a focus on the American Revolution, leading major excavations at Fort Motte, Camden, Ninety Six, Dunham's Bluff, Wadboo Plantation, Williamson's Plantation, and Parkers Ferry. He has published extensively on the archaeology of warfare, lately focusing on the camps and battlefields of Francis Marion. He has published six other books, and recently co-edited the book *Partisans, Guerillas, and Irregulars: Historical Archaeology of Asymmetric Warfare*, published by the University of Alabama Press (2019).

www.ingramcontent.com/pod-product-compliance
Lightning Source LLC
Chambersburg PA
CBHW040251090526